The United Nations Transitional Authority in Cambodia (UNTAC): Debriefing and Lessons

The United Nations Transitional Authority in Cambodia (UNTAC): Debriefing and Lessons

Report and Recommendations of the
International Conference
Singapore, August 1994

The Institute of Policy Studies (IPS)
of Singapore

and

The United Nations Institute for
Training and Research (UNITAR)

Publication series prepared under the direction of

Nassrine Azimi

LONDON – THE HAGUE – BOSTON

Published by Kluwer Law International
Sterling House
66 Wilton Road
London SW1V 1DE
United Kingdom

Sold and distributed in the USA and Canada by
Kluwer Law International
675 Massachusetts Avenue
Cambridge MA 02139
USA

Kluwer Law International incorporates
the publishing programmes of
Graham & Trotman Ltd,
Kluwer Law & Taxation Publishers
and Martinus Nijhoff Publishers.

In all other countries, sold and distributed by
Kluwer Law International
P.O. Box 85889
2508 CN The Hague
The Netherlands

© The United Nations Institute for Training and Research (UNITAR) 1995
First published in 1995

ISBN 90-411-0886-6

British Library Cataloguing in Publication Data and Library of Congress Cataloging-in-Publication Data is available

Opinions expressed in the contributions to this volume are those of the authors and do not necessarily reflect the views of the United Nations Secretariat, UNITAR, or any other United Nations organs and agencies mentioned in this volume. This general disclaimer applies to all contributions.

The designations employed and the presentation of material in this publication do not imply the expression of any opinion whatsoever on the part of the Secretariat of the United Nations concerning the legal status of any country, territory, city or area or of its authorities, or concerning the delimitation of its frontiers or boundaries.

This publication is protected by international copyright law. All rights reserved. No part of this publication may be reproduced, stored in a retrieval system, or transmitted in any form or by any means, electronic, mechanical, photocopying, recording or otherwise, without the prior permission of the publisher.

Typeset in 10/11 pt Palatino by BookEns Ltd, Royston, Herts.
Printed and bound in Great Britain by Hartnolls Ltd, Bodmin, Cornwall.

Table of Contents

Selected Biographies ix
Foreword xv
Explanatory Note and Acknowledgements xix
List of Abbreviations xxi

PART I: REPORT AND RECOMMENDATIONS

1. The Cambodian peace process and the role of the United Nations 3

History of the peace process 3
New requirements in peace-keeping 4
UNTAC: a complex and comprehensive operation 4
The advance survey mission 5
The UNTAC start-up 6
The four Cambodian political factions 7

2. The UNTAC components 9

The Military Component 9
The Police Component 16
The Civil Administration Component 19
The Human Rights Component 23
The Repatriation Component 28
The Component for Rehabilitation and Economic Affairs 33
The Electoral Component 36
The Information/Education Division 39

3. General lessons and recommendations from UNTAC 45

A sound peace plan 46
Early deployment of staff and resources 46
Speeding up approvals 47
Clear and achievable goals 48
Support from the parties to the conflict 49
Enlisting external support 50
Personnel qualifications and relations 50
Role of United Nations Volunteers 51
Improving the financing and logistical efficiency of peace-keeping operations 52

4. Conclusions 53

PART II: CONFERENCE PAPERS

5. UN peace-keeping and the new world disorder 57
   Professor S. Jayakumar

6. Message 61
   Dr Boutros Boutros-Ghali

7. Message 63
   Ambassador Samuel R. Insanally

8. The Paris Agreements and their implementation 65
   Ambassador Yukio Imagawa

9. Crafting the Paris Agreements on Cambodia 71
   Sylvie Bermann

10. The UN's role in bringing about peace in Cambodia (an insider's view) 75
    USG Rafeeuddin Ahmed

11. The Cambodian factions in the democratic process 79
    Khieu Kanharith

12. The Paris Agreements on Cambodia: a retrospect 85
    Mark Hong

13. The UN's role in bringing about peace in Cambodia (an observer's view) 91
    Dr Hrach Gregorian

14. Exercising the Transitional Authority 95
    Takahisa Kawakami

15. Lessons from exercising the Transitional Authority 103
    Tan Lian Choo

16. The ASEAN role – a historical perspective 107
    Ambassador Zainal A. Sulong

17. The Cambodian perspective 111
    HRH Prince Sisowath Sirirath

18. **How the Paris Agreements affected UNTAC operations**   115
    Ambassador Nana S. Sutresna

19. **A political analysis of the Cambodian situation**   119
    Ambassador Ataul Karim

20. **UNTAC: the Military Component view**   125
    Lieutenant-General John M. Sanderson

21. **UNTAC's civilian police operation**   139
    Brigadier-General Klaas C. Roos

22. **Refugee repatriation and reintegration in Cambodia**   147
    Sergio Vieira de Mello

23. **Economics/rehabilitation**   157
    Roger C. Lawrence

24. **The protection and promotion of human rights**   165
    Dennis McNamara

25. **UNTAC's information/education programme**   171
    Timothy M. Carney

26. **Election-monitoring: preparation and conduct**   177
    Professor Reginald Austin

27. **A legal perspective on UNTAC – an overview**   191
    Vishakan Krishnadasan

28. **Drafting the Cambodian Constitution**   205
    Ambassador Tan Boon Teik

29. **Perspective from the Department of Peace-Keeping Operations (DPKO)**   211
    Hisako Shimura

30. **UNITAR's Program of Correspondence Instruction (POCI) in Peace-Keeping Operations**   217
    Dr Harvey J. Langholtz

31. A French perspective on peace-keeping   227
Lieutenant-Colonel Xavier Guérin

32. Cambodia today   231
Benny Widyono

33. UNTAC: a flawed paradigm/success   237
Ken Berry

34. UNTAC: a paradigm for future UN peace-keeping operations?   249
John Pace

35. UN peace-keeping operations in the future   253
Ambassador Hisashi Owada

PART III: ANNEXES

Annex 1: List of conference participants   261
Annex 2: Agenda of the conference   265

Selected Biographies

(functions as at end of 1994)

Rafeeuddin Ahmed
Under-Secretary-General Rafeeuddin Ahmed was the chief negotiator of the UN throughout the Cambodian peace process, and later Executive Secretary of the Economic and Social Commission for Asia and the Pacific (ESCAP). He is currently Associate Administrator of the United Nations Development Program (UNDP).

Reginald Austin
Professor Reginald Austin graduated from the Universities of Cape Town and London. He took part in different peace-keeping operations as Legal Adviser or Elections Consultant (Namibia, Angola, Mozambique). In 1992, he was appointed Director of the Electoral Component and Chief Electoral Officer in UNTAC. At present he is Director of Legal Affairs at the Commonwealth Secretariat.

Nassrine Azimi
Nassrine Azimi graduated from the University of Lausanne and from the Graduate Institute of International Studies of Geneva. She has been Coordinator of the Environmental Training Programs at the United Nations Institute for Training and Research (UNITAR), and is currently Deputy to the Acting Executive Director of the Institute.

Sylvie Bermann
Sylvie Bermann graduated in political science, history and oriental languages. She is currently Counsellor at the Permanent Mission of France to the United Nations in New York.

Ken Berry
Ken Berry was closely involved in the Cambodian peace process since its inception and was, in 1990 and 1991, Australian Foreign Minister Senator Gareth Evans's legal adviser on Cambodia. He is currently a Senior Adviser to Senator Evans and is also writing a book on Australia's role in the Cambodian peace process.

Marcel A. Boisard
Dr Marcel A. Boisard graduated from the Graduate Institute of International Studies of Geneva and was formerly Chief Delegate of the International

Committee of the Red Cross (ICRC). He is currently Acting Executive Director of the United Nations Institute for Training and Research (UNITAR).

Timothy M. Carney

Timothy M. Carney graduated from MIT. His publications include monographs and essays related to current Cambodian history. He was the senior US government official seconded to UNTAC and served as Director of the Information/Education Division of UNTAC from March 1992 to August 1993. A career officer of the Foreign Service of the United States, he was designated Deputy Assistant Secretary of State in the South Asia Bureau in July 1994.

Hrach Gregorian

Dr Hrach Gregorian graduated from Boston and Brandeis Universities. He is currently Director of the Education & Training Program at the United States Institute of Peace (USIP). His principal areas of academic and professional interest are international relations, political philosophy and American political institutions and thought.

Xavier Guérin

Lieutenant-Colonel Xavier Guérin graduated from the *Ecole Spéciale Militaire de Saint-Cyr* in 1975. His different postings include Chad, Senegal and former Yugoslavia. At present, he is in charge of the studies on the peace-keeping operations in the Recruitment Section of the Headquarters of the French Army.

Mark Hong

Mark Hong is a graduate of Cambridge University, and of Georgetown University in Washington DC. He joined the Foreign Ministry of Singapore in 1969. His overseas postings include Cambodia, Hong Kong, Paris and New York. He is currently Director of Directorate IV, Singapore Ministry of Foreign Affairs (International Organizations and Developing Countries).

Yukio Imagawa

Ambassador Yukio Imagawa graduated from Waseda University and joined the Ministry of Foreign Affairs in 1956. As Minister of the Embassy of Japan in France, he was Co-President of the third Committee of the Paris International Conference on Cambodia. In September 1991, he was appointed Permanent Representative of Japan to the Supreme National Council (SNC) and is currently Ambassador Extraordinary and Plenipotentiary of Japan in Cambodia.

Khieu Kanharith

Khieu Kanharith graduated in Law and Economics and from the National School of Administration. From 1979 to 1990, he was Chief Editor of *Kampuchea Weekly* and, from 1981, a member of the National Assembly and Rapporteur of its Commission for Education and Social Welfare. At present, he is Secretary of State of the Ministry of Information of Cambodia.

Ataul Karim

Ambassador Ataul Karim graduated from the University of Dhaka in 1954. He joined the Foreign Office in 1955 and thereafter obtained a Certificate of Graduate Studies from the Fletcher School of Law and Diplomacy in Massachusetts. He was appointed Chief Liaison Officer and Head of Mission of UNAMIC in October 1991, and served afterwards as Senior Political Adviser in UNTAC. At present he is Director, Political Affairs Division, UNOSOM II (UN Operation in Somalia).

Takahisa Kawakami

Takahisa Kawakami was Senior Political Officer in UNAMIC and, from March 1992 to September 1993, Assistant to the Special Representative of the Secretary-General for Cambodia and Senior Political Officer in UNTAC. He is currently Assistant Director, UN Policy Division, Ministry of Foreign Affairs, Japan.

Tommy Koh

Ambassador Tommy Koh graduated from the University of Singapore, from Harvard University and from Cambridge University. He is currently Ambassador-at-Large at the Ministry of Foreign Affairs, Director of the Institute of Policy Studies (IPS), and Chairman of the National Art Council of Singapore.

Vishakan Krishnadasan

Vishakan Krishnadasan graduated from the University of Ceylon and from the University of London. He was Legal Adviser to the Special Representative of the Secretary-General of the United Nations, on all legal aspects of UNTAC's activities and responsibilities. He is currently in the Legal Council and Secretary of the Council of the United Nations University in Tokyo.

Harvey J. Langholtz

Dr Harvey J. Langholtz holds a degree in decision theory. He served as Political Officer at the United States mission to the United Nations from 1991 to 1993, and was the primary US Delegate to the UN Special Committee for Peace-Keeping Operations. He has been the Director of UNITAR's Program of Correspondence Instruction in Peace-Keeping Operations (POCI) since its inception.

Roger C. Lawrence

Roger C. Lawrence previously held the responsibilities for the work of the UN Conference on Trade and Development (UNCTAD) on macro-economics, international finance and external indebtedness. Within UNTAC, he was Economic Advisor of the SRSG and, consequently, Director of the Rehabilitation Component. Roger Lawrence is presently Deputy to the Secretary-General of UNCTAD, and Director-in-Charge of UNCTAD's Division for Transnational Corporations and Investment. Recently, he has also been appointed Economic Advisor of the SRSG to Haiti.

Dennis McNamara

Dennis McNamara graduated from the University of Auckland and joined the UN High Commissioner for Refugees (UNHCR) in 1975, where he undertook numerous responsibilities, particularly in Southeast Asia. From 1990 to 1993, he was seconded to the United Nations as Deputy Special Representative for Humanitarian Assistance to Cambodia and, subsequently, as Director of the Human Rights Component for UNTAC, from March 1992 to August 1993. He is currently the Director of External Relations at UNHCR.

Hisashi Owada

Ambassador Hisashi Owada graduated from Tokyo University and continued his post-graduate studies at Cambridge University. From 1991 to 1993, he held the post of Vice-Minister for Foreign Affairs of Japan. At present, he is Permanent Representative of Japan to the United Nations in New York.

Steve Pieczenik

Dr Steve Pieczenik graduated from Cornell University and from Harvard Medical College. He was for some time appointed as psychiatrist/political scientist at the State Department. Deputy Assistant Secretary of State for East Asian and Pacific Affairs, he was one of the participants of the International Paris Peace Conference on Cambodia. He is currently Consultant to the United States Institute of Peace.

Klaas C. Roos

Brigadier-General Klaas Roos was Police Commissioner of the Police Component of UNTAC, and commanded the UN Civil Police Force during the 18-month mission in Cambodia. Since October 1993, Brigadier-General Roos has served as the Deputy Commandant of the Netherlands Royal Marechaussee.

John M. Sanderson

Lieutenant-General John M. Sanderson graduated into the Royal Australian Engineers from the Royal Military College Duntroon in 1961. His regimental appointments have included active service in East Malaysia and in South

Vietnam. He was Commander of the Military Component of UNTAC from March 1992 to October 1993. Lieutenant General Sanderson was made a Companion of the Order of Australia in January 1994, and is currently Commander, Joint Forces, Australia.

Hisako Shimura

Hisako Shimura graduated from the University of California at Berkeley, and from the Universities of Toledo and Iowa. Since 1978, she has been at the Office for Special Political Affairs (renamed Department of Peace-Keeping Operations – DPKO – in March 1992). She was involved in many UN peace-keeping operations (especially in the Middle East and Cambodia) and in conflict resolution (Afghanistan, Iran/Iraq). Currently, Ms Shimura is Director of the Europe/Latin America Division at UNDPKO.

Zainal A. Sulong

Ambassador Zainal A. Sulong served as Malaysia's Ambassador to Indonesia and to the USSR, and was Permanent Representative of his country to the UN in New York, before being appointed Secretary-General at the Ministry of Foreign Affairs in April 1984. Among many tasks and functions, he is currently the Chairman of the Malaysian Industrial Development Authority (MIDA), and the Institute of Strategic and International Studies of Malaysia (ISIS).

Nana S. Sutresna

Ambassador-at-Large Nana S. Sutresna is currently Head Executive Assistant to President Soeharto in his capacity as Chairman of the Non-Aligned Movement. Previously he served as Ambassador/Permanent Representative of Indonesia to the UN, and later as Secretary-General of the Tenth Conference of Heads of State or Government of Non-Aligned Countries in Jakarta.

Tan Boon Teik

Ambassador Tan Boon Teik graduated from University College, London. He took part and represented Singapore in various UN and Commonwealth Ministers' Meetings. Currently, he is Singapore's Ambassador to Hungary, Austria and the Slovak Republic, and Chairman of the Singapore International Arbitration Center (SIAC).

Tan Lian Choo

Tan Lian Choo graduated from Paris University in international economic relations. From 1988 to 1993, she was correspondent for *The Straits Times* of Bangkok. At present, she is the Senior Correspondent attached to *The Strait Times*' Foreign Desk.

Sergio Vieira de Mello

Sergio Vieira de Mello graduated from Paris University and joined the UNHCR in 1969. Between 1991 and 1993, he was Special Envoy of the High Commissioner to Cambodia, UNTAC Director of Repatriation, and Director *ad interim* of the Cambodian Mine Action Center. In October 1993, he was appointed as Delegate in Bosnia-Herzegovina of the Special Representative of the Secretary-General in former Yugoslavia, and later Head of Civil Affairs of the United Nations Protection Force (UNPROFOR). Mr Vieira de Mello is currently back at the UNHCR Headquarters in Geneva.

Benny Widyono

Benny Widyono graduated from the Universities of Texas, Kansas and Indonesia. From April 1992 to September 1993, he was seconded to UNTAC where he served as Provincial Director of Siem Reap. He is currently the UN Secretary-General's Representative in Cambodia.

Foreword

The "International Conference on the United Nations Transitional Authority in Cambodia (UNTAC): Debriefing and Lessons" was organized jointly by the Institute of Policy Studies (IPS) of Singapore and the United Nations Institute for Training and Research (UNITAR). It was held in Singapore from 2–4 August 1994, and brought together some 50 resource persons and participants.

When we convened this conference, questions about the future of United Nations peace-keeping operations (UNPKOs) had already been raised in various circles. Over the last few months, in view of the difficulties experienced in Somalia, Bosnia and elsewhere, these questions have become yet more urgent. The international community is now under even stronger pressure to try to identify, amidst apparent discord and confusion, ways of containing crisis and turmoil through United Nations peace-keeping operations and preventive diplomacy.

With the benefit of hindsight, the initiative of the international community to respond to the call of Cambodia seems to have created one of the more successful undertakings of United Nations peace-keeping. UNTAC was the fruit of many years of negotiations which had resulted in the Paris Agreements on Cambodia, and a sincere attempt to reach out to a country devastated by conflict. That in this attempt not all the aspirations were achieved, that some things went wrong, and that the unexpected always took precedence over the planned, should not detract from the initial *élan vital*. Cambodia is, we hope, a better place for most Cambodians because of UNTAC.

The present report is the synthesis of the discussions and papers presented at the Singapore Conference, which was unique in having gathered, for the first time, many of the key protagonists and UNTAC component heads to reflect and debrief jointly on the important lessons of UNTAC, both positive and negative. The objective of this report is to reflect as faithfully as possible the analysis and observations of the conference participants, and to draw overall lessons and recommendations from that exercise, in the hope that these could be of use to future undertakings of the United Nations. It is not intended to be an exhaustive review, either of UNTAC, or of United Nations peace-keeping operations.

A number of points need to be expressed at the outset, to outline both the limits and the scope of this document.

Firstly, the report is the collective work of the resource persons present at the Conference. A few key UNTAC staff could not attend, with the ensuing result that not all perspectives and opinions have been gathered here. We take full responsibility for these shortcomings, and hope that they will be brought to our attention and amended in future reports.

Secondly, individuals from many institutions have conducted studies on

UNTAC, and many continue to do so. Although we have consulted with some of them in the preparation of this report, it is not intended to be a review of these studies, but rather a reflection of the Singapore Conference. We hope that as the IPS/UNITAR cycle of conferences on the evaluation of peace-keeping operations continues, the informal and fruitful contacts already established with many of these scholars will be strengthened, and that this new forum will be an on-going platform for consultation and exchange of information to ease the task of those dealing with peace-keeping issues within the United Nations.

Thirdly, many events have occurred in Cambodia since the elections of May 1993, and the subsequent establishment of the new Government. Some of these events, as well as "post-operation" hindsight, could make it easy to conclude that things should have been done "otherwise". This report does not consider the current economic and political situation in Cambodia, for we felt that addressing these would take us too far away from the specific scope of this study, which aims to assess a particular peace-keeping operation of the United Nations. We hope that others will continue to study the lessons to be learned from Cambodia, and that gradually these different analyses will provide a complete picture.

Fourthly, in the wake of UNTAC, many reforms have already been initiated at the United Nations Secretariat. The Department of Peace-Keeping Operations (DPKO) has been strengthened and the Field Operations Division (FOD) integrated into it, the number of staff dealing with political analysis and training has increased, and the involvement of Member States, through secondments and the provision of national expertise, has become institutionalized. Some major issues, such as the question of stand-by forces and of specially-trained national civil servants at the disposal of the United Nations, are still not resolved. Without a clear commitment by Member States, the task of the United Nations remains daunting. If recent events are any indication, resources provided to the Organization for its peace-keeping operations are not increasing, and may even decline significantly in the future. This trend could seriously limit the United Nations' ability to provide peace-keeping as a vital instrument for the peaceful settlement of disputes. It would deny millions of people the assistance they need for reconstructing war-torn and fragmented societies. A sober analysis of each peace-keeping operation – not only of its failures but also of its successes – is a necessity. We hope that this report contributes in some small way to that analysis.

Finally, we wish to thank sincerely the many resource persons, at the United Nations, in Cambodia, and elsewhere, for their contributions. This report is the collective work of many individuals, who generously and with honesty shared their thoughts with us. We cannot thank them each separately, but they have our heartfelt gratitude. Cambodia and UNTAC remain in the hearts and minds of many of these individuals – such is the nature of this country, and the nature of this particular peace-keeping operation. Exercising "transitional authority" demands a far-reaching involvement. Our purpose, in presenting this report, is to ensure that the experience of that involvement remains a part of the United Nations' institutional memory, and one which could be called upon to refine the future initiatives of the Organization. Whilst the world seems to be in disarray, and the United Nations weakened by the many unrealistic demands put on it, we believe it necessary to remember and to record what has already been achieved, and the lessons which have been learned from the past. It is also necessary to keep the faith in the midst of adversity.

Marcel A. Boisard
Tommy Koh
Hisashi Owada
Conference Co-Chairs

Explanatory Note and Acknowledgements

This work is, in the best sense of the word, the result of a collective effort. It was made possible thanks to the many contributions of the 1994 Singapore Conference participants, and they each have our heartfelt gratitude for writing the relevant segments, for their valuable insights, and for their patience with the endless revisions.

Part I of this book is a synthesis of the various papers, positions and discussions held at that conference, and is not meant to be an exact rendition of UNTAC itself. Part II reproduces all the papers presented in Singapore and should provide the reader with a sense of the complexity of UNTAC, and the diversity of views of the different actors.

Due to the fact that Under-Secretary-General Yasushi Akashi, Special Representative of the Secretary-General (SRSG) to Cambodia, could not participate in the Singapore Conference, the ensuing report, though rich in its component-oriented evaluation, could not benefit from his overall analysis. In particular, the crucial relationship between the SRSG and the Supreme National Council, and political groups represented there, as well as the special relationship between the SRSG and HRH King Sihanouk, could certainly have been exposed in more detail. In this regard, readers may wish to refer to various articles written by USG Akashi, to gain a more comprehensive picture of the forces at play.

The conduct of the Singapore Conference and the preparation of this book was made possible thanks to generous contributions from The Asia Foundation and from the United States Institute of Peace. Both institutions have our deep appreciation for their trust, and our commitment to pursue the IPS/UNITAR cycle of debriefing conferences, in the hope that these will help improve the peace-keeping efforts of the United Nations.

Finally, our boundless gratitude to Evgeni Chossudovsky, Jacques Lemoine, Connie Peck and Michael Doyle for priceless advice given throughout the preparation of the Conference and thereafter, to Marione Kazimirsky for her many contributions, to Valérie Fournier for remaining, tirelessly and always cheerfully, the backbone of the project, and to the three Co-chairs, Marcel A. Boisard, Tommy Koh and Hisashi Owada, for their unwavering commitment and support throughout.

Nassrine Azimi
Geneva, November 1995

List of Abbreviations

ACABQ	Advisory Committee on Administrative and Budgetary Questions
ADB	Asian Development Bank
ADD	Action pour la Démocratie et pour le Développement
ASEAN	Association of South-East Asian Nations
BLDP	Buddhist Liberal Democratic Party
CGDK	Coalition Government of Democratic Kampuchea
CIVADMIN	Civil Administration Component
CIVPOL	Civilian Police Component
CMAC	Cambodian Mine Action Centre
CPAF	Cambodian People's Armed Forces
CPP	Cambodian People's Party
CSCE	Conference for Security and Cooperation in Europe
CTO	Compensatory Time Off
DEO	District Electoral Officer
DPKO	United Nations Department of Peace-Keeping Operations
DSRSG	Deputy to the Special Representative of the Secretary-General
EP5	Extended Permanent Five
ESCAP	United Nations Economic and Social Commission for Asia and the Pacific
FOD	Field Operation Division
FUNCINPEC	French acronym for the National Union Front for an Independent, Neutral, Peaceful and Cooperative Cambodia
IBRD	International Bank for Reconstruction and Development (World Bank)
ICK	International Conference on Kampuchea
ICORC	International Committee on the Reconstruction of Cambodia
ICRC	International Committee of the Red Cross
ILO	International Labour Office
IMC	Informal Meeting on Cambodia
IMF	International Monetary Fund
INFO/ED	Information/Education Division
IPD	Institute for Professional Development
IPS	Institute of Policy Studies
ISIS	Institute of Strategic and International Studies of Malaysia
JIM	Jakarta Informal Meeting
KPNLF	Khmer Rouge National Liberation Front
KR	Khmer Rouge

MCP	Malaysian Communist Party
MIDA	Malaysian Industrial Development Authority
MINURSO	United Nations Mission for the Referendum in Western Sahara
MLO	Military Liaison Officer
MMWG	Mixed Military Working Group
MOU	Memorandum of Understanding
NADK	National Army of Democratic Kampuchea
NAM	Non-Aligned Movement
NATO	North Atlantic Treaty Organisation
NCO	Non-Commissioned Officer
NGO	Non-Governmental Organisation
NHPAC	National Heritage Protection Authority in Cambodia
ONUC	United Nations Operation in the Congo
ONUMOZ	United Nations Operation in Mozambique
ONUSAL	United Nations Observer Mission in El Salvador
P5	Five Permanent Members of the Security Council
PDK	Party of Democratic Kampuchea
PEO	Provincial Electoral Officer
PICC	Paris International Conference on Cambodia
PKO	Peace-Keeping Operation
POCI	Programme of Correspondence Instruction in Peace-Keeping Operations
POW	Prisoner of War
PRK	People's Republic of Kampuchea
QIP	Quick Impact Project
RCAF	Royal Cambodian Armed Forces
RCG	Royal Cambodian Government
SDR	Special Drawing Rights
SIAC	Singapore International Arbitration Center
SIT	Strategic Investigation Teams
SNC	Supreme National Council
SOC	State of Cambodia
SRSG	Special Representative of the Secretary-General
TAC	Technical Advisory Committees
UN	United Nations
UNAMIC	United Nations Advance Mission in Cambodia
UNCTAD	United Nations Conference on Trade and Development
UNDP	United Nations Development Programme
UNESCO	United Nations Educational, Scientific and Cultural Organization
UNIFICYP	United Nations Peace-Keeping Force in Cyprus
UNGA	United Nations General Assembly
UNHCR	United Nations High Commissioner for Refugees
UNHQ	United Nations Headquarters
UNICEF	United Nations Children's Fund
UNIFIL	United Nations Interim Force in Lebanon
UNIKOM	United Nations Iraq-Kuwait Observation Mission

UNITAR	United Nations Institute for Training and Research
UNOSOM	United Nations Operation in Somalia
UNPROFOR	United Nations Protection Force (in the former Yugoslavia)
UNSC	United Nations Security Council
UNSG	United Nations Secertary-General
UNTAC	United Nations Transitional Authority in Cambodia
UNTAG	United Nations Transition Assistance Group (in Namibia)
UNTSO	United Nations Truce Supervision Organisation
UNV	United Nations Volunteers
USG	Under-Secretary-General
USIA	United States Information Agency
USIP	United States Institute of Peace
WEU	Western European Union
WFP	World Food Program
ZOPFAN	Zone of Peace, Freedom, and Neutrality

Part I

*Report and Recommendations
of the International Conference
in Singapore, August 1994*

1. The Cambodian Peace Process and the Role of the United Nations

HISTORY OF THE PEACE PROCESS

It took Member States, regional organizations and the United Nations more than 12 years to bring the different Cambodian factions to the negotiating table. As of 1979, the Secretary-General of the United Nations was offering the good offices of the Organization to broker peace; at the request of the General Assembly, he convened an International Conference on Kampuchea (ICK) in 1981. Though Vietnam and its allies did not participate, the peace process was set in motion. Throughout the 1980s the Special Representative of the Secretary-General (SRSG) attended the annual meetings of the foreign ministers of the Association of South East Asian Nations (ASEAN), thus providing a channel of communication between ASEAN and Vietnam. It is worth noting the key role played by ASEAN throughout this period in helping to mobilize the international community through diplomatic action to support and eventually achieve a comprehensive settlement of the Cambodian conflict. Amidst on-going diplomatic efforts, the Secretary-General visited the region in 1985 and, in the report subsequently submitted to the General Assembly, he identified the major elements of a possible comprehensive political settlement. The report outlined many of the conditions that would ultimately become part of the final Peace Plan:

(a) the withdrawal of foreign forces;
(b) the right of the Cambodian people to decide their future through free and fair elections;
(c) national reconciliation as proposed by the ASEAN foreign ministers;
(d) renunciation of the universally condemned policies and practices of the past;
(e) the formation of a non-aligned, independent and neutral sovereign State;
(f) international guarantees.

The Jakarta Informal Meetings (JIM I and JIM II) of July 1988 and February 1989, as well as the first Paris Conference of July 1989, though inconclusive, paved the way for both a more comprehensive peace plan, and for an enhanced role of the United Nations in the process. The five Permanent Members of the Security Council undertook to negotiate, as a first step, an understanding among themselves, and thereafter an agreement with the Cambodian factions. Between 1989 and 1991, amidst a rapidly changing world situation, the different parties, under the co-chairmanship of France and Indonesia, negotiated a framework document that was ultimately to become the "Paris Agreements". They also agreed that the instruments for implementing their decision would be the United Nations Transitional Authority in Cambodia (UNTAC) and the Supreme National Council (SNC), composed of representatives of each of the Cambodian factions. The Agreements were signed by all Cambodian factions in Paris in October 1991. The establishment of UNTAC was approved by the Security Council in February 1992.

NEW REQUIREMENTS IN PEACE-KEEPING

Over the last decade, United Nations peace-keeping operations have undergone drastic modifications to cope with the many international and regional conflicts that have erupted since the ending of East–West confrontation.

Firstly, the mandates have become more complex and comprehensive, as the United Nations is no longer expected simply to maintain a cease-fire. Mandates such as that of UNTAC covered a broad range of diverse activities, including election-monitoring, mine-clearance, repatriation of refugees and displaced persons, troop demobilization, protection of human rights, and support for national reconstruction.

Secondly, the size of peace-keeping operations has increased and, as a result, such operations are far more costly. UNTAC and UNOSOM II each deployed more than 20,000 personnel, and UNPROFOR more than 30,000. The cost of each of these operations exceeded US$1 billion. As might be expected, these large-scale operations have placed a tremendous financial burden on the United Nations. They have also raised pertinent questions in terms of the expertise and general preparedness of the Organization to meet such demands. Today, two of the most urgent issues facing the United Nations and its Member States relate to the organizational aspects of peace-keeping operations and to their financing.

Finally, the civilian component in all peace-keeping operations has grown. As these operations become more comprehensive, the role of civilian personnel, particularly in the fields of election-monitoring, security, administration, and humanitarian aid, has become crucial. The mobilization and training of such personnel and their deployment in the field in an integrated manner, as well as their protection and security, demand careful study.

UNTAC: A COMPLEX AND COMPREHENSIVE OPERATION

Although not the largest, the operation in Cambodia was arguably the United Nations' most complex and comprehensive undertaking to date. It called for some 15,900 military personnel, 3600 civilian police and 1020 civilian personnel from more than 30 countries.

UNTAC's mandate went far beyond that of traditional peace-keeping. It postulated major tasks in institution-building and social reconstruction as integral parts of a peace-building "package" designed to secure an end to armed conflict, and a transition to genuine democracy. To this end, UNTAC was endowed with significant legislative and electoral, civil administration, police, human rights, repatriation, rehabilitation, and reconstruction functions.

UNTAC achieved its primary objective of organizing and conducting free and fair elections in May 1993. This was no mean achievement: it provided for some 365,000 displaced Cambodians from the Thai border to be successfully repatriated, and for some 200,000 internally displaced persons to return to their villages. Since the end of the UNTAC mandate, external powers have largely withdrawn material support for the various Cambodian political groupings, thereby at least reducing the possibility of a destructive civil war continuing endlessly.

As in all pioneering ventures, there were a number of serious flaws in UNTAC itself, both in its conception and in its implementation: the tardy deployment of some inefficiently planned central elements inhibited the aims of the operation from the outset. Civil administration control over the key areas of government was late in coming and not fully achieved throughout the mission. The civilian police element, with some exceptions, proved to be largely unsatisfactory, and the adequate prosecution of human rights abuses proved impossible, making it difficult to create a minimum human rights basis for the new Government.

A detailed study of the UNTAC process inevitably raises the broader question of the need for a clear definition of the objectives of peace-keeping and peace-making undertakings, especially those that can be classified as major operations. In the case of UNTAC, such a study requires an understanding of what the international community, the United Nations, the parties to the Paris Agreements, the regional groupings, the factions and the Permanent Five set out to achieve through the Peace Plan, and what instruments for delivery and management of that process they had in mind. Any inquiry of such a nature, if it is to provide valid lessons for the future, must address the question of the gap between those who conceive and decide to mount a peace-keeping operation, and those who have the task of its implementation and of safeguarding its viability.

THE ADVANCE SURVEY MISSION

Once the final round of negotiations among all parties to the Paris Agreements was under way, preparations for the implementation of UNTAC began. In October 1991 and immediately following the signature of the Agreements, the Security Council established the United Nations Advance Mission in Cambodia (UNAMIC). A US$200 million fund was set up to facilitate early procurement of equipment and materials for UNTAC itself.

UNAMIC consisted of civilian and military liaison staff, a military mine-awareness unit, and logistics and support personnel. In January 1992 the Security Council, in its resolution 728, extended the mandate of UNAMIC to include training in mine-clearance for Cambodians. UNAMIC's mandate was to maintain the existing cease-fire through liaison and communication (though with only 50 military liaison officers (MLOs) in the whole country), establish relations with the SNC with a view to the setting-up of UNTAC, and to institute a mine-awareness programme, which was subsequently enlarged to mine-clearance training.

The MLOs were deployed almost immediately to the State of Cambodia (SOC) general headquarters in Phnom Penh, in the two regimental centres of Battambang and Siem Reap, and in the general headquarters of the three other factions. In preparation for UNTAC, reconnaissance for the cantonment sites was conducted in the territories of all four factions.

The Mixed Military Working Group (MMWG), composed of United Nations officers from several nations and the liaison officers of the armed forces of the Cambodian parties, was established under the auspices of UNAMIC. It set up the Cambodian Mine Action Centre (CMAC) to act as a focal point for mine information, coordinate the training of Cambodian mine-clearers, and channel funds for mine-clearing and the actual long-term mine-clearance programme. The MMWG was also called upon to deal with the already occurring cease-fire violations.

Furthermore, UNAMIC carried out civil operations and had to address a number of immediate issues: release of political prisoners and prisoners of war, freedom of the press and freedom of movement including free entry and exit of foreign journalists, as well as practical arrangements for the repatriation of the returnees. Over 600 political prisoners and prisoners of war were released throughout Cambodia before the establishment of UNTAC.

THE UNTAC START-UP

UNTAC became operational on 15 March 1992, somewhat earlier than expected, and absorbed UNAMIC. Its first manifestation was, however, symbolic: the SRSG, though successful in gathering a senior team, had few support staff and little equipment at his disposal. It took almost six months to get the basic structure of men and material in place.

There were numerous reasons for the substantive delays in the deployment of UNTAC. Despite close involvement in and monitoring of the peace process by United Nations officials, no concrete planning or preparation had been undertaken at Headquarters, nor were adequate budgetary or human resources allocated to allow for this. In addition, a number of events, such as the appointment of a new Secretary-General at the beginning of 1992, and the pressures put on the United Nations due to the emerging crisis in the former Yugoslavia, further accentuated these delays.

In terms of the management of the operation, the SRSG was the key officer responsible for its conduct and success. Assisted by a few advisers and the component directors, and reporting directly to the Secretary-General, the SRSG had the task of interacting with the SNC, the factions, and the representatives of the "Extended Permanent Five" (EP5) in Phnom Penh. The EP5 comprised, along with the ambassadors of the five Permanent Members of the Security Council, ambassadors from Australia, Germany, Indonesia, Japan and Thailand, and served to ensure that the Cambodian parties fulfilled their obligations. It must be underlined that the EP5 was instrumental in ensuring that the realities on the ground were being communicated to the missions in New York, and through them to the

Security Council. This precluded over-reactions at United Nations Headquarters, and ensured that Security Council resolutions reflected the actual situation in the field and were framed to be implemented. Although not in a position to implement the Paris Agreements as envisaged, UNTAC was nevertheless able to move towards the goal of the Agreements enjoying a degree of legitimacy from the international community. It is noteworthy that such a degree of involvement of Member States in the implementation of the mandate did not occur in most other major United Nations peace-keeping operations.

On the military side, demilitarization of the country was envisaged through regroupment, cantonment, disarmament and demobilization of different military forces in order to facilitate the creation of a neutral political environment and peaceful conditions for the holding of free and fair elections. These objectives could be achieved only partially.

One of the primary responsibilities of UNTAC was to establish a neutral political environment, conducive to the holding of free and fair general elections. This was to be achieved by ensuring strict impartiality through relevant administrative structures, and a sufficient number of adequately trained personnel was needed to perform this task. At that time emphasis was given to recruiting the personnel from within the United Nations system. Given the size of the requirements, as well as the range of expertise needed, the United Nations system could not meet the demand. In the end, Member States provided personnel, but it took time to get them in place.

Peace-keeping operations require prompt availability and dispatch of men and material. Under current United Nations rules and procedures, which were followed (and which are still used in other peace-keeping operations), it was not possible to assemble the personnel and equipment rapidly enough, for no procedures can guarantee quick responses on the part of governments. On the practical plane, the planning for UNTAC's structure was based on the advanced analysis by UNAMIC. However, this analysis was not always accurate and it proved most difficult to cope with the magnitude of the operation once it unfolded.

THE FOUR CAMBODIAN POLITICAL FACTIONS

FUNCINPEC: French acronym for the *National Union Front for an Independent, Neutral, Peaceful and Cooperative Cambodia*, the royalist party of Prince (now King) Norodom Sihanouk under the leadership of his son, Prince Norodom Ranariddh.

KPNLF: the *Khmer People's National Liberation Front* of former Prime Minister Son Sann, comprising the remnants of the Lon Nol regime whose political and military elements had meanwhile split. This group launched the *Buddhist Liberal Democratic Party* (BLDP).

PDK (Khmer Rouge): the *Party of Democratic Kampuchea*, under the nominal presidency of Khieu Samphan but with Pol Pot still considerably involved in the background.

SOC: the *State of Cambodia* (prior to 1989, People's Republic of Kampuchea – PRK), with Prime Minister Hun Sen and Communist party chief, Chea Sim. As of 1991 the political party for this group was called the *Cambodian People's Party* (CPP).

2. The UNTAC Components

In February 1992, the Secretary-General submitted a report to the Security Council that contained his proposed implementation plan for the Paris Agreements. The Council approved this by its resolution 745 of February 1992, establishing UNTAC under its authority for a period not to exceed 18 months. UNTAC became operational in March 1992, absorbing UNAMIC.

UNTAC consisted of seven distinct components, with responsibilities in the fields of human rights, electoral activities, military, civil administration, civilian police, repatriation and rehabilitation. UNTAC's strength varied according to the phase of the operation, with over 21,000 military and civilian personnel present at maximum strength.

THE MILITARY COMPONENT

Number of staff: 16,000 in 270 locations.

Mandate and structure

The military was charged with the following main functions:
(a) verification of the withdrawal and non-return of foreign forces, their arms and equipment from Cambodia;
(b) supervision of the cease-fire and related measures, including the regrouping, cantonment and disarming of the armed forces of the Cambodian parties, and demobilization of at least 70% of these armed forces;
(c) weapons control, including monitoring the cessation of outside military assistance, locating and confiscating caches of weapons and military supplies throughout Cambodia and storing of the arms and equipment of the cantoned and demobilized military forces;
(d) assisting with mine-clearance, including training and mine-awareness programmes.

In addition, the military was responsible for providing assistance in the release of prisoners of war and in the repatriation of Cambodian refugees and displaced persons.

The Military Component was the most visible face of UNTAC. It was deployed throughout Cambodia in such a manner as to generate confidence in the United Nations' commitment to proceed with the mandate. In areas where security was at risk, the military provided a firm base and protection as well as logistic support for the other UNTAC components. This was particularly important for the UNTAC's Electoral Component as voter registration (October 1992) and the polling process started.

Once the cease-fire provisions of the Paris Agreements were recognized as being no longer viable, it became clear that a secure environment for the elections could not be guaranteed without the back-up of the Military Component. This meant maintaining the UNTAC force at full strength. Accordingly, in December 1992, the Military Component was redeployed to align its command structure with that of the Civil Administration Component.

At a sector commanders' conference in January 1993, with UNTAC provincial directors and electoral officers, the Head of the Civil Administration Component observed that although the Paris Agreements did not rule out an election in the absence of disarmament, such a situation was likely to lead to a climate of violence. He stated:

Ensuring the security of the electoral process in its entirety is now ... the principal mission of the Military Component ... . Our respective activities ... are becoming complementary and profoundly linked. From our viewpoint, this participation of military personnel in the realization of civilian objectives is a veritable godsend: free of the constraints of the tasks ... originally assigned, the Military Component can utilize its technical competence (which is large), its important material and personnel capabilities, as well as its remarkable faculty for organization resulting from its own technique of military command, which together act to enhance the control activity normally carried out by the Civil Administration Component.

There was no strategic coordination in the planning for UNTAC, with each component proceeding in isolation with its own plan. This resulted in many problems. For example, the repatriation programme proceeded before the Military Component was deployed into a countryside in which the cease-fire was breaking down and some areas were still heavily mined. A Malaysian battalion had to be deployed urgently in order to provide escort and security to the repatriation convoys. This escort duty was an essential role which the military performed throughout the operation.[1]

The Military Component played a key role in using civic action to gain the respect of the Cambodian people. "Hearts and minds" activities formed an essential part of the Military Component's method of operation. Unfortunately, there was great difficulty in convincing the United Nations Secretariat and mission administration that the Military Component had a role to play in civic action, the prevailing view being that this was the role of other United Nations agencies and non-governmental organizations (NGOs). The Military Component's presence and the protection it provided facilitated humanitarian tasks and helped convince the Cambodian people of UNTAC's commitment. Civic action programmes were set up with the help of donations from individual countries. Close cooperation with other United Nations agencies and NGOs, as well as effective use of the nation-building

---

[1] Lieutenant General Sanderson has emphasized that, in this context, he is referring to a weakness at the strategic level, specifically in the disconnection in the planning process leading to the compilation of the report of the Secretary-General on Cambodia, dated 19 February 1992. He does not refer to the efforts to effect coordination in the conduct of the mission, made at the operational level in Phnom Penh, after UNTAC was established in March 1992.

and other skills that many of the United Nations soldiers brought to Cambodia, helped improve the situation in a number of ways. An essential lesson that emerged from the UNTAC mission was the need for an integrated approach to be adopted in the planning and conduct of peacekeeping operations, all the way from the Secretariat to the forward area, and from the beginning of the mandate to its conclusion.

One of the more valuable tools in reinforcing UNTAC policy was the Mixed Military Working Group (MMWG) Secretariat. The MMWG was a forum set up under the Paris Agreements to resolve problems relating to the cease-fire. However, owing to the difficulties faced, it became the Force Commander's main instrument for dealing with the armed forces of the Cambodian parties. The creation of a fully functioning and pro-active Secretariat to support negotiations was a key decision. This was composed mainly of a small core of professional officers from Southeast Asian nations. This deliberate decision created confidence among the liaison officers of the armed forces of the Cambodian parties.

The MMWG Secretariat issued a considerable volume of correspondence, agendas and other papers, in English and in Khmer, designed to keep UNTAC well ahead of developments. It maintained continuous liaison and conducted frequent complex negotiations with the military staff of all the Cambodian factions and was particularly active in resolving difficult situations. It also acted as a coordinating agency with the civilian components, other United Nations agencies and NGOs.

The MMWG Secretariat's work enabled UNTAC to be more pro-active in negotiations, and made a strong contribution to creating trust between the UNTAC Military Component and the military personnel of all parties, including the Khmer Rouge liaison officers who came into contact with it. The MMWG placed considerable emphasis on the reconciliation of the armed forces of the parties, and actively encouraged the unification of the armed forces of the three parties which participated in the UNTAC sponsored elections (the PDK declined to participate) leading, after the elections, to the formation of a national army which was committed to the constitutional process. The MMWG thus provided a major stabilizing influence at a critical time, when the losers of the election threatened to overturn the outcome. The pro-active approach of the MMWG and its Secretariat requires particularly close scrutiny since such mechanisms are highly likely to be applicable to many other peace-keeping missions.

As regards the Force Commander's relationship with the Extended Permanent Five (EP5), it must be noted that meetings were frequent and the representatives in Phnom Penh were briefed regularly. On many occasions, the EP5 representatives attended meetings of the MMWG; this was instrumental in generating confidence in what the UNTAC Military Component was trying to achieve, namely, the maintenance of strict impartiality and the implementation of the Paris Agreements as faithfully as possible under the circumstances. The EP5 closely paralleled the grouping of ambassadors in New York known as the "Core Group". The Security Council was also in receipt of mission reports processed by UNTAC military liaison officers deployed to New York for the purpose.

The involvement of ambassadors was also important in aspects concerning force discipline. United Nations Force Commanders have no jurisdiction over the international contingents under their operational command, and must therefore rely on a rapid response by the contributing countries to such issues, or their intervening with their national contingents as and when necessary.

As regards the Cambodian military forces, according to information provided by the four parties, their regular military forces totalled over 200,000, with another 250,000 militia operating throughout the country. These forces were armed with over 300,000 weapons and some 80 million rounds of ammunition. Although by mid-November 1992 UNTAC had cantoned some 55,000 troops of the three cooperating parties, the refusal of the Party of Democratic Kampuchea (PDK) to participate fully in the peace process made the full implementation of Phase II of the cease-fire uncertain. This resulted in the suspension of the cantonment and demobilization of the armed forces of the four parties.

Safeguarding unity and impartiality

One of the key goals of the UNTAC Military Component was the preservation of its unity and impartiality through strict adherence to the peace-keeping ethos. Unity of purpose, command and understanding were the principles under which the Military Component had to function so as to represent the will of the international community. Without such unity, it would not have been possible for the force to remain impartial.

A United Nations force needs to maintain cohesion – it cannot afford to be a collection of national contingents, each following a separate agenda; it must be seen as pursuing the agreed objectives of its mandate. Some elements of the Military Component were influenced by their national governments to take positions which were not in harmony with the overall directive of the Force Commander. This allowed the Khmer Rouge to classify some units as "good UNTAC" and others as "bad UNTAC", in its attempts to widen divisions within the force.

The cultural diversity of 16,000 troops, drawn from 34 Member States, made cohesion difficult. Efforts at generating cohesion were made by involving everyone in the planning process, by continuous briefings, and by clear directives and strict adherence to the peace-keeping ethos. There were also advantages to this diversity. Troops from countries with similar economic and social problems and an affinity with Cambodian culture were more attuned to Cambodian needs and sensitivities, and were thus able to strengthen UNTAC's relationships with the people.

Mine-clearance

The mine-clearing resources of UNTAC were very limited: the Military Component was supposed only to "assist ... with clearing mines and undertaking training programmes in mine-clearance and a mine-awareness programme among the Cambodian people".

The magnitude of the mine problem became clear during the UNAMIC survey; only a long-term coordinated approach would work. The Cambodian Mine Action Centre (CMAC) was then set up and designed to continue well beyond the expiry of the UNTAC mandate. The fundamental objectives of CMAC were:

(a) to act as a focal point for mine information;
(b) to coordinate the training of Cambodian mine-clearers (10,000 was the target), the funds provided for mine-clearing, and the clearing of mines over the long term.

The repatriation programme and the appeals of the NGOs concerned with the mine problem soon brought calls for the diversion of scarce training resources to mine-clearing, so as to avoid an immediate crisis and save lives. The effect, however, was the opposite of that intended, and slowed progress toward the overall objective of clearing the mines from the Cambodian countryside. With an integrated approach to planning and conduct of the mission, immediate objectives could have been given their proper perspective and appropriately resourced in order to avoid their drawing away resources from the attainment of longer-term objectives.

Standardization of equipment

In any sizeable peace-keeping mission, and in operations such as UNTAC *a fortiori*, it is necessary to establish a check-list for donors of military equipment to ensure, to the extent reasonably possible, standardization and compatibility of equipment. Some units of the UNTAC Military Component arrived with equipment which was old, and thus required more spare parts/replacements. Others brought equipment that was totally inappropriate (for example, electrical equipment running on 110V, rather than UNTAC's 220V, thus necessitating the purchase of extra generators). Some contingents were well equipped, while others arrived with almost no equipment at all. There were also complaints about engineering support arriving with inappropriate equipment.

Logistics

Adequate logistic support was not always available, and there were delays in the setting-up of an efficient logistics chain. This was particularly apparent in procurement and maintenance. Religious conventions with regard to food also presented problems for some contingents. Others expressed concern that spare parts were not provided in time. For all these reasons, a thorough review of procurement procedures and preparation of check-lists is essential.

Military personnel problems

The issue of pay and allowances created serious difficulties in two areas: the first of these was the huge discrepancy between subsistence payments to United Nations civilians (including CIVPOL), which varied between US$130 and US$160 per day, and the much lower subsistence payments to military personnel designated members of "contingents". Instances occurred where

United Nations police earned more in a day than military officers of the same country could earn in a month. In a country where the average income was about US$100 per annum, such high payments were difficult to justify. The issue of subsistence equity needs close examination. The second issue was that of the delay in reimbursement of troop costs. A number of developing countries relied on these payments to pay their contingents and the delay meant that their troops were not paid for up to nine months. Reimbursement processes need streamlining, especially in such cases.

Although misbehaviour was not widespread in the Military Component, the actions of a few, and their potential impact on the mission, gave cause for concern. A military code of conduct and professional standards should be drawn up by the United Nations to cover troop behaviour. It was difficult to produce a consistent set of standards of professionalism and behaviour among UNTAC's blue berets. How they related to the local population was also crucial. Invariably the Cambodian parties made propaganda use of incidents of poor troop discipline to vilify the United Nations' effort. More directly, the international press showed a tendency to condemn the entire force on the basis of its inability to correct the actions of a small minority. The United Nations Secretariat alone reserves the right, in the light of the views of the Permanent Five, to decide which troops come from which countries. This is done in accordance with the Secretariat's priorities, which, in the case of UNTAC, were not always consistent with the needs of the mission. Issues of professionalism, discipline and the human rights record of the armed forces concerned should, of necessity, be considerations in contingent selection.

Misbehaviour was not exclusive to the Military Component; some CIVPOL and other civilians acted in unacceptable ways. Codes of conduct are warranted for these personnel and should include disciplinary arrangements for non-compliance.

The military future in Cambodia

Payment of the wages of the Cambodian troops and police (and, for that matter, of the Cambodian civil service) was a major question that arose throughout the mandate but, in particular, after the elections. The factional administrations had effectively emptied their treasuries to pay for their electoral campaigns. There was a real danger of the military forces fragmenting into autonomous local armies or bandit groups and the police taking matters into their own hands in order to survive. The immediate problem was resolved by arranging for budget support from the remnants of the 1991 UNAMIC trust fund. "Operation Paymaster", planned and executed by the MMWG, was a great success. It provided salaries to the armed forces in the final months of the UNTAC mandate. To receive such pay, the recipients had to make a formal pledge of allegiance to the new Government. This was the major incentive for the unification of the armed forces, and proved a stabilizing factor.

The formation and effective training of the Royal Cambodian Armed Forces (RCAF) is still an outstanding issue. It was one which was recognized by the parties when drafting the Paris Agreements, but it was decided then that it was a matter more properly left to the sovereign Cambodian Government when it was installed. Pay (or lack of it) is also still a central problem affecting morale, encouraging corruption, and to an extent even perpetuating the factionalism of the former armies now comprising the RCAF. This sets back efforts to build the RCAF into a cohesive force.

The international community has devoted considerable resources to the reconstruction and rehabilitation of Cambodia; effectively ignoring one of the principal institutions on which the country's future security and stability clearly depends would be counter-productive. Military assistance is not ruled out by Agreement III on Cambodian neutrality. The drafting was quite careful on this point, as there was no wider agreement on specific references to building a new national army. Under Article V of that Agreement there is a duty on the signatories – and even on the United Nations – to take action to prevent or suppress the sort of massive violations of human rights which occurred in Cambodia in the past. To date, however, only a handful of States have shown any willingness to extend military assistance to Cambodia. Comprehensive arrangements for armed forces and police need to be given careful consideration in any mission which focuses on nation-building or rebuilding, particularly in the post-election period and perhaps even post-mandate.

Recommendations

Major issues to be addressed are those of self-defence and the use of force, which remain recurrent problems in all peace-keeping operations. Confusion over these issues plagues many missions. Standing operating procedures and continuous briefings need to provide clear definitions. This was the case in UNTAC, where self-defence meant defence by anyone going about their legitimate business under the Paris Agreements. However, some contributing countries and analysts had differing interpretations. Eventually, the majority of the military units were prepared and equipped to follow the UNTAC definition. It was important that operations were seen to be conducted strictly within these constraints, in order to maintain international consensus behind the mission and unity within it, especially as concerns increased over time. At various times, however, suggestions were made that the UNTAC Military Component should somehow become engaged in internal security operations, for which it was neither structured nor equipped and, most importantly, for which it had no legal mandate. For such operations a force many times larger would have been required, equipped with the array of combat and support systems needed for a protracted conflict, and at significantly greater cost. There was no consensus for the use of force – internationally, in the Security Council, in UNTAC, or in the contributing countries. Had attempts been made to use force, both UNTAC and the international support behind it would have been very likely to have been torn apart and the Cambodian peace process, the result of years of diplomatic effort and a huge expenditure in international funds, would have unravelled.

A peace-keeping force is an instrument of diplomacy, not of war. Its acceptability, both internationally and among the parties to the dispute, comes about because it is impartial. Enforcement action requires much stronger international consensus and domestic political support in the contributing countries. In the event that this is not possible, it is necessary to ensure that the message is clearly understood. Unless forthright measures are taken to preserve its impartiality, a formal body of international troops could become a factor in the conflict, whether this was intended or not. There is potential disaster in a military force being caught up in a conflict, if there is no clearly identified or achievable operational objective which will allow honourable termination of involvement.

Contributing countries have repeatedly requested to be involved in military planning at the highest level. They have correctly argued that time is needed to equip, train and otherwise ready their troops for peace-keeping operations. The critical issues are early warning and forward planning, to allow timely national decision-making processes and preparation of forces to occur.

Training is seen to be a national responsibility of the contributing countries. Some countries would like United Nations assistance in providing standardized courses in military peace-keeping. There is a need for specialized military courses in subjects like mine-clearance. Member States should also be able to rely on the United Nations to provide guidance on mission-oriented background information on the politics, culture, customs and language of the area or country where the peace-keeping force will be deployed. Regional training centres would be useful in preparing troops for peace-keeping actions in specific geographic areas. They would also help officers of the area's contributing nations to make and keep contacts.

THE POLICE COMPONENT

Number of staff: 3,600 civilian police monitors.

Mandate and structure

The UNTAC police monitors were charged with supervising or controlling the local civil police, thus ensuring that law and order were maintained effectively and impartially, and that human rights and fundamental freedoms were fully protected. There was a Policy and Management Unit at headquarters in Phnom Penh, 21 units at the provincial level and 200 district-level units. This gave an estimated ratio of one UNTAC police monitor in the field to approximately 15 local civil police.

By the end of December 1992, the Civilian Police Component (CIVPOL) of UNTAC had reached almost full deployment of its personnel. About two-thirds of the force were employed in assisting with first the voter registration process and later the actual elections. UNTAC provided the local police with training in basic police methods and traffic-control procedures. Special instruction was also given to police officers and judiciary in the implementation of the new penal code adopted by the SNC in September 1992. Some 90 Cambodian police officers, including 24 from the Party of Democratic Kampuchea (PDK), were awarded certificates after these courses.

The Police Component's duties also included directing the efforts of the local police force against banditry in the interior. It participated, in cooperation with the Military Component, in supervising the checkpoints and patrols of the existing police forces in sensitive areas. It investigated cases of human rights abuses and was meant to promote a neutral political environment in Cambodia. Before the May 1993 elections, it instigated the static guarding of political party offices against night attacks.

The police monitoring action was one of the United Nations' first attempts of this sort, and there were numerous problems. CIVPOL's experience, however, provided a number of lessons that could benefit similar missions in the future. They are divided into two groups: lessons primarily for the United Nations, and lessons for countries contributing police contingents.

Appointments, qualifications and training

Appointment of key officials is needed at a much earlier stage than that at which it took place in UNTAC. CIVPOL's commander was requested to come to New York by the end of February 1992 and was officially appointed by the Secretary-General on 6 March. That same day the official police contributors' conference was held. The mission started on 15 March.

It took the Police Component eight months to reach full deployment. From the operational point of view, this created an impossible situation. Although the United Nations cannot enforce personnel contributions in any way, it is vital to approach potential contributor countries as early as possible, to anable them to accelerate their selection and training programmes.

The Police Component had to face considerable problems throughout the mandated period in meeting official requirements for police monitors. The United Nations requested six years of police experience, possession of a valid national driver's licence, additional experience with four-wheel drive vehicles, and sufficient proficiency in the official languages of the mission.

The level of police experience required was too general, in view of the substantial differences among various national police forces. Depending on the police mandate, this requirement should be defined more accurately, specifically requesting experience in "community policing". In addition various other special police skills were required, e.g. training experience, investigation, technical and forensic experience, communications, traffic, and crime-scene handling. Practical requirements such as a driver's licence and experience are essential for the proper performance of the police mission and also for safety. Of all the policemen lost in three major recent United Nations missions, most casualties resulted from traffic accidents. Non-drivers in national contingents should not be accepted.

The language requirement

Although in most cases language problems are not as potentially life-threatening as a lack of driving skills, they do seriously hamper the effectiveness of a police mission. By the nature of their mandate, United Nations police personnel must communicate directly with their local counterparts and with the local population (sometimes through interpreters).

Language should be taken into account in the selection of potential police-contributing countries. If there is an English-speaking mission, junior personnel from non-English speaking countries could have trouble communicating. Provision for competent interpreters must also be made, as necessary.

Two sorts of training experience are needed: training of local police as part of the mandate, and training of CIVPOL personnel before actual deployment in their police districts and stations of the mission area.

Training of local police is an essential element in the reconstruction of a country and its administration. Reconstruction of a country's infrastructure, civil service, health care and education will all be of little use in a lawless environment. Close cooperation and joint planning between law-makers, judicial experts, human rights experts and United Nations police is therefore necessary. This will help in setting up a comprehensive system of law enforcement and will enable local police to play their part in the reconstruction process. Training of CIVPOL personnel is essential to realize the goals set out in the mandate. This should already start in the home countries with United Nations assistance where needed, for example, with the help of police training manuals developed by the United Nations.

Relations with other components

For a multi-component mission like UNTAC, policy-level conferences are essential, in order to allow senior officials (e.g. component directors) to brief each other on developments in their sectors and to find ways to forestall or resolve problems. Certain administrative procedures should be standardized between components. A problem of this type existed with regard to provisions for leave and time off. Compensatory time off (CTO), for example, should be replaced by a straightforward regulation for days off. The CTO system was never designed for large organizations such as CIVPOL, but rather for small groups operating individually, such as United Nations military observers.

Recommendations

A commanders' conference prior to deployment is likely to produce more and better information which is needed for the preparation of the contingents. Such a conference was held before the Namibian mission, with good results.

Training of police contingents prior to deployment is of the utmost importance. It should focus on specific items: the mandate of the mission; knowledge of the problems in the mission area (the reasons for deployment of a United Nations mission); the nature of the police operation; the environment in which the police must operate (climate, health risks, security situation); and a refresher course on various police skills.

Discipline is a major part of preparatory training, starting with an appropriate national selection procedure. An offer to volunteer is a useful factor, but personnel files should be systematically checked. A first selection should be followed by observations during the entire training period. Contributing nations must ensure discipline directly during the policeman's tour of duty with the United Nations.

During training, national contingents must be provided with information on the cultural, religious and racial differences to be found in a multinational police operation. Instructors should point out the importance of cooperation between different nationalities.

Background information on the local population is also essential. On this issue, the United Nations can be of assistance by making this information available as early and as comprehensively as possible.

Contributing countries should strictly follow the United Nations requirements for police monitors. Contingent members should be professional community police with several years' experience, have a driver's licence and several years of driving experience, and speak at least one of the official languages of the mission.

Contributors should also follow the United Nations rules for the medical examination, based on the existing United Nations regulations and inoculation programme. Valuable UNTAC time was lost because countries did not follow the United Nations medical requirements.

The setting-up of a police planning group containing relevant expertise under United Nations auspices would be useful. Many Member States may be willing to provide expertise on a voluntary basis. Relevant "field experience" should be a necessary qualification for each member of the planning team. The planning staff could also be reinforced on a temporary basis by police officers likely to be deployed in forthcoming missions.

In the few days allowed for practical police planning for the UNTAC mission, the Police Commissioner gathered a small staff who later served as his assistants in Cambodia. This proved to be of significant help, particularly as the Police Commissioner designate was not a member of the UNAMIC survey team, which led to problems in fulfilling the mission guidelines established in the first place. Integrated planning with other designated component leaders is essential when setting up a mission. Except for the experts taking part in UNAMIC, the rest of the senior UNTAC management only met on the plane from Bangkok to Phnom Penh at the official start of the mission.

THE CIVIL ADMINISTRATION COMPONENT

Number of staff: 95 international staff in Phnom Penh and 123 in the provinces.

Mandate and structure

Article 6 of the Paris Peace Agreements stipulates that:

in order to ensure a neutral political environment conducive to free and fair elections, administrative agencies, bodies and offices which could directly influence the outcome of the elections will be placed under direct United Nations supervision or control. In that context, special attention will be given to foreign affairs, national defence, finance, public security and information.

The range of UNTAC's mandate in this area, particularly as regards the five key areas mentioned, which came to be known as "direct control", was unique, and despite UNTAC's discernible effort to exercise such control, it was hampered from the outset by insufficient numbers of staff. There was a substantial delay in recruitment for the civil administration. Priority was given to the Military Component, and the Civil Administration Component (CIVADMIN) staff was not complete until October 1992.

The Civil Administration Component had, in theory, three complementary means of control: control *a posteriori*, control *a priori*, and appraisal. The first was to be achieved through the receipt of all documentation dealing with the operation of the existing administrative structures, the second through the authority to change decisions dealing, for instance, with personnel, finance and the sale of assets, and the last was to be achieved through the proposal of improvements in the operations of the existing administrative structures. In reality, however, CIVADMIN never had the means or resources to meet these objectives. Each provincial director had only three international staff working for him/her: one deputy, one human rights expert and one financial controller, in addition to two international secretaries. These human resources were clearly inadequate.

According to CIVADMIN's Deputy Director:

in Phnom Penh, a city of one million people, the centre of all administrative and political decisions, not to mention the financial hub and the one point where all political parties set up their headquarters, Civil Administration was initially allocated four persons for the municipal office. Eventually, there were 18 international staff. They were to control and monitor the budget and financial transactions of the city administration, register and monitor all aspiring political parties, investigate all complaints, monitor and control the judicial process, prevent political intimidation and harassment, control corruption and abuse of power, not to mention putting in place free media and guarantee rights of assembly ... From the start, it was clear that the mandate as written could not be fulfilled. A selective application was necessary.

Some flexibility is therefore required in establishing an optimum-sized administrative staff.

Control mechanisms

The Civil Administration Component set up a Complaints Clarification Committee with UNTAC representatives from CIVPOL, Human Rights and CIVADMIN, and Cambodian representatives from the police, military, prosecutor's office, court and mayor/governor. The Committee jointly considered all data relative to a claim, and the joint Cambodian–UNTAC Implementation Teams carried out the judicial or administrative decisions. Later, more pro-active measures included a Joint Standing Committee on Public Security set up to determine and authorize actions for the control of public order, guarantee security of political party offices and at rallies, and to investigate alleged abuses by police or military. Relations with provincial governors made it possible to determine which reports had to be sent periodically to UNTAC, while round-table meetings with political parties provided forums for discussion and for airing complaints.

CIVADMIN had some success in controlling foreign affairs, and proved effective in dealing with finance and information. However, this was accomplished by the Rehabilitation and Information Components, rather than by CIVADMIN *per se*. Direct control was probably most difficult in internal security and the military sectors, but it moved along the lines foreseen by the Paris Agreements. This control was meant to ensure a neutral political environment that would lead to free and fair general elections. The implementation of the provisions of the Agreements called for experienced personnel, capable of managing and understanding the affairs of government, in particular those of a one-party police state with some scope for mismanagement. Direct control would certainly have been more successful if there had been more human resources available, especially in the provinces.

There was a fundamental divergence between the actual political situation and the control mandate, for the SOC regime did not cooperate in matters of security. This led to major problems in enforcing human rights rules.

Flaws in the administrative structure

Inadequate pre-mission analysis failed to show that power lay with individual leaders, primarily the State of Cambodia (SOC) provincial governors. The ministries in Phnom Penh were largely ineffective, while UNTAC's own structure was centralized in Phnom Penh. It took Civil Administration until December 1992 to realize that the Ministry of the Interior in Phnom Penh was merely an empty shell, and that instructions to provincial governors were conveyed through party channels. In general, the negotiators of the Peace Plan and the planners of UNTAC had gravely underestimated the level of human resources and expertise needed to impose a United Nations presence within the provincial and local administrative offices. Furthermore, a larger than expected number of existing staff was used for UNTAC's own administration, leaving limited staff resources with which to influence the provincial administrators.

The provincial offices of the different components reported directly to the component headquarters in the capital, leaving little opportunity for UNTAC coordination at provincial level. In the future, provincial directors should report directly to the SRSG or his deputy, rather than to the Civil Administration Component head. Once the power structure was understood, UNTAC did make an effort to strengthen the provincial offices, but such coordination generally failed because most component reporting lines still went directly to the capital.

The difficulties of coordinating action at provincial level were compounded by administrative problems of recruitment and deployment; lack of qualified staff; inadequate guidance to and coordination of the provincial offices; a difficult local language; and dependence on insufficiently qualified interpreters. In short, UNTAC needed more experienced administrators to survey the various branches of the local administration.

Recommendations

Plans drawn up for the administrative control of Cambodia during the

UNTAC period were not always realistic and achievable. It is, furthermore, difficult to envision that the United Nations would be able, in future operations, to obtain enough resources to conduct any such detailed "administration" of a given country. But whilst complete administration may be difficult, a well-functioning mechanism for "monitoring", and the authority and will to apply the rule of law and reduce political manipulation, is an alternative which, in the case of UNTAC, was not fully exercised and which could provide an option for future operations.

In selecting its priorities, the SRSG was quoted as saying, when considering the need for voter security and a secret ballot for rebuilding a country through free and fair elections: "public security (for the voter's physical well-being) together with civic education and information about the voting process, become crucial ... Control of finance and other administrative elements are of lesser import." Such action would "demand a tighter, more well-defined and achievable mandate that emphasizes security and information issues. Detailed and integrated planning between CIVPOL and CIVADMIN before deployment is essential." Civil administrators would scrutinize and monitor, rather than attempt to control, the local administration. If there were misdemeanours, publicizing these abuses through a United Nations media system would probably be more effective than trying to work through an inefficient or biased judiciary.

The exercise of an unspecified "management" of the key areas in a nation's administrative structure could, in future, be a determining executive role for the United Nations to play in creating an effective neutral environment conducive to the peaceful resolution of internal conflicts.

The civil administrations that are established to carry out such tasks should look at the following points:

Separate administrative power from political power

The SOC Government was the only effective administrative structure in Cambodia. UNTAC should have attempted to "monitor", rather than unsuccessfully control administrative actions to remove political bias wherever possible. Training courses could help local officials in facilitating the transition from a one-party state to a pluralistic democracy. Such courses should include curricula in impartial civil-service administration and loyalty to a government rather than a political party, and could be developed and standardized by the United Nations itself.

Set up an institution to promote national reconciliation

The Supreme National Council (SNC) was designed to play a key role in national reconciliation. It was composed of 12 members: six SOC representatives and two each from the three opposition parties. It gave the former enemies a forum in which to discuss problems and to begin to work together. The SRSG consulted with the SNC to reach a consensus on proposed legislation.

Set up a standby force of experienced civilian personnel

Such a qualified and experienced personnel should be ready to establish and staff similar mandates. This could be promoted in the same manner as the military standby force. Parallel to such an effort, contracts for future United Nations administrative personnel should include a clause stating that officials must be willing and ready to serve for short periods in peace-keeping operations abroad. The United Nations should provide on-going training and preparation for its staff on peace-keeping issues.

THE HUMAN RIGHTS COMPONENT

Number of staff: Initially ten professionals. With voluntary contributions, additional 15 professionals in Phnom Penh, 21 professionals and 21 Khmer-speaking assistants in the provinces.

Mandate and structure

The Human Rights Component was established to prevent any recurrence of the gross human rights violations of the past and to establish the "neutral political environment" necessary for the conduct of free and fair general elections. The Human Rights Component was expected to deliver concrete results in terms of dissemination and education, institution-building, legislative development, prevention of political violence, and even penal enforcement.

UNTAC was given the most comprehensive human rights mandate ever entrusted to a United Nations peace-keeping operation. This ambitious programme was to be carried out by the smallest UNTAC component, consisting initially of only ten professional staff. The reasoning behind this initial modesty, as indicated by the Secretary-General, was that "all [18,000] UNTAC staff would be charged with carrying out human rights functions, as an integral part of their primary duties". However, only a few had received any human rights training before coming to Cambodia. With voluntary contributions from Member States, this group was later strengthened.

While one of the major goals of the human rights mandate was the training of all UNTAC staff as well as the Cambodian civil administration, the limited resources and time available made this goal impossible. There had been no pre-mission human rights training or even basic human rights briefing for United Nations or non-United Nations staff assigned to the peace-keeping mission in Cambodia. The Human Rights Component arranged *ad hoc* human rights briefing sessions for arriving UNTAC civilian police and for all District Electoral Supervisors. Some 2000 CIVPOL staff were briefed in this limited way, but it was not adequate for their key support role in human rights monitoring and investigation.

Setting up a human rights legal framework

The Cambodian peace settlement provided that the country would become a party to international human rights instruments. Within a month of

UNTAC's arrival, the Supreme National Council (SNC) signed the International Covenants on Civil and Political Rights and on Economic, Social and Cultural Rights. In September 1992, the SNC signed a further five major human rights accords, at UNTAC's request. All these documents were translated into Khmer and widely circulated with the assistance of local human rights groups.

Political control of the judiciary and unsatisfactory penal legislation prompted UNTAC to prepare a transitional criminal law, which was adopted by SNC in September 1992. While this law called for an independent judiciary, Cambodia's judges remained under tight political control. The comprehensive electoral law and rules and the electoral code of conduct drafted by UNTAC and adopted by the SNC also contained some human rights provisions and sanctions. These were used during the electoral period to prevent abuses.

When local authorities failed to take action to stop political violence during the pre-electoral period (and in fact often were responsible for it), the Special Representative of the Secretary-General (SRSG) took the radical step of setting up a Special Prosecutor's Office, in January 1993, despite opposition from both the State of Cambodia (SOC) and non-SOC parties. It had the power to arrest, prosecute and detain persons suspected of serious human rights violations.

Monitoring, investigation, and "corrective actions"

Within this minimum legal framework, the Human Rights Component tried to monitor key institutions and actions by officials. Limited resources meant that priorities had to be set to concentrate the Component's effort on prison conditions, politically or ethnically motivated acts of violence or intimidation, and on judicial and police processes.

In accordance with the Paris Agreements, all known "civilian internees" and prisoners of war were reportedly released prior to UNTAC's arrival. The Human Rights Component, aided by CIVPOL, undertook systematic visits to all known prisons in Phnom Penh and later in the provinces. All of the prisons visited failed to meet the most basic international standards, partly because of inadequate resources. Lack of funds primarily accounted for the low health and other standards, and the shortage of staff. The non-functioning judicial system meant that prisons were constantly overcrowded.

All these prisons were under the authority of SOC. Other factions denied the existence of prisons in their areas, although UNTAC believed that there were military-run detention camps in various sections of the country. The SOC authorities agreed with UNTAC on basic guidelines for prison conditions and visits. UNTAC generally could obtain access to prisons without prior notice.

UNTAC was able to achieve some improvement in prison conditions and the release of some untried prisoners on humanitarian grounds, but the overall health, medical and penal situation remained far from satisfactory. Almost all prisoners had been detained without a trial – not even the most basic judicial requirements were met. Thus prisoners were effectively detained as "civilian internees", in contravention of the Paris Agreements.

UNTAC investigated and intervened in other situations of human rights violations connected with politically motivated attacks on opposition party members before the elections, and attacks on Cambodians of ethnic Vietnamese origin. Direct attacks on UNTAC personnel by Cambodians were also investigated.

CIVPOL investigated the killing of 442 Cambodians, including persons of ethnic Vietnamese origin, during the mission, with the Human Rights Component surveying the most serious attacks and those with human rights implications. A further 633 Cambodians were injured in these attacks and 200 Cambodians were abducted or disappeared. The United Nations Military, CIVPOL and Human Rights Components also investigated cases of UNTAC personnel killed or injured by armed Cambodians. The lack of effective legal punishment and the failure to pursue these investigations, however, deeply affected UNTAC staff morale.

In total, the Component investigated some 1300 complaints or violations, many referred by CIVPOL and the Military Component. In view of the limited resources, investigations were often carried out jointly by CIVPOL and the military. The lack of trained investigators among UNTAC personnel sometimes led to difficulties and delays. The results of these investigations were shared with the SNC, the SOC and other parties, as well as with the press, United Nations headquarters and interested human rights non-governmental organizations (NGOs). Initially, the SOC accepted some remedial measures at UNTAC's request, but later the normal response was a strong denial of responsibility.

Racial violence against ethnic Vietnamese in Cambodia, many of them long-term residents, was a clear Khmer Rouge policy in the months preceding the election. In view of the political sensitivities involved, SOC officials were usually unwilling to investigate or prosecute these atrocities or to take preventive measures. Other Cambodian factions and even Cambodian human rights groups were equally hesitant to denounce these attacks publicly. Attacks on ethnic Vietnamese remained one of the major preoccupations of the Human Rights Component. The SRSG for Human Rights in Cambodia has continued to focus on this problem, particularly as these people have been denied the protection of the new Cambodian Constitution.

Training

Training was an essential element of the programme in Cambodia. In addition to its briefing/training of UNTAC staff, the Human Rights Component developed special training programmes for local police which it carried out in six provinces. These were supplemented by several two-week long "train-the-trainer" programmes.

After the adoption of the transitional criminal code, the Human Rights Component worked with the Civil Administration Component on the joint training of judges and prosecutors. In July 1993, a three-week Component-funded programme was organized by the International Commission of Jurists for judges who had been or who might be appointed to the Court of Appeal and to the Supreme Court.

Complementing the judicial programme was one designed for training defenders. The transitional criminal law guaranteed the right to legal assistance for any person accused of a crime or misdemeanour. Since there had been no private attorneys or public defenders in Cambodia since 1975, the transitional provisions allowed anyone with a secondary school diploma or who was a family member to represent the accused. The Human Rights Component created a special training programme to provide a minimal level of competency for these defenders.

An extensive human rights education programme in all the provinces was conducted by two mobile training teams, once the human rights staff had been strengthened. However, even with its expanded staff, the Human Rights Component could not implement a human rights education strategy that would have made any measurable impact on the prevailing situation. It therefore appealed for extra financing to 18 governments and received US$1.85 million to set up a trust fund for a human rights education programme. This allowed the human rights programme to reach the teacher training colleges, the faculty of medicine and the nurses' college, and to prepare a course for teachers.

Recommendations

The Human Rights Component of UNTAC was able to achieve a number of its objectives, most notably by assisting in the conduct of a widely supported election, but failed in others. Arguably, its mandate was too ambitious, and it certainly could not have been achieved in the absence of proper cooperation by the Cambodian parties. The human rights activities for Cambodia were, in many ways, experimental and innovative, and could provide far-reaching lessons for future operations. Some achievements were notable, while in other areas work remained to be done.

There are central human rights concerns in all peace-keeping operations, which need to be addressed. In peace-keeping operations intended to promote transition from conflict to a democratic civil society, the need to actively address these concerns is fundamental. There are different, but important, human rights concerns in peace-keeping operations as regards the actions and conduct of United Nations personnel, particularly the military, which also need to be addressed. Ideally, human rights promotion and protection should take place in a post-conflict situation, and can face serious difficulties if the conflict continues. It is also important for United Nations human rights activities that effective control is exercised by the civilian over the military components of United Nations peace-keeping operations.

The international system is ill-equipped, both conceptually and operationally, to undertake effective human rights action in peace-keeping operations. A number of governments actively oppose such action and the United Nations needs to review urgently its approach and capacity in this area. Arguments of cultural and regional relativism in this respect need to be more systematically addressed, especially through the more active involvement of local NGOs and other community groups.

Because of the contentions and potentially conflictual nature of international human rights actions, it is essential that the mandate and objectives of the human rights aspects of any peace settlement/peace-keeping operation are spelled out in broad detail and formally endorsed by all key parties concerned. Where possible, these should be linked to future constitutional arrangements which should be actively promoted by the United Nations.

Human rights promotion and protection activities must be recognized as labour-intensive and often specialized. The Centre for Human Rights needs to be encouraged to become more familiar with human rights actions in peace-keeping operations in the field, and to re-orientate itself in a more operational and pragmatic manner in order to provide proper support to future operations. The High Commissioner for Human Rights should be involved at the policy level in the formulation of future peace-keeping operations, and should have access to a reserve pool of experienced personnel to be called upon urgently for future peace-keeping operations.

Where United Nations human rights actions are part of a broader political settlement, it is important that they do not outrun the political will of Member States to support them. Key Member States should be regularly informed of actions in this area, and urged to provide proper political support. Human rights must be positively linked to the political process, while every effort must be made to avoid the dilution of human rights responsibilities by the diplomatic and political environment.

Specific financial resources, additional to regular administrative costs, must be available to enable human rights education, training and information programmes to be undertaken as an integral part of any monitoring and investigatory role. A special United Nations trust fund should be urgently established for this purpose.

Human rights monitoring and investigation activities must be supported by credible enforcement mechanisms, whether locally or internationally. Human rights actions, especially in peace-keeping operations, without effective redress measures are likely to be counter-productive. The responsible use of the media is a key point of this response, and guidelines in this area should be prepared for all United Nations human rights staff.

The international human rights support structures, including the Centre for Human Rights, the Commission on Human Rights, the various thematic special rapporteurs and international and regional NGOs, as well as the media, need to be more fully utilized to respond actively and promptly in support of United Nations human rights operations. A proper appreciation of the local realities surrounding such operations is an essential aspect of this response.

The human rights implications of peace-keeping operations, especially those with enforcement mandates, should be systematically monitored by the United Nations, possibly through the establishment of a United Nations ombudsman-type system in each operation.

The staffing, training and administrative support provided for United Nations human rights field operations should be comprehensively reviewed. A pool of experienced staff and an inventory of essential material should be established, supported if necessary by an emergency trust fund to enable immediate deployment of key staff.

Broad policy and priority guidelines for human rights activities in peace-keeping operations should be established, and should be reviewed in detail at United Nations Headquarters at a senior level, with key staff assigned to new missions prior to the deployment of the mission.

Systematic training courses in basic human rights should be provided to all senior peace-keeping operations staff, including all senior military, police and civilian personnel. A basic guidebook or training manual should be prepared for this purpose, in addition to any national guidelines. Human rights responsibilities should be formally spelled out in military and police standard operating instructions in peace-keeping operations.

At the outset of human rights programmes in conflict or post-conflict situations, there should be an agreed assessment of the related institution-building and longer-term training activities required in the country concerned to support the (re-)establishment of the rule of law. The cost of these should form an integral part of rehabilitation and reconstruction appeals to donor countries.

Human rights NGOs, both international and regional, should be encouraged and supported to establish an international operational capacity, which could provide human rights monitors, investigators and trainers for field assignments at short notice.

THE REPATRIATION COMPONENT

Number of staff: approximately 127 professional, consultant and general staff.

Mandate and structure

The Repatriation Component of UNTAC was charged with the repatriation and resettlement of refugees and internally displaced persons. Estimates are that some 370,000 refugees and another 200,000 displaced persons were assisted in returning to their former homes. The repatriation and resettlement was an inter-agency effort under the overall authority of UNTAC. The Office of the United Nations High Commissioner for Refugees (UNHCR), acting as the lead agency, supervised the movement of returnees, the provision of immediate assistance and food, and a reintegration programme. The Repatriation Component Director was appointed by the Secretary-General and reported to the Special Representative as well as to the High Commissioner.

The repatriation goals

UNHCR's objectives, of paramount importance for the success of the overall Peace Plan, were as follows:

(a) All the refugees in Thailand, especially the tens of thousands sheltered in Khmer Rouge-controlled camps, required protection from manipulation

and forcible return, practices which had developed into a scandalous pattern over the years. The refugees had to be given the possibility of freely choosing the time and means of return, as well as their final destination inside Cambodia.
(b) Returnee convoys had to be organized. There were, in total, nearly 500 travelling by road, river, railway and air. Reception centres had to be prepared, and areas of settlement had to be protected from any sort of threat or attack.
(c) All those who freely opted to return to areas under Khmer Rouge control had to be permitted to do so. This required UNHCR logistical support and unhindered monitoring.
(d) Those returning to State of Cambodia (SOC)-controlled areas could not be harassed in any way for leaving the country or for their stay in camps in Thailand administered by non-SOC factions. They were also to enjoy freedom of choice of their final destination.

To achieve these goals, UNHCR had to maintain a dialogue with the Khmer Rouge, while also keeping the other parties fully informed of every step so as to secure their cooperation. The SOC party, for instance, extended full assistance in the return, registration, transit and onward transportation of those refugees wishing to settle in the Khmer Rouge area. But the return was mainly possible thanks to the Cambodian people themselves: returnees, mainly relatives, were by and large welcomed and supported in their readjustment to normal life.

UNHCR/UNTAC waged an effective mass information campaign and made efforts to depoliticize the refugee question. This received substantial support from Prince Sihanouk. His personal interest since late 1991, his influence over all the parties, and his attendance and supportive public statements at repatriation-related working meetings and ceremonies helped UNHCR avoid many difficulties.

Finally, UNHCR, its non-governmental organization (NGO) partners and UNTAC took all possible precautions to reduce risks such as physical security, health and mine hazards. They also undertook to improve the state of roads and the communications infrastructure, and to provide legal protection and children's education. The returnees were back in Cambodia in time to vote in the May 1993 elections.

Reintegration problems

Insecurity from cease-fire violations

Clearly, the failure to respect the cease-fire since early 1992, coupled with the disarmament failure, led to a general climate of insecurity and to the emergence of areas of chronic military activity which continued into late 1994. This fighting caused the renewed uprooting of civilians and led large numbers to flee once again to Thailand, albeit for a short time. These events did not disrupt the resolve of Cambodian refugees to return home. Fighting did, however, make the return of thousands of families to their places of origin risky as a result of on-going military activity or because it rendered impossible the de-mining of areas adjacent to the conflict zone. As a result, many of those families became internally displaced persons, despite UNHCR's systematic attempts to find alternative solutions.

Violations of the cease-fire and the consequent non-demobilization of unpaid troops, coupled with the absence of any far-reaching rehabilitation and employment scheme, led to a pervasive phenomenon of banditry. Criminality in Cambodia became as dangerous a threat to the security of the people as military activity.

Casualties from anti-personnel mines

The slow pace of de-mining of arable land in more peaceful areas was also a factor that made reintegration of returnees problematic. Until the Cambodian Mine Action Centre (CMAC) became operational, United Nations agencies and major NGOs such as Handicap International, Halo Trust, Norwegian People's Aid and Mine Action Group resorted to *ad hoc* arrangements that were certainly commendable, but insufficient. De-mining activities are still on-going and will take many years to complete.

Mine-awareness campaigns and "no-go areas" also helped reduce loss of life from anti-personnel mines. However, many Cambodian villages have again resorted to mining certain areas at night, for self-defence purposes.

Lack of arable land

The shortage of arable land for returning rural refugees was due not only to the continued existence of areas of active or sporadic conflicts and to the related problem of landmines. UNHCR mistakenly assumed that an average of 2.5 hectares of land could be made available to all returnee families with a rural background. It did not take into account the pressure on land in certain areas – especially Battambang Province – and the resistance of authorities at the provincial, district, commune or village level. Years of conflict had enhanced the autonomy and powers of provincial civilian and military governments. In the SOC areas, where the majority of refugees were returning, Prime Minister Hun Sen and his ministers were entirely supportive of the agreed policy of providing available land free of charge to returnees with a rural background. This policy was frustrated in some provinces and districts, thereby increasing the dependence of certain categories of returnees on continued food assistance and reducing their ability to attain self-sufficiency. In areas controlled by the three non-SOC parties, no particular problems were encountered.

UNHCR has remained committed, well beyond the conclusion of the repatriation operation, to the allocation of land, including titles, to returnees and renewed efforts were made in the post-electoral period with the help of the Government of the Kingdom of Cambodia.

Recommendations

The repatriation programme was successful for a number of reasons: it had countrywide support from the people and the political factions, it had close cooperation with all the other components, and UNHCR had maintained an impartial and neutral position during the entire UNTAC period.

Support from all factions

First of all, repatriation was an area in which agreement was reached by all four Cambodian parties, including the Khmer Rouge (Party of Democratic Kampuchea – PDK). This led to all refugees returning in freedom, without a single serious accident or deliberately disruptive incident, by April 1993.

UNHCR's long experience in Cambodia

UNHCR had been in Cambodia for a decade and took part in the UNAMIC survey. On 15 March 1992, UNHCR agreed to act as its operational arm.

Independent financing

The UNHCR-led repatriation operation was entirely funded through voluntary contributions of almost US$120 million, separate from the UNTAC-assessed budget. This risky approach proved to be the right one, and provided UNHCR with an early and essential financial operational and administrative independence.

Close cooperation with other UNTAC components and NGOs

UNHCR cooperated closely with the Military, Civilian Police and Electoral Components of UNTAC, as well as with those responsible for human rights, civil administration and information/education.

Strict adherence to impartiality

The two humanitarian agencies, UNHCR and the International Committee of the Red Cross (ICRC), had specific roles assigned to them in the Paris Agreements. This was essential in order to ensure, at all times and *vis-à-vis* the four parties to the Cambodian conflict, that the independent, neutral, non-political and impartial nature of their humanitarian concerns and action was preserved, perceived and respected by all. Equal treatment of all affected populations and strict respect for their freedom of choice also called for even-handedness combined with firmness in the dealings with the four Cambodian parties.

Soon after the establishment of UNTAC, the Khmer Rouge became suspicious and later hostile towards the Transitional Authority. Even though UNHCR remained UNTAC's humanitarian arm, it was able to maintain its impartial identity and its channels of communication with the Khmer Rouge, with the full support of the SRSG.

Using Quick Impact Projects (QIPs) for rehabilitation

The lack of arable land was one of the main reasons why UNHCR, together with UNDP and NGOs, set up an ambitious, albeit financially modest programme of QIPs in Cambodia. The "QIPs for land" approach was often used as an incentive to greater cooperation at the village level.

By the end of 1994 UNHCR had invested over US$10 million in nearly 100 QIPs covering ten sectors of assistance. Projects were undertaken in all of the 21 provinces of Cambodia and in the three areas controlled by the non-Khmer Rouge parties.

Among the projects funded were the repair or construction of tertiary roads, bridges, hospitals and dispensaries as well as schools. Hundreds of wells and ponds were dug. QIPs funded preparation of large areas of land, including the provision of rice seeds and, where appropriate, fertilizers. Vegetable seeds were also provided to tens of thousands of vulnerable families. Moreover, large quantities of fishery equipment, water jars and mosquito nets were distributed. Income-generating activities included the provision of start-up loans. Targeted assistance was also extended, through specialized NGOs, to vulnerable families and their dependants such as the elderly, female heads of households, orphans and amputees.

These joint endeavours have significantly contributed to facilitating a dignified reintegration of returnees and internally displaced persons within their receiving communities. Indeed, the impact of QIPs far exceeds the limited investment involved.

With the experience gained in the joint UNHCR/UNDP scheme QIP programme in Cambodia, UNHCR and other aid agencies have observed that similar rehabilitation activities are an essential consolidating ingredient in the early stages of implementing a comprehensive peace settlement, especially in countries affected by protracted warfare.

The need for immediate, modest and concrete input in the sectors of communications, water, education, health/nutrition, shelter, community services, land preparation and crop production, sanitation, livestock, small start-up loans and assistance to vulnerable categories of persons – including war victims – is beyond dispute. Moreover, such visible assistance to labour-intensive projects provides a tangible confirmation of international concern to uninformed populations residing in remote and often sorely affected rural areas. They also constitute an important bridge between, on the one hand, relief assistance and, on the other, reconstruction and development aid. For the latter, no significant cash contributions can be expected until lasting military and political stability is achieved.

The experiences gained have highlighted the importance of the early identification of funding sources for a broader QIPs strategy which can both supplement UNHCR's efforts (by targeting other local vulnerable populations) and prolong its rehabilitation programmes after it phases out. In the case of UNTAC a specific rehabilitation QIP-type fund was to have been specifically included in the appeal submitted to the June 1992 Tokyo Conference.

THE COMPONENT FOR REHABILITATION AND ECONOMIC AFFAIRS

Number of staff: 30–50 professionals.

Mandate and structure

The Rehabilitation and Economic Affairs Component was organized so as to allow the achievement of sets of short-term and long-term goals. The former activities were directly linked to ensuring the success of the electoral process, and included tasks such as maintaining the stability of key macroeconomic variables, direct control over administrative expenditures, and the control of the sale of state property.

The longer-term objectives, i.e. those linked to the rehabilitation of the Cambodian economy, encompassed raising resources through donor contributions, natural resource management, developing human resources and institution-building.

The Declaration on the Rehabilitation and Reconstruction of Cambodia was one of the three instruments comprising the Paris Agreements. Chronologically, the rehabilitation phase ran from the signing of the Agreements and the establishment of UNTAC until the formation of the Royal Cambodian Government, following the May 1993 elections, the Constituent Assembly and the new Constitution of Cambodia.

The exercise of direct control over the administration's finance and the efforts aimed at macroeconomic stabilization were areas where UNTAC achieved substantial results. In contrast, the rehabilitation programme was only partially successful. To a large extent, this was due to the discontinuity in the leadership and staffing of the component. During the 18-month UNTAC mission, the component had three directors. By the end of 1992, it had lost two-thirds of its professional staff. As a result, rehabilitation activities were integrated into the Office of Economic Affairs, and some progress was achieved in the second part of the mission.

Macroeconomic stabilization

The expenditure of government agencies was supposed to be election-neutral. The Component for Rehabilitation and Economic Affairs undertook a survey of expenditures which showed that the administration was printing money to help pay for the budget deficit. (The State of Cambodia administration's revenues covered only 40% of spending, once financial support from the former USSR stopped and the Vietnamese troops had withdrawn.) Money creation – and to some extent the influx of United Nations troops and local UNTAC payments for salaries of Cambodian employees and other expenses – resulted in sharp inflation. To create the conditions for a fair and free election, the country needed a reasonably orderly economy, and activities were undertaken to achieve this objective.

In May–August 1992, inflation was running at a rate of 10–20% per month. But by September 1992, the UNTAC effort practically stopped currency creation and both the inflation and the exchange rate were stabilized.

Stopping the sell-off of state property

As Cambodia moved from a centrally planned economy to a market economy, a number of property sales took place. The UNTAC team wanted to set up a privatization system that would provide clarity and transparency for such sales. While the Supreme National Council (SNC) adopted a proposal of this type, SOC objected and compliance was not forthcoming. SNC was asked to issue a statement indicating that any transaction made outside the system would not be recognized by the new Government. This may have slowed down sales to international investors. Internally, however, many SOC assets were transferred to the Cambodian People's Party (CPP) and then sold or rented to finance its election expenses.

Management of natural resources

Cambodia has two important natural resources: tropical timber and gemstones. Its three neighbours, Laos, Thailand and Vietnam, have lost much of their forested areas and now control or ban logging or exports of logs or sawn timber. Also, recent ecological movements have created pressure on timber-exporting nations to stop irreparable damage to tropical forests. This has resulted in a shortage of tropical hardwoods. Illegal exporters took advantage of this scarcity and shipped out an estimated 1.2 million cubic feet in 1992, according to UNDP. Since then, large-scale deforestation has continued in Cambodia, and unprofessional logging practices are causing serious environmental damage to watersheds and forest areas.

The staff of the Rehabilitation Component considered that it would be difficult to seek aid when Cambodia's own resources were not being used for the rebuilding of the country. Resources were squandered and depleted in a way that threatened the country's future economic stability. At UNTAC's suggestion, SNC set up a Technical Advisory Committee to review and examine the contracts for exploiting natural resources. This led to a moratorium on log exports (September 1992) and a ceiling on sawn timber exports for 1993 (February 1993). However, UNTAC reported 103 violations of the export ban in January–May 1993. There were probably many more illegal exports across the long Cambodian border that were not recorded.

Gemstone quarrying has led to similar damage. Despite protests from the Khmer Rouge, SNC adopted a moratorium on the export of minerals and gems in February 1993.

External assistance

Many rehabilitation objectives were not met within the 18 months set for the UNTAC mission. For example, the Tokyo ICORC meeting in June 1992 pledged some US$800 million for reconstruction and rehabilitation, but funds dribbled in very slowly. Only US$95 million had actually arrived by early 1993; much of the delay came from the lengthy and often rigid bureaucratic procedures in the donor countries.

Unsettled conditions in Cambodia may also have contributed to the delays in disbursements. Donor countries were reluctant to disburse funds when unrest could damage projects. As another Rehabilitation Component leader pointed out, "for [reconstruction and development aid], no significant cash contributions can be expected before lasting military and political stability is achieved."

Implementing direct controls

The UNTAC team had to move rapidly to establish a control mechanism over government spending. This was done with an intensive technical assistance effort to reshape procedures in the Ministry of Finance. Professionals in the national administration of taxes, government finance and customs procedures were brought to Cambodia to set up the new system and oversee its operation. Financial control was exercised both at the central and provincial levels. Local staff had to be trained, and the UNTAC team instituted follow-up procedures to make sure that the controls were in place and were being used.

Recommendations

Political pressure was brought on the SOC administration to comply with the controls. This approach worked well in stopping the creation of money. UNTAC linked inflation primarily to the lack of monetary management. SOC attributed the inflation to the UNTAC presence and its demand for local goods and services. This was widely debated, but the UNTAC team remained adamant. Finally, the administration agreed to the direct controls over money creation and, in effect, stopped the printing of money.

UNTAC created another linkage between compliance and financial assistance from international agencies such as the World Bank (IBRD) and the International Monetary Fund (IMF). The UNTAC team contacted IBRD and ensured that the precondition for any disbursement was that suitable financial controls were in place and operating well. This clause was written into the loan agreements and was understood by Cambodian authorities. The SRSG twice warned SNC that there would be no IBRD disbursements until UNTAC was satisfied with financial controls.

The IMF discussed UNTAC controls and whether they were compatible with IMF loan conditions. Eventually, the UNTAC control levels were integrated into IMF conditions and accepted voluntarily by the Cambodian authorities.

When appropriate, in future peace-keeping missions, it might prove useful to link financial assistance explicitly to compliance with the political objectives of the mission.

Although the Rehabilitation and Economic Affairs Component did not fully accomplish all of its objectives, the areas where it was successful have had a lasting impact. For example, the system of vetoing government payments that was set up in the Ministry of Finance is still working. Also, some of the staff who were trained by the UNTAC team are still in place. The foreign exchange value of the riel, Cambodia's currency, has remained stable since December 1992.

THE ELECTORAL COMPONENT

Number of staff: about 300 initial international staff, 1000 international polling observers seconded from Member States, and some 50,000 Cambodians recruited for the polling process.

Mandate and structure

The Paris Agreements entrusted UNTAC with the organization of free and fair general elections of 120 members to the Constituent Assembly. The Electoral Component of UNTAC was responsible for designing and implementing a system for every phase of the electoral process, starting with the establishment, in consultation with the Supreme National Council (SNC), of a legal framework including electoral law and regulations to govern the electoral process, and an electoral code of conduct. Other charges included civic education and training, registration of voters and political parties and the polling process itself.

Responsible for the successful carrying out of the voter registration and polling process, the Electoral Component faced tremendous obstacles in terms of terrain, climate and political complications. It received excellent cooperation from the Military Component and the information staff. Without the military's security and logistic help, the election process could certainly have failed.

Since Cambodia's election was the first actually conducted by the United Nations (in Namibia the role of the United Nations was one of observation only), there were inevitably a number of problems. Those of a general nature are discussed in the next chapter.

Political problems

The election, planned to take place under peaceful conditions, was *de facto* turned into an election in time of war. There was a huge security risk for all the provincial and district staffs. Opposing factions made numerous demands that threatened the election's impartiality. Firstly, the draft electoral law was held up for four months by disagreement on who should vote. The demand was that only Khmers should vote, but the parties could not define who and what exactly a Khmer was. Secondly, it was demanded that all overseas Khmers should be provided with registration facilities universally.

UNTAC allowed the possibility of negotiations on these points, which was probably a mistake as this created a pattern and incurred a political cost, with the parties threatening to boycott the elections at various critical stages. Up to 36 hours before polling time, electoral rules and procedures were still being negotiated.

Electoral staffing problems

The contribution of the United Nations Volunteers (UNVs) to the success of the electoral process was immeasurable. Certainly, the elections of May 1993 could not have taken place without the work, throughout the country, of the UNVs. Serious problems, however, hampered their work, and require redress if the best use of their contribution to future peace-keeping operations is to be made.

Although UNVs were regarded as electoral officers in all respects, the conditions of their work and retribution were unsatisfactory. UNVs were paid only a minimum sum, insufficient for long missions. For the benefit of the UNTAC mission, it was essential that they not be rotated; consequently, many endured difficult living conditions for long periods. They also lost out on compensatory time off (CTO), their duties involving a virtually seven-day week, 24-hour day. An initial promise that CTO could be accumulated was arbitrarily changed by an administrative decision.

UNV electoral officers were diverted to inappropriate jobs. They recruited the 50,000 local election staff, and had to interview 200,000 candidates. Revenge over job disappointment probably led to the murder of district staff. Recruiting also undermined their strictly electoral identity, as did their employment as the distributors of free radios.

Suggestions for procurement, transport and communications

The Electoral Component initially used turn-key procurement to solve its need for rapid acquisition of the computer equipment needed for the election. In order to overcome the effects of the United Nations' tardy and piecemeal logistical support in the field, it resorted again to turn-key procurement for electoral materials, including delivery to Cambodia. This put the responsibility on the supplier for as many aspects as possible, reducing the need to rely on the mission's civilian organization. Even so, specialists had to watch over such suppliers, to make sure that equipment was delivered on time and in good condition. Another benefit of turn-key contracts was that it required only one passage through the United Nations' procurement process, and through the Headquarters Contracts Committee, thus avoiding bottlenecks at UNTAC's procurement section.

Communications were a basic need for preparing and implementing the electoral system, and its functioning was a constant concern. Most messages were sent by radio and messengers – phones and faxes never effectively reached the districts. Provincial telephones were only connected nine months after the mission had started, and after the main registration was over. The radios provided to district election officers often did not work; repeaters broke down as regularly as the promises made that they would not. This was exacerbated by a serious lack of radio discipline; future missions should ensure that a code of radio use is set up and enforced. A possible solution to the communication problem would be to have the military provide a simpler service. This would also enhance security.

Recommendations

The Electoral Component successfully tested the decentralization of election management to the provincial level and the delegation of decision-making to the Provincial Electoral Officers (PEOs). Initially, the main reason for this move was the severely limited communication facilities, but later the need for greater security strengthened its importance. When the location of polling stations was being fixed, the close relations of the PEOs with sector military commanders was essential in getting the task done rapidly and efficiently. This could not have been achieved from the Phnom Penh headquarters.

The decision to staff the districts with UNVs also proved successful. The UNVs were motivated, flexible and professional. They were rapidly recruited and deployed, and given intensive training in the Cambodian culture and language. After a UNV was murdered, the group's morale naturally suffered and some 40 staff resigned. The situation was markedly improved by very frank briefings that allowed personnel in the field to share real information.

The electoral plan's flexible and dynamic coordination system helped the component to solve problems which had been foreseen and to absorb those that had not. Coordination with, and support from, the Military and Information/Education Components was vital to the success of the election. One high-level electoral officer stated:

there was a clear consensus that the involvement of the Military Component in the conduct of the polling was absolutely critical to the success of the election ... the military, being outcome-oriented, accustomed to working in a systematic, planned environment, and familiar with the importance of logistics were in tune with practical electoral issues and well placed to provide the Electoral Component with the support it needed.

Voters' education was critically dependent on Radio UNTAC. At the same time, other Information/Education staff supplied culturally and politically sensitive analysis. Future electoral ventures should be planned with particular attention to such support.

One of the lessons for the Electoral Component was the need to ensure availability of satisfactory technical equipment. The United Nations' Electoral Assistance Unit should review with its suppliers the needs specific for elections and set up guidelines that provide quality products to meet the climatic and other conditions encountered in each peace-keeping mission. In addition, such suppliers must be ready to provide special logistic back-up needs in the mission area and for as long a period as needed.

To meet the criteria for impartiality, political parties need the reassurance of tamper-proof ballot boxes; voters' credibility should be strengthened by all the usual paraphernalia – seals, security ink, appropriate polling booths, etc.

Should the United Nations be required once again to conduct, rather than merely supervise, elections as part of a comprehensive peace-making process, it should ensure that a proper degree of independence for its Electoral Component from its political and administrative institutions is assured. This isolation of electoral from other "governmental" functions of a peace-keeping operation is as important as the credible independence of a national electoral commission from the government of the day. Failure to understand and provide for this will jeopardize the vital image of the electoral institution as absolutely neutral and separate from even a United Nations administration which may have to negotiate and make difficult political and "governmental" decisions.

THE INFORMATION/EDUCATION DIVISION

Number of staff: 45 international staff, 100 Cambodians.

Mandate and structure

The main task of the Information/Education (INFO/ED) Division of UNTAC was to inform the Cambodians about the essence of the Paris Agreements and about UNTAC's role, objectives and activities, and to provide the production and broadcasting facilities to spread voter education. The Division also implemented UNTAC's mandate for direct control of the field of information and devoted considerable resources and programme time to broadcasting political parties' platforms and messages. A vital aspect of the mandate was in helping to establish and maintain UNTAC's credibility through the understanding of the Cambodian popular view of the mission. After two decades of fighting and isolation, many Cambodians were hardly aware of the international community's efforts to assist their country, and were understandably sceptical about the applicability to Cambodia of basic concepts of human rights, including free and fair elections and multi-party political campaigning. The flow of information between UNTAC and the grass roots was considered essential to the success of the UNTAC operation.

UNTAC sought to establish countrywide communications using all forms of media. As part of planning for the UNTAC phase, the United Nations Department of Public Information (DPI) proposed nationwide radio coverage under UNTAC's control. Following the United Nations Headquarters' approval of an UNTAC broadcast facility in July 1992, the mission encountered many bureaucratic and logistical obstacles, which delayed inauguration of UNTAC's own studios and relay transmitters until April 1993, one month before the elections. Meanwhile, Radio UNTAC delivered prerecorded tapes for twice daily prime-time broadcast to a Thai/US facility and to four Cambodian factions before going on the air itself in November 1992, using a borrowed transmitter in Phnom Penh. Of the four factions, only the PDK refused to broadcast UNTAC programming on the peace process and the United Nations' role.

The broadcasts initially concentrated on the Paris Agreements and the composition of the UNTAC mission and its goals. Radio UNTAC actually began programming with the announcement of the June date for regroupment and cantonment. Programming centred thereafter on aspects of voter registration and the electoral process, emphasising the secrecy of the ballot. Radio UNTAC also featured human rights and other aspects of the UNTAC mandate and activities. In the actual campaign period, political parties broadcast on Radio UNTAC and recorded at UNTAC TV studios under the "equal access equal time" formula.

The Division also undertook a range of other activities to keep the Cambodians informed and to counteract negative propaganda aimed at UNTAC. These included audio-visual materials in the Khmer language and posters on voter registration and on the work of UNTAC.

To provide local households with radios, a campaign brought forth a donation of hundreds of thousands of radios and batteries from both the Japanese Government and people for distribution among the population.

There was clear evidence that Radio UNTAC broadcasts, emphasizing that the ballots were secret, were instrumental in convincing many Cambodians to register and vote. Radio UNTAC probably also persuaded opponents not to interfere in the election.

Major information steps

Implementing the UNTAC mandate for direct control of the field of information demanded a consultative approach with not only the factions, but also other elements of the media in Phnom Penh. To ensure transparency and to make absolutely certain the goals of the media and the limits on what might be said or written in the media, the Division created a Working Group which contributed to drafting a set of guidelines for the media. Only the Democratic Kampuchea faction refused to participate in this effort.

In its own productions, UNTAC had to provide timely, transparent and accurate information that was as censorship-free as possible. In this way, it could build credibility and create a local audience among Cambodians. To plan its work, it had to look at specific themes amidst a rapidly evolving political and military situation. This meant keeping in touch with as many official sources and contacts as possible. The creation of a foundation of media freedom, before UNTAC left, was one of the major legacies of the operation.

One difficulty lay in the fact that few, if any, UNTAC officials spoke Cambodian. INFO/ED international Khmer-speaking staff vetted all translated broadcast and videos internally, both for factual accuracy and to ensure that the texts were "politically correct", not only in terms of United Nations policy and strategy, but to avoid the use of politically loaded Khmer terminology. The Division used the Khmer-language text of the Paris Agreements where possible, and even cobbled together important political terms such as "the people", in a conscious effort at impartiality in vocabulary.

Handling the international media

Reporting in an accurate and timely manner on complex and often volatile peace-keeping, peace-enforcement or peace-building efforts can be difficult for many reporters. The international press covering any peace-keeping operation is going to make an impact on public opinion. Whether this is negative or positive depends on how the mission's information is handled.

The UNTAC mission divided the information effort into an internal audience managed by the INFO/ED Division itself, and an external audience handled by a separate spokesman attached to the Office of the SRSG.

Underlining the complexity of the information factor for UNTAC, the Force Commander stated that:

... the media in all its forms presents a problem of large magnitude for a United Nations commander. He is required to respond to the press of all contributing countries. The extent of the interest is governed by the extent of the national consensus for the contribution to the mission. This can vary as the mission proceeds, particularly if there is dissent within the force, if there are casualties, or if there is bad press. The potential impact on the unity of the force is evident and it is salutary for a

Force Commander to realize that he has become a factor in the domestic politics of some countries.

Similar emphasis was put on the importance of the role of United Nations spokesperson, who had to understand the complexities of the military strategy, but also the sensitivities — at times contradictory — of the different contributing countries.

Each medium — television, radio, newspaper — has its specific needs and demands. For example, a reporter looking for an in-depth profile of one of the mission's leaders will need different information than that required for making a brief daily radio broadcast. Journalists usually represent the national press of their own countries and are thus obliged to adapt the news focus so that it appeals to the home audience or readership. The press wants hard news or information, but it is difficult to disseminate information about a complex situation or operation. United Nations personnel must themselves clearly understand the complexity of the situation at hand, so as to be able to influence the dissemination of accurate information about it.

Coping with journalists

There were three categories of journalists who covered UNTAC, roughly divided into:

(a) "War veterans" — those who had covered the war in Cambodia, from the time of the American bombings to the Khmer Rouge atrocities. Because of the duration of the Cambodian story, these veteran journalists returning to cover the peace-keeping operation had a long historical "memory". They also often had definite ideas on what the political development of the country should be.
(b) Journalists with an open and "impartial" stand on the issue — willing to acquire a more complete picture of the situation.
(c) Journalists unable to cope with the complexity of a multi-faceted peace-keeping operation, preparing nuggets of information to provide a daily dose of news.

One method of handling such a mixed group would have been to set up a unified public information office with sole authority to handle press relations for all of the components. This office would refer journalists to the specialized personnel in each component trained to deal with the press and dispense accurate information in a form suitable to the different categories of journalists.

Recommendations

As was the case with UNTAC, United Nations personnel on all peace-keeping missions could be constantly approached by the media. To respond to this pressure and opportunity in an effective manner, peace-keepers should receive advance training and practical guidelines to deal with this situation. Such training should highlight the need to explain the dynamics of the complex local situation, and the intricacies of international relations. It should also minimize the "public relations" aspect and reduce the emphasis on showing journalists "how the United Nations operation works". There were also suggestions that regional training centres should be set up to handle information training. This would allow for regional differences in the way journalists handle news, and instruct press officers in regional specificities.

An independent broadcast capacity should be standard for missions similar to UNTAC. Radio UNTAC was a revolutionary innovation and it created an important precedent for United Nations peace-keeping operations providing the means to get the UNTAC message to the local population in a way which would bypass the propaganda of the Cambodian factions. There is also no doubt that the international press will continue to play a key role in future peace-keeping operations. This is now apparent, with on-going operations in Rwanda, Mozambique, Haiti and others, requiring that the training of United Nations personnel be addressed in the most professional settings.

Mandate

Interpreting the mandate, or more specifically interpreting the implementation of a given mandate, demands flexibility. Historically the United Nations has been a "strict constructionist" concerning mandates. That is not adequate for modern operations. At the same time, a mandate cannot be realized without consensus on its measures of implementation by the concerned parties, as the media guidelines demonstrated in the Cambodian case.

Analysis

A political analytical element, best based in the SRSG's office, is indispensable to avoid elementary mistakes in dealing with the host culture, and ensuring real-time understanding of public positions in nations where United Nations languages are not widely used.

Procurement/personnel

The Field Operations Division (FOD) was too slow and inadequate in the Cambodian case. On the procurement side, even expanding purchasing authority in the mission area to US$500,000 proved inadequate for radio or television. On the personnel side, the new idea of a United Nations reserve could address the problem of recruiting appropriate and competent personnel. It could also help realize the new developing "can-do" ethos of United Nations mission staff.

Media themes

Regular meetings, about every six weeks with the SRSG, enabled a check on the direction of themes, and intake of suggestions for new ones. The exclusive broadcast in Khmer usefully limited second-guessing and potential micro-management, as no senior or mid-level expertise in the language existed outside the INDO/ED Division. The down-side was a doubt among colleagues that the division was doing much of anything. Translation and screening of selected television production aimed to redress such doubts.

Content

Timely, accurate and, above all, transparent programming that was as censorship-free as possible ensured UNTAC credibility and built its audience. At the same time, a very careful political vetoing of drafts, translations and final broadcasts by Khmer-speaking international staff ensured its political appropriateness on the basis of the Khmer-language text of the Paris Agreements.

Training

United Nations reporters who had worked on General Assembly and Security Council sessions proved inadequately prepared for the mix of news and features needed for Radio UNTAC. Training in elementary journalism as well as the mechanics of radio and television production could well address this problem.

3. General Lessons and Recommendations from UNTAC

The UNTAC experience provides a range of lessons that have immense value for current and future peace-keeping operations of the United Nations. The relative success of UNTAC lay in its comprehensive and multifaceted approach, and the intense diplomatic efforts undertaken to bring about a degree of national reconciliation. The ASEAN nations, as well as Australia, Japan and other like-minded countries, played a decisive role in these efforts which were pursued in close coordination with the Permanent Members of the Security Council.

Under the Paris Agreements, a framework for the efforts to restore peace in Cambodia was established. UNTAC was launched with a mandate that included a wide range of tasks, from the organization and conduct of elections to civil administration. Involving some 22,000 personnel, it was until then one of the two costliest operations in the history of the United Nations. Equally important, however, were the parallel and concerted diplomatic efforts to create a political environment that would be conducive to durable peace, as well as the provision of economic assistance for the rehabilitation and reconstruction of the war-torn nation.

Before focusing on the lessons that were learned from UNTAC, a few general considerations need to be highlighted.

Firstly, the use of preventive measures still remains the most pertinent tool at the disposal of the United Nations, and should continue to be applied even throughout a peace-keeping mission. Many experts increasingly feel that such preventive mechanisms should be more fully and frequently utilized in situations likely to threaten international peace and security, and that United Nations analytical investigation and mediation missions should be sent with more alacrity to areas where there is the danger of a conflict erupting. The Organization needs to have enough resources to closely monitor even subtle changes in politically volatile regions, and to request neighbouring countries to provide up-to-date information on these regions. Such measures, along with economic and humanitarian assistance, could certainly prove effective in defusing tense situations that might lead to conflict.

Secondly, there is increased pressure to establish some mechanism of selectivity in choosing peace-keeping operations. In the post-Cold War period, the number of regional hostilities is on the rise, outrunning the United Nations' financial and human resources, and requiring strict selectivity criteria. The question is: which criteria are appropriate? This enters into a delicate area where the national interests of individual Member States or the members of the Security Council may not be the same as the broader interests of the international community. In the case of Cambodia, there was an unprecedented consensus on the necessity of involvement.

Finally, what a peace-keeping operation can achieve depends not only on the political will but also on the amount of financing and human resources available from Member States. Practical considerations and political wisdom would advocate that the United Nations should draw a line between sowing the seeds of reconstruction, and rebuilding the whole structure of a nation. The completion of Cambodia's election was not the end of the process to restore a democratic Cambodia, but rather its beginning.

Some of the specific lessons of UNTAC that need careful attention can be summarized as follows.

A SOUND PEACE PLAN

The first condition needed for a successful peace-keeping operation is a conceptually sound and appropriately detailed peace plan. The UNTAC peace-keeping operation was itself the outcome of a successful peace-making exercise conducted over a number of years, bringing together a wide group of countries as well as the internal players, and producing a very complex peace blueprint, the Paris Agreements.

The essence of the Peace Plan – and what distinguished it from other United Nations operations – was the mandate given to the United Nations itself to assume responsibility for the internal administration of Cambodia during its transition to elected government, as the warring parties could not agree on interim power-sharing arrangements.

Although some of the Plan's assumptions – especially the aspect of military demobilization – were undermined by Khmer Rouge intransigence, it proved sufficiently detailed and robust in practice to give effective guidance to UNTAC. There were, however, significant exceptions, including the lack of definition of, and clear directions on, the role of the Supreme National Council (SNC). Furthermore, the possibility of non-compliance by one or more of the parties was not given adequate consideration. Perhaps the most obvious shortcoming was the lack of an alternative plan that would have allowed UNTAC to set out conditions for pulling up stakes or leaving Cambodia, should the various factions have failed to provide the cooperation required.

EARLY DEPLOYMENT OF STAFF AND RESOURCES

It is crucial that adequate resources be deployed as rapidly as possible after the parties have reached an agreement and immediately following the formal approval of the operation by the Security Council. This will build and maintain the confidence of not only the parties, but also the local population, thus enabling the effective implementation of the mandate. The United Nations operation in Cambodia could not satisfy this prerequisite. The period between the signing of the Paris Agreements in October 1991 and the arrival in Cambodia of the first UNTAC elements in mid-April 1992 was five months, and it was another five to six months before UNTAC was fully operational, particularly in the all-important Civil Administration Component (CIVADMIN).

The delays in UNTAC's deployment were not surprising. In general, the time gap between the Security Council's announcement of a peace-keeping operation, the Secretary-General's solicitation from the Member States of troops and civilian contingents, and the funding needed for the peace-keeping operation has, so far, been incompatible with a rapid and effective deployment. The stand-by troop agreement, with no more than a few committed donors and only 5,500 troops, produced no response for the months following the Secretary-General's initial call for support for the Rwandan peace-keeping operation.

Currently, established mechanisms at the United Nations do not provide for adequate planning time. This again led to delays in UNTAC's deployment. There were deficiencies in the work of the United Nations Advance Mission in Cambodia (UNAMIC), though it could not be entirely blamed, being itself short of resources and having been ill-prepared at United Nations Headquarters in New York. Headquarters, on the other hand, had not received timely human and financial resources, and lacked the training to react promptly as developments took place.

An essential part of adequate preparation is the early designation of senior staff – both civilian and military – and their rapid involvement in the design and planning of the operation. In the case of UNTAC, the Special Representative of the Secretary-General (SRSG) was only appointed in January 1992; the Police Commissioner and the Civil Administration and Human Rights Directors in March 1992. UNTAC subsequently suffered from a lack of both continuity and institutional memory, due largely to the even later appointment of many of its subsidiary staff and their subsequent rapid – and often arbitrarily timed – rotation.

SPEEDING UP APPROVALS

The slow and cumbersome legislative and budgetary procedures, even for the clearly most essential items, remained a serious problem throughout the duration of UNTAC, highlighting the need for a number of reforms in this area. In general, once the Security Council approves a peace-keeping operation, the budget is prepared and has to go through the Advisory Committee on Administrative and Budgetary Questions (ACABQ), the Fifth Committee, and the General Assembly. This procedure normally takes several weeks. Theoretically, until the approval of the budget, the Secretary-General has no authority to spend. In the case of UNTAC, this handicap was partially offset by the advance commitment of US$200 million – though this was a commitment only, and not cash.

As regards the day-to-day administration and financing of the operation, it should be noted that peace-keeping operations are guided by the established rules and regulations of the United Nations. These, however, were designed for the regular, more static, United Nations operations and are far from adequate for the current needs of peace-keeping operations. Here, too, the much needed reforms must be supported by the Member States.

Further structural changes could also be considered at the Secretariat itself, in order to prepare it to meet the increasing demands being placed on it, and to improve the administration of peace-keeping operations in general. The view of many of those working in the various sectors of the UNTAC operation was that multi-dimensional peace-keeping requires a new or revamped planning structure at the United Nations Secretariat. There should be additional or strengthened planning units dedicated to the various sectors: military and political affairs, human rights, electoral, police and administration. These changes, some of which have already been implemented, will require increased staff and financing. However, there is also room for the better deployment of existing Secretariat personnel and resources. The alternative is the continuation of wasteful *ad hoc* planning for multi-dimensional and multi-billion-dollar operations.

More flexibility and greater direct authority over fund allocations should be given to operation commanders (civilian and military). They are best aware of the complicated conditions on the ground and most immediately concerned by the need for speedy reactions. A cogent example was the delay of well over a year in the establishment of the important UNTAC civilian radio station. Much of the delay was due to the United Nations Headquarters' ponderous tendering processes, which further complicated matters. In the mean time, the propaganda of two of the factions, who controlled their own transmitters, was broadcast essentially without challenge.

Better guidelines for donor countries would ensure greater uniformity (and utility) of the equipment national units bring along. The recent appointment of a "Force Inspector General" to oversee standards and the use of check-lists should help address this problem.

Regional considerations might lead to such trends as the greater use of engineering units from countries close to the current operation, in order to ensure speedy deployment. Joint regional training centres in certain useful specialities deployed at present in most United Nations operations might also be a way of ensuring minimum uniform standards for troops and civilian staff.

Some observers felt that the cumulative delays were critical, and cut into the tight (and equally tightly-funded) timetable outlined in the Paris Agreements. Such delays affected UNTAC's credibility in the eyes of the Cambodian people, as well as some donors and other countries.

CLEAR AND ACHIEVABLE GOALS

Another basic condition for ensuring an effective peace-keeping operation is the establishment of clear and achievable goals. In Cambodia, there were serious weaknesses in the actual implementation of what was in many ways the most innovative single element of the Paris Agreements – the Civil Administration Component. This was largely due to the mandate being overly ambitious and in some respects clearly not achievable in view of the United Nations' over-stretched resources and the situation in Cambodia, where years of armed struggle had caused enormous damage both to the population and to the basic infrastructure of the country.

UNTAC failed to take rapid and, in some cases, adequate control of the key areas of the civil administrations of the factions – particularly that of the SOC, which was the largest and only effective one – and to initiate corrective action when necessary. This meant that UNTAC was unable to deal effectively with corruption and with the continuing SOC intimidation of political figures from other parties during the election period. It also allowed the PDK – the Khmer Rouge – to justify its non-compliance with key provisions of the Paris Agreements, including the demobilization process; the Khmer Rouge itself claimed that the United Nations was not implementing essential elements of the settlement. This in turn meant that the elections could not be held in a strictly neutral political environment. While the debate over whether the Khmer Rouge would ever have complied with the Paris Agreements could be endless, it must be acknowledged that the United Nations did give them a tailor-made excuse for their non-compliance.

The situation of the civil service in Cambodia is, even today, still far from ideal. Factionalism is rife and there are many instances of discrimination in favour of former SOC civil servants and against those of FUNCINPEC or the KPNLF. There is clearly scope, in the context of assistance to Cambodia in its nation-building effort, for training courses designed not only to improve the efficiency of individuals, but also to imbue them with loyalty to the State, rather than to specific parties.

SUPPORT FROM THE PARTIES TO THE CONFLICT

Support of the parties to the conflict is essential for a successful peace-keeping operation. As was shown by the operation in Cambodia, the non-compliance of the Khmer Rouge with key provisions of the Paris Agreements, and the less than full compliance of the other parties, affected every aspect of the UNTAC operation.

When the Khmer Rouge effectively withdrew from the process, there were three options open to the United Nations. Firstly, it could choose to change the peace-keeping mandate to one of peace-enforcement. Secondly, it could soldier on in a peace-keeping role, re-emphasizing the peace-making functions, at the risk of both placing the peace-keeping force in physical danger and having the peace process bogged down indefinitely. Thirdly, it could withdraw, which would have meant abandoning the advances that were being made in returning Cambodia to the community of nations.

The United Nations Secretary-General decided to continue on to the elections. This was not an easy decision, for it meant that UNTAC had to compromise on a number of important issues which together could have entailed serious consequences for the operation. The elections had to be held with a central element of the Paris Agreements missing, namely demobilization of the factional armed forces. This effectively left two of the largest armed forces still in place. As a result, United Nations military forces had to spend most of their time protecting the voter registration process and the polling stations, rather than monitoring other aspects of the Agreements.

There were few advocates for converting the peace-keeping mandate of UNTAC to one of peace-enforcement. The general consensus was that a midstream change of this kind was bound to cause major and dramatic problems for the troop-contributing countries, in terms of the safety of troops involved. Despite the numbers already deployed, it had to be recognized that an enforcement operation probably faced a most uncertain outcome. It was recalled that over 300,000 well-trained Vietnamese troops had not succeeded in ten years within Cambodia in eradicating the Khmer Rouge.

ENLISTING EXTERNAL SUPPORT

Another basic condition for a successful peace-keeping operation is the need for external support for the undertaking. In the Cambodian peace-keeping operation the internal parties were at war, so the support of external players, who had been involved previously in helping one side or another in the conflict, was essential to ensure that the operation could be carried through. One reason for the successful elections in Cambodia was that the external backers of the various factions pressed their clients not to return to violence. It was only with developments such as the Gorbachev "Initiative" of July 1986 that individual members of the Permanent Five (P5) began to see Cambodia no longer as an excuse to keep apart, but as a good reason to get together on the wider issues.

In addition, the Core Group or "Extended P5" (EP5) maintained a commitment to Cambodia's future within the international community. They were also useful in focusing and maintaining pressure and persuasion on the Cambodian factions to comply with the terms of the Paris Agreements.

Future peace-keeping operations will have to develop similar international back-up from Member States to ensure success. The lack of a real international consensus and actual support in troops and equipment can, as evidenced by subsequent United Nations operations in other parts of the world, lead to major problems or even failure.

PERSONNEL QUALIFICATIONS AND RELATIONS

The United Nations and Member States must ensure that the best-qualified, well-disciplined and professional personnel are recruited in order to maintain the credibility of the operation. There should be an obligation on the part of the contributing countries to meet the criteria set by the United Nations for personnel. There should also be a right and an obligation on the part of the United Nations to provide appropriate guidelines on standards and the training necessary to meet the required standards so as to be able to reject unsuitable or unqualified personnel at the contributing country's expense.

There is need for an updated and widely accessible database of qualified personnel from both within and outside the United Nations, which would identify candidates with the required competence or qualifications to meet the established standards in a given subject.

Pre-deployment training to a common United Nations standard should also be regarded as essential. At the very least, efforts should be made to ensure the use of a common language by United Nations personnel in particular areas. This did not always occur in UNTAC, and its absence completely undermined any utility that those personnel lacking the necessary language skills might otherwise have had.

UNTAC's 21,000 personnel ranged from highly qualified to incompetent professionals. The latter were, in some cases, a menace to their colleagues and to the Cambodian population. Unfortunately, there were far too many instances of personnel in the latter category being retained in the mission, possibly for fear of offending contributing countries, or simply because there were no replacements available. Worse for morale within UNTAC was the appointment (or even "promotion") of such personnel to more comfortable jobs (for example, in Phnom Penh), simply to move them out of sensitive areas.

It is essential that a code of conduct should be established for United Nations personnel in future operations. Mission personnel must be informed about the code, and made aware that failure to respect it would result in disciplinary action. The unacceptable behaviour of some military and CIVPOL personnel caused much resentment and alienated many Cambodians.

The appointment of a personnel "ombudsman", to whom all mission personnel could submit problems that cannot be resolved by their own superiors, should be considered. This would establish an impartial platform for resolving such issues.

The safety of personnel engaged in peace-keeping is another serious issue. Whenever the Security Council contemplates launching a peace-keeping operation, it should take into consideration the safety of the personnel involved. Renewed efforts should be made to achieve a degree of integration and accountability among various bodies to ensure the security of personnel. To this end, the activities of the Office of Security Coordinator at United Nations Headquarters should be strengthened and expert staff recruited to assist the Security Coordinator and his designated officials in the field.

ROLE OF UNITED NATIONS VOLUNTEERS

UNTAC was also one of the first peace-keeping operation in which United Nations Volunteers (UNVs) participated on a large scale. Some of them had arrived even before UNTAC was in place, and when the security situation in the whole country was volatile. There were mines everywhere, the infrastructure was fragile and no telecommunication links existed between Phnom Penh and the countryside.

The UNVs did an admirable job, covering all of Cambodia to collect the basic data on which the electoral plan was drawn up. They were the District Electoral Officers who spread the message of democracy from door to door. UNVs later made a significant contribution in Somalia, and could be a major source for recruitment of personnel in future operations.

IMPROVING THE FINANCING AND LOGISTIC EFFICIENCY OF PEACE-KEEPING OPERATIONS

One of the more critical issues for United Nations peace-keeping efforts is that of securing adequate financing, and it bears repeating that Member States must recognize this problem as their collective responsibility. Without the payment of assessed contributions, in full and on time, the conduct of a peace-keeping operation is bound to come to a halt.

At present, the financing of each operation is budgeted for only a few months at a time. This partly explains the inadequate planning and poor administration of peace-keeping operations. Member States might be much more willing to extend their financial commitments to peace-keeping operations for longer periods if financial control of an operation were to be more transparent. This would ensure that the operation is efficiently implemented.

At the same time, the Secretariat must be helped to improve its administrative and budgetary management of the operations. It should also strengthen the system of audit and inspection in order to ensure accountability and transparency, and enhance the mechanisms for financial control.

The Secretary-General has proposed that Member States be assessed for a third of the total estimated costs of an operation as soon as it is approved by the Security Council. He has also called for the raising of the ceiling of the Peace-Keeping Reserve Fund, from US$150 million to US$800 million – a sum equivalent to about four months' expenditures under the 1993 peace-keeping budget. Before considering these two ideas, Member States should first thoroughly scrutinize the present system of planning, budgeting and administration, and consider ways of streamlining it. Moreover, the Reserve Fund should be fully funded at its present level before its ceiling is raised.

There is obviously no substitute for the efficient spending of scarce funds, once they are made available. UNTAC suffered many inefficiencies, such as too many vehicles of one type, not enough of another; too few computers arriving too late; the high cost of supplying water to United Nations personnel all over Cambodia; radios of insufficient range. Such examples, though not entirely avoidable in operations of such a scale, are useful in pin-pointing flaws in the preparation and planning processes for peace-keeping operations generally.

Among the reforms at the United Nations Secretariat that have come about in the wake of UNTAC is the integration of the Field Operations Division (FOD) into the Department of Peace-Keeping Operations (DPKO). Whilst UNTAC had received sufficient resources for its operations, the support structure in UNHQ was not given resources in tune with the magnitude of the operation to be supported. This created immense problems in the areas of personnel and procurement, where the urgency and immediacy of the needs in the field were not matched by a rapid response from UNHQ. Whilst the recent strengthening of the DPKO and other relevant departments is a step in the right direction, much remains to be done.

4. Conclusions

UNTAC was the United Nations' most complex and comprehensive operation to date in terms of its mandate, its tasks and its structure. In many ways it was a "first", and was made possible to a large extent because it occurred at a critical time in recent history, in the immediate aftermath of the Cold War. The objectives of UNTAC were ambitious. Its Civilian Police Component was the largest ever, and the variety of tasks and expertise required of its other civilian components was equally unprecedented.

UNTAC was the outcome of a lengthy phase of negotiations. It had taken 12 years to reach an agreement on the peaceful settlement of the Cambodian conflict, and to draft the Paris Agreements. With hindsight, it might seem that the expectation that the terms of those Agreements be implemented in 18 months was unrealistic. UNTAC aimed at no less than establishing a democratic society in a country ravaged by war. Was that ambition impossible? Could it have been achieved differently? Did UNTAC do the best it could? There are no easy answers to these questions, but they are certainly worth raising.

The positive legacies of UNTAC were many and far-reaching. It established the basis for a free press in Cambodia, put the question of human rights on the national agenda, and most importantly, succeeded in conducting free and fair elections, bringing more than 90% of the population to the voting polls. None of these achievements is minor; all have left their mark on the country.

On the other hand, the fact that key problems plaguing the country remain unresolved facilitates further criticisms of the operation. Some of these problems go beyond UNTAC *per se*, and relate to the lack of a clear position of the international community in the face of unresolved dilemmas, such as the role of the Khmer Rouge and the support given to them from military forces outside Cambodia, the large influence of the former SOC/CPP in the army and national civil service, and the difficulty presented by widespread corruption. The operation itself has at times been judged severely, besides being considered slow and wasteful in delivery, and short-sighted in scope.

There are, however, many different ways of appraising the facts, and this task is always easier with hindsight. An assessment of a complex operation such as UNTAC, if compiled by the United Nations Secretariat, might tend to be too specific and even narrow, due to a certain lack of distance from the daily on-going operational activities. On the other hand, an evaluation by the contributing countries may well appear contradictory, since not all countries necessarily had the same agenda. Because UNTAC was a "first" in so many ways, it had to break new ground continuously. Being multi-dimensional, it remained largely dependent on the goodwill of contributing countries to provide the range of expertise needed for the implementation of its mandate. UNTAC was in fact requested to undertake the exercise of government in Cambodia for a specific period of time, and the practical aspects of that exercise have been assessed to some degree in this report. It is clear that an honest analysis has pointed to both great achievements and serious flaws.

The consideration of those practical aspects, however, should not override the broader question of the actual objectives of particular peace-keeping and peace-making operations. As was asked by one of the Singapore conference participants, what did the international community, the parties to the Paris Agreements, the region, the factions and the Permanent Five actually expect to achieve in Cambodia? If, through UNTAC, they intended to set Cambodia on an irreversible path to democracy, political and economic stability, and good governance, the "plan" was inadequate from the start, and too limited in its scope. One of its more obvious shortcomings, for example, was the lack of provision for the constitution-making process and the "start-up" for a newly-elected government.

As long as fundamental questions of such a nature are not addressed, the systems for delivery and management designed by the United Nations (or others) will fail to attain objectives. This is one of the more important lessons to retain from UNTAC. Despite some flaws the operation was successful, but it was successful only in meeting those objectives that were achievable.

Part II

*Conference Papers
of the International Conference
in Singapore, August 1994*

UN Peace-Keeping and the New World Disorder

Part II

Conference Papers
of the International Conference,
Singapore, August 1993

5. UN Peace-Keeping and the New World Disorder

Professor S. Jayakumar[1]

Far from seeing global peace and tranquillity that many expected to follow the end of the Cold War, we have seen an upsurge in localized internal conflicts in various parts of the world. Everyday, the international print and TV media bring to our attention reports of anarchy, death, misery, and destruction.

Faced with these challenges, the world has turned to two sources for leadership, organization and resources to address these problems: firstly, the major powers which have traditionally provided the means to address global problems. Today, however, these countries are themselves burdened by severe domestic economic, political and social problems. The political will to address problems with international consequences has been eroded or lacks support from their public. Western governments, faced with these constraints, have become introspective. They are now more reluctant to engage themselves in international conflict resolution and management.

The second source is the United Nations. But the UN, as an intergovernmental organization, can only reflect the collective political will and resolve of its Member States, and act on the resources that Member States are prepared to allocate to it. The overall effectiveness of the UN depends on many factors, such as the leadership and support of the Permanent Members; the Security Council's effectiveness in decision-making; the UN Secretary-General's leadership; and the availability of financial and material resources for UN developmental and peace-keeping functions.

Therefore, when we talk of UN peace-keeping, there should be a clear link between the overall effectiveness of the UN, and effective UN peace-keeping. Improvements in UN peace-keeping cannot be separated from improvements in the overall effectiveness of the UN. This means strengthening financing as well as reforms to the UN Security Council and UN Secretariat. Moreover, faced with ever-increasing UN peace-keeping bills, Member States are asking whether there are limits to UN peace-keeping, and under what terms and conditions and criteria UN peace-keeping operations should be launched and terminated.

The UN is presently faced with weakening and inadequate financial, political and manpower resources for ever-increasing UN peace-keeping operations. The sad and depressing example of the unprecedented tragedy in Rwanda illustrates this quandary. The UNSG and the Secretariat have attempted to cope with the difficult conditions by launching various urgent appeals to Member States.

They have also reorganized the Secretariat departments dealing with peace-keeping, making improvements in "command and control", communications

---

[1] Minister for Foreign Affairs and for Law, Singapore.

and monitoring, and political analytical functions. Thus, the UN Department of Peace-Keeping Operations now monitors and controls all UN peace-keeping operations.

Despite all these constructive efforts, however, the UN peace-keeping situation is still in a critical state as a result of political and financial difficulties. Unpaid assessments totalled US$2.1 billion as of 30 June 1994. A minimum of US$200 million is needed every month to sustain the on-going peace-keeping operations.

In response to this critical state of peace-keeping, in his report "An agenda for peace", the UNSG suggested innovations such as peace-enforcement and a UN Standby Force. Others have proposed a UN Standing Army composed of volunteers. While these ideas are interesting, the crux of the matter is:

(a) Will the major players demonstrate sufficient political will to carry out UN peace-keeping operations, especially where these have international repercussions?
(b) Is there a need for the UN to assist states to govern themselves in such a way as to prevent internal conflicts from occurring?

The answers to these two questions will determine if there can be combined pro-active and preventive approaches by those who have the means and by those who may need assistance. The big and middle-sized developed powers could provide the UN with commitments under the UN Standby Scheme to provide airlift, logistics and financial support, so that UN peace-keeping operations can be launched quickly. The second approach would require the UN to exercise quiet and discreet preventive diplomacy, to advise and assist those states identified to be in danger of impending collapse.

A third approach is to build a new support base of countries willing and ready to assist the UN in peace-keeping matters. In addition to the traditional big and middle-sized powers such as the US, UK, Canada, Australia and the Nordic states which have made vital contributions in peace-keeping, a new group of active Member States has emerged which are able to contribute troops to UN peace-keeping operations. These include Spain, Uruguay, Malaysia, Indonesia, Turkey, Pakistan and South Korea. Small states like Singapore and Brunei have also chipped in with small contingents of civilian police in operations such as UNTAC and UNIKOM. In this way, the peace-keeping burdens are spread more widely.

These three approaches can help the UN in addressing the phenomenon of increasing internal conflicts and growing humanitarian disasters. These approaches are important because the UN must play a central role in upholding international law and world peace. Together with the restructuring of the UN Secretariat to provide better peace-keeping services, they offer the promise of restoring some stability to the post-Cold War era.

It would be remiss of me if I do not refer to the issues of sovereignty and consent. It is clear that "second generation" UN peace-keeping is very intrusive and upsets traditional concepts of sovereignty and independence of nation-states. Is it then important for the success of a peace-keeping operation that UN involvement takes place only with the consent of the parties to a conflict? If the answer is yes, then how can the consent requirement apply in cases where there is no effective central government capable of ruling and providing the most basic functions of law and order? For example, in the new anarchic conditions, such as in Somalia and Rwanda, the UN does not know who will perform the "request and consent" function. In such a situation, who will invite the UN to rescue the people?

CONCLUSION

I have posed some questions which I hope may be of interest to you. Your conference, of course, is to discuss and analyse UNTAC and Cambodia. UNTAC operations in Cambodia may not be the same as other peace-keeping operations elsewhere. But your discussions and conclusions will be most timely and useful, as the UN and the international community are still confronted with difficult decisions in UNPROFOR, UNOSOM, and elsewhere. You will need to ask the right questions, even if they are difficult ones, and to draw accurate lessons from UNTAC's complex and difficult operations.

In closing, let me thank all the sponsors, organizers, and the participants whose support and effort have made this conference possible. I hope you have a good conference.

6. Message

Dr Boutros Boutros-Ghali[1]

The United Nations is leading the way into a new era. To the role of peace-keeping as created and defined by the world organization during the Cold War decades has been added vast new responsibilities in peace operations. In this second generation of peace-keeping every mission is unique, yet each has in common a greater scale, more extensive civilian participation, and a far more comprehensive approach to address the problems which at times afflict an entire society and state. The United Nations mission in Cambodia over the past few years has served as the flagship for this United Nations-led voyage to the future. This seminar therefore can itself be of far-reaching significance.

The efforts of the United Nations to resolve the long-standing political conflict in Cambodia involved new and unparalleled forms of international diplomatic action. Massive in size, comprehensive in scope, and precise in its mandate, the United Nations Transitional Authority in Cambodia (UNTAC) set a new standard for peace-keeping operations undertaken by the international community. Clearly, because it was breaking new ground, UNTAC, and the Paris Peace Agreements which articulated its mandate, involved both risk and experimentation.

In Paris, the international community negotiated a framework for peace in Cambodia which depended for its success on the conflicting parties' willingness to adhere to the agreements reached and on the freedom of the Cambodian people to decide for themselves on the future of their country. Unforeseen diplomatic and logistical hurdles presented almost daily challenges to UNTAC's operational mandate.

It has already become clear that the ultimate success of UNTAC was the result of a combination of factors, including a unified decision-making apparatus in New York, the work of competent and dedicated personnel in the field and, in Cambodia itself, a political atmosphere of conciliation and an acceptance of the need for change.

The experience of UNTAC has also shown, however, the need for operational plans to be based on a full understanding of the conditions – social, political, and infrastructural – on the ground; for clearer institutional procedures for equipping and maintaining large overseas operations; and for a command structure in the field that can coordinate diverse groups of professionals while remaining flexible enough to meet changing needs.

A careful evaluation of the operation is therefore necessary so that lessons may be learned for future United Nations peace-keeping missions. In addition, lessons may be learned from a study of the process of translating diplomatic decision-making into practical action.

---

[1] Secretary-General of the United Nations.

Today you are beginning that process of lesson-learning and analysis. I congratulate the Institute of Policy Studies and UNITAR on their initiative in organizing this seminar. I look forward to reading the report of your deliberations and proceedings, and I wish all participants an enjoyable and profitable seminar.

7. Message

Ambassador Samuel R. Insanally[1]

I welcome this opportunity to send a message to this important conference which seeks to undertake an analysis of the United Nations Transitional Authority in Cambodia (UNTAC) peace-keeping operation, to draw lessons for future peace-keeping operations of the United Nations and to propose new training concepts and methodologies to ensure the better preparation, through training, of the personnel to be involved in these operations.

The Institute of Policy Studies of Singapore and UNITAR are to be congratulated on this initiative since it offers a timely opportunity of examining ways and means of enhancing the capacity of the United Nations in the areas of peace-keeping, peace-making and preventive diplomacy. The Cambodia operation which, by all accounts, proved generally successful can offer many important lessons for the future.

At a dinner held in my honor by ASEAN in New York in October 1993, I strongly commended the early initiatives which its member countries have taken to enhance the prospect of political stability in their region. I noted that since the United Nations was now hard pressed, by lack of adequate resources, to guarantee world peace and security, regional groups such as ASEAN can play an important complementary role, in keeping with Chapter VIII of the Charter, to achieve the "pacific settlement of local disputes". I referred then to the success of the Cambodia operation.

On that occasion, I proposed an early meeting, under the auspices of the United Nations, of relevant regional organizations which can contribute to the maintenance of international peace and security. More recently, I have come to the conclusion, substantiated by the World Hearings on Development, which I convened last month in New York, that in the field of peace and security formal mechanisms should be established for the greater use of regional organizations in peace-keeping, conflict prevention and in forging confidence-building at the regional level.

I am pleased that plans are underway for a first meeting in New York among officials of the United Nations and the regional organizations with which the UN has cooperated in matters of international peace and security in recent years, to undertake a joint assessment of that cooperation and to exchange views about how it might be improved. In assessing such cooperation I believe that the case of UNTAC offers many lessons and can therefore be instructive in handling similar situations in the future. The United Nations, it may be recalled, had been involved in finding a peaceful solution to the situation in Cambodia from 1978. For the next decade the Secretary-General, at the request of the General Assembly, exercised his

---

[1] President of the 1993–94 United Nations General Assembly.

good offices in trying to assist all parties concerned in the search for a negotiated settlement.

During this period, the mechanisms of the good offices of the Secretary-General and the contacts made by his Special Representative produced the framework for a comprehensive settlement plan. Of great significance also was the involvement of ASEAN in the first face-to-face talks on the occasion of the Jakarta Informal Meeting (JIM), held in Indonesia in July 1988, between all four Cambodian parties. Later, in 1989, another JIM addressed the general understanding that an international mechanism should play a role in supervising and controlling the implementation of agreements reached by the parties.

The authority to establish this international control mechanism was given by the Agreements on a Comprehensive Political Settlement of the Cambodia Conflict which entered into force on 23 October 1991, and which invited the Security Council to establish UNTAC – one of the largest operations conducted by the UN.

I believe that the comprehensiveness, the thorough planning and the well-judged execution of this operation were the hallmarks of its success.

The review which you will undertake should be of great help in shaping a new paradigm for peace-keeping operations. With the increasing proliferation of conflicts throughout the world, there is a certain urgency to determine how best the United Nations can help to preserve peace and stability.

Special attention must be given to the period after a peace-keeping operation has been concluded. The groundwork laid, and the institutions put in place, would be threatened if there were no assurances of sustained social and economic development. The United Nations has the urgent task of balancing its peace and development agenda so that adequate conditions for gaining and maintaining stability are created. In commending these thoughts for your consideration, I would like to wish the conference much success.

8. The Paris Agreements and their Implementation

Ambassador Yukio Imagawa[1]

CAMBODIA: A SUCCESS STORY OF THE UNITED NATIONS PEACE-KEEPING OPERATIONS

The United Nations peace-keeping operations (PKO) which were carried out in Cambodia from 15 March 1992 to 24 September 1993 were considered a great success. Of course that does not mean they were 100% triumphant, but they can be said to have been 80% successful. No one can expect a 100% victory in such a complicated and difficult mission, and an 80% result was surely enough to achieve a big success.

What contributed to the 20% that failed? The answer is simple: problems with the Khmer Rouge. Even the serious efforts made by UNTAC, which had deployed more than 22,000 military and civilian peace-keepers all over Cambodia, could neither disarm nor demobilize the Khmer Rouge nor make them participate in the elections organized by the UN.

Nevertheless, I think it is better not to overestimate the Khmer Rouge influence, but to recognize the fact that in most parts of Cambodia since the end of the UN's PKO, people are enjoying peaceful and normal daily life and making their contribution to national reconstruction under the guidance of the democratically elected government which controls more than 90% of the whole territory. If you look at the actual situation in Cambodia, you can clearly see the fact that the Cambodian PKO was a UN success story.

THE PARIS AGREEMENTS: THE BASIS OF THE SUCCESSFUL UNPKO IN CAMBODIA

It is often said that the success of the UN's PKO in Cambodia was due to Prince Norodom Sihanouk, the incontestable leader respected by all the warring factions, and also due to the capable leadership of Mr Yasushi Akashi, the UN Secretary-General's Special Representative. These facts are true. However, I think the most important reason why the UN's PKO in Cambodia could achieve such a great success is that it was legally based on good and well-built international agreements, the Agreements on a Comprehensive Political Settlement of the Cambodia Conflict, usually called the "Paris Agreements". These Agreements had been carefully drafted and adopted on 23 October 1991 in Paris by Cambodia and 18 other nations.

---

[1] Ambassador Extraordinary and Plenipotentiary of Japan in Cambodia, Phnom Penh.

DRAFTING THE PARIS AGREEMENTS

In December 1987 in a small French village called Ferre en Tardenois, some 120 kilometers north of Paris, Prince Norodom Sihanouk, then head of the three factions' anti-Vietnam coalition, met with Mr Hun Sen, then Prime Minister of the Vietnam-supported Phnom Penh Government. After nearly two decades of warfare between Cambodians backed by different foreign powers, they began for the first time to conduct a direct dialogue of reconciliation and to consult about peace in Cambodia.

After these first historic Sihanouk–Hun Sen talks, they again met in France, in January 1988 at Saint Germain en Laye, in November 1988 once more at Ferre en Tardenois, and in July 1989 at La Celle Saint Cloud. On the other hand, the Indonesian Government convened and organized the "Jakarta Informal Meetings" on Cambodia, where representatives of all four Cambodian factions participated, first in July 1988, and then in February and May 1989. In these talks and meetings, progress on substantive issues was rather slow, but understanding between Cambodians was steadily created.

Both France and Indonesia made enormous efforts in setting up the framework of Cambodian peace negotiations, and jointly proposed and then invited Cambodia's four factions, two other Indochinese states, the Permanent Five and six ASEAN countries, as well as Japan, Australia, India, Canada and the Chairman of the Non-Aligned Movement to participate in the Paris International Conference on Cambodia (PICC) usually called the "Paris Conference". The Cambodian factions were Prince Sihanouk's faction, Mr Son San's faction, Mr Hun Sen's faction (the Phnom Penh Government) and Mr Khieu Samphan's faction (the Khmer Rouge). The Paris Conference was opened on 30 July 1989 and serious discussions continued daily for a month. Besides the plenary session, discussions took place in three committees: the First Committee for military affairs, the Second Committee for political affairs and the Third Committee for rehabilitation, reconstruction and repatriation of refugees. After one month's talks and negotiations, only the Third Committee, co-chaired by Japan and Australia, could reach agreement and adopt unanimously an official document. The First and Second Committees could not achieve any conclusion or understanding in their fields. Therefore the first phase of the Paris Conference was suspended on 30 August 1989.

After this suspension, discussions between the Cambodian parties were revived and took place in Pattaya (Thailand), Jakarta and Bangkok. As of November 1990, there were many active international consultations to help Cambodians. The Permanent Five and the co-chair Indonesia met frequently, almost every month, alternatively in Paris and in New York. The result of the Cambodian and international efforts to find ways to solve the remaining problems and narrow the gap between partners, over two years two months, led to the second phase of the Paris Conference convened by France on 21 October 1991, 22 days after the adjournment of the first phase. On 23 October 1991, all the Cambodian delegates and representatives of the 18 participating countries adopted and signed, in the presence of the UN

Secretary-General, four documents composing the Agreements on the Comprehensive Political Settlement of the Cambodia Conflict, usually called the "Paris Agreements", which became the legal basis for the peace process in Cambodia.

IMPLEMENTATION OF PARIS AGREEMENTS (1)

The four documents of the Paris Agreements on Cambodia were: 1) Final Act; 2) Agreement on a Comprehensive Political Settlement of the Cambodian Conflict; 3) Agreement concerning the Sovereignty, Independence, Territorial Integrity and Inviolability, Neutrality and National Unity of Cambodia, and 4) Declaration on the Rehabilitation and Reconstruction of Cambodia. Of these four documents, the second seemed to be the most important, mentioning the formation and the activities of the two main bodies for its implementation, the United Nations Transitional Authority in Cambodia and the Supreme National Council.

According to the second document, the period between the entry into force of the Agreements and the promulgation of the new Constitution was to be called the transitional period. During this period, the UN peace-keeping operations were deployed all over Cambodia by the United Nations Transitional Authority in Cambodia (UNTAC), with civilian and military components. UNTAC was put under the direct responsibility of the UN Secretary-General and led by his Special Representative. According to the Agreements' second document, UNTAC was given the mandate to implement the Agreements and was also delegated by the Supreme National Council of Cambodia (SNC) with all power necessary to ensure this implementation. UNTAC had, at its peak, more than 22,000 international staff, of which about 6,000 were civilian and 16,000 were military. The head office of UNTAC was located at Cambodia's capital, Phnom Penh, where the civilian components were Electoral, Legal, Human Rights, Information, Rehabilitation, Repatriation and Civilian Police. The Military Component was headquartered at the High Command. Local offices of UNTAC were installed in every province (*Khet*); military control posts were spotted along frontiers and civilian police stations were in all cantons (*Srok*). All the peace-keepers of UNTAC worked hard to implement the Paris Agreements. They had one supreme objective: to organize and conduct free and fair elections in Cambodia.

In addition to UNTAC, there was the Supreme National Council (SNC) of Cambodia. The SNC was in the transitional period the unique legitimate body and source of authority in which the sovereignty, independence and unity of Cambodia were enshrined. The SNC was first composed of 12 members, six from the resistance coalition including its president (Prince Norodom Sihanouk) and six from the Phnom Penh Government. It later increased to 13 members, a neutral president (again, Prince Sihanouk) plus six from each side. SNC meetings were held, about once a week or every two weeks, usually at the Royal Palace in Phnom Penh, but sometimes outside, at Siem Reap or even in foreign countries (Thailand, China, Japan, USA). SNC meetings were co-chaired by its president, Prince Norodom Sihanouk and Mr Yasushi Akashi, Head of UNTAC. Also present were high-ranking UNTAC officials and representatives of the Permanent Five, Indonesia and other countries.

In the transitional period, the existing administration of the Phnom Penh Government was primarily responsible for the normal day-to-day life of the Cambodian people. More than 90% of Cambodia's territory, including the capital Phnom Penh and all other provincial capitals, was under the control of the Government of the State of Cambodia (the Phnom Penh Government). This Administration was put under the general control of UNTAC and SNC. But the second document of the Paris Agreements gave UNTAC direct control over the fields of foreign affairs, national defence, finance, public security and information in order to ensure a neutral political environment leading to free and fair elections.

The Expanded Permanent Five (EP5) played an important role in the diplomatic circle at Phnom Penh. To cooperate with UNTAC, diplomatic representatives of the Permanent Five plus other influential countries such as Indonesia, Japan, Australia, Thailand and, later, Germany formed a unique consulting and coordinating body called EP5 or Core Group. They met once, twice or even three times a week to discuss measures for cooperation and exchange opinions about the peace process, in Phnom Penh or sometimes in foreign countries. EP5 member countries also consulted with each other and cooperated with UNTAC, concentrating on their common interest: peace in Cambodia, regardless of their political or ideological standpoints.

IMPLEMENTATION OF PARIS AGREEMENTS (2)

Mr Yasushi Akashi, Special Representative of the UN Secretary-General, accompanied by General Sanderson, Commander in Chief of the Military Component of UNTAC, arrived in Phnom Penh on 15 March 1992 and, on this date, UNTAC commenced UN's PKO activities in Cambodia. Both civilian and military components began their activities to implement the Paris Agreements in the field immediately. According to the dispositions of the Agreements (second document), the Military Component tried to advance the cease-fire into its second phase for the purpose of realizing the regrouping, disarmament and demobilization of the Cambodian factions' forces. But strong objections from the Khmer Rouge forced UNTAC to abandon the second phase in June 1992.

Despite the uncooperative attitude of the Khmer Rouge, UNTAC's Chief Akashi and his colleagues did their best to prepare the way for organizing free and fair elections. UN volunteers devotedly and successfully promoted the registration of voters all over the territory. In August 1992, UNTAC's electoral law was adopted, despite tough objections from the Khmer Rouge. From the beginning of 1993, Khmer Rouge harassment accelerated sharply and Cambodia's security environment became very disturbed. Though the surrounding situation was not favorable and the Khmer Rouge publicly denounced the UN-organized elections, Akashi and his colleagues stood firm and decided to conduct the election from 23 to 28 May 1993 all over Cambodia, except in a very few areas controlled by the Khmer Rouge.

The results of the election were far better than even UNTAC expected. Polling was conducted on a nationwide scale almost without harassment, hindrance, threat or attack by the Khmer Rouge, and the voter turnout rate was recorded at more than 90%. The Constituent Assembly was established with a total of 120 elected members, whose seats were shared by the FUNCINPEC party (ex-Sihanouk faction) 58, People's Party (Phnom Penh Government) 51, and others 11, and worked for six months to formulate a new Constitution. On 21 September 1993, the Constituent Assembly adopted a new Constitution based on the principles of democracy and constitutional monarchy. On 24 September 1993, the new Constitution of the Kingdom of Cambodia was promulgated. Prince Norodom Sihanouk, who had been President of the SNC, acceded to the throne. King Sihanouk nominated Prince Norodom Ranariddh of the FUNCINPEC party as First Prime Minister and Mr Hun Sen of the People's Party as Second Prime Minister and together they formed a new coalition Royal Government. On 24 September 1993, UNTAC completed its supreme mission of the PKO in Cambodia, winning high praise for a great success, and Mr Akashi left Cambodia two days later.

CAMBODIA OF TODAY AND TOMORROW: PEACE AND DEVELOPMENT

After the formation of the new Kingdom and its Royal Government of Cambodia on 24 September 1993, the reconciliation of Cambodian parties, except for the Khmer Rouge who did not participate in the UN-organized elections, seemed to be making good progress. But following the failure of attacks by government forces on the Khmer Rouge main base at Pailin on April 1994, the military and political situation became tense again. Aiming to try to reconcile the Royal Government with the Khmer Rouge, King Sihanouk organized round-table talks in May and June 1994. Unhappily the good intentions of the King were unsuccessful. Nowadays, many speak of the menace of the Khmer Rouge in Cambodia, but in reality, more than 90% of Cambodia's territory is under the control of the Royal Government, where the inhabitants enjoy a poor but peaceful daily life.

To cope successfully with the Khmer Rouge danger, if it truly exists, the most important action for the Cambodian Government and citizens is to make serious efforts for economic and social development in order to raise the Cambodian people's standard of living. They will be helped, if necessary, by economic and technical assistance from friendly countries. To close my speech, I want to mention that "There is no peace without development and no development without peace".

9. Crafting the Paris Agreements on Cambodia

Sylvie Bermann[1]

More than two years and numerous meetings with different configurations in Paris, Jakarta, Beijing and Pattaya were necessary to conclude the Paris Agreements on Cambodia, which were signed on 23 October 1991 in Paris. They are based on what appeared to be, in the last day of the first session of the Paris Conference, a desperate *boutade* of Prince Sihanouk. He said that the only solution for Cambodia would be to place the country under United Nations trusteeship. At that time, nobody took this remark seriously, because such a formula was unprecedented in international law for a sovereign and independent country. The idea in fact made its way into the minds of the people involved in this issue and, as failure of the peace process was unthinkable, it was "publicized" first by US Congressman Stephen Solarz, and then by the Australian Foreign Minister, Senator Gareth Evans. This idea of an enhanced role of the United Nations led to the involvement of the countries most responsible for the maintenance of peace and security, namely the five Permanent Members of the Security Council, which started to draft a framework agreement. This draft was later transformed with the cooperation of the Co-chairman of the Paris Conference, Indonesia, the Cambodian parties and finally the other states participating in the Paris Conference into a final agreement signed in Paris on 23 October 1991 (the Paris Agreements).

These Agreements constitute a tremendous innovation in international law, because they were drafted by diplomats and politicians, who knew they had to be flexible and pragmatic, and not by lawyers. The most innovative point was the creation of a body, absolutely *sui generis*, known as the Supreme National Council. It was composed of representatives of all the factions and entitled to represent the sovereignty of Cambodia both internally and externally and defined as the "unique legitimate body and source of authority enshrining the sovereignty, independence and unity of Cambodia". This body delegated all powers "necessary to ensure the implementation of this agreement" to the United Nations Transitional Authority (UNTAC). And so UNTAC was in fact for 18 months the guardian of Cambodia, with enormous powers not only in the military field but mostly in domestic affairs and civilian administration, and in the monitoring of human rights. The success which culminated with the election process was due, in particular, to the comprehensive nature of this operation. The success has been such that it has been envisaged as a model for other conflicts.

Looking back to the history of these Agreements, it started in fact during the first phase of the Paris Conference on Cambodia, which was also an idea of Prince Sihanouk who thought that only the pressure imposed by the bigger powers would convince the Cambodian factions to work towards

---

[1] Counsellor, Permanent Mission of France to the United Nations, New York.

national reconciliation. The conference started well. The international situation at that time was rather encouraging.

The Vietnamese decided to withdraw their troops from Cambodia and there was a beginning of reconciliation between Beijing and Moscow, who started to put aside what was called the "third obstacle to the Sino-Soviet reconciliation". Of course the position of China a short time after the Tiananmen incidents raised doubts. But the hope was that the countries that were supposed to have influence over their "Cambodian friends" would exercise it in a positive way so that a comprehensive political settlement could be signed at the end of August 1989. The countries that participated in the conference had been carefully chosen to this end: the Indonesian Co-chairman, who earlier had organized the "JIM meetings of Jakarta", the Permanent Five, ASEAN countries, Vietnam and Laos, and Japan, Australia, India and Canada, as well as the current chairman of the Non-Aligned Movement. There was also a United Nations delegation, led by Mr Rafeeuddin Ahmed; at the beginning, he was only present as a representative of the Secretary-General in his personal capacity, because one of the Cambodian parties and Vietnam did not agree on the role foreseen for the United Nations. This shows that the involvement of the UN was not inevitable.

Despite the positive start to the conference, the positions of the actors hardened. Apparently, they thought they could achieve new gains by reopening military action. In these circumstances, the conference adjourned on 30 August 1989, deciding only to reconvene when the conditions were ripe. In fact, some of the ideas and the content which constituted the final Agreements were envisaged during this conference and some parts of the Agreements were even agreed in the various committees set up by the conference: some basic military provisions and the declarations on rehabilitation and reconstruction and on the repatriation of refugees and displaced persons, as well as the agreement on international guarantees ("the Agreement concerning the Sovereignty, Independence, Territorial Integrity and Inviolability, Neutrality and National Unity of Cambodia"). The conference, however, failed on what has been qualified as "GAPS" by one participant: Genocide, Authority (which was the problem of a UN involvement), Power Sharing (but the idea of a quadripartite authority, which constituted the basis for the Supreme National Council, was defined at that time) and the question of the Vietnamese settlers (close to solution).

All the elements were nonetheless in place for restarting the negotiations. The new idea was a more important presence of the United Nations. And this started to be discussed during the meetings of the Permanent Five on Cambodia which took place from January to August 1990. It was based on the idea that the main objective was to create a neutral environment for the organization of free and fair elections, which would permit the Cambodian people to choose their own destiny. It resulted in a series of communiques defining all the fundamental components of the solution and was finally assembled in a framework document. This text, agreed upon on 28 August 1990, promptly endorsed by the Security Council and the General Assembly, and accepted by the Cambodian parties, constituted the basis for the negotiations. The fact was that beside the personal influence of one or another country on its "Cambodian friends", the authority of the Permanent Five was fully recognized by the Cambodian parties. The document was quickly elaborated in a comprehensive agreement with the participation of the UN experts and at appropriate times the other participants of the Paris Conference. The agreement was completed in November 1990 but the negotiations with the Cambodian parties to get their full support took one more year because they were assessing the relative strength of their armed forces and their chances in the elections. The evolution of the international situation and, in particular, the collapse of the Soviet Union, which deprived one party of its full support, helped a lot. The final revisions of the agreement at Pattaya in August 1991 defined the demobilization at the level of 70% and the definition of the electoral system, paving the way for the signing of the Agreements.

Of the four instruments constituting the Paris Agreements, the most important and binding agreement was the Agreement on a Comprehensive Political Settlement of the Cambodian Conflict and its Annexes defining in particular the mandate of UNTAC, military matters, the election system and even the principles for a new Constitution. The most interesting innovation in this agreement concerns the power of the United Nations through the Special Representative of the Secretary-General and UNTAC over the whole civil administration of Cambodia. It was decided to exercise a three-level control over the administration, taking into account the importance of the sector for the elections. The first degree of control (direct) concerned five key sectors: foreign affairs, national defence, finance, information and public security. The second concerned supervision over the governmental elements which could directly influence the outcome of election, those bodies to be determined by the Special Representative "in cooperation with the SNC" (for example, education, public health, transportation and communications). The last degree of intervention of UNTAC was reserved for those agencies that, according to the Special Representative, could continue to operate in order to ensure normal day-to-day life in Cambodia (for example, cultural affairs). But even in this field the UN could decide to conduct investigations and, if necessary, take corrective steps which would include placing these organs under greater supervision or control. And what is interesting and unusual is that the Special Representative had specific prerogatives – generally those of governments – which permitted him to issue binding directives, to put in place UN personnel with unrestricted access to all administrative operations and documents and to require the reassignment or removal of any Cambodian personnel. Furthermore, in order to prevent any obstruction in the process, the Special Representative had in law the final decision, after consultation with SNC which was supposed to give advice by consensus, on all issues relating to the implementation of the Agreements.

Another aspect of the Agreements which was unprecedented and covered specifically was the protection and promotion of human rights and fundamental freedoms – even programmes of education in this field. This decision was taken because of the tragedy suffered by this country and the great sensitivity of the international community on this question. A complete section of the Agreements was devoted to this issue. These provisions appeared to be very effective during the electoral campaign and in terms of restoring real political life and democracy in the country. The continuing presence of UN specialists for human rights in this country, through the Centre for Human Rights, which was decided in the agreements, is still very useful. And finally UNTAC had the full responsibility for the organization and conduct of the election. This differed from other UN operations, Angola for instance, where the UN was supposed only to monitor the process. In this regard it is interesting to note that UNTAC had the prerogative of suspending or abrogating existing laws deemed contrary to the objectives of the Agreements. It also had the responsibility to establish a system of laws and procedures and administrative measures, including the adoption of an electoral law and a code of conduct for the holding of elections.

Of course, implementation was not as complete as foreseen by the authors of the Paris Agreements, because of the realities on the ground. Nevertheless, these Agreements and the settlement plan, which was drawn up by the United Nations, could serve as a model for the resolution of other conflicts. But the personality of King Sihanouk, who was accepted by all the factions, was one of the main reasons why the SNC was effective, and this condition does not apply in other countries where United Nations operations have been set up (e.g. Somalia). It was also one of the first big operations of the UN, and proved very costly. In view of the increasing involvement of the UN around the world, it would probably not be possible nowadays to establish another such operation. And lastly, countries were enthusiastic in contributing peace-keeping troops or civilian personnel to this operation; this might not be the case in the future.

10. The UN's Role in Bringing about Peace in Cambodia (An Insider's View)

USG Rafeeuddin Ahmed[1]

The General Assembly of the United Nations, the Security Council, the Secretary-General and the Human Rights Commission played a role in the United Nations' effort in the Cambodian affair. This presentation aims to focus on the role of the Secretary-General. The Security Council had failed to act on two occasions because of the Soviet veto in 1979. However, the General Assembly repeatedly adopted each year from 1979 on, with an increasing voting majority, resolutions that enunciated the key elements of a settlement. In addition, the Human Rights Commission also adopted resolutions almost every year with regard to the human rights situation in Cambodia.

In late 1978 when reports about increasing hostilities between Vietnam and Democratic Kampuchea began to appear, the Secretary-General, Dr Kurt Waldheim, decided to pay a visit to Cambodia and Vietnam. He sought the acceptance of the two countries to allow his visit in December 1978. The Cambodian response was positive. However, the Vietnamese answered by suggesting that the visit should take place later. The Secretary-General felt that perhaps his presence in the region might avoid an open war, so he decided to restrict his visit to Cambodia. At that time, the Cambodian side considered that the risk of a big war did not exist, and concurred with postponing the Secretary-General's visit to a later date.

On 25 December 1978, open hostilities broke out. The Government of the Democratic Republic of Kampuchea fled and a new regime, the National United Front for the National Salvation of Kampuchea, came to power, installed by Vietnamese forces. As the Security Council considered the matter, Prince Sihanouk appeared personally before the Council and made a passionate appeal. Unfortunately, the resolution put forward by the non-aligned members was not adopted, due to a Soviet veto. Between 17 February and 16 March 1979, hostilities took place between Chinese and Vietnamese forces. The Secretary-General expressed his concern over this situation and on 23 February he offered his good offices to bring about a settlement in the region. Later that month, the Security Council again resumed its consideration of the matter. In March, an ASEAN draft resolution calling upon all parties to withdraw their forces to their own countries was also vetoed by the Soviet Union. In the course of April and May, the Secretary-General visited the ASEAN countries, Laos, Vietnam, China, Japan and both Koreas.

In Beijing, the Secretary-General met with Prince Sihanouk on the Cambodian issue. Soon after, there was an increase in the outflow of refugees from Indochina. First the Secretary-General appointed Mr Iiter Turkmen as

---

[1] Associate Administrator, United Nations Development Programme, New York.

his Special Representative for Humanitarian Affairs in Southeast Asia. Later UN conferences were convened to deal with the Kampuchean humanitarian situation and Sir Robert Jackson was appointed as Coordinator for Assistance to the Kampuchean People.

Meanwhile the situation inside Cambodia became rather desperate. Relief was therefore provided by the international community, both inside Cambodia and to refugee or "displaced persons" camps situated on the border of Cambodia and Thailand. At that time, the Phnom Penh authorities considered the United Nations to be a neutral organization.

In 1980 the General Assembly asked the Secretary-General to convene an International Conference on Kampuchea (ICK). The Secretary-General directed his Special Representative for Humanitarian Affairs in Southeast Asia, Mr Hamed Essafi, to visit the ASEAN countries as well as Vietnam, Laos and China to undertake consultations on the conference. That was the first follow-up of the 1979 visit of the Secretary-General by a high-level representative of the Secretary-General. Held in 1981, the ICK was boycotted by Vietnam and its allies. Under the ASEAN countries' leadership, the conference took an objective position in dealing with the substance of the issue. It kept the door open in order to permit the different Cambodian political factions to participate. As it was boycotted, the participants decided that, instead of ending the conference, it should be kept alive so that one day it could reconvene with full participation. They also created an *ad hoc* committee that would be a continuing mechanism within the United Nations at the inter-governmental level to deal with the issue of Cambodia.

Following the conference, and to show the UN flag, the Secretary-General sent Mr Pérez de Cuéllar, the USG for Special Political Affairs to the region, and Ms Shimura. The Thai Government had requested the Secretary-General to send a representative. They stayed for a number of weeks in Bangkok as they felt tension growing between Thailand and Cambodia. After Mr Pérez de Cuéllar became Secretary-General in 1982, Mr Essafi and I exchanged functions. That is to say, he took over my function as Chief of Cabinet to the Secretary-General, and I became Special Representative for Humanitarian Affairs in Southeast Asia. The Secretary-General asked me to undertake a trip to the region. We agreed that I should try to focus on reaching an agreement on a formula that would begin a dialogue among the parties concerned under a changed form which would enable Vietnam and its allies to participate. As they were insisting on a regional conference, while the ASEAN countries and China held to an international conference format, we decided to propose a limited international conference. The participants would include the Cambodian parties, ASEAN countries, Vietnam, Laos, the five Permanent Members and a few other interested countries. I discussed this idea with the ASEAN countries, Vietnam, Laos, China, Japan and USSR. The ASEAN countries individually agreed to it. China, Japan and Vietnam agreed to consider it, but the USSR rejected it. Another problem arose: the three Indochinese Foreign Ministers announced this limited international conference as their own idea. Immediately, it was rejected by the other parties. We had little choice but to make further investigation and wait for a more propitious moment to revive the idea.

The Secretary-General visited the region in 1985. On the basis of his talks, he presented a report to the United Nations General Assembly. In this report, he identified the elements of a comprehensive political settlement on which he felt there was convergence. Among these elements there were those which had been there from the very beginning, namely withdrawal of foreign forces and the right of the Cambodian people to decide their future through free and fair elections. Another element was national reconciliation, which was first mentioned by the ASEAN Foreign Ministers at the time of the Jakarta meeting in September 1983 and later also accepted by the Indochinese Foreign Ministers. In addition to these three points, the Secretary-General also mentioned the non-return to the universally condemned policies and practices of the recent past. Moreover, the report mentioned that Cambodia should become a non-aligned independent and neutral sovereign state, and that there should be international guarantees. We developed these ideas during the course of the next couple of years. For ten years, I attended annual meetings of the ASEAN Foreign Ministers to help to transmit messages between ASEAN countries and Vietnam. In the beginning, no direct dialogue took place at all. The United Nations had the role of an intermediary and honest broker in terms of interpreting the positions of the different parties to each other. Regularly, we also met with the three factions constituting the Coalition Government of Democratic Kampuchea, which was formed in 1982.

In 1988, we felt that the time had come to build upon these elements as the basis of a tentative peace plan. We also thought that it was very important that the human rights situation should be added to other elements. The international community could assure Cambodia that it would recognize and guarantee its independence and sovereignty. Cambodia in turn would give guarantees that it would never return to the universally condemned policies and practices of the Khmer Rouge period. This was a kind of conditionality between the two sets of guarantees which was incorporated in the peace plan.

In June 1988, for the first time, I went to Phnom Penh, although the regime in Phnom Penh was not recognized by the United Nations. I relied upon a precedent, the visit of Mr Dag Hammarskjöld to Beijing to secure the release of certain American airmen who had been shot down during the Korean war. In a note, he explained that he was not there under a General Assembly resolution but he was there under his authority as Secretary-General under the UN Charter. On this basis, I made my recommendation to Mr Pérez de Cuéllar that I should be allowed to go to Phnom Penh — otherwise the credibility of our proposal might well be questioned. So I made my first visit to Phnom Penh and introduced this plan to Mr Hun Sen. Following this, I presented it in Bangkok to the ASEAN Foreign Ministers and to the three other Cambodian factions. In July, I gave the plan to the Permanent Representative in Geneva of the five Permanent Members, as well as to countries like Japan and Australia which had shown a lot of interest in this matter.

We were very closely involved in discussions with the French Government when it was planning to organise the Paris Conference. The

UN Secretariat prepared documents on each item on the agenda of the conference. After the five Permanent Members began their consultations in January 1990, I was invited to meet with them to share the United Nations' perceptions on the various issues under consideration. Once the framework was drawn up and issued in August, it was endorsed by the Security Council. Indonesia and the United Nations were asked to join the Permanent Five in the elaboration of a comprehensive political settlement agreement. We made a lot of input, especially in areas like the military and elections. We anticipated problems at the meeting with the State of Cambodia in Paris from 21 to 23 December, especially with Mr Hun Sen. I had to speak to him personally and explain to him how we intended to implement the agreement. Then he asked me to say the same thing at the SOC meeting itself. Then he, together with Prince Ranariddh, asked if I could put it in writing, which I did in the form of an explanatory note. This statement led Mr Hun Sen to agree with what was being proposed. We again compromised, on the issue of representation, agreeing to proportional representation on a provincial basis; this was then accepted by Mr Hun Sen. So we were in any case very much involved throughout this process leading up to the finalization of the Agreements and their acceptance by the parties. On 23 October 1991, at the final meeting of the resumed Paris Conference; the Agreements were signed.

We tried to anticipate some of the problems which would arise and sent a number of advance missions to Cambodia. Two missions were sent by UNDP to look at the situation of the infrastructure, a mission was sent by me to look at the administrative structures, and a mission was sent by UNHCR to look at the situation regarding the return of the refugees. Military missions headed by General Dibuama were also fielded. We also discussed how we could get some money ahead of time. I received some money from the Scandinavian countries to carry out advanced work in relation to the elections and was able to send an advance team on elections headed by William Clive. I also talked to the United Nations Volunteers, which was the first time they were approached by anyone to provide UNVs to a peace-keeping operation. They immediately and enthusiastically agreed to send 400 UNVs, who worked especially in the Electoral Component. The matter was taken to the Security Council, requesting the establishment of the United Nations Advanced Mission in Cambodia (UNAMIC) as a precedent to UNTAC. This proposal was accepted by the Security Council, and under Ambassador Ataul Karim, UNAMIC was established in Cambodia. It remained in place until UNTAC was deployed under the Special Representative of the Secretary-General, Mr Yasushi Akashi.

11. The Cambodian Factions in the Democratic Process

Khieu Kanharith[1]

Asked about democracy in the 1950s, Cambodians from that generation would call to mind the assassination of the leading figure of the opposition groups and the chairman of the most influential party of that time, Mr Jeu Koeus, in 1950; the fatal shooting of Mr Nop Bophann, director of the leftist newspaper, the *Pracheachon* ("People"), in 1959; and also the more or less perfidious manoeuvres to monopolize power and to sideline the factions considered most threatening by the regime. For the 1960s generation, it was the moral and physical violence against those journalists and politicians who were opposing the regime; the vote-buying and the internal splits encouraged by different political options. And all these deviations from the democratic process led to the most horrible tragedy in contemporary Cambodian history: two decades of fratricidal war culminating in genocide on a scale unprecedented since the end of World War II.

The year 1987 saw the first breakthrough in the Cambodian conflict, with the appeal made by the Phnom Penh Government for a national reconciliation "except for the principal leaders responsible for the genocide". This opening would bring about a series of diplomatic shuttles: the Sihanouk–Hun Sen meeting, the four warring factions meeting with various concerned countries, the sessions of the Permanent Members of the UN Security Council and the international conferences to try to settle the Cambodian conflict in Paris and Jakarta.

Finally, in Paris on 23 October 1991, the four Cambodian factions and 18 foreign ministers signed four documents:

(a) an Agreement on a Comprehensive Political Settlement of the Cambodian Conflict;
(b) an Agreement concerning the Sovereignty, Independence, Territorial Integrity and Inviolability, Neutrality and National Unity of Cambodia;
(c) a Declaration on the Rebuilding and Reconstruction of Cambodia; and
(d) a Final Act on the Paris Conference on Cambodia.

These Paris Agreements were implemented by two main mechanisms:

(a) the Supreme National Council (SNC), composed of six representatives of the Government of the State of Cambodia (SOC) and six others representing the three opposition factions: the Khmer Rouge of Mr Pol Pot, the monarchist FUNCINPEC of Prince Sihanouk, and the republican KPNLF of Mr Son San;
(b) the UN transitional force charged with monitoring the cease-fire and the dismantling of 70% of the various military forces and the creation of a

---

[1] Secretary of State, Ministry of Information, Phnom Penh.

neutral environment for a fair and free election by taking under its control certain administrative bodies that might influence the electoral process.

The UN was to be deployed in two stages:

(a) After the signing of the peace agreement, a UN Advanced Mission in Cambodia (UNAMIC) of 268 persons was dispatched to Cambodia to facilitate the commitment to the cease-fire of the four factions and to collect data concerning the strength and the equipment of different troops, to launch the de-mining and mine-awareness programs and to provide all the necessary information for the deployment of the UN Transitional Authority in Cambodia (UNTAC).
(b) Once having defined and funded the necessary and sufficient human and financial needs, UNTAC began to assure a full implementation of these peace agreements.

Could all these projects be implemented? If yes, could they assure a stable and lasting peace in Cambodia? Could the long-martyred Cambodian people finally enjoy true democracy or not? I think the answer to these questions depended on the attitude of the four existing Cambodian factions that composed the SNC. This did not mean that the other factions were to be neglected or that they had no role or influence in society. But the fact was that these four factions possessed all the means — political, financial, organizational and military — that could and will decisively influence the peace process in Cambodia. Moreover, we must also mention the importance of Prince Sihanouk's role in contributing to the success or failure of the Cambodian peace plan. Now, let us try to analyse one by one these various actors on the Cambodian political scene.

PRINCE SIHANOUK: DANCING ON A TIGHTROPE

At the beginning the Prince's strategy was to rely on the Khmer Rouge's might to weaken the Phnom Penh Government in order to impose his conditions and become the sole architect of a Cambodian peace. But after his return to Phnom Penh and his understanding of the reality on the ground, continuation of this strategy appeared to be doing more harm than good. Sihanouk's decision to stay neutral, above all the political confrontations, reinforced his new role as the main guarantor of peace. Enjoying support from many foreign governments and benefiting from the respect accorded to his age (very important in Cambodia), the Prince could play a crucial stabilizing role in this first stage of the peace, if he can maintain his neutrality. But the Prince has to overcome three main obstacles to succeed in dancing on this tightrope: his myth, the republicans, and his entourage.

In fact, if we take a look at the reality of things, what makes the strength of the Prince is his myth. He is supposed to be a symbol of the independence and unity of the nation, the benefactor king and the messiah bringing peace, stability and even prosperity to the country. But confronted with reality, myths fade away. And adding to this is the fact that today everybody has invested so much hope in him without noticing that he is also trapped in the global geopolitical torments.

Furthermore, the age that gives him a certain respectability on the political scene becomes a handicap in the preparation of his successor. Combining these two factors, at the point when the Prince feels his power fading away or when he cannot realize the hopes placed on him, he might be tempted to concentrate power in his hands or in his groups and that, in the long run, would once again tip the country back into chaos.

The republicans would also give a hard time. Whether Sihanouk becomes a king or president of a republic, the republicans will always put obstacles in his way. Although right now every faction is trying to please him, the conflicts arising from time to time with the republicans of the old generation are a good illustration of this hidden animosity.

Most of all, the entourage, who were his downfall in 1970, are the main danger to the Prince today. This phenomenon is not typical only of Cambodia, nor does it have implications for Sihanouk alone but, due to his current role and the need of his moral authority in this very fragile situation, the Prince's best interests lie in avoiding as much as possible his name being used for the narrow or byzantine interests of a clan or group in such a way that could affect his whole credibility. Currently, it seems that the Prince is adopting a "wait and see" policy, tiptoeing through the political maze. At the same time, he is showing preference for cooperation between FUNCINPEC and the CPP (the ruling Cambodian People's Party), because the Prince well knows that the CPP is an unavoidable factor in the process and, what is more, he has more trust in Hun Sen's Government that in any other faction.

FUNCINPEC: WHAT DEGREE OF COOPERATION?

Since Prince Sihanouk decided to quit this faction and become neutral, FUNCINPEC has run into a leadership crisis. Formed mostly by Cambodian expatriates, this faction lacks popular local figures and has no strong popular base inside the country. Adding to this, the internal conflict has considerably reduced FUNCINPEC's capacity for action to gain strong support for its cause. It is clear that the threat to FUNCINPEC comes not from the Phnom Penh (CPP) group, but rather from the KPNLF and the KR. But the difference lies in the evaluation of this threat and the degree of cooperation with the CPP during the transitional period and the coming electoral campaign.

The FUNCINPEC group that supports the idea of a coalition with Phnom Penh think that it will bring more advantage than harm. The reason is that because of the proportional voting system in the UN-sponsored agreement, there is a possibility that no faction will get a majority in the new assembly to enable it to form a government alone. And the cooperation of these two factions (CPP and FUNCINPEC) will boost the group's chances to get a majority to form a relatively stable government and not depend too much on a hung Parliament subject to changing moods. Secondly, because of the many uncertainties that could hinder an effective implementation of the peace agreement, Phnom Penh will be the best life insurance should something go wrong in the future.

For the non-cooperating FUNCINPEC group, its first concern is the risk of FUNCINPEC being swallowed by the CPP and then losing its identity. Secondly, there is a risk of its losing the support of its rank-and-file members by making an alliance with the Government, which is considered as a Vietnamese creation and also corrupt. But it is probable that this last point is only a justification of a position, rather than a political and philosophical concept. The real reason behind this group's attitude is rather a conflict of personalities existing within this faction itself. Nonetheless, in the long run this conflict could be settled by mutual consensus and sacrifice, in the long-term interest of all sides.

THE KPNLF: THE REPUBLICAN ALTERNATIVE

At the beginning, the Khmer People's National Liberation Front enjoyed a lot of support from many Cambodian expatriates and also some people inside Cambodia; it represented an alternative between the monarchy, viewed as obsolete, and despotic KR-style Communism. This illusion is fading and will continue to fade very quickly, because of the intra-factional power struggle plaguing the KPNLF and the widespread corruption in its camps and its army. Despite this situation, this faction could maintain its existence due to the support of the USA and Thailand, which wish to counterbalance the power of the KR and to keep a margin of manoeuvre against the regional strategy of China and Vietnam.

With the split within the KPNLF between Mr Son Sann and General Sak Sutsakhan, it is premature to accurately assess the balance of forces between these two groups. But General Sak's strategy now is to establish and consolidate his popular base by renewing contact with former republican officers and soldiers and also those intellectuals who are displeased with the Phnom Penh Government. These groups, in the near future, could become efficient propagandists among the local masses in the elections.

For Mr Son Sann, his strategy has both short-term and long-term aims. In the short term, knowing he has little chance of winning the election – the emergence of new political groups supporting democratic institutions will seriously undermine his republican alternative – he will try to present himself as the leader of the republican and democratic groups in order to form so strong an opposition that any government will have to deal with him in the future National Assembly. This position would secure him a chance, if the President and Vice-President of a republic are to be elected by the National Assembly, to gain the post of Vice-President under Sihanouk and to give him more room to manoeuvre against both the President and the Government. His long-term strategy aims to reduce the influence of Hun Sen, who might be appointed as Prime Minister if the cooperation between the CPP and FUNCINPEC proves successful (wishes of Prince Sihanouk).

THE KHMER ROUGE: THE TWO-TRACK POLICY

Pol Pot has been prepared for many years for the Cambodian conflict's being resolved — for good or bad — by a political solution that would inevitably end up in some form of an electoral contest. But at the same time he insists that the situation is temporary, and sooner or later the civil war will break out again. From this analysis, the KR have changed their purely military strategy to a strategy that has electoral as well as military goals.

For their electoral strategy, the KR have adopted three priorities: to consolidate the area under their control, to exploit the dissensions among the different factions and their weak points; and to lead a campaign of education, both political and economic, among their cadres.

For their military strategy, they have two essential goals: to keep secretly hidden part of their elite troops, with two distinct tasks. In the case of a general election supervised by the UN, these forces along with their political propagandists will exert pressure in the areas controlled by the other factions in order to influence the vote toward the Khmer Rouge, at the same time eliminating their most dangerous rivals and also their own cadres not totally immersed in Khmer Rouge policies. The second task is a sort of emergency exit. In case things get out of control, these hidden forces will go into battle immediately, first of all to destroy the elite forces of the other factions.

But the KR also face three uncertainties concerning the degree of efficiency of their strategy. The first is that, although the other factions will see a dispersion of the Khmer Rouge vote resulting from the emergence of new political parties, the Khmer Rouge political monolith could be seriously threatened by the free communication of ideas and by opening up to the outside world. Their second uncertainty is, if the international community chooses to give the aid necessary for the reconstruction of Cambodia, the living conditions of the people would be noticeably improved. This could attract many KR soldiers to return to a normal life, thus weakening this faction's fighting capacity. The third uncertainty is the degree of efficiency of the UN's control and also the length of the presence of UN forces on the ground.

THE CAMBODIAN PEOPLE'S PARTY: IN SEARCH OF COALITIONS

For more than ten years, the CPP has been the only faction which has fought against the return of the Khmer Rouge. It is also the faction which controls the most territory and population in Cambodia, and at the same time it is the most structured of the factions. Although it previously had a structure and ideology which closely resembled those of most Communist parties, the CPP is seeking a future that is appropriate to Cambodian society. Further, it was the first ruling Marxist party to recognize individual private property rights for agricultural and urban land. The recent changes in the CPP's political platform, dropping references to Communist ideology, demonstrate this continuing effort towards a broader accommodation with the social and political reality of the country.

But this faction is facing many problems; primarily, the erosion of its authority after a decade in power; secondly, the image of a government installed by Vietnam; and thirdly, the economic difficulties caused by the Western trade embargo and the ending of aid from the former Communist countries of Eastern Europe and the USSR.

In this context, the CPP is trying to establish an alliance with other groups politically closer to its ideas, to face its most dangerous adversary. The success of this coalition will considerably influence the political process of the country. There are two reasons for this:

(a) The first is that without a genuine coalition the Government could find itself in an unstable situation. And without stability, one cannot ensure a sound environment for guaranteeing a democratic election in the country.
(b) The second reason is that no matter which other faction wins the election, the CPP must be included, if one wants relatively stable government to tackle effectively the task of reconstruction and creation of lasting peace.

In short, despite some reluctance on all sides, and some accidental eventualities such as we have seen in the past two months, the four factions which compose the SNC know well that an election is inevitable and they are preparing, each in their own way, to face a political confrontation.

Certainly, there will be new factions appearing, but they will encounter three serious handicaps. They will lack an organizational structure, funds and candidates who know the country well. It is too soon yet to assess the potential of such groups because, in the course of the electoral process, alliances between parties will inevitably come into play.

This multi-party image does not necessarily signify democracy, but at least constitutes the first step towards the democratization of Cambodian society. Democracy is a process which is not achieved in one or two elections. Other factors will also influence this process: the place of the army on the future political scene; the effectiveness of various pillars of democracy such as the press; the degree of respect for human rights; the degree of popular participation in political life; the equitable distribution of national wealth; and especially the determination of the international community to encourage a real and genuine democracy appropriate for Cambodia.

12. The Paris Agreements on Cambodia: A Retrospect

Mark Hong[1]

INTRODUCTION

The road to agreement in Paris was a very long, winding and difficult path. There were many cul de sacs or dead ends such as JIM I and JIM II, Bangkok Informal Meeting, Tokyo Informal Meeting and intra-Cambodian discussions and negotiations. In a way, they prepared the way for the Paris Agreements to succeed, because they showed in what areas agreement was not possible. Also, before the actual process of negotiations could begin, there was a long phase (ten years) of diplomatic and military battles to deny the Vietnamese claim of a *fait accompli* in Cambodia. These diplomatic battles in international forums were fought by ASEAN, which sought to persuade Vietnam to leave Cambodia peacefully. The Paris Agreements were achieved over three phases: Paris I (which began on 30 July 1989), the Australian Initiative and Paris II, the final and successful agreements, signed in October 1991. The Australian Initiative was launched by Australian Foreign Minister Gareth Evans in November 1989 after the failure of Paris I. It was based on the concept advocated by US Congressman Stephen Solarz, to set up a UN Interim Administration that would neutralize the political environment in Cambodia, and prepare for free and fair elections.

PARIS I

The Paris Agreements were co-chaired by France and Indonesia. France had offered to host the conference after Vietnam and the People's Republic of Kampuchea (later the State of Cambodia) had stated that they would not attend a peace conference convened by the UN, which they accused of bias. Indonesia was acceptable to Vietnam and the PRK, as JIM I and II had narrowed the gap between the two sides. Thus because of the major contributions of Indonesia to the Cambodian peace negotiations, France invited Indonesia to be co-chair. The peace negotiations took an increased urgency and also appeared more likely to succeed when Vietnam announced that it would withdraw all its troops from Cambodia by 30 September 1989.

Paris I failed because Vietnam and the four Cambodian parties could not agree on five critical issues. These were: power-sharing in the quadripartite interim authority, a compromise between the resistance's demand for a coalition government and the PRK's insistence on an advisory council subordinate to itself; the auspices under which the International Control Mechanism (a proposal by the Permanent Five) would be set up; the use of

---

[1] Director, Directorate IV, Ministry of Foreign Affairs, Singapore.

the term "genocide" to describe the Khmer Rouge atrocities; the question of Vietnamese settlers in Cambodia; and the modalities of a cease-fire. The most critical issue was that of power-sharing. Hun Sen was then not prepared to concede substantial executive power to Prince Sihanouk, but could only accept him in a figurehead role.

Besides the five critical areas, it appeared that the timing of the Paris I conference was premature, even though many of the parties involved appeared ready for a settlement. A third factor was a hardening of the Vietnamese position in the midst of Paris I, arising from a hardliner victory in the Hanoi Politburo.

Thus, one lesson of Paris I was that even though the Permanent Five were ready to settle a regional conflict, the agreement and support of regional parties such as Vietnam was also necessary. The failure of Paris I was a great disappointment, as it showed that the Cambodian factions were still not ready for power-sharing or national reconciliation.

PARIS II

Why did Paris II succeed? It succeeded because the Permanent Five undertook first to negotiate an agreement amongst themselves, and then to pressure their proteges and allies to accept their agreement. The Permanent Five adopted the Solarz-Evans approach in January 1990 in New York. They amplified it into what they called "an enhanced UN role". They negotiated amongst themselves and over four meetings agreed that UNTAC would supervise five key ministries. They also accepted that the two rival governments could continue to exist but would be supervised to ensure "a neutral political environment" for elections. On 28 August 1990, the Permanent Five issued their plan, entitled the "Framework Document". This became the basis of the Paris II Agreements.

Other important factors underlie the success of Paris II. First, Vietnam and China agreed to improve their bilateral relations, which meant resolving the Cambodian conflict at a meeting in Chengdu in September 1990. Both understood that with the end of the Cold War, times had changed. The key to Paris II was in the hands of Vietnam and China. Once they decided to make peace amongst themselves, a peace settlement in Cambodia became possible. The Soviet Union had also changed its support for the PRK to acceptance of the Permanent Five proposal. Soviet support was a necessary but not sufficient factor in the Paris peace negotiations. ASEAN countries, particularly Thailand, the frontline state, also accepted the need for compromise. Thus, both the Permanent Five and the regional parties were in agreement on how to resolve the Cambodian dilemma of power-sharing: through UNTAC and the Supreme National Council. The four Cambodian factions accepted the framework document in September 1990, and agreed to form the SNC. There were some delays, caused by PRK objections to the requirement of full demobilization of its forces. This was resolved by various compromises which enabled Prince Sihanouk to be named President of the SNC, with the casting vote to break deadlocks.

This paved the way for the Paris II Agreements to be signed on 23 October 1991. At the crux of the Paris II Agreements were two aspects: firstly, a set of commitments aimed at resolving the international aspects, and secondly, another set directed at the internal aspects. The key instruments to achieve these commitments were UNTAC and SNC. The key issue of request and consent to an intrusive and complex UN peace-keeping operation (UNTAC) was resolved by getting the invitation from both sides of the dispute. Another key invention was the creation of the SNC, which circumvented the question of whether the PRK or the CGDK constituted the legal government of Cambodia, since the SNC included representatives of all four factions. The SNC embodied the sovereignty of Cambodia, pending the formation of a legitimate government following free and fair elections. The SNC thus had the authority to delegate to UNTAC the powers needed to implement the Paris Agreements.

THE PRESENT SITUATION

Having surveyed above the process and factors behind the Paris peace negotiations, we now come to the present situation in Cambodia, which can be described as:

(a) a situation of political fluidity, as shown in the attempted coup in July 1994, by persons whose motivations are still unknown (Nate Thayer, writing in *Jane's Defence Weekly* (23 July 1994), opined that "the murky plot appears to have been led by powerful figures connected with the Interior Ministry". He wrote that the attempted coup appeared to be aimed at FUNCINPEC, King Sihanouk and also at Hun Sen);

(b) political alienation of the Khmer Rouge, the Cambodian Parliament having passed a bill outlawing them, and the subsequent declaration of a KR government in July 1994;

(c) attempts by the Royal Cambodian Government to concentrate on economic development and to attract foreign investment (a long-term strategy to defeat the KR);

(d) attempts to contain the KR through a military solution by the Royal Cambodian Government, and with the support of some foreign governments which are prepared to offer arms and training to the Phnom Penh armed forces.

Obviously, the KR issue remains salient, because they were allowed to renege on their commitment to disarm and demobilize and to canton their forces under Phase Two of the Paris Agreements. It was unlikely that UNTAC could have forced the KR to honor their Phase Two commitment, because UNTAC lacked the large forces that would have been needed to confront the KR. Also, UNTAC was not equipped to fight the guerilla war that the KR would have waged. Thus, a key part of the Paris Agreements was not fulfilled. The Paris Agreements remain incomplete as long as the KR issue remains unresolved. The continued political fluidity in Cambodia arises from the failure of national reconciliation between the factions, which was another key component of the Paris Agreements. In other words, the set of commitments which were directed at the internal aspects of the Cambodian problem have not been fulfilled. The role of King Sihanouk still remains critical to the process of national reconciliation.

Despite reports of maladministration and political infighting, the Royal Cambodian Government deserves the support of the international community because it obtained its legitimacy through UNTAC-organized "free and fair" elections. The ICORC commitments should be honored to provide funds to support the Royal Cambodian Government's efforts in the economic development of Cambodia and in attracting foreign investments. The Royal Cambodian Government should be commended on the progress it has made so far, for instance the steps it has taken towards building a legal framework for foreign investments. This is a major achievement, given the past background of the breakdown of society and the economy, and the short time that has passed since UNTAC left in late 1993.

LESSONS FOR CAMBODIA

In retrospect, there appears to be three main lessons for Cambodia from the Paris Agreements. Firstly, Cambodia needs to maximize the opportunities created by the Paris Agreements and UNTAC's success in organizing free and fair elections. World attention is transitory and is now focused on the dramas in Rwanda, Bosnia and Somalia. There are also limits to UN peacekeeping efforts and financial resources. The future of Cambodia is in the hands of the Cambodians themselves. It is very unlikely that the UN can find the political and financial resources for another UNTAC. There will be no second "second chance".

Secondly, the progress toward a government of national unity should continue, in order to consolidate the advances already achieved in building a new Cambodian national identity.

Thirdly, the Royal Cambodian Government must not let the KR win by default – the KR are betting that the Royal Cambodian Government will lose the support of the people because of maladministration and factional infighting, and thereafter the people will accept the KR's return to power. Thus, the Royal Cambodian Government must deliver to the people economic progress and development, which depend on political stability.

LESSONS FOR THE UN

In retrospect, there appear to be three main lessons also for the UN from the Paris peace negotiations. Firstly, there is the power of the local factions to derail the peace settlement – the phenomenon of the tail wagging the dog. Thus, although the Permanent Five could agree among themselves and draw up a detailed peace plan, both the SOC and the KR could sabotage the peace plan by not honoring their commitments. In other conflicts, such as Bosnia and Afghanistan, the same process of political dissonance between external supporters and parties to the conflict can also be observed. The political process of getting all parties to stay on board the peace process and not to renege on their commitments needs to be handled by skilled UN negotiators who can wield effective carrots and sticks.

Secondly, the Paris Agreements' bold and imaginative innovations in setting up UNTAC and the SNC show the UN how such political sophistication can help to resolve complex conflicts such as Cambodia. As described earlier, the UNTAC–SNC solution circumvented difficult problems of sovereignty, request and consent, the competing claims of rival governments and national reconciliation. Perhaps the Cambodian case is unique – there may be no equivalent of Prince Sihanouk to act as a political center, in other conflicts.

Thirdly, with the benefit of hindsight, we can argue that the question of the KR reneging on their commitment to disarm, demobilize and to canton their forces should have been foreseen by the Permanent Five negotiators during their discussions on the framework document. Not being privy to Permanent Five secrets, we can only guess that perhaps an assessment was made of the probabilities of KR disarming, based perhaps on secret assurances to "deliver" the KR. The KR are committed ideologues, and the lesson here is that in future cases of dealing with similar groups, the UN needs to adopt long-term solutions. The KR and similar groups like the Sandinistas can only be expected to outwardly comply with disarming and demobilizing, but will hide their arms and keep alive their military organizations in secret. The UN efforts to neutralize committed and ideological guerrillas should include firmness in insisting on disarming, demobilization and cantonment. This process needs to be supported by two other efforts: firstly, providing economic support to enable former guerrillas to get jobs; secondly, eliminating external support for the guerrillas. Thus, UN peace-making needs to be succeeded by UN peace-building efforts over a short, defined period of (perhaps) three years. In the context of Cambodia, the saliency of the KR threat appears to be a function of the state of Sino-Vietnam relations, which are currently sensitive because of the South China Sea disputes.

CONCLUSION

After all the efforts and billions of dollars invested in UNTAC, the final phase of the Cambodian saga is now in the hands of the Cambodian people. The UN had delivered a second chance for Cambodia, which has achieved its independence and sovereignty. In order to defeat the KR, the Royal Cambodian Government needs to deliver economic growth and political stability to the people. The international community should not abandon the new Cambodia, which is after all the creation of the Paris Agreements, but continue to support and encourage Cambodia.

13. The UN's Role in Bringing about Peace in Cambodia (An Observer's View)

Dr Hrach Gregorian[1]

INTRODUCTION

The Cambodian election of 23–28 May 1993 closed a chapter in one of this century's most tragic episodes. The long-suffering people of Cambodia who had survived foreign invasion, a civil war and the genocidal policies of the Khmer Rouge (KR) were finally given an opportunity to directly voice their political preferences. The UN-administered election was the capstone of a peace process begun in the late 1980s that had resulted in the 1991 Paris Agreements. The Agreements had among other things given the United Nations Transitional Authority in Cambodia (UNTAC) extraordinary power to virtually govern the country for the 15 months preceding the May election.

Until the election was held there was widespread concern about the likely impact of UNTAC, whether the investment of close to US$2 billion (some have placed the figure as high as US$3 billion) and over 20,000 military and civilian personnel from more than 30 countries would yield desired results. However, upon the successful conclusion of the election process, and despite numerous setbacks that have been suffered since, there is general agreement that the UN played an extremely important role in bringing about peace in Cambodia. Michael Maley of the Australian Electoral Commission who served in the Electoral Component of UNTAC has gone as far as to observe that "Cambodia is widely regarded as the brightest jewel currently to be found in the crown of UN peace-keeping". And US Deputy Assistant Secretary of State Peter Tornsen characterized UNTAC as "a stunning peace-keeping success".

HISTORY

The UN was active in promoting peace in Cambodia as far back as 1982. Then Secretary-General Javier Pérez de Cuéllar dispatched an aide, Mr Rafeeuddin Ahmed, to offer the UN's good offices to Mr Hun Sen. For three years, Ahmed labored with the major Cambodian factions and interested regional powers to hammer out the general contours of a comprehensive

---

[1] Director, Education and Training, United States Institute of Peace, Washington DC.

solution to the conflict. It was not until 1987, however, that a major breakthrough came, with the decision by Prince Sihanouk and Hun Sen to begin peace discussions in Paris. Thereafter, the two Jakarta informal meetings were held. These were followed by the Paris Conference of 1989, co-sponsored by French Foreign Minister Roland Dumas and Indonesian Foreign Minister Ali Alatas.

The Paris Conference and subsequent regional talks in Jakarta and Tokyo, in 1990, proved inconclusive. At this time Prince Sihanouk floated an idea developed by Congressman Stephen Solarz of the United States that would have given the UN a virtual trusteeship in Cambodia upon the conclusion of hostilities and the holding of elections. The Australians too were active in developing various options for UN involvement during a period of transition.

The Vietnamese withdrawal from Cambodia and the resumption of hostilities in the country brought all these efforts to a head. The Permanent Five members of the UN Security Council (the P5) now became very active in moving forward a Peace Plan. Their work began with a meeting in Paris in January 1990 and resulted eight months and many consultations later in the development of a "framework" for peace. In September 1990 the four Cambodian factions met in Jakarta whereupon they accepted the P5's Peace Plan and formed a Supreme National Council that was to embody Cambodian sovereignty during a transition period. Months of negotiations then ensued, leading to the signing of the Paris Agreements on 23 October 1991. The Paris peace settlement called for unprecedented UN authority in such spheres as human rights, civil administration, elections, refugee repatriation and economic reconstruction. UNTAC was given the authority to implement these arrangements as well as various security measures, including the monitoring of the cease-fire, the withdrawal of external military forces, and containment and demobilization of the four factions' troops.

SUCCESSES AND FAILURES

In a recent briefing paper prepared for the United States Institute of Peace (USIP), Dr Craig Etcheson of the Cambodian Campaign enumerated the following accomplishments of the peace-makers in Cambodia:

- the Cambodian embroglio was decoupled from larger geopolitical conflicts;
- Chinese military aid to the Khmer Rouge was terminated;
- Cambodia's two decades of international isolation ended;
- refugees left camps in Thailand and returned to their homeland;
- the three-faction rebel coalition challenging the Cambodian Government was reduced to a single faction (KR);
- political pluralism has begun to take root;
- haltingly, there is movement toward greater freedom of the press;
- indigenous human rights groups have been founded and are growing;
- 90% of eligible Cambodians registered to vote and 89% of them voted in free and fair elections, despite Khmer Rouge threats to kill anyone who participated;
- a liberal constitutional monarchy has been promulgated; and

- a coalition government is functioning, albeit in fits and starts.

The observations of an USIP team that was in Cambodia very recently to conduct a conflict resolution training seminar essentially confirm Etcheson's analysis. Cambodia is on the road to recovery, politically, economically and psychologically. However, problems still abound. They grow out of UNTAC's failure to see a cease-fire implemented and then to canton, demobilize, and disarm the military forces of the four factions. They also result from UNTAC's failure to control such areas of administration as defence, public security, finance, information and foreign affairs, as stipulated in the Paris Agreements. These failures have resulted in the creation of a coalition government that is unstable, the continued presence of a heavily armed Khmer Rouge faction alienated from and threatening to central government, foreign economic penetration and exploitation, meager development, and party and clan control of many state institutions. The rule of law has yet to be fully realized in Cambodia. Demobilized soldiers desperate for money have increasingly turned to banditry and armed robbery. Corruption, involving government officials and military leaders, continues unabated. The judicial system needs to be substantially upgraded (most of the judges and magistrates have little or no professional training) and depoliticized. Finally, the press is by no means entirely free from manipulation and intimidation.

CONCLUSION

There is every reason to believe that if the election of May 1993 had not produced a satisfactory outcome, the UN operation in Cambodia would have been written off as a very costly failure. Thus the significance of the work of the thousands of men and women who contributed to the achievement of UNTAC's primary goal of organizing and overseeing fair and free elections cannot be overstated. There is little doubt too that without UNTAC, Cambodia could still be in the throes of a totally enervating internal conflict. What hope there is for the future of Cambodia is directly linked to the positive achievements of the UN peace-keeping and peace-building effort there.

The Cambodia experience also raises a fundamental question about how far UN peace-keeping operations should and can be stretched. Should they be extended to the creation of civil society in so-called failed states? Who will foot the bill for such comprehensive, sustained interventions?

Apart from practical questions relating to the establishment of civil and legal administration, can comprehensive "state-building" by external actors be defended on ethical and legal grounds? These are obviously large, complex questions that will continue to challenge policy-makers. The danger is that they will not – perhaps cannot – be addressed definitively. Thus the general parameters of so-called "second generation" peace-keeping operations of the type carried out in Cambodia will remain vague, sending mixed or, worse, wrong signals as to whether the UN was "successful" in executing various peace-keeping plans.

14. Exercising the Transitional Authority

Takahisa Kawakami[1]

It is a great honour to be given this opportunity to address you. I feel particularly honoured to have been assigned one of the most important topics in this seminar, "Exercising the Transitional Authority", one that goes to the very heart of UNTAC's *raison d'être*. It is most unfortunate that Mr Akashi, Special Representative of the Secretary-General for Cambodia during the UNTAC operation, should have been unable to be here with us. No one could brief us better on the subject than Mr Akashi, the man who had ultimate responsibility for "exercising transitional authority" and who, if I may borrow the wording of the Paris Agreements, was "the source of authority" in UNTAC. I have consulted Mr Akashi, who very kindly gave me extremely useful advice. However, I should make it clear that the responsibility for anything said here is mine alone.

THREE ASPECTS OF THE EXERCISE OF TRANSITIONAL AUTHORITY

I would like to focus on three aspects which characterized the exercise of transitional authority in Cambodia. Firstly, the transitional authority was exercised through, and in close consultation with, the Supreme National Council. Here, the working relationship between UNTAC and the SNC is particularly important. Secondly, the transitional authority was exercised through implementing various distinct mandates given to UNTAC by a Security Council resolution, itself based on the Paris Agreements. The differences in the ways the various mandates were exercised merit careful study. Thirdly, regardless of differences in the various mandates, one can see certain principles that guided the operation as a whole.

THE RELATIONSHIP OF UNTAC AND THE SNC

Transitional authority was exercised through and in close consultation with the SNC. There are two important references in the Paris Agreements regarding UNTAC's relationship with the SNC:

- Firstly, after the SNC is defined, in Article 3 of the Agreements, as "the unique legitimate body and source of authority in which, throughout the transitional period, the sovereignty of Cambodia is enshrined", in Article 6, the SNC delegates to the UN "all powers necessary to ensure the implementation of" the Agreements. This mechanism was necessary in

---

[1] Assistant Director, United Nations Policy Division, Ministry of Foreign Affairs, Tokyo.

order for the UN to exercise authority over the country, which was not a colony but a sovereign state.
- Secondly, the Agreements provide in detail for a decision-making formula, part of which involved the SNC's "advising" UNTAC. That formula was a compromise between the Cambodian parties and the drafters of the Agreements (the Five Permanent Members and others), who had feared that the SNC would find itself at an impasse because of a failure to achieve consensus. There was a pessimistic view that the role of the SNC was simply to delegate its power to UNTAC and it would not matter if the SNC were to be merely a symbolic entity with no real function.

Let me mention some very significant facts. During the period of the UNTAC operation (March 92–September 93, 18 months), 25 SNC meetings were held in Cambodia. There were, in addition, five meetings outside Cambodia (one Special Meeting in Tokyo, and two Special Meetings and one Informal Meeting in Beijing). There were, in addition, a total of eight working sessions of the SNC. If we examine the chronological distribution of these meetings, we find a very significant pattern. The SNC met on 16 occasions between March and September 1992. This coincided with the period when UNTAC was striving to obtain the consent of all the parties, including the PDK, to full implementation of the Agreements. It was during this period that many decisions were arrived at by consensus, which I will speak of in more detail later. Throughout the SNC meetings, the changing positions of the two opposing parties, the SOC and the PDK, had shown a sharp contrast. In the very early stage, the PDK was willing to cooperate with UNTAC. At least, the leaders pledged their cooperation and urged the SRSG to hasten the deployment of UNTAC. On the other hand, the SOC party was not very cooperative in the deployment of UNTAC and did more to obstruct SNC discussion. On working on the communiques of the SNC, I had more difficulties with the SOC than with the PDK during early days of the operation. However, as preparation proceeded for entry into Phase II involving the cantonment, disarmament and demobilization, the PDK began to show increasing intransigence. And as the attitude of the PDK changed, the SOC began to show some flexibility and became more cooperative.

There were positive and negative aspects to the SNC and its meetings. On the positive side, it is a fact that a certain number of decisions and actions were actually achieved in the SNC. Surprisingly, most were by consensus. They included: ratification of the human rights conventions, including the International Convention on Civil and Political Rights and on Economic, Social and Cultural Rights (Convention against Torture, Convention on the Elimination of All Forms of Discrimination Against Women, etc.), announcement of a humanitarian amnesty, declaration of the rights of freedom of speech, assembly and association, approval of rehabilitation programs and creation of the Cambodian Mine Action Center. On the "negative" side (the quotation marks are there to indicate my reservations regarding the negative character), those who attended the SNC meetings observed that the discussion became polemicized, ending without any positive results, or only in bitterness among the members. Some members did no more than insist on their views, which were no more than the "party lines" of their parties. The SNC discussed crucially important issues, such as the question of foreign forces and foreign residents and a neutral political environment, but, owing to divergence in views and uncompromising attitudes, could not arrive at mutually acceptable solutions. It was a central tenet of the policy of the SRSG that "the SNC should be fully utilized".[2] He believed that the SNC should be encouraged to make decisions and take action itself, which would not only help implementation of the Agreements, but also serve the cause of national reconciliation. The SRSG believed it was vitally important to cultivate a spirit of dialogue and give-and-take in Cambodia.

There were, in addition, some issues so intimately connected with Cambodian sovereignty that the decision was one that had to be taken by the SNC itself. The SRSG, for example, presented to the SNC, for the Council's decision, a proposal on the management and preservation of natural resources. After a series of discussions, the SNC decided, firstly, on a moratorium on the export of logs and timber, and, later, on a declaration on the mining and export of minerals and gems. These measures adopted by the SNC were not adopted by consensus, because of the strong opposition by the PDK, but by the decision of the Chairman of the SNC, Prince Sihanouk. On other important issues, too, UNTAC consulted with the SNC and endeavored to obtain its consent, seeking to avoid unilateral decisions to the greatest extent possible. Many will, however, be surprised to learn that on only two occasions did the SRSG exercise the decision-making power stipulated in the Agreements. The first case was that of adoption of the SG's appeal for the rehabilitation programme for Cambodia (the decision was, in fact, made by the DSRSG, the SRSG not being in Cambodia at the time). The other case was the adoption of the electoral law, on which I will touch later.

The creation of the "working session", a formula not provided for in the Agreements, was based on this policy too. In the absence of Prince Sihanouk, the SRSG could have exercised his power, without having an SNC meeting. Instead, the SRSG held working sessions in order to "promote free discussion, even if it often seemed to be just an arena for futile polemical exchanges".[3] This view of the SRSG was also relevant to the "negative aspects". Although discussion was unproductive, if there had not been discussion in the SNC, the situation would have been worse. If there had been no open discussion of such issues as the question of foreign forces and residents, a neutral political environment and various problems related to the electoral process, the dissatisfaction would have culminated in parties' non-participation in the peace process as a whole. In the case of the PDK, if the only channel of communication with it had been written, in all probability its opposition to the electoral process would have been even more violent.

UNTAC facilitated the holding of the SNC meetings. This was, of course, done in close consultation with the SNC. Agenda items were shown to and approved by the parties in advance. Members themselves proposed topics,

---

[2] Yasushi Akashi, UNTAC in Cambodia: "Lessons for UN Peace-keeping", Speech to the Third Charles Rostov Lecture on Asian Affairs, The Paul H. Nitze School of Advanced International Studies, Johns Hopkins University, 14 October 1993 (p.20).

[3] *Op. cit.* n. 2 above (pp.20–21).

many of which were adopted as agenda items. Some technical advisory committees were established in response to requests from the parties. After each meeting, a communique was issued in the name of the SNC. Except on three occasions (twice when the SRSG exercised his decision-making power, once when the parties could not agree on what to call "the SOC administration"), every word in the communique was discussed and adopted by consensus.

I would like to stress the importance of the role of the Secretariat of the SNC, which was created by the SNC itself. Although the Secretariat's mandate was rather limited, it met continuously during the transitional period until the opening of the Constituent Assembly. It not only served the SNC as its permanent secretariat, but also functioned as the executive arm of the SNC, which represented Cambodia during the transitional period. It dealt with communications from diplomatic missions and visa and immigration matters, and such practical matters as overseas scholarships and training programme places. I can say that I saw a very pragmatic working relationship established among all the parties' members, including the PDK representative. I felt there were signs that national reconciliation would prove possible. Unfortunately, they died out when the PDK stopped participating in the work. I am not at all surprised to see members of the Secretariat now occupying very important positions in the present Government. To sum up, in its relationship with the SNC, UNTAC exercised its authority taking great care to ensure that the SNC might play as substantial a role as possible.

IMPLEMENTATION OF THE UNTAC MANDATES

UNTAC's exercise of its authority was defined by the terms of its various mandates. There was a very clear difference between UNTAC's civilian and military mandates. UNTAC had an unprecedented mandate in terms of control and supervision of civil administration and the planning and organization of elections. On the other hand, in the military area, its role continued to be of a traditional PKO type, although it included an especially ambitious objective: disarmament and demobilization of the armed forces of the parties to the conflict. Leaving detailed explanation of these mandates to later briefings by the respective components, let me make a few points which are relevant to my briefing topic.

The control and supervision of civil administration had to be carried out under certain constraints. Firstly, UNTAC worked under quite serious personnel constraints. As the UN Secretariat did not have the specialists needed, they had to be obtained from various governments and specialized agencies, which resulted in serious delays in the actual deployment of specialists. It was only at a late stage in the operation that UNTAC had a satisfactory number of the specialists it needed. Secondly, UNTAC's exercise of the control that was its mandate encountered varying degrees of resistance from the existing administrative entities, which resulted in considerable difficulty for the operation. The degree of resistance differed from entity to entity. In some cases, UNTAC and the entity enjoyed a good working relationship. In some exceptional cases, the existing administrative entity actually became dependent on UNTAC, even requesting financial assistance. However, in many fields, UNTAC had to overcome various forms of non-cooperation and resistance. Thirdly, UNTAC had to consider and try to satisfy the complaints of anti-SOC people. The PDK claimed that UNTAC's control over the SOC administration was weak and inadequate. The PDK even demanded that the SNC take direct control of the administration.

Faced with these constraints, UNTAC opted for a mixed approach. Firstly, UNTAC worked to obtain the maximum possible cooperation from the existing administrative machinery, by means of both explanation and persuasion. UNTAC established a presence in various offices of the central administration and in all the provincial capitals. UNTAC civil officers, through their daily contacts with their Cambodian counterparts, strove to enhance the latter's understanding of and cooperation with UNTAC. Secondly, whenever necessary, UNTAC issued some directives overriding existing laws. Thirdly, UNTAC used more direct means to implement its policy in such fields as immigration and border control, where UNTAC officers were present on the spot, prepared to intervene whenever necessary. Lastly, in exceptional cases, UNTAC even used enforcement measures. The SRSG made clear his intention to remove certain personnel in accordance with paragraph 4b), section B, Annex 1, of the Agreements. A Special Prosecutor's Office was established to "press charges against and detain suspects for flagrant political and human rights crimes".[4] UNTAC actually arrested a number of offenders, among them a PDK soldier and a SOC policeman, under warrants issued by the UNTAC Special Prosecutor.

UNTAC, for the first time in the history of the UN, conducted elections. The term "UNTACist election", used by Prince Sihanouk, was accurate in this sense. However, the expression was misinterpreted by some as suggesting that the elections were held ignoring the wishes of the Cambodian people. In fact, UNTAC's planning and organization of the elections was carried out in close consultation with the Cambodian parties and people. The electoral law was a good example of this. The draft law was presented to the Cambodian side at a 1 April SNC meeting, but was not adopted until four months later, at the meeting held on 5 August. Following a series of consultations in the SNC and other consultative bodies, two significant amendments were introduced, even amending provisions of the Paris Agreements: one dealing with the franchise, the other with voting by overseas Cambodians. This approach was based on the SRSG's conviction that it would be absurd to impose an electoral law on reluctant Cambodians in order to bring democracy to Cambodia. He believed that democracy could not be imposed on Cambodia. It should, however be noted that the law was finally adopted without a 100% consensus on the Cambodian side. At the 5 August 1992 meeting of the SNC, with the PDK expressing its opposition and the BLDP stating it was 85% satisfied, not 100%, the SRSG exercised his powers under section A of the Agreements, believing that further delay in adopting the law might result in serious harm to the electoral process.

---

[4] *Op. cit.* n. 2 above (p.15).

For treatment of UNTAC's military mandate, we had better wait for the briefing by UNTAC's Force Commander, General Sanderson, who is in the best position to give us the view of the UNTAC Military Component. However, with his permission, I will just touch on a few points that are particularly relevant to my briefing topic. When I said that the military role of UNTAC was rather of the traditional PKO type, in which everything depends on the consent of the conflicting parties, I did not mean that the Military Component just sat there, waiting for agreement of the parties to come. Quite the contrary; the Military Component actively engaged in the promotion of agreement. The Mixed Military Working Group (MMWG) met regularly to discuss and agree on all military matters. The MMWG, in this sense, looked quite like the SNC, except that the Force Commander, of course, had no corresponding decision-making power. Although it was not possible to attain the original ambitious goal – disarmament and demobilization of all armed forces – the work of the MMWG contributed to the reconciliation of the armed wings of the parties, except the NADK, the armed wing of the PDK, and, thus, to the unification of three armed forces and the formation of a new national army after the elections.

In the field, if one may put it that way, UNTAC's Military Component remained strictly impartial throughout. Even in a hostile situation, it kept calm. When the NADK detained UNTAC military observers, UNTAC succeeded in freeing them through negotiation. However, that does not mean that UNTAC was at anybody's mercy. When UNTAC was actually attacked, it did not hesitate to exercise its right of self-defence. Mr Akashi said: "When the challenge of the Khmer Rouge became a more serious impediment to the accomplishment of its duties, UNTAC commanders were permitted to offer resistance for legitimate self-defence, and some Khmer Rouge soldiers had to be killed during the process."[5] At the same time, it should be stressed that the use of force was kept strictly within the limits of legitimate self-defence and did not result in any escalation of fighting.

OPERATIONAL PRINCIPLES

The Paris Agreements provided UNTAC with a solid foundation for exercising authority. However, the Agreements did not contain any provision regarding non-compliance or violation of the Agreements, except for Article 28, in which it was stated that "the two co-Chairmen of the Paris Conference on Cambodia, in the event of a violation or threat of violation of this Agreement, will immediately undertake appropriate consultations, with a view to taking appropriate steps to ensure respect for these commitments." To ensure that the Agreements were implemented, it was clearly better to encourage (if not, indeed, to "coax"), rather than to threaten. It was on the basis of this view that UNTAC laid down its operational principles. Officially speaking, there were no fixed principles. I believe that one can, however, point to three basic elements: obtaining the cooperation of the Cambodian

---

[5] *Op. cit.* n. 2 above (p.24).

parties through flexible implementation of the Agreements; promotion of understanding of UNTAC's purpose and practice; making clear UNTAC's determination to carry out its mandate. (With regard to the first principle, seeking the cooperation of the Cambodian parties and flexibility in implementing the Agreements, I have already mentioned various examples in my review of UNTAC's relations with the SNC and UNTAC's mandates.)

Regarding promoting understanding of the objectives and activities of UNTAC, as the Information and Education Department was mainly responsible for this, I will leave all explanation and comment regarding that activity to the briefing by the representative of that component. I will say only that at all levels every effort was made to dispel misconceptions and correct misunderstanding. It is true that there were a few cases in which certain UNTAC personnel actions were called in question. I believe that one may say quite objectively, however, that most criticism of UNTAC was unfounded, the result of misunderstanding, and on occasion bad faith. There were certainly some people, or groups, who deliberately set out to exploit misunderstandings. The PDK attempted to damage UNTAC's image by accusing UNTAC of a "pro-Vietnamese attitude". Such criticism could have destroyed UNTAC's credibility, making it very difficult to carry out its mandates. Fortunately, UNTAC was able to disarm such criticism by developing better understanding among the Cambodian people.

While making every effort to gain the cooperation and understanding of the Cambodian parties and people, UNTAC also made clear its determination to carry out its mandates. UNTAC consistently showed flexibility, but refused to be moved on certain matters. I have already mentioned a few examples: the determination that the elections would be held, arrest of criminals and exercise of its right of self-defence. It might be felt that the latter two cases, in particular, were very exceptional. Nevertheless, UNTAC undoubtedly succeeded in demonstrating to the parties and the people of Cambodia, and to the international community, its firm determination to do its job.

CONCLUSION

A transition is a passage from one stage to another. Cambodia had suffered years and years of the direst distress. Oppression and disorder had dominated the entire country. What UNTAC sought to do was to replace tyranny with democracy and chaos with stability. It is true that the primary objective of the UNTAC operation was to help to establish a democratic government through elections. At the same time, the SRSG was equally concerned about the stability of the government that would come into being following those elections. Even if elections were conducted in a free and fair manner, and a democratic government established as a result, one could not claim success if that government failed to survive after the departure of the UN.

Convinced of this, the SRSG worked actively to help to resolve post-electoral disputes. Immediately after the announcement of the election results, the CPP began to criticize the elections and there were moves to establish "autonomous zones" in the eastern provinces. The leaders of FUNCINPEC, the winning party, were not able to return to Cambodia, because of the possibility of attack by the CPP. The SRSG, having obtained the support of Prince Sihanouk, endeavoured to mediate between the two parties. Contacting Prince Ranariddh, the SRSG persuaded him to issue a message expressing his desire for reconciliation with the CPP. He met Mr Hun Sen and Mr Chea Sim and asked them to refrain from any action that might exacerbate the situation. To go some way towards meeting the CPP's demands, he suggested a mechanism to study the question of alleged irregularities. The SRSG also requested Prince Sihanouk for his cooperation to improve the situation. The Prince immediately agreed, issuing a message over the radio, with the desired result. A few days later, the parties agreed on a formula in which the two major parties were treated equally and the third party was also given favourable treatment. There has been some criticism of this – in particular, over the formation of the Joint Interim Administration, in terms of "orthodox democracy". However, I believed then, and still believe, that it was a necessary compromise between the requirements of democracy and the need for national stability.

Rather than seeking to draw "conclusions", I would like to end my presentation by quoting Mr Akashi. While warning that "every conflict is unique and the methods that were successfully employed by UNTAC in Cambodia cannot necessarily be automatically applied to other areas or situations,"[6] he said that UNTAC served very important functions, as a bridge between the factions, as a catalyst for the attainment of democracy, and as a transitional "cushion" leading to the establishment of a new government of national unity.[7] Also, Mr Akashi, said, "we [UNTAC] provided an indispensable international guarantee for the kind of independence which Cambodia needed and wanted".[8] He said, in effect, that UNTAC showed a new direction, one that would mean that the UN would be stronger in the future – that UNTAC would, in fact, be an important model for future operations.

---

[6] *Op. cit.* n. 2 above (p.17).
[7] Yasushi Akashi (1993) *An Agenda for Hope: the UN in a New Era*, The Simul Press (p.34).
[8] *Ibid.*

15. Lessons from Exercising the Transitional Authority

Tan Lian Choo[1]

Mr Takahisa Kawakami has described at great length how UNTAC exercised its authority in Cambodia after Yasushi Akashi arrived in Phnom Penh on 15 March 1992 as the Special Representative of the UN Secretary-General. To focus my discussion, I have chosen to dwell on two points he touched on, namely, decision-making within the Supreme National Council (SNC) and direct control over the administration.

THE SNC WAS A POWERLESS ARRANGEMENT

This was due, in part, to the inherent weakness of the arrangement, which had been crafted at the Paris Agreements to break a stalemate. In the accords, the SNC was conceived merely as a repository of Cambodian sovereignty while the UN exercised transitional authority.

How it would function later, in reality, was left to our imagination. Certainly, each rival Khmer faction planned to interpret that, and act accordingly with its own interests. Crucial in what was left unsaid was the fact that its effectiveness would depend almost entirely on Prince Norodom Sihanouk – on his being able to act as a dependable final arbiter in any "dispute" between UNTAC and any one of the Khmer parties that was a signatory to the Paris Agreements. Now, how it could possibly blur the line between being solely a repository of sovereignty and act closely with UNTAC in exercising executive authority was largely left to Sihanouk, on whom rested the moral authority. But, as we all know, this was easier conceived and said than done.

Sihanouk's continued absence from Phnom Penh for most of 1992 rendered the SNC useless as an instrument of political balance. But his attacks on UNTAC, while he was in Beijing, for not wresting control from the Phnom Penh authorities were, in my view, legitimate. He had initially counted on the State of Cambodia (SOC) faction to yield power to him. Without it, he could not manoeuvre within the SNC. SOC did not yield. UNTAC stood aside while this opportunity for Sihanouk to regain true leadership slipped away from him. And the moment the Khmer Rouge saw this, they decided they wanted out of the Paris Agreements. That was when they decided they would not give up their arms.

---

[1] Senior Correspondent, *The Straits Times*, Singapore.

ON IMPLEMENTATION OF THE UNTAC MANDATES

The weakest aspect was that of exercising authority over the administration. The civil and defence administrations were not effectively neutralized by UNTAC's presence. Again, this ineffectiveness was crucial. It hardened the Khmer Rouge's decisions. What UNTAC needed were a lot more administrators to populate various branches of the local administration. But again, this was definitely easier said than done. Recruitment of such personnel was not easy.

So, for future reference, there should perhaps be new contracts worked out for UN administrative personnel – contracts that include a clause that says that you must be willing or ready to serve short-term stints at such peace-keeping operations abroad! The one overwhelming impression I had from UNTAC's operation was that it needed much more support staff and logistics for its own operation, compared to what would have been needed to impose a UN presence within the local administration.

Military

Coordination of such multi-national forces can only be difficult, albeit challenging. But the inability to produce a consistency of standards of professionalism and behavior among UNTAC's blue berets was jarring. How they related to the local population was also crucial.

Summing up

UNTAC was slow to take off. It was badly immobilized and was at risk of being a vast flop. There was a positive reaction following that from within. I could sense the "We've got to do everything now to save it" sort of commitment, and all UNTAC's energy was focused then on holding the election despite the failed disarmament phase. Now, if only there had been this kind of UNTAC energy from the start, we might have seen a happier outcome altogether.

LESSONS FROM UNTAC FOR FUTURE PEACE-KEEPING OPERATIONS

While the refugee issue should be totally depoliticized (on this count, UNTAC was successful), the leadership within a UN transitional authority (i.e. directors of components) should be highly politicized. They must even be "political animals", able to read the ground situation, and respond accordingly by applying the spirit of the mandate. They must grasp the local political culture in order to be effective while handling the local players. In the case of UNTAC, many of its early setbacks came because it was unable to appreciate Khmer intransigence, unable to read Sihanouk (politically or otherwise), unable to discount the regime in Phnom Penh, and unable to flex its muscle within the local administration. This is due, in large measure, to the lack of background of key UN personnel in dealing with Cambodians. Future peace-keeping operations and arrangements would do well if this aspect of early familiarization is taken into consideration.

Internal debate within UNTAC on the interpretation of its mandate

There was some soul-searching during difficult moments on whether UNTAC could go beyond peace-keeping to peace-enforcement. Hence much of its effectiveness depended on individual personalities, their own value systems and their own notions of how to get the job done. To ensure a certain consistency, some head-hunting might be necessary. UNITAR could step in here, giving pointers on how to find the right person for the job. Perhaps UNITAR can, after some careful study, draw up a suitable profile for each individual post, making it easier to source for such positions worldwide. There must be some kind of criteria to select or approach the right candidates by casting the net widely.

Failure of the crucial disarmament phase

Much has been made of the flexibility of UNTAC to respond to continued cease-fire violations, kidnaps, etc. (at one point, UNTAC even had to agree to return arms to the factions that complained that they needed them). Maybe future UN operations may want to consider a built-in, damage-control clause: let the international community decide at which crucial point in the peace-keeping process the UN should cut loose if all the involved warring parties do not respond by making progress according to the peace-keeping timetable. This may be expensive (and harsh), but it could be more effective in the long run. It would be the largest "stick" in a carrot-and-stick approach taken by a transitional authority.

Handling the international press

Just as rebuilding peace is difficult, reporting on peace-keeping, peace-enforcement or peace-building is also difficult for reporters. Of course journalists often represent the national press of their own countries, and will want some narrow focus pertaining to the home audience or readership. Each medium also has its specific needs and demands. The international press covering any peace-keeping operation is likely to make an impact, whether one likes it or not. It is important to understand that the press wants hard news information. But how to disseminate information about a complex situation or operation? If UN personnel do not themselves understand the complexity of the situation at hand, then it would be difficult, if not impossible, to accurately disseminate information about it.

The international press that covered UNTAC included:

- "War veterans" – those who had covered the war in Cambodia, from the time of the American bombings to the Khmer Rouge atrocities. Because of the duration of the Cambodian story, such veteran journalists returning to cover the peace-keeping operation had a long historical reference. They also often had definite ideas on what the political development of the country should be. (If the situation in Bosnia becomes a protracted

one, then you will also eventually have such media "veterans" covering it.)
- Journalists who genuinely had an open mind and wanted to get a more complete picture of the situation.
- Those who couldn't cope with the complexity — all they needed were nuggets of information to make a daily dose of news.

There's no easy way to handle such a mixed group. But more thought needs to be given to this, since UN personnel will be constantly approached by the media.

UNITAR will have to train peace-keepers to deal with the press in a more complex way. It can minimize the public relations exercise, reduce the emphasis on showing journalists "how the UN operation works" and instead highlight the need to explain the dynamics of a complex situation. There's no doubt that the international press will play an increasing role in future peace-keeping operations, but UN personnel should move away from the love-hate relationship that so often characterizes their dealings with the press.

16. The ASEAN Role – A Historical Perspective

Ambassador Tan Zainal A. Sulong[1]

HISTORICAL PERSPECTIVE

- Regionalism or regional cooperation form the corner-stone of foreign policy of the ASEAN member states, to ensure peace and security for the ASEAN region and for Southeast Asia.
- The concept of national and regional resilience – *zopfan* – forms part of the framework for this peace and security.
- ASEAN and regional cooperation are founded upon the lofty principles of the UN Charter, such as non-aggression, respect for sovereignty and integrity of nations.
- The Treaty of Amity and Concord encompasses all these principles and is a framework to guarantee peace and stability, cooperation and progress for the region of Southeast Asia.
- The invasion of Cambodia by Vietnam was seen by ASEAN as a direct violation of the principles and programme for peace and security in the region.
- ASEAN therefore had to respond and to act quickly and decisively and with considerable vehemence.
- ASEAN's first diplomatic initiative was to establish the Government in Exile of Kampuchea, the CGDK. The inclusion of Khmer Rouge in this coalition was a legal necessity to ensure the recognition and legitimacy of the exiled Government.
- ASEAN acted in concert and with considerable effectiveness in championing the cause of the CGDK at the United Nations, international fora and the capitals of the world. Over the years ASEAN had successfully developed its skill and expertise as a lobby group. It was recognized as the most effective group at the United Nations. ASEAN pursued the cause of Cambodia with such fervor and seriousness that it was soon labelled as a "one-issue" organization, concerned only with Cambodia. In this campaign, the Cambodian factions were always presented to the world fora as a group.
- Meanwhile ASEAN countries also offered various aid to refugees, training facilities, arms and ammunitions to sustain resistance on the ground.
- Clearly the major issue confronting ASEAN in mounting initiatives to seek a viable solution to the Cambodian question was and still is simply what to do with the Khmer Rouge. The Khmer Rouge was seen as the best-armed and most effective forces against the Vietnamese invasion.

---

[1] Chairman, Malaysian Industrial Development Authority, Kuala Lumpur.

Indeed, efforts to strengthen and reinforce the two other factions were regarded as not so successful.
- It was obvious that two strategic options were open to ASEAN. Option one was to ensure trends and development that would lead to the control and management of the Khmer Rouge forces so that eventually such Khmer Rouge elements would be absorbed into the mainstream and body politic of Cambodia so that it would achieve permanent peace and security; option two was to ensure trends and developments that would lend legitimacy to the Government in Phnom Penh and that would at the same time isolate the Khmer Rouge faction and eventually eliminate it and its threat within the body politic of the mainstream of Cambodian society.
- The ASEAN countries, and I believe particularly Malaysia, opted for strategic option one for two main reasons: (a) within the context of the Cold War ideological conflict, an isolated Khmer Rouge faction could establish ties with the Thai Communist Party and the Malaysian Communist Party (MCP) and could pose a threat to the entire region, and (b) the Khmer Rouge as a dissident force or outlawed group would have the capacity to undermine the stability of Cambodia for the next two decades, as Malaysia's experience with the MCP had shown. (I am not sure, however, whether the Malaysian Government still holds this view.)

COMMENT ON UNTAC

It is within this context that we tend to view the success or otherwise of UNTAC operations. I endorse the general stand that UNTAC was unique in its varied activities. UNTAC was given a comprehensive mandate by the Paris Agreements. Nevertheless, in the context of the strategic objective of option one, we have to conclude that, despite the tactics of the Party of Democratic Kampuchea in the electoral process, or in the post-election government, UNTAC was not able to bring the Khmer Rouge into the peace process. This was contrary therefore to the provisions of the Paris Agreements. The pros and cons of this aspect of the question could of course be debated at length. The fact of the matter remains that the Khmer Rouge faction has not been brought into the peace-keeping process, with, I am convinced, dire implications and consequences. In addition, UNTAC was not able to disarm the Khmer Rouge, again as was required by the Paris Agreements. This aspect of the question could also be debated at length. However, the fact of the matter remains that the Khmer Rouge was able to keep out of the peace process with arms intact and remains a threat, the consequences of which are yet to be seen. I believe it is wrong to underestimate the potential or the threat of the Khmer Rouge by discounting them in terms of percentages.

The question we ask is should UNTAC not have persevered, or should ASEAN not have exerted influence for UNTAC to persist and persevere? This is a long-term crucial and strategic issue and is clearly provided for in the multi-lateral peace agreement. Some observers believe that it was wrong of UNTAC to proceed with the elections even after the Khmer Rouge had withdrawn from the process. Again, the Paris Agreements required the elections to be an-all party process.

It is said that to restore and legitimize the Government in Phnom Penh through a process of elections is the *raison d'être* of the UN operations. I contend that this is insufficient. As Mr Rafeeuddin has said, the objective of the UN exercise is to bring about national reconciliation and to disarm the Khmer Rouge forces so that they could eventually be absorbed into the Cambodian national armed forces. To bring permanent peace and stability to Cambodia through political reconciliation and through democratic process is the ultimate objective. The Khmer Rouge was and is the main problem in Cambodia. The fact that it remains a thorn on the side of everyone should be a matter of concern not only for the Cambodian people but for all of us in ASEAN as well. We cannot afford to be suffering from what is often described as "Cambodia fatigue", especially now, when we are promoting the Group of Southeast Asia Ten or ASEAN Ten in the near future. Following this line of argument, it is possible to conclude that UNTAC had not achieved any diplomatic breakthrough on Cambodia's most pressing problem, i.e. the Khmer Rouge forces; UNTAC had also not dealt militarily with the issue and likewise UNTAC had not achieved or offered any diplomatic alternative.

I would conclude that much that had occurred throughout the peace process depended on political will: a perception among some analysts, for example, was that the entire UNTAC project was overwhelmingly "influenced by Western countries, and the consequences of which accorded largely with the wishes of these countries". It has also been said that what transpired was quite predictable. There is even the contention that some of these countries want to see Cambodia or Indochina in perpetual disarray. I am convinced that this cannot be an objective of ASEAN, particularly if ASEAN is to realize its hope of incorporating the countries of Indochina as part of a peaceful, prosperous and integrated region of Southeast Asia. It has been contended that economic developments will bring about peace and stability in Cambodia. I disagree. On the contrary, peace and security and political stability are the prerequisite for economic development and progress. In the context of the UNTAC operation, it is regrettable that overall ASEAN did not assert itself more, throughout the entire peace process. In this sense, whatever problems and weaknesses UNTAC might have could also be attributed to ASEAN's passivity. The future remains uncertain for Cambodia. It was a missed opportunity. UNTAC is now ended. We can no longer expect another UNTAC.

17. The Cambodian Perspective

HRH Prince Sisowath Sirirath[1]

It is an honor for me to be invited by UNITAR and IPS (United Nations Institute for Training and Research, and Institute of Policy Studies of Singapore) to this important international conference entitled "UNTAC: Debriefing and Lessons". May I also be permitted to express my sincere thanks to my good friends, Pr Tommy Koh and Mr Marcel A. Boisard, for this kind invitation. I am also very happy to see many of our friends here today whom I had not met since the early days of the Paris Conference on Cambodia in 1991. I wish to express my warm welcome to you all and I am sure as always that I will once again benefit from our discussions here during these next three days.

The Cambodian problem is unique in its own way. Each peace-keeping operation differs from one country to another. UNTAC was able to operate smoothly without too much difficulty due mainly to the support rendered to it by the Cambodian people on the one hand and the international community on the other. After 21 years of bloody conflict, the Cambodians thought it was time to pack up and settle for a peaceful solution. This desire for peace, however, could not immediately be realized. At first each faction took a stubborn stance and was trying to out-maneuver the other for a better deal. But, the Cold War and the East–West conflict were things of the past. With the collapse of the defunct Soviet Union, the time was ripe. Cambodia, as many world leaders saw, should have its peace. Then, finally came the success of the PICC and the decision of the Security Council to send UNTAC to Cambodia. It was the most costly operation that the UN had undertaken in all of its history of peace-keeping operations. And it was worth every penny of it. Cambodia received an independent, democratic government and development and rehabilitation funds from the international community.

Cambodia as a former protectorate of France is used to foreigners and in particular Europeans. The Cambodian people adapted well to the situation during the presence of UN peace-keeping forces. After the long ordeal of suffering the people welcomed the international peace-keepers with open arms and prayers for the success of their duty in the country. They look to the peace-keepers as their saviors and protectors from harm. No doubt, UNTAC brought about a success story in Cambodia last year. This phase has been praised by many world leaders alike. Many thought that the suffering of the Cambodian people ended there, and that now is the time for national reconciliation, development and rehabilitation. But it was only a part of the success story.

One of the four Cambodian factions, namely the DK Party (Khmer Rouge)

---

[1] Ambassador, Permanent Representative of the Kingdom of Cambodia to the United Nations, New York.

which was a co-signatory of the Paris Peace Agreements, did not agree to the call for the 70% demobilization of their troops. And things went a little bit further when the DK Party refused to allow the UN peace-keeping forces to enter their zones of control and denied the people there their right to vote. The DK finally refused to participate in the UN-organized and supervised election because they knew full well beforehand what the outcome of the vote would be. Under the chairmanship of the honorable Yasushi Akashi, UNTAC has not failed in its mission, in the eyes of many Cambodians. But it was the Cambodians themselves — namely the party which refused to cooperate with UNTAC — that failed and disappointed the international community. I still can recall the endless smile, the hope and the enthusiasm of the Cambodian people when the first UN peace-keeping operation, the (UNAMIC) UN Advance Mission in Cambodia, arrived in Cambodia in mid-November 1991. It was thought that the end of 21 years of bloody conflict had finally arrived.

Mr Ataul Karim and Mr Akashi were commended by Cambodian people from all walks of life and their leadership was continuously praised by His Majesty, King Norodom Sihanouk Varman, as well as from leaders of the various Cambodian parties that contested the elections. UNTAC was right not to enter into bloody confrontation with the KR. The UNTAC Commanding General, John Sanderson, won great admiration from Cambodia's peace-loving people in keeping his men safe and at the same time protecting the innocent Cambodian people from possible danger. The KR was challenging UNTAC in every aspect of the way and frustrating many people who were seeking a peaceful solution of the conflict. They had often arrested and detained quite a number of UNTAC military and civilian personnel and caused great alarm each time within the international community. When they released these people, the KR expressed strong disappointment at UNTAC's handling of the Cambodian situation, yet a number of UNTAC staff had lost their lives needlessly in ambushes and attacks from irresponsible armed elements. The KR had always denied involvement. However, the Cambodian authorities had always condemned in the strongest terms the irresponsible acts that caused the loss of life of UNTAC personnel. After learning of these acts, the Cambodian people expressed a great sorrow to the international community. Their names and courageous services are enshrined, deep in the heart of the Cambodian people.

No Cambodian in his or her right mind supported the KR's action in detaining UN personnel. It was just a threat. What the KR wanted was for UNTAC to check the so-called Vietnamese illegal immigrants and their secret army presence in Cambodia. Without taking their complaints into consideration, the KR refused all other cooperation with UNTAC. It caught everybody by surprise. When the KR first agreed to enter the peace process, many Cambodians doubted their real intention. Could their words be matched by their deeds? It was too good to be true that the KR had at last accepted joining the national reconciliation and the rebuilding of the new Cambodian society and nation under the very high leadership of His Majesty King Sihanouk, the revered father of the Cambodian nation.

Choosing or asking member countries to participate in the peace-keeping forces is a very important role for the UN, because that alone could determine the outcome of the success and failure of the international community. Watching a country suffer and having compassion for that particular unfortunate country and its people is not enough. Member countries ought to brief their soldiers and civilians on their role before sending them to participate in the peace-keeping operation. Information on the geographic location of the troubled country is not enough; a short history on its cultural and religious beliefs should also be given to the peace-keepers before they embark for their assigned destination.

Cambodia has a long proud history as a civilization which once dominated most of present Southeast Asia. Nations in the region which took part in the peace-keeping operation in Cambodia were warmly welcomed and embraced by the Cambodian people. This derives mainly from the historical good relations between the peoples of the regions and their leaders. One should know about the cultural heritage of the Cambodian people in order to fit in well with their everyday life.

As a war-torn country, Cambodia was left neglected for more than two decades and its people were burdened with tremendous suffering and hardships. Yet the Cambodian people are very proud of their heritage. Cambodians as a whole are very satisfied and grateful to the international peace-keepers, with the exception of a few isolated cases in which poor peasants in some remote areas encountered mistreatment by some young inexperienced East European soldiers. Their behavior was sometimes troublesome and most disappointing to Cambodians and UNTAC officials alike.

Before we can determine the success or failure of UNTAC, we must first look at the role it was assigned to play. The Paris conference on Cambodia wanted to see a 70% reduction of troops of the four Cambodian factions. This was never realized. It should not be considered as one of the failures of UNTAC either. What should UNTAC have done then remains a question that still puzzles many Cambodian scholars: strike against the faction that refused to cooperate for not abiding by the peace accord, or leave it alone and hope that this particular faction would not disturb the on-going peace process and would soon perhaps join in the national reconciliation once UNTAC departed from Cambodia? It was a difficult decision for Mr Akashi to make; his views were not accepted by his former deputy commander who packed up his bag and left the country. Can we call this a failure, or a test of will to challenge the credibility of UNTAC to operate by the KR?

But, on the other hand, the Cambodian people themselves did not fully understand the role of UNTAC. Many out of ignorance perhaps or out of contact with the rest of the world for many years thought that UNTAC would punish those who refused to disarm and cooperate with them. The KR was just buying more time and was looking for a way to disrupt UNTAC's ability to perform. It was definitely a frustrating duty for the peace-keepers as a whole. Their job was not easy as far as the KR was concerned.

Most Cambodians and foreign observers alike believed that UNTAC would have a greater success story if the KR had joined in the national reconciliation and abided by the Paris Conference. Personally, I always wonder why the KR, so indomitable in war, had been unable to benefit from their remarkable victories when they were rulers of the country in the mid-1970s. Why do they continue in a mess now, why have they let themselves become bogged down in killing their own innocent people, and why have they become so isolated and ostracized in this region and in the rest of the world? Are they so addicted to violence and struggle that they are simply incapable of adjusting to peace? Are they, after all, compulsively self-destructive or just purely hungry for power, even at the cost of destroying their own country?

As an Asian, Mr Akashi understood full well the Cambodian problem. He has the charisma to get along well with the leaders of the Cambodian factions. But, despite all his tireless efforts and sincere offers, he constantly ran into a brick wall of being ignored or rejected by the KR. A little more than a year has passed since the world welcomed and supported the democratic elections in Cambodia. But now the world is once again witnessing a humanitarian disaster in my country. I am sure that the international community is appalled and dismayed by the recent plight of thousands of Cambodians displaced internally, who face a situation of hunger, disease and death, when small-scale war erupted last month and has continued until now along the Khmer–Thai border. Sadly, it looks as though the Cambodian dilemma does not end here. As we speak today, Cambodia remains very much a problem for the UN, and particularly the ASEAN states. During the past two decades ASEAN has remained an uncompromising and steadfast ally of the Cambodian people, and helped broker the Peace Agreements of 1991. But the problems of Cambodia cannot be solved overnight. Peace must bring about the real social and economic reconstruction of the country. We hope that the UN, ASEAN and the international community will work hand in hand with the Cambodian people to consolidate the peace dividend.

18. How the Paris Agreements Affected UNTAC Operations

Ambassador Nana S. Sutresna[1]

I should like to congratulate the Institute of Policy Studies (IPS) and the United Nations Institute for Training and Research (UNITAR) for organizing this conference and to thank them kindly for inviting me to participate.

I am aware that, as stated in the Note to Resource Persons, the main focus of the conference is on the operation of the UNTAC (United Nations Transitional Authority in Cambodia). I believe, however that some reflections at this point about how the UNTAC was created would be both relevant and useful as it could shed light on why the UNTAC operated in the way that it did. On a personal note, it is in this earlier respect that I could make my contribution as I had the privilege of being involved in the activities which led to the establishment of the UNTAC, but not in its operation.

The signing of the Agreements on Cambodia in Paris on 23 October 1991 was hailed as a historic milestone; it prefigured the end to hostilities and bloodshed that had plagued the country for decades, and promised to usher in an era of peace, stability and cooperation in the Southeast Asian region and beyond. It represented the culmination of long and arduous efforts initiated by regional countries, ASEAN members primarily, to help achieve a comprehensive political settlement of an exceedingly complex and intractable problem.

The Agreements which gave birth to the UNTAC and also to the SNC (the Supreme National Council of Cambodia) were unique in many respects. For instance, while a large part of the Cambodian (then called Kampuchean) problem was caused by the invasion and occupation of a sovereign and independent country by an outside power – or at least this was seen to be so in the eyes of many other nations – it is noteworthy that the agreements expressed no condemnation of the perceived invading power. Their references to the issue of withdrawal and non-return of foreign forces and subsequent verification were carefully worded so that they did not single out a particular foreign force but were applicable to any or all foreign forces. In this regard, Vietnam indicated as early as April 1991 that its forces would be withdrawn from Cambodia by September of the same year. This may indeed have been the case, but the withdrawal was carried out without international verification.

Another unique feature of the Agreements is that instead of lamenting the past, they set their sight firmly on the future. In their wisdom, those who crafted the Agreements set aside the question of who was to blame for the tragedy. Instead, they concentrated on how to prevent further deterioration

---

[1] Ambassador-at-Large, Head Executive Assistant to the Chairman of the Non-Aligned Movement, Jakarta.

of the situation and promptly addressed the urgent tasks of restoring peace and order, ensuring the exercise of the right to self-determination through free and fair elections, guaranteeing respect for and observance of human rights and fundamental freedoms, and contributing to the rehabilitation and reconstruction of Cambodia.

This comprehensive and non-accusatory approach, which would prove to be very successful, can be traced back to a much earlier stage. At the very beginning of the conflict, Indonesia and the other ASEAN countries based their stand not on animosity toward any state or group of states, but on internationally recognized principles. Thus they held that on the basis of the principle of equality of states, self-determination of peoples and peaceful co-existence, all enshrined in the UN Charter and held sacred by the Non-Aligned Movement, no foreign intervention in the internal affairs of another state for any reason or under any pretext can be justified or condoned. Moreover, Indonesia was firmly convinced that priority attention should be directed towards ensuring peace and harmony in our region, which had a long history of internecine conflicts. Indonesia therefore endeavored to explore all possible avenues which could realistically and effectively lead to a viable solution of the Cambodian conflict and also contribute to strengthening the framework for peace and stability in Southeast Asia.

As early as on 22 August 1985, Indonesia and Vietnam agreed to initiate, through the existing Indonesia–Vietnam Working Group at senior officials level, a more detailed and systematic discussion on the Kampuchean problem with a view to narrowing the differences then prevailing among the parties involved and the countries concerned. This was pursued in parallel with the ASEAN's unsuccessful efforts to pressure Vietnam through sponsorship of a series of resolutions in the United Nations. Thus with ASEAN's continuous support, Indonesia had from the very outset sought Vietnam's participation in the efforts to find a way out of the Kampuchean problem as if Vietnam was not a directly involved party. This approach made it possible for Indonesia and Vietnam to arrive at the Ho Chi Minh City Understanding of 1987, the thrust of which constituted the precursor of the JIM (Jakarta Informal Meeting) processes.

Section II, Article 2 of the Agreement on a Comprehensive Political Settlement of the Cambodia Conflict, including Annex 1 on UNTAC's mandate and the UN Security Council resolution no. 718 (28 February 1992) regarding its establishment, were the authoritative sources from which the UNTAC derived its powers and responsibilities. The UNTAC in consultation with the SNC – in which the sovereignty, independence and unity of Cambodia were to be enshrined throughout the transition period – was responsible for the implementation of the Agreement, including the organization and conduct of free and fair elections. This Agreement was approved and duly signed by all 12 representatives of the four Cambodian parties, including the Khmer Rouge, to the SNC and witnessed by all participating states in the Paris Conference.

The question has been raised why the Khmer Rouge, one of the main opposition parties, with a rather formidable fighting force, was subsequently excluded from the Cambodian Government which emerged from the peace process, and eventually outlawed. It should be recalled, in this context, that the Khmer Rouge was involved in the negotiation process from the very beginning and Mr Yasushi Akashi, the Special Representative on Cambodia, said during a briefing on the UNTAC on 20 February 1992 that "all parties seemed willing to shift from a military to a democratic background".

In reply, some would say that the Khmer Rouge leaders brought this upon themselves, as they put insurmountable obstacles to the cantonment and regrouping of forces as envisaged by the Agreement and ultimately refused to participate in the UN-supervised general elections. As a result, the provisions on the cantonment and regrouping of forces, which constituted an important military measure in the implementation of the Agreement, were practically put aside because, in the face of the Khmer Rouge's obstructionism, the other parties also became reluctant to comply with the provisions. Considering that, by signing the Paris Agreements, the Khmer Rouge, like all the other Cambodian parties, had already acceded to its political future being decided through the exercise of the right of self-determination by the Cambodian people in free and fair elections, the UN Secretary-General arrived at a decision to go ahead with the elections in May 1993 as originally scheduled, in spite of the refusal of the Khmer Rouge to participate. The decision, reflecting a new emphasis in implementation of the Paris Agreements on their "fundamental objectives", was subsequently endorsed by the UN Security Council and was successfully carried out.

It could be argued that more time should have been given to the consultation process within the SNC as well as outside it, through the intervention of the two co-chairmen of the Paris Conference upon the request of the UN Secretary-General. This would have allowed the Khmer Rouge to be part of the entire peace process. We were made to understand that the demands put forward by the Khmer Rouge which the UNTAC apparently found to be out of reach were the following:

- that the SNC would take over the administration of the state from the Hun Sen Government;
- that a verification operation would be held which would lead to the inclusion of Vietnamese settlers among those foreign forces that had to leave the country; and
- that a neutral political environment would be created to make possible the conduct of free and fair elections.

I should appreciate it if the distinguished participants of this conference who had direct involvement in the field could shed some light on how these issues were subsequently dealt with.

It may be worthwhile and it may give further comprehensiveness and depth to our discussions if this conference could put to rest a supposition which is held in some circles to this effect: that the present situation is the result of a deliberate and rather meticulous scheme of those who from the very beginning had opposed the inclusion of the Khmer Rouge in the peace process and eventually in the new Cambodian Government following general elections. It has been asserted that the Western countries, especially after the center of peace initiatives on Cambodia shifted from Jakarta to Paris, prompted by the record of atrocities and violations of human rights perpetrated by the Khmer Rouge, systematically prepared the ground for an eventual exclusion of the Khmer Rouge from the entire peace process. It may be recalled that even during the signing ceremony, some statements were already being made which had the effect of stirring distrust of the Khmer Rouge. If there are facts available that can put this supposition to rest, then they should be brought out to shed light on and ensure a proper appreciation of the work of the UNTAC.

Another important factor which had a considerable impact on the situation were the international developments which coincided with the concluding stages of the peace process: this development led to a widespread perception that the value system of the West had emerged victorious in the ideological conflict of the Cold War, thus giving impetus to the drive for human rights promotion and democratization. This perception was reinforced by the fact that the principal actors in charge of the implementation in the field were those who were regarded as inclined to be receptive to concepts based on the value system of the West.

Perhaps the present conference could be a good occasion to make a real evaluation of what Mr Yasushi Akashi termed "the largest United Nations operation ever mounted". As we all know, the program included seven different components: Military (including a contingent of 15,900 troops), Human Rights, Civil Administration, Electoral, Police (about 3,600 police monitors), Repatriation and Rehabilitation. The total cost of implementing all these elements has been estimated at roughly US$2 billion. In the light of both the peace process and stipulations of the Agreements, was this whole exercise of the UNTAC operation politically worthwhile? The question is worth raising and answering. To many outsiders, it appears that the achievement of peace and security in Cambodia, which would usher in a new era of peace and stability and cooperation in Southeast Asia, is still elusive.

19. A Political Analysis of the Cambodian Situation

Ambassador Ataul Karim[1]

UNTAC was mandated to implement the Agreements on a Comprehensive Political Settlement of the Cambodian Conflict. This can be considered to have been a successful peace-keeping operation. UNTAC was able to organize and conduct successfully a free and fair election leading to the establishment of a democratically elected and legitimate government in Cambodia. However, a residual problem has remained.

This paper will try to evaluate the situation in Cambodia, political and otherwise, at the beginning of the peace process and prior to the establishment of UNTAC. It will try to analyze the political will, the sensitivities and the expectations of the four Cambodian parties. The residual problem remained primarily because of the intransigence of the Democratic Kampuchea Party. An attempt will be made to explore whether there was any possibility of surmounting this difficulty.

On the practical plane, the paper will try to examine whether the planning and preparatory stages were based on realistic considerations leading to establishing a rational and pragmatic physical structure to implement all aspects of the Agreements, the nature of the actual structure and the manner in which it was set up. It will also examine whether the existing United Nations system was capable of performing the task and whether any deficiency in this respect materially affected implementation of the Agreements.

The United Nations' intervention in Cambodia amounted to its most comprehensive and multi-dimensional peace-keeping operation ever, to resolve an essentially domestic unravelling of the economic, political and social systems following a long period of upheaval resulting from foreign intervention and internal conflict. At the end of the day, there was a successful, free and fair election with massive participation of the electorate leading to the establishment of a democratically elected legitimate government in Cambodia. UNTAC was a successful peace-keeping operation. But a residual problem remained. It is this context that I would like to touch upon some of the basic issues and perhaps raise some questions.

Political will, a spirit of cooperation and mutual accommodation on the part of the signatories to an agreement have been some of the essential prerequisites for the successful implementation of the Agreements. What was it like at the beginning of the peace process? Memories were still fresh and bitterness still perceptible when the United Nations Advance Mission in Cambodia was established on 9 November 1991.

Phnom Penh, where the presence of the existing administrative structure was predominant, was a cheerless city bearing the scars of a long conflict.

---

[1] Director of Political Affairs Division, United Nations Operation in Somalia II, Mogadishu.

Phnom Penh had to be the seat of the Supreme National Council of a Cambodia committed to holding the free and fair elections organized and conducted by the United Nations as the basis for forming a new and legitimate government.

The return of Prince Sihanouk – now His Majesty King Sihanouk, the President of the Supreme National Council and the father of the nation – was a joyous national celebration which relaxed the atmosphere. The effect of his moral authority could be felt immediately. It appeared that people started to live again. The return of the faction leaders, however, was a different matter. Mr Son Sann had to face a barrage of criticism on his return, but the real test for the peace process came on 27 November 1991 when Mr Khieu Samphan was severely assaulted and sent out of the country. The mission could have collapsed at that time because the Supreme National Council could not become operational without the presence in Phnom Penh of the representatives of all the Cambodian parties, including the Democratic Kampuchea Party. But the mission did not collapse. The United Nations provided its good offices and the Cambodian parties, under the wise leadership of Prince Sihanouk, mastered the political will to resolve the issue honorably. Prince Sihanouk's moral authority and persuasive power prevailed.

The Supreme National Council held its first session on Cambodian soil in Phnom Penh before the year was out, on 30 December 1991. Similarly, the Mixed Military Working Group (MMWG) also held its first session on 28 December 1991 with the participation of all four Cambodian parties. The message, it appeared, was that the Cambodian parties would no doubt play power politics, they might even try brinkmanship, but none of the parties would go as far as to wreck the peace process.

UNAMIC's mandate was simple: to maintain the cease-fire existing on the ground. This was to be done only through liaison and communication. There were only 50 military liaison officers in the whole country to perform this task; to establish relations with the Supreme National Council with a view to prepare for the establishment of UNTAC; and to set up a programme of mine-awareness, which was subsequently enlarged to mine-clearance training.

By gaining the full support of Prince Sihanouk and the confidence of the four Cambodian parties, and through the exercise of Prince Sihanouk's moral authority, such sensitive issues as the release of political prisoners and prisoners of war, freedom of the press and freedom of movement, including free entry and exit of foreign journalists, as well as practical arrangements for the repatriation of the returnees, which were beyond the mandate of UNAMIC, could be dealt with. Over 600 political prisoners and POWs were released throughout Cambodia before the establishment of UNTAC. This was possible through the innovative operation of the SNC with the blessing of its president. Unity and territorial integrity of Cambodia and the fact that the Supreme National Council represented one Cambodia was symbolized by visits of SNC's president to all the factional territories across the boundaries of these territories.

On the military side, MLOs had been deployed almost immediately in the General Headquarters of CPAF in Phnom Penh; similar deployment in the two regimental centers in Battambang and Siem Reap had been completed by early December. Simultaneous deployment of MLOs in the General Headquarters of the three other factions took place on 22 December 1991. In preparation for UNTAC, reconnaissance for the cantonment sites were conducted in the territories of all the four factions including the PDK. However, there were problems. Cease-fire violations — both major — and the first hostile act against a UN helicopter while on a reconnaissance mission took place during this time. The positive factor was that the MMWG was meeting regularly in a business-like manner to deal with cease-fire violations. On the whole, an air of expectancy and the will to cooperate were perceptible on the eve of the establishment of UNTAC.

I would now like to examine the sensitivities and expectations of the four Cambodian parties. CPP, being the largest party in term of control of territory and population, as well as administrative structure (which would provide most of the facilities for the establishment and preferential functioning of UNTAC), expected somewhat special treatment. They tried to assert their rights, perceived or real, with a view to safeguarding their autonomy. This was to be expected because they were very apprehensive that the control mechanism of UNTAC would affect them most.

On the other hand, the other three parties — FUNCINPEC, KPNLF and as pronounced repeatedly by PDK at that time — were looking forward to early establishment of UNTAC. FUNCINPEC and KPNLF, the two moderate parties, expected UNTAC to take control of the existing administrative structures so as to create a neutral political environment to facilitate their political activities throughout the country. PDK, although demanding the earliest establishment of UNTAC, was apprehensive about opening up their territory. However, they were keenly looking forward to UNTAC ensuring strict neutrality of the Phnom Penh Administration so as to make it an even field for all the parties as well as for their own security.

PDK, it would appear, had three main objectives in signing the agreement: firstly, to gain legitimacy; secondly, to neutralize the State of Cambodia; and thirdly, to obtain the withdrawal and non-return of foreign forces through the intervention of UNTAC. The latter was the most sensitive issue and I shall come back to it later.

FUNCINPEC, KPNLF and PDK fully expected to be treated as equal partners in the peace process as signatories to the agreement. They were very sensitive about this issue, PDK the most sensitive. PDK had gained legitimacy but they had grave doubts as to whether the international community had indeed accepted them as such. They were watching all the time for even the slightest nuances in this respect. This sensitivity had to be kept in mind in any attempt to gain their confidence.

UNTAC was established on 15 March 1992, much earlier than expected. UNAMIC was merged with UNTAC. The study missions to finalize the structure of UNTAC, both civil and military, were conducted in November and December 1991. The Security Council expeditiously approved the mandate and for the first time in a peace-keeping operation, funds — some US$200 million — were sanctioned in advance to facilitate early procurement of equipment and materials. However, UNTAC, when it was established, only arrived. The Special Representative was highly successful in gathering his senior team but there were hardly any support staff as well as equipment. It took months, in fact almost six months, for the basic structure, in terms of men and material, to be in place.

The expectation among the Cambodian people was that UNTAC, the transitional authority, would take control of the situation immediately after its establishment. This was perhaps an unrealistic expectation but that was the perception, which is sometime more important than reality. However, this did not happen. The State of Cambodia took full advantage of the situation and consolidated its control. FUNCINPEC and KPNLF, in particular, were very keen to cooperate at the beginning, but became more and more frustrated because they neither felt secure, nor could they conduct their political activities as they wished. Political harassment, intimidation and even killings continued and the much-awaited neutral political environment was not in sight. One may therefore wonder whether it was wise for UNTAC to appear symbolically or whether it would have been wiser to have come a little later when it would have been in a position to establish at least a semblance of control over the existing administrative structures.

UNTAC was vested with the authority to require the reassignment or removal of any personnel of the administrative agencies, bodies and offices of the existing administrative structures that it deemed necessary to ensure strict neutrality. Cambodians expected this authority to be exercised but they felt somewhat disappointed. In July 1992, a member of the Supreme National Council, while travelling in the countryside on a legitimate political mission, after giving due notice to UNTAC and the existing administrative structure, was arrested, detained for some time and accused of banditry. To set an example, disciplinary action at least against the minor official directly responsible for such conduct could have been taken. Later that year, some consideration was given by UNTAC to removing the governor, but the idea was given up. Subsequently, during the electoral campaign, some disciplinary actions were taken which restored a measure of confidence.

On the military side, demilitarization of the country was envisaged through regroupment, cantonment, disarmament and demobilization of the forces of the parties in order to facilitate creation of a neutral political environment and to create peaceful conditions for holding a free and fair election. This could be achieved only partially because the Democratic Kampuchea Party refused to participate in this process although, after the establishment of UNTAC, they were the ones who insisted on the earliest fixing of the date of commencement of Phase Two of the cease-fire. Consequently, the other parties, particularly CPP, demanded retention of their right of self-defence, which was acknowledged. Factional armed forces in Cambodia, therefore, remained operative.

PDK refused to participate, mainly on the ground that foreign forces – Vietnamese – were still present in Cambodia. PDK insisted that they could not disarm under such circumstances. They asserted that UNTAC was mandated to undertake verification of withdrawal from Cambodia and non-return of all categories of foreign forces, but UNTAC took no action. The other two resistance parties also held the same view but they did not make it a condition for their participation in Phase Two.

As stated earlier, foreign forces were a highly sensitive issue for all three resistance parties. With PDK it was an obsession. It was stated that the Cambodian parties should provide information in this aspect to enable UNTAC to conduct such verification. The three parties maintained that they had provided such information from time to time, but without result. In any case, the Agreements obliged UNTAC to undertake investigations on its own. UNTAC did set up a special unit in due course to undertake this task, but it was not until the beginning of 1993 that a few members of the foreign forces were identified. The Agreements provided that such members of foreign forces should be conducted by UNTAC out of the country, but they remained in Cambodia.

The question of foreign forces escalated into a highly emotional issue concerning the presence of Vietnamese civilians residing in Cambodia and participating in economic activities. According to a bilateral agreement between the State of Cambodia and Vietnam, the citizens of the two countries were free to cross the border and reside in either country without restriction. The three resistance parties and many other Cambodians maintained that a very large number of such Vietnamese were present in Cambodia and that they would participate in the political process, including the election. Thus the issue was affecting the neutral political process, including the electoral environment.

The Democratic Kampuchea Party became a signatory to the Paris Agreements, but a lingering doubt remained as to whether they did so in good faith. PDK insisted that they were fully prepared to cooperate, provided the Agreements were implemented according to the letter and spirit. Early on they did permit deployment of military liaison officers who were still there and operating as military observers, but under very severe restrictions. Alleging that UNTAC was not implementing the Agreements in good faith, they subsequently refused entry even to civilian staff who would have exercised control over their existing administrative structure. They refused to participate in Phase Two of the cease-fire and denied access to UNTAC's military elements on similar grounds. Could PDK's real intentions be tested early in the day, so that they could be exposed publicly and their true identity established if they were not acting in good faith?

Soon after the establishment of UNTAC, when decisions were being made on deployment of military elements in various factional territories, PDK requested deployment of a particular contingent from a developing country, instead of the force which had been earmarked for their territory. They assured facilitating immediate deployment if their request was acceded to. This request was denied, on the ground that UNTAC must have the final say on such matters and the parties had no right to choose. Had this request been accepted and PDK kept its promise, UNTAC forces would have commenced Phase Two of the cease-fire. The Khmer Rouge's real intention would have become known if they had refused, as was suspected, to honor their promise. Perhaps early establishment of PDK's bona fides without giving them any benefit of doubt could have made it possible to draw up contingency plans to deal with the changed circumstances, instead of reacting to an evolving situation or taking things for granted.

On the practical plane, the planning for the structure of UNTAC was based on realistic studies. However, the system could not cope with the vast magnitude of the operation. Peace-keeping operations need quick delivery of men and material. The rules and procedures, which had been followed, and are still being followed, did not permit that.

The primary responsibility of UNTAC was to establish a neutral political environment, conducive to holding free and fair general election. This was to be achieved by ensuring strict neutrality of the existing administrative structures. Adequate trained personnel were required to perform this task. Emphasis at that time was given to recruiting the personnel from within the UN system. Given the dimension of the requirement, the system could not meet the demand. Member States provided personnel, but it took time to deploy them.

In order to deal with similar situations, Member States could be requested to select personnel and keep them on call so that they could be deployed at short notice. Such personnel would require some orientation and training, say by UNITAR, to enable them to function effectively in a peace-keeping operation.

UNTAC was the first peace-keeping operation in which UN volunteers participated. Some of them arrived even before UNTAC, when the security situation in the whole country was volatile, mines were everywhere, the infrastructure was fragile and there was no telecommunication link between Phnom Penh and the countryside. The UNVs went all over Cambodia to collect the basic data on which the electoral plan was drawn up. They were the District Electoral Officers, who spread the message of democracy from door to door. The UNVs did an admirable job in Cambodia. UNVs could be a significant source for recruitment of personnel, and I was happy to see some of them in Somalia.

The Cambodian people had been brutalized for two decades by successive authoritarian regimes. Intimidation and violence continued until the election. They were threatened with dire consequences by the Democratic Kampuchea Party if they participated in the election, but the people of Cambodia stood up for their democratic rights. It was the will of the Cambodian people that prevailed, and the peace process was a success. Cambodia is blessed with the presence of a personality who reigns in the hearts of the people as the father of the nation. The total commitment of this neutral father figure to the peace process, his devotion to his people and his moral authority held the peace process together. His moral authority saved many a situation, inspired the people and enabled the peace process to go forward until it reached its final goal.

20. UNTAC: The Military Component View

Lieutenant-General John M. Sanderson[1]

INTRODUCTION

I was grateful for the opportunity to speak to the IPS/UNITAR conference in Singapore a little over one year after the end of the mandate of the United Nations Transitional Authority in Cambodia (UNTAC). The Singapore conference was an important initiative, drawing together as it did many of the component heads from UNTAC, as well as diplomats, officials and academics from a number of interested countries around the world. For all of us, there was a deep sense of satisfaction to see the representatives of the Kingdom of Cambodia actively participating – since the fundamental purpose of the operation had been to restore that shattered nation to the status of a complete international actor, as a first essential step on the road to recovery.

I have made many presentations on the subject of peace-keeping in Cambodia since I left Phnom Penh at the end of September 1993, in many places around the world, but mostly in Australia, where interest among the Australian people remains high. At the professional level, there is an increasing interest in peace-keeping generally, generated by Australia's involvement in a number of operations, but in Cambodia in particular, in view of Australia's major contribution to the diplomatic and operational resolution of the conflict.

On a broader dimension, the book *Cooperating for Peace* by Australia's Foreign Minister, Senator Gareth Evans, has sought to put peace-keeping into the context of multi-national conflict resolution and preventative diplomacy generally. We have been encouraged by the interest which this has aroused and look forward to the wide international cooperation which it urges since, as the UNTAC experience shows, cooperation is the key ingredient of success.

During many of the presentations I have given, I have stressed the importance of developing skills in the planning and conduct of peace-keeping operations at the operational level, that is the level between the strategic level, where higher political direction occurs, and the tactical operations in the field. As in war, it is at the operational level that peace-keeping operations are won or lost. I have a growing feeling that the problem with many other missions is due to something of a disconnection between the strategic and tactical levels, which is almost inevitable if the operational art, which brings the capabilities of diverse elements into harmony to work towards the common objective, is not exploited to its fullest extent. Despite enormous difficulties, in UNTAC we were able to establish this essential link and I hope that this will become clear from what follows.

---

[1] Commander, Australian Joint Forces, Canberra.

UNTAC IN CONTEXT

It is important to make the point early in any discussion about UNTAC that it was unequivocally a success. While even at the time it was not the biggest United Nations operation – ONUC in the Congo was marginally larger – it was, and remains at the time of writing, the most complex to date. Despite the difficulties, we were able to repatriate nearly 370,000 refugees, and we were able to allow the Cambodian people to have their voice heard in determining their future. The UNTAC-sponsored electoral process led to the formation of a constitutional authority, which could be recognised as the legitimate Cambodian Government – the fundamental purpose of the Paris Agreements of October 1991. This has removed any ambiguity over sovereign authority in Cambodia. While many problems remain, they are beyond the scope of a United Nations transitional authority.

There is a tendency to look at UNTAC in terms of Cambodia's tragic past. However, I would like to make the point that UNTAC was about the future of Cambodia, not the past. Through the process made possible by the Paris Agreements, UNTAC was able to act as a stabilising influence on the Cambodian parties. We were able to moderate the effects of almost 30 years of instability and war, to give Cambodia the opportunity to become a united Member State of the United Nations, rather than continue as a potential regional destabilising influence and an international humanitarian concern.

Nevertheless, it is important that we ask ourselves if a better outcome might have been achieved:

- Could we have left Cambodia in better shape if we had done things differently? Perhaps more importantly:
- Could we have prevented some of the problems experienced and their enduring effects, if the mission had been approached differently?

There is inevitably considerable interest in the operations of the Military Component, which was by far the largest and most visible element of UNTAC. From my perspective as Force Commander, UNTAC was an exciting and challenging experience of enormous significance to Cambodia, to the Asia-Pacific region, and to the world.

To a large degree, the significance was reflected in the diversity of the 34 nation-force under my command. Many nations were participating in a United Nations peace-keeping mission for the first time. Both Germany and Japan deployed troops outside their sovereign territories for the first time since the end of the Second World War, against a background of intense domestic political scrutiny. It was also China's first such mission. A number of former Iron Curtain countries also participated. All three nations of the Indian sub-continent were represented together for the first time. Uruguay's involvement saw it deploy troops outside its borders for the first time in over 100 years. Shortly before the elections, Namibia, the most recent beneficiary of United Nations peace-keeping efforts, deployed a small contingent.

It was clear that the maintenance of the commitment of contributing countries and the readiness of many nations to contribute troops to future missions would be influenced by the outcomes. There was therefore a heavy responsibility on the Force Commander to ensure success. In many respects, UNTAC was as important to the future of United Nations peace-keeping as it was to Cambodia. Accordingly, I think that it would miss the point to focus on the Military Component alone and I therefore intend to focus on its activities in the context of UNTAC as a complete operation.

GENERAL UNTAC FRAMEWORK

When I arrived with the Special Representative of the Secretary-General, Mr Yusushi Akashi, on 15 March 1992 to establish UNTAC, the political climate had deteriorated to one of extreme volatility. The Paris Agreements had been signed five months earlier. Their purpose was to enable the international community to sponsor a comprehensive settlement agreed by the Cambodian parties. UNTAC's role was to generate confidence through neutral oversight of agreed mechanisms. However, things were not going according to plan and an examination of those Agreements helps to explain why the situation had deteriorated to the extent that it had.

The central pillars were the stabilisation of the security environment and the creation of a neutral political environment. These were not sequential, but *parallel and interdependent* military and civil actions designed to open the way for the repatriation of the refugees and the electoral process, followed by a constitutional process leading to a legitimate government. In essence, the difficulties resulted because the Khmer Rouge were unwilling to participate in the military actions on the basis that the civil actions had not been implemented.

The fragile climate of trust reflected in the Agreements was undermined very early in the process. What does not seem to have been foreseen was the dynamics created by the Agreements themselves, as the Cambodian parties, and some nations, manoeuvred to gain advantage from the new political framework. These dynamics were manifested in November 1991 when attempts were made to form an alliance between the State of Cambodia (SOC) Prime Minister, Hun Sen, and the leader of the royalist party FUNCINPEC, Prince Norodom Ranariddh; and when the Khmer Rouge were driven from Phnom Penh following orchestrated demonstrations. At about the same time, the SOC launched military operations against the Khmer Rouge in the countryside.

In this climate, the influence of the moderates, which had probably been instrumental in bringing the major parties to accept the Agreements, was weakened by the inability to deploy substantial United Nations resources at an early date. The planning and preparation for UNTAC had only been *initiated* by the signing of the Agreements but proceeded all too slowly. The advance mission, UNAMIC, proved powerless to influence events. Its presence was far too small even to attribute responsibility for disturbances in the countryside. As a consequence, the Khmer Rouge were blamed for everything, which led them in turn to question the neutrality of the United Nations. With the Agreements only a few months old, they already appeared to be stillborn.

MILITARY COMPONENT OPERATIONS

In essence, the functions of the Military Component were concerned with cease-fire supervision and other confidence-building measures. Their centrepiece was the Phase Two cease-fire, involving regroupment, cantonment and disarming of the armed forces of the Cambodian parties, and demobilisation of at least 70% of them.

Phase Two was only partially carried out because, as is well known, the Khmer Rouge refused to participate, for reasons which still require a great deal of analysis. The right of self-defence meant that substantial elements of the other armed forces had to remain in the field. The continuing confrontation and the inherent security risks impacted on the other UNTAC programmes.

However, the Phase Two cease-fire was not a stand-alone activity. It was linked to other provisions for the control of the machinery of government. In particular, the SOC police forces were a matter of concern. These were not community police, but the politicised forces of a one-party state, designed to protect the interests of the regime. Moreover, with the armed forces of the parties cantoned, disarmed and largely demobilised as the Agreements required, the relative power of the police would have been markedly increased.

The Paris Agreements placed the police forces of the parties under UNTAC supervision or control, "to ensure strict neutrality"; "to ensure that law and order [were] maintained effectively and impartially"; and that "human rights and fundamental freedoms [were] fully protected". However, the Agreements did not specify any control measures similar, for example, to those measures governing the disposal of the armed forces. This proved to be a major omission.

Agreed, unambiguous provisions could have been aimed at ensuring the creation of non-political police forces, for example through training schemes and the provision of funding, which would have removed their dependence on the parties and could have facilitated UNTAC control. In addition, a system of laws and an independent judiciary similarly held accountable to UNTAC would have enabled these police to prosecute offenders effectively.

If you look at the situation from the Khmer Rouge perspective, you will quickly recognise that the National Army of Democratic Kampuchea (NADK) is their protective shield. In the terms of their fanatical nationalist ideology, the SOC equated with the hated Vietnamese presence which had forced them from power in 1979. With the SOC police intact and still under party control, the Khmer Rouge could not allow UNTAC to disarm the NADK without making themselves vulnerable. It is important to recall that the Khmer Rouge only accepted compromise on this issue in 1991 because of the inclusion of the control provisions in the Paris Agreements.

By August 1992, the Khmer Rouge were calling for power to be given to the Supreme National Council (SNC – the quadripartite body enshrining Cambodian sovereignty during the UNTAC mandate); for the SNC and UNTAC jointly to control the "five fields" of SOC administration (finance, foreign affairs, information, defence and public security); and for the withdrawal of Vietnamese forces, which in effect meant the neutralisation of the SOC. The demands relating to the authority of the SNC and administrative control were beyond the scope of the Military Component. In accordance with its mandate to verify the withdrawal and non-return of foreign forces, the Military Component tried to find the Vietnamese forces which the Khmer Rouge said were in Cambodia, but they never helped in any way — no allegation was ever substantiated — and no forces with any significance in the terms of the Agreements were ever found.

These conditions were all prerequisites established by Khmer Rouge for their cooperation in the process. A little later, in early 1993, they called for quadripartite military and police forces. In essence, these were the power-sharing proposals which had been rejected by the SOC at the first Paris Conference in 1989 and were clearly beyond the Paris Agreements. Evidently, the Khmer Rouge thought that they were achievable in the light of the new dynamics. By 1993 they were the only conditions with which the Khmer Rouge could feel safe — they left the NADK intact until the SOC Police could be somehow neutralised, either by UNTAC and the SNC, or by the SOC's ultimate collapse as the peace process lost direction.

The Khmer Rouge evidently reasoned that, threatened by a loss of power in the election, elements of the still well-armed SOC could be expected to resort to violence and intimidation. By not disarming, the Khmer Rouge sought to increase the SOC's unpopularity and made it easier to defeat politically, with the added potential of avoiding an election in which the Khmer Rouge could itself expect to be marginalised. Although it is noteworthy that all parties declared their full support for the Agreements, the delay in UNTAC deployment simply made it easier for elements within the parties to evade their responsibilities. *Both* the SOC and the Khmer Rouge stated that they could not implement the Agreements because of UNTAC's failure to control the other. These were continuing themes.

As Force Commander, in early 1992 I could feel the ground moving away from under myself and those moderates of all military factions who were committed to the process. I held numerous discussions with the Khmer Rouge military commander, General Son Sen, about this time, but it was clear that he could no longer deliver all his forces in the countryside to the process. This undermining of the moderates was due partly to a new-found assertiveness by reactionaries in the factions, and partly to a rapid decline in confidence in the United Nations.

The Military Component deployed in the period May to July 1992 in a climate of growing mistrust. The Civil Police Component deployed even later. The Civil Administration Component was not complete until nearly one year after the Agreements were signed, its staff of some 170 woefully inadequate for the task in any case. By then the repatriation programme was only proceeding with difficulty, into a countryside with the armed forces still holding the field and some areas heavily mined.

The point to be drawn from this is not whose fault it might have been, but simply that the signing of the Agreements should have been a "trigger" for the execution of integrated and comprehensive set of plans already in place —

plans which gave the United Nations the means to exercise transitional authority in Cambodia from the outset.

Regrettably, for almost everyone in UNTAC, the process was one of on-the-job training, while implementing plans prepared by someone else. Such arrangements are not conducive to success and should not be repeated. In my view, such plans need to be prepared by the people who will be responsible for their execution – people who are aware of the subtleties within the peace agreement, and the interrelation of its provisions. This is an important lesson for future peace-keeping missions and requires a clear break with the practices of the past.

ENFORCEMENT OR PEACE-KEEPING?

Although UNTAC had started badly, it still had a number of options available to it. These options did *not* include enforcement action by United Nations peace-keepers. To do so would have required a force several times larger than the one we had, one structured and equipped for a protracted conflict, and at a significantly greater cost.

I take the view that such a mission would have been doomed to disaster, even if it had been given wide international support, since it would have required a United Nations force to take sides in an internal conflict. While the Khmer Rouge was usually seen as the disturbing party, there were nevertheless deep divisions internationally, within the Security Council and within UNTAC about who really was at fault. Both UNTAC and the international unity which had been built up behind the Cambodian peace process would have been very likely to have been torn apart on this issue.

Enforcement action requires much stronger consensus than peace-keeping, both internationally and within the contributing countries. Enforcement is, after all, war by another name, and there have to be interests of severe magnitude at stake before the international consensus will reach the necessary fervour to provide the forces and funds, and possibly to accept casualties on a significant scale. Anyone who thinks they can bluff their way through these things with a mandate and a force designed for peace-keeping has little understanding of the nature of conflict and the consequences of the use of force at the international level. Regrettably, as Force Commander, from beginning to end I was plagued by appeals for the UNTAC Military Component to become involved in internal security operations.

Peace-keepers are instruments of diplomacy – not of war. They are part of an agreement between parties which have been in conflict and are protected by that agreement. They operate in the open as an expression of their international neutrality – this gives them acceptability and great strength. When used for enforcement, they lose their neutrality, are stripped of their political protection and the wavering international support for whatever new objectives are chosen will make the command weak and vulnerable. It is no way to go to war.

I hasten to emphasise my deep concern with respect to the advocates of violence on peace-keeping missions. I think that we can all understand the frustration of people when they cannot achieve results, or others who see atrocities committed within their reach and vision. We can recall the disturbing images of Belgian United Nations troops cutting up their blue berets in disgust on their return from Rwanda in May 1994.

But it seems to me that the difficulty here really lies in ensuring that everyone has to understand the purpose of peace-keeping operations, why the peace-keepers are deployed to these volatile areas in the first place, and what they are legally entitled to do. Closely related to this is the need for all concerned to understand the effects of the use of force by peace-keepers, on all United Nations personnel in the mission area as they implement their part of the mandate, on their ability to resolve the causes of the conflict, and on the future capacity of the United Nations to resolve conflict generally.

Much of the basis of criticism of the philosophy which eschews the use of force by peace-keepers other than in self-defence might be due to passion over events which blind the advocates of violence to the realities of the situation. Some might also be due to the remnants, in some armed forces, of an interventionist tradition developed in colonial times, which sees peace-keeping operations as a dilution of military potency. It should be a matter of concern for us all that such an approach could be seriously proposed as a future form of United Nations peace-keeping. In true peace-keeping, Member States deploy an international force with the agreement of the parties to a conflict, to assist them in the resolution of a dispute between them. Whether it is due to diplomatic pressure, economic sanctions, or exhaustion, the parties want resolution of the conflict, or at least its suspension, while the diplomatic process works to find an agreed solution.

Even if the agreement is broken, or in the case of some humanitarian missions, where peace-keepers might be deployed without a formal agreement being reached among the parties, it is difficult to argue that peace-keepers have the right to kill people in their own country without proper sanction under either international or domestic law. Everyone has the right of self-defence and peace-keepers are lightly armed in view of the increased threats in world spots. But it seems difficult to argue that a mandate which draws its authority from a Charter designed to defend the sovereignty of states can authorise hostile intervention against any party within a state.

UNITY AND NEUTRALITY

A better option for Cambodia was the one we followed – namely, to preserve the unity and neutrality of the force through strict adherence to the peace-keeping ethos. Without unity of purpose, unity of command, unity of understanding, the force fractures very quickly and can no longer truly represent the will of the international community. From that point on, the force's ability to retain its neutrality is doubtful. Unity and neutrality represent the true strength of a peace-keeping force. Without unity and neutrality, you either go to war or go home. And in UNTAC, it would have been the civilian components which would have been the most exposed and vulnerable in such a climate. Other than in the climate of a peace-keeping mission, they could not have done their job in any way.

The good fortune in Cambodia was in having a clear objective – the election. No matter how circumstances changed, the conduct of the election stood out and it was critical not to be diverted from it. The problem was to convince everybody that the election could be held within the framework of the mandate.

There were many distorted views among influential expatriates in Cambodia about why we were there, including from some United Nations personnel, members of non-government organisations and journalists. Some of these actually succumbed to faction propaganda and took partisan positions. The diversity of views served to confuse the international community and made our task among the Cambodian people even more difficult, since their confidence in the United Nations tended to be undermined.

The Khmer Rouge recognised the importance of these issues and there were definite attempts to break the unity of the force. Very early in the mission, the Khmer Rouge began classifying some units as "good UNTAC", and others as "bad UNTAC". Some elements of UNTAC were acceptable in their areas and others were not. There is no doubt that some contingents were directed by national interests to take positions which were not in harmony with the overall directive of the Force Commander, and perhaps the Khmer Rouge were seeking to widen these divisions. This is a serious matter. A *United Nations* force cannot afford to be a collection of national contingents each pursuing their own agenda – it has to be seen to be pursuing the objectives of the agreements which grant it authority to be there.

This has to be recognised by the parties also. The United Nations Force Commander cannot be seen to be discriminating between the members of his force. To have done so in UNTAC would have almost certainly led to further demands aimed at dividing the force and weakening the Agreements. It is important to note that while some were urging us to meet the demands of the Khmer Rouge, they began firing on UNTAC helicopters.

Generating cohesion among 16,000 troops, representing 34 Member States of the United Nations, was not an easy task. Despite this, in many respects the cultural diversity was an advantage – we truly represented the international community. Many troops came from countries with similar economic and social problems to Cambodia, or similar cultural backgrounds. As a result, they were often more attuned to Cambodian needs and sensitivities, strengthening our relationship with the people. However, a small number of contingents, one in particular, held very different attitudes about the relationship between the military and the population. These caused serious problems which also affected United Nations civilians and members of the non-government organisation community.

Cohesion was generated by involving everyone in the planning process, by continuous briefings, and by clear directives and orders. In the end, it was the desire of most soldiers to be seen as military professionals, the one thing we all had in common, which overcame the more serious difficulties.

The United Nations Secretariat alone reserves the right, in the light of the views of the Permanent Five, to decide which troops come from which countries. This is done in accordance with the Secretariat's priorities, which in the case of UNTAC were not always consistent with the needs of the mission. The Force Commander is held accountable before the international community for the actions of the members of his force, but he has no say in the selection. There might be good reasons for this, but it is an important question to be addressed, if the risks of splitting command and undermining unity are to be avoided on future missions.

AN ALLIANCE WITH THE PEOPLE

What became clear was that the Cambodian people desperately wanted peace. The essential task was to forge an alliance between UNTAC and the people which would overcome the distortions created by the power struggles between and within the faction leaderships.

The first requirement was an information programme which was undistorted by faction propaganda. The difficulty in convincing the United Nations Secretariat that UNTAC needed its own radio station meant that "Radio UNTAC" did not commence operation until more than one year after the signing of the Agreements. I do not believe that anyone could now deny the criticality of Radio UNTAC to the whole process. In my view, this was obvious from the start and only the United Nations bureaucracy delayed it.

When we started to develop a penetration into the countryside, the Khmer Rouge, realising that they had a highly plausible competitor for the hearts and minds of the people, staged a series of intimidatory hostage situations designed to establish control over the way UNTAC interfaced with the people in the countryside. Despite the widespread diplomatic concerns for their safety, UNTAC troops continued to push out into the villages and into remote corners, including along the fringes of the Khmer Rouge-controlled zones.

Of greater concern was the SOC propaganda which sought to erode respect for UNTAC by asserting that it lacked the commitment to face up to the Khmer Rouge. But peace-keepers can only use their weapons for self-defence. So other, neutral ways of gaining respect among the people had to be found.

We all know that large groups of people who are disadvantaged by circumstances are in a highly exploitable state. Often they see no choice but to lend what weight they have to the support of a party to a conflict. Alleviating the cause of these grievances can often only be possible with the intervention of outside agencies. This is where the partnership between peace-keepers and humanitarian agencies comes into play. Civic action programmes which bring improvements to conditions of life are one obvious way. Unfortunately, there seemed to be a prevailing view that this sort of activity was the responsibility of other United Nations agencies and non-government organisations – not the business of the Military Component.

This misses the point – the military has a much deeper presence, and "hearts and minds" activities always form an essential part of a military component's method of operation in these circumstances. In the event, we were able to establish a reasonable programme through the generosity of donations from individual countries and close cooperation with other United Nations agencies and non-governmental organisations, as well as effective use of the nation-building and other skills that many of the United Nations soldiers brought to Cambodia. The protection afforded by peace-keepers and the manpower they provided also enabled the humanitarian agencies to reach more members of the population than would have been possible otherwise.

I stress that humanitarian and peace-keeping objectives are not in opposition, but rather they are different instruments of the same purpose. The humanitarian effort must itself be the subject of properly constructed plans which themselves form part of an overall integrated plan working towards the common objective.

CIVIL–MILITARY INTEGRATION

Although we continued to seek the parties' compliance with the cease-fire provisions of the Agreements, in September 1992, it became clear to me that the Khmer Rouge were unlikely to enter the Phase Two cease-fire and that a secure environment for the elections could not be guaranteed without the Military Component behind it. Initially, it had been planned to reduce the strength of the Military Component by more than one-half after the demobilisation of the armed forces of the parties. But the changed circumstances now necessitated the maintenance of the force at full strength. Accordingly, in December 1992 the Military Component was redeployed to align its command structure with administrative boundaries of the Civil Administration Component.

At a Sector Commanders' conference in January 1993, to which I had invited UNTAC provincial directors and electoral officers, the Head of the Civil Administration Component, M. Gérard Porcell, observed that although the Paris Agreements did not rule out an election in the absence of disarmament, this reality nevertheless steered it towards a climate of violence. He went on:

> Ensuring the security of the electoral process in its entirety is now ... the principal mission of the Military Component .... Our respective activities ... are becoming complementary and profoundly linked. From our viewpoint, this participation of military personnel in the realisation of civilian objectives is a veritable godsend: free of the constraints of the tasks ... originally assigned, the Military Component can utilise its technical competence (which is large), its important material and personnel capabilities, as well as its remarkable faculty for organisation resulting from its own technique of military command, which together act to enhance the control activity normally carried out by the Civil Administration Component.

The security situation had imposed the requirement for close collaboration. The Military Component had to provide not only security for civilians and military alike, but a logistic support structure which penetrated to district level. An integrated approach was adopted which established a planning and control alliance for the electoral process between the Electoral and Military Components, and Information and Education Division. Centred around Military Plans in Phnom Penh, and Sector Headquarters in the field, this also drew in the Civil Police Component. These arrangements were instrumental in the effective conduct of the election. Without them, United Nations civilian casualties would have resulted and there could not have been an election.

The UNTAC arrangements also drew in the armed forces of the Cambodian parties which participated in the elections. Agreement was reached in April 1993 for them to use minimum force and proportionate response to help protect the electoral process against any threats. Military operations which went beyond this were unacceptable. In effect, the Cambodian armed forces became an extension of the UNTAC peace-keeping force. A division of responsibility was also agreed in which the Cambodian armed forces secured the countryside to enable the people to vote, while UNTAC secured the electoral process itself and guaranteed its integrity. Consistent with neutrality, this was open to all parties. But the Khmer Rouge maintained their opposition to the elections.

An encouraging aspect to this was that by establishing our credentials as neutral peace-keepers who intended to implement the mandate, we had won the confidence of patriotic Cambodian military leaders, among them men of integrity, who were now willing to bind their forces to Cambodia's future. Shortly after the elections, we concluded negotiations in Phnom Penh which led to the unification of the three armed forces. We had been conducting negotiations to this end for many months, but without much progress. Now the shared experience of supporting this truly democratic process, in concert with the international community, had engendered great professional pride and had drawn former enemies together. This unification paid critical dividends in the politically ambiguous period immediately after the elections, when some of the losers tried to unravel the process. No political arrangements had been foreshadowed in the Agreements and nothing substantial had been prepared, but the united armed forces provided essential stability. No coup attempt could have been sure of success without the support of an army. I believe that up to the time of writing, the unified armed forces and general staff continue to provide the major stabilising influence in Cambodia.

This initiative was supported by a number of Member States of the United Nations which offered to fund salaries of the armed forces, as well as of the police and bureaucracy, as long as they committed themselves to the constitutional Government which was to emerge from the electoral process. My view is that such pro-active initiatives are an essential element in peace-building and can have enduring benefits long after the end of the mission.

Of particular importance in all this was the Mixed Military Working Group Secretariat. The forum of the Mixed Military Working Group was set up under the Paris Agreements to resolve problems relating to the cease-fire, but due to the difficulties confronted in the peace process, it became my main instrument for dealing with the military forces of the parties. The Mixed

Military Working Group Secretariat was a mixed grouping of officers from many nations which prepared agendum papers, maintained continuous liaison with military staff of all factions and acted as a coordination agency with the civil components and other United Nations agencies. The main work of the Secretariat was directed at supporting the meetings I held with the military liaison officers and leaders of the military of the Cambodian parties.

The Mixed Military Working Group Secretariat's work enabled me to seize the initiative in negotiations and was a valuable tool in establishing the correctness of the UNTAC position. The effective liaison work made a strong contribution to the establishment of a climate of trust between the UNTAC Military Component and the military of all factions – even the Khmer Rouge. No other component had an effective secretariat and this area warrants very close study to determine its applicability to other peace-keeping missions.

COALITION-BUILDING

A crucial element was the maintenance of the international coalition behind the Paris Agreements. In Cambodia, the coalition was reflected in the Expanded Permanent Five (EP5), which had been established soon after signing the Paris Agreements. This body grouped around the representatives of the Permanent Five Members of the Security Council the representatives of Indonesia, Australia, Germany, Thailand and Japan; India and Malaysia eventually joined too. My relationship with the EP5 was a corporate one, as was the SRSG's. The EP5 received regular briefings to ensure it was fully and accurately informed of our activities.

The EP5 closely paralleled the grouping in New York known as the "Core Group", and was instrumental in ensuring that the realities on the ground were communicated to the missions in New York and, through them, to the Security Council. The Security Council was also in receipt of mission reports processed by our own military liaison officers deployed to New York for the purpose.

Through these mechanisms, UNTAC was able to proceed towards the elections and the formation of a constitutional government, the goal of the Paris Agreements, despite the difficulties, confident of the legitimacy of its actions and of the support of the world community. Such a process became necessary for UNTAC because the United Nations Secretariat was constantly distracted by other missions, particularly in the former Yugoslavia. In effect, we were able to overcome the difficulties experienced by the hard-pressed United Nations Secretariat in conducting a number of complex missions simultaneously. The Secretariat simply does not have enough qualified staff to act as a strategic headquarters. Accordingly, it must be ready to be supplemented by skilled manpower from Member States for this purpose.

It is regrettable that there was no strategic integration and planning for the UNTAC mission, nor was there broad consultation in the preparation of the Secretary-General's report which could have linked the programmes of the various components in an ordered way, or effective strategic integration once the mission started. This imposed penalties throughout the mission and was only overcome by component heads networking as problems arose, and by the Military Component becoming the focal point for the planning and conduct of the operations of UNTAC as a whole. I believe that the effectiveness of an integrated approach is an essential lesson for other peace-keeping missions to be drawn from the UNTAC experience.

CONCLUSION

Cambodia was an operation in which we were able to implement the mandate and withdraw in good order, under budget and on time. We had no authority to remain and, had we done so, it is likely that we would have been progressively drawn into the continuing internal strife. In any case, internal security had become a matter for the legitimate Government, which we had helped to establish, and their armed forces, which we had helped to bring together. Internal conflict in a sovereign Member State is not a matter for the United Nations, without authorisation from the legitimate authority and the support of the international community.

In the implementation of the mandate, strict adherence to the peace-keeping ethos was an essential ingredient of success. If unity and neutrality had not been scrupulously preserved in a multi-faceted mission of such complexity, the prospects of an outcome which met the aspirations of the Cambodian people and the international community would have been gravely prejudiced.

If it can be accepted that unity and neutrality extend beyond peace-keepers to all participants working towards the mission objective, then it becomes clear that the effectiveness of the United Nations can be markedly improved by cooperative arrangements which bring their operations into harmony. Specific opportunities exist in areas such as civic action programmes to raise the condition of the population, public information and education, logistics, electoral activities, and establishment of a system of justice to maintain law and order and to defend human rights. One can only imagine what might have eventuated if the integrated approach had been used from the outset and maintained throughout. If this central lesson can be learnt, peace-keeping operations, rather than being the confused and directionless affairs they often are, can become an effective instrument for conflict resolution by the international community. The lesson from UNTAC is a lesson of *unity*.

My own conviction to emerge from the UNTAC operation is the need for a strategic alliance between peace-keepers, both military and civilian, humanitarian organisations, and those non-government organisations which feel that they have a role to play in pursuing common objectives. An integrated approach needs to be adopted all the way from the United Nations Secretariat to the forward area, across the components and interested agencies, for the duration of the mission. This means that both civilian and military personnel must be trained to operate in an integrated environment. This strategic alliance must be aimed at the development and execution of timely plans which include building structures which help sustain the outcomes of the mission after it has ended. The plans need to be dynamic, with clearly signposted exits for the various components and agencies once their programmes are completed.

In the end, UNTAC was a great success. But the greatest triumph of UNTAC has been essentially one for the Cambodian people who had the courage to come forward and vote in overwhelming numbers, despite the efforts to thwart their will. Convincing the people of our commitment by securing the mechanism in the countryside was the challenge UNTAC faced. It was through cooperation that we were able to fulfil our obligations to them.

21. UNTAC's Civilian Police Operation

Brigadier-General Klaas C. Roos[1]

INTRODUCTORY REMARKS

First of all I would like to thank the Institute of Policy Studies (IPS) of Singapore and the UN Institute for Training and Research (UNITAR) for inviting me here to participate in this conference, which I regard as very important because it can contribute significantly to better prepared and performed UN peace-keeping missions. Previous experience in UN missions – especially short-term missions – has convinced me that a thorough study of previous missions ought to be a first activity before starting a new mission. I sincerely hope that the contribution of all former UNTAC officials present here and the overall outcome of the conference will be a firm support to our future peace-keeping colleagues, military and civilian alike. I also hope that the final report of this conference will be a good guide for the decision-makers in New York and eventually for the relevant authorities in the troop-contributing countries.

DEBRIEFING REMARKS

Before the UNTAC mission ended, my headquarters compiled a 63-page evaluation report on CIVPOL's mission in Cambodia and submitted it to UN Headquarters in New York. In terms of a proper debriefing, it would have been advisable to call the head of the Component to New York to elucidate and explain the contents of the report and give him the opportunity to present additional explanations. Such an action would have shown a genuine interest in practical experience. Unfortunately, for reasons unknown to me, no personal debriefing took place.

In the context of this conference it would take too much time to elaborate extensively on this evaluation report. Considering CIVPOL's mission and the extent to which its goals, according to mandate, have been achieved, I propose to follow the formal wording of the CIVPOL mission as embodied in Chapter II, paragraph E of the report of the Secretary-General (SG) on Cambodia of 19 February 1992. Although I will specially deal with "lessons learned" in my presentation, it is hard to avoid lessons learned in the following debriefing remarks.

---

[1] Deputy Commandant, The Netherlands Royal Marechaussee, The Hague.

In a proper and logical procedure in an integrated planning process, the four pages on the Police Component contained in the 43-page SG report were mainly drawn from the report drafted by the survey team that visited Cambodia in December 1991. However, when the senior CIVPOL team (the Commissioner and his senior staff officers, all police officers with long-standing experience and much practice in leading large police organizations) arrived in the mission area and started to assess the actual situation on the ground, they soon reached the conclusion that there were various errors in the survey report and therefore also in the tasks for the Police Component.

A few examples: there was no Khmer Rouge police; there were no FUNCINPEC or KPNLF police (at best, some of their military performed certain police-like activities); the remarks on the notorious "A-3" forces (paragraph 116, SG report) were highly suggestive and caused many problems in the daily management of UNTAC. The "A-3 ghost" was there on many occasions, despite professional police investigations concluding the non-existence of A-3.

The main functions of CIVPOL were the supervision and control of local civil police, in particular focussing on protection of human rights and fundamental freedoms. In order to execute this important task effectively it is necessary to arrange for executive police powers (e.g. the powers of arrest) and the logical follow-up of prosecution within the UN structure. This was necessary since it was quite clear that none of the factions operated an impartial and effective system of law and order or an independent judiciary. With a growing increase in political violence and violations of human rights, UNTAC eventually reacted by appointing a special UN prosecutor, assigning the powers of arrest to CIVPOL and, even before that, designing a basic penal code and criminal procedures. Toward the end of the mission, a UN detention centre was established. An independent court, however, never came into being, thus frustrating the attempts to upgrade law and order procedures in Cambodia.

The form of CIVPOL police monitoring as determined by the SG report was almost entirely based on the structure of the civil police of one faction (SOC), formally disregarding the need for CIVPOL presence in the areas controlled by other factions as well as a training organization for local police. Once the fact was established that the smaller factions had no police and the larger faction had a poorly trained force, it became obvious that our training efforts needed high priority. In addition to country-wide training, a special police training school in the north-west Thmar Pouk area was established. Managing this training school effectively, CIVPOL achieved interfactional integration by training and educating local police students from all four factions in integrated training courses. The inflexibility of the UN administration's procedures unfortunately interfered with the success of this achievement. The police integration achieved here was in my opinion an important political achievement as well, and therefore should have been given priority in UNTAC's overall policy. Financially it was difficult or sometimes impossible to arrange for the necessary logistical aspects like food, lodging, basic police equipment for trainees, transport to and from the UN police training school and even some sort of substitute for a salary or allowance. Luckily, the CIVPOL monitors used a lot of private initiative (sometimes not in line with UN rules and regulations) and private money to make this small but significant part of CIVPOL's mission a success. All in all, the total training effort of CIVPOL resulted in some 10,000 local police officers trained in various police skills ranging from basic training to all sorts of specialized courses. I must add that, in the initial phase of the mission, there was no clear indication of the availability of training expertise within CIVPOL, but fortunately quite a number of experienced police officers had acquired training expertise during their national careers.

The chapter on the police component refers several times to some sort of joint operation with other components. No guidance for this cooperation, however, not even basic and general indications, was given in the SG report. It had therefore to be accomplished in the course of the mission, which often took quite some effort because components were busy with setting up their own parts of the total operation. Frequently there was lack of knowledge of the mission and organization of the other components. Integral planning and pre-mission inter-component consultations could have avoided a lot of these types of problems.

The more difficult part of my debriefing remarks is to come to a conclusion on the degree of success of the Police Component in relation to the mandate. As said before, there were deficiencies noted in the mandate as we deployed in Cambodia, deficiencies mainly caused by an incorrect survey and the resulting errors. Also the lessons learned, mentioned below, had an impact on the success of the police mission. However, the 18-month mandate of UNTAC was a partial success, taking into account that a peace-keeping operation can only be successful if the parties involved offer and execute full cooperation. We all know that one of the factions refused to cooperate, thus hindering the achievement of UNTAC's goals. Given the natural and unavoidable limitations every international operation shows, I dare say the police contributed positively to UNTAC's success. However, the contribution could have been better if the lessons learned had been dealt with at the onset of the mission.

LESSONS TO BE LEARNED

The debriefing remarks already contain some lessons, but there are more, although the list will be far from complete. The lessons learned will be divided in two groups: lessons primarily for the UN and a second group for police-contributing countries.

Lessons applying to the UN

One important lesson the UN has already learned since UNTAC concerns the appointment of a Police Adviser. In early 1993, a Nigerian senior police officer was assigned to DPKO in New York. Within a year he was followed by a Dutch colleague to reinforce the police presence in DPKO. Compared to the arrangements Namibian and Cambodian UN police components had to work with, this definitely is an improvement, and will no doubt lead to better mission preparation. In addition, professional planning is essential. It is therefore necessary to establish a Police Planning Group which contains all the relevant expertise. Although I realize that the UN's financial position could be an impediment, I am convinced that many Member States are willing to provide voluntary contributions of expertise. And each member of the planning team should have relevant "field experience".

Apart from the police experts mentioned above, the planning staff should be reinforced on a temporary basis with police officers who are likely to be deployed in the forthcoming mission. In the few days I had to do some practical police planning, I managed to convince the USG that I needed a small staff around me to assist in some fundamental planning activities. Thanks to my previous CIVPOL experience, I was able to handpick some fine colleagues from various countries by simply calling them on a personal basis and then submitting the list of names to the UN to ask for their secondment through normal diplomatic channels. It gave me a significant lead to enlist these colleagues.

Integrated and integral planning is an essential part of the planning process. The few days I spent in New York before deployment gave me only a little opportunity to work on some basic coordination with the administration and other components. By sheer accident I met a gentleman in New York who turned out to be the Force Commander designate. But even generals need more than just an accidental meeting to coordinate strategies and operations. As far as the SRSG is concerned I was only in a position to make a courtesy call. The rest of the top management met each other on the plane from Bangkok to Phnom Penh when the mission officially started. However, recent adjustments in the structure of the peace-keeping department in New York provide better scope for this planning concept.

Appointment of key officials is needed much earlier than was the case with UNTAC. I was requested to come to New York by the end of February 1992 and officially appointed by the SG on 6 March. That same day, the official police contributors' conference was held. The mission started on 15 March.

It took the police component eight months to reach full deployment. From the operational point of view this was absolutely unacceptable. Although the UN cannot enforce contingent contributions in any way, it would help to approach potential contributors earlier. Countries could accelerate their selection and training programmes if the information needed is made available on a timely basis.

As mentioned in my debriefing remarks, the survey reports on the police were drafted without the input of the Commissioner designate, who was not part of the survey team. Here of course police experts who were actually going to participate in UNTAC should have been part of the survey mission. If I recall correctly, this did happen in the military survey. Obviously the presence of a military staff in New York helped bring this about.

Requirements and training

The UN officially laid down some specific requirements for police monitors:
- six years of police experience;

- possession of a valid national driver's licence and additional experience with four wheel-drive vehicles;
- sufficient proficiency in the official language(s) of the mission.

We had considerable problems with these requirements throughout the mandate period. First of all, the experience requirement is too general when one takes into account the many sorts of police and the differences between various national police forces. Depending on the police mandate, this requirement should be defined more accurately in terms of experience in "community policing". In addition various special police skills are required, e.g. training, investigation, technical and forensic experience, communications, traffic, crime scene specialists and so on.

A driver's licence and driving experience is essential for the proper performance of the police mission and also for safety. Of all the policemen I lost in three missions, most casualties resulted from traffic accidents. Non-drivers in national contingents should not be accepted. Police-contributing countries should be informed in advance that non-drivers will be returned, at that country's expense.

Language problems, although in most cases not as life-threatening as a lack of driving skills, nevertheless seriously downgrade the effectiveness of a police mission. UN police personnel, by the nature of their mandate, communicate directly with their local counterparts and with the local population (sometimes through interpreters). Language should be taken into account in the selection of potential police-contributing countries. If the UN requests, for example, a South American country to contribute to a mission where English is spoken, the chances are that language could present a problem, particularly among junior personnel.

Training is a two-pronged effort: training of local police as part of the mandate and training of CIVPOL personnel before actual deployment to their police districts and stations in the mission area. Training of local police is an essential element in the reconstruction of the country and its administration. A close cooperation and joint planning between law-makers, judicial experts, human rights experts and UN police is therefore necessary. Thus a comprehensive system of law enforcement can be set up and will enable local police to play their part in the reconstruction. Let us keep in mind that reconstruction of other fields like infrastructure, civil service, health care and education will all be in vain if the environment is lawless. Training of CIVPOL personnel is essential to realize the goals set in the mandate. This should already start in the home countries with proper UN assistance, at least in the form of police-training manuals developed by the UN. I will return to this subject in the section below about lessons for police-contributing countries.

For a multi-component mission like UNTAC, an essential point of good planning is a policy-level conference, where senior officials (e.g. component directors) can brief each other on their component mandate, as well as having a chance to get to know the others and get used to their ways of working and/or management.

Between components, certain administrative procedures should be standardized. A problem in this field existed concerning leave and time off. Experience in Namibia with this confusing system caused much criticism, and the final evaluation report advised New York to abolish this complicated system and introduce a straightforward regulation for days off. The infamous compensatory time off (CTO) system was nevertheless used again in UNTAC. Those who made that decision did not listen to advice from the field and forgot that the CTO system was never designed for large organizations such as CIVPOL, but for small groups operating on a strictly individual basis, e.g. UNMOs.

Lessons learned for police-contributing countries

Finally, ladies and gentlemen, I would like to touch upon a few lessons for the police contributors. As I have already mentioned, training of police contingents prior to deployment is of the utmost importance. This training should focus on specific items like:

- the mandate of the mission;
- the police operation;
- the environment in which the police has to operate (climate, health risks, security situation);
- the problems in the mission area (the reasons for deployment of a UN mission);
- a refresher course on various police skills.

Although actually part of preparatory training, the discipline topic is so important that I regard it as a separate lesson. All nations must ensure good discipline during the policeman's tour of duty with the UN. Also, much can be done through national disciplinary systems. In this respect, the contingent commander has to cooperate closely with the Police Commissioner.

A logical way to guarantee good discipline is by using a good national selection procedure to man the contingent. Volunteers are not necessarily useful members of a contingent. Personnel files are helpful, but the whole training period should in fact be used for selection.

In addition, the medical examination based on the existing UN regulations and the inoculation programme should be accurate. In UNTAC, a lot of valuable time was lost because countries did not follow the UN medical requirements.

Quite a few visiting officials from police-contributing countries asked me why I did not arrange for a commanders' conference prior to deployment. They felt such a conference could have produced more and better-quality information for the preparation of their contingents. I agreed with them and in fact I had proposed such a conference, because my personal experience in this respect before going to Namibia was positive. Unfortunately the UN did not agree. Strangely enough such a conference was organized for the military. This problem contains a lesson both for the UN and the Member States. The UN should simply organize it and the countries in their negotiations with the UN should insist on such a pre-deployment meeting before future operations.

With regard to the general requirements for police monitors, contributing countries should follow UN requirements strictly. Thus a perfect

French-speaking foreign affairs diplomat, without a driver's licence, will not arrive as part of a police contingent in police uniform.

Finally, during training it is of the utmost importance to provide national contingents with good information on the cultural, religious and racial differences in the multi-national police force and to point out the importance of good cooperation between all those nationalities. I expelled one CIVPOL member for committing racial discrimination against a colleague. At the same time similar information on the local population is essential. The UN can be of assistance in this very important issue by making this type of information available.

CLOSING REMARKS

Ladies and gentlemen, at the start of my presentation I pointed out that my list of lessons learned would be far from complete. Although the presentation has contained critical remarks, it was meant to be constructive. I merely tried to make a small contribution for better future peace-keeping, aiming at better conditions and circumstances for field commanders. Needless to say, this will reflect in a positive way on the UN's efforts to bring peace to war-torn countries.

22. Refugee Repatriation and Reintegration in Cambodia

Sergio Vieira de Mello[1]

INTRODUCTION

Why was the Third Committee, dealing with repatriation of refugees and reconstruction, the only one to have achieved consensus on a written document, at the end of the first Paris International Conference on Cambodia (PICC) in late August 1989? After weeks of laborious negotiations and with the support of major international and regional partners – including the Committee's Co-chairmen, China and ASEAN – the four Cambodian parties adopted a set of principles and operational guidelines that represented a radical departure from the unacceptable practices that had affected Cambodian refugees and displaced populations over the years. In a nutshell, all participants surprisingly agreed to depoliticize humanitarian issues, after nearly two decades of brutal conflict and exploitation of civilian populations for political and military purposes. The text adopted in 1989, which UNHCR found acceptable, became, word for word, Annex 3 of the Agreement on a Comprehensive Political Settlement of the Cambodian Conflict, adopted on 23 October 1991.

In the negotiation process, as well as in the implementation of the Paris Agreements, humanitarian issues – the repatriation of refugees and displaced persons and the release of prisoners of war – were perhaps the only ones on which early agreement and delivery could be achieved by the four parties, including the Khmer Rouge (Party of Democratic Kampuchea – PDK). Conversely, they could have been fatal to the Peace Plan as a whole had the parties refused to cooperate. In fact, the principles and operational modalities adopted in 1989 were scrupulously respected by all the Cambodian parties in the late 1991–1993 implementation phase, even though other provisions of the peace agreements were being blatantly violated. As a result, all prisoners were set free in early 1992 and all refugees returned in freedom, without a single serious accident or deliberately disruptive incident, by April 1993.

INTEGRATED OPERATIONS AND INDIVIDUAL MANDATES

Why was this possible in the case of Cambodia or, for that matter, in Central America and particularly El Salvador, virtually at the same time?

Firstly, as UNHCR had been insisting for a number of years, the Paris Conference process (1989–1991) adopted an integrated and comprehensive approach where humanitarian and human rights facets were perceived and

---

[1] Director, Policy Planning and Operations, United Nations High Commissioner for Refugees, Geneva.

resolved in conjunction with their root causes, that is in the framework of an overall political and military agreement.

Secondly, the implementation process was likewise integrated. The solution of the refugee problem and, whenever possible, of the problem of internally displaced persons, the release of prisoners of war under International Committee of the Red Cross (ICRC) supervision and the active promotion of respect for human rights – including institution-building, release of prisoners, creation of an investigatory and independent prosecution capacity – were integral parts of the United Nations Transitional Authority in Cambodia (UNTAC) mandate and structure. Although, or perhaps because, UNHCR had been in Cambodia for a decade and had commenced its preparatory work in the UN Advance Mission (UNAMIC) days, it had no difficulty in merging with UNTAC on 15 March 1992 and in becoming its first operational arm.[2] UNHCR cooperated closely with the Military, Civilian Police and Electoral Components of UNTAC, as well as with the Human Rights, Civil Administration and Information/Education Components in ensuring the free, safe and dignified return of over 370,000 refugees. The Human Rights and Military Components of UNTAC were mutually reinforcing. In fact, the first UNTAC contingent – a self-contained Malaysian Ranger battalion – arrived ahead of schedule in late March 1992 in order to provide escort and security to the early repatriation convoys, an essential role which the military performed with distinction throughout the operation. UNHCR also provided an important link between UNTAC, UNDP and WFP (which also had other functions as part of the cantonment and demobilization mandate), UNICEF and a host of non-governmental organizations that acted as its operational partners.

With a view to increasing the ability of UNHCR to respond swiftly and in a non-bureaucratic fashion to changing realities, the High Commissioner delegated ample policy and operational authority to a senior Special Envoy who assumed regional responsibility for the repatriation operation and who was also appointed by the Secretary-General as UNTAC Director for Repatriation.

The importance of good personal relations among senior UN staff in achieving success in such a large and multi-faceted undertaking should not be underestimated. Indeed, the remarkable degree of integration and coherence was largely due to the equally remarkable team spirit and empathy that existed between the various key figures within UNTAC and in other branches of the United Nations.

Thirdly, it was essential for the two humanitarian agencies – UNHCR and the ICRC – that had specific roles assigned to them in the Comprehensive Political Settlement to ensure, at all times and *vis-à-vis* the four parties to the Cambodian conflict, that the independent, neutral, non-political and impartial nature of their humanitarian concerns and action was preserved, perceived

---

[2] The UNHCR-led repatriation operation was entirely funded through voluntary contributions of almost US$120 million, that is separately from the UNTAC-assessed budget. This risky approach proved to be the right one and provided UNHCR with an early and essential financial operational and administrative independence.

and respected by all. Equal treatment of all affected populations and strict respect of their freedom of choice also called for even-handedness and firmness in the dealings with the four Cambodian parties. Contrary to the unfortunate simultaneous experience in the former Yugoslavia, fundamental principles, such as free access, presence and movement for the agencies, freedom of choice and of movement for individuals and non-linkage and non-conditionality of protection and assistance had to be, and indeed were, recognized and observed by all. In other words, full cooperation on the ground at every stage of such a tortuous implementation period was predicated on the ability of humanitarian agencies to establish and maintain their credibility and build confidence with the parties.

In this context, the increasingly acute problem of potential confusion stemming from the integration of humanitarian and political or military operations comes to the fore. Indeed, what was described above as a successful, integrated achievement could also have led to a tragic failure, had the distinction between mandates not been preserved. Soon after the establishment of UNTAC, the Khmer Rouge became suspicious and later utterly hostile towards the Transitional Authority, to the extent that it estranged itself from the peace process, refused to canton, disarm and demobilize its troops, did not participate in the electoral campaign and general elections, launched a major information campaign vilifying UNTAC and eventually carried out numerous aggressive actions against UNTAC's military and civilian personnel. On its part, and with the full cognizance and support of the Special Representative of the Secretary-General, UNHCR – even though it remained at all times the humanitarian component of UNTAC – was able to maintain its impartial identity and its channels of communication with the Khmer Rouge. The objectives were clear and of paramount importance for the success of the Peace Plan as a whole:

- all the refugees in Thailand, especially the tens of thousands sheltered in Khmer Rouge-controlled camps, required protection from manipulation and forcible return – practices which had turned into a scandalous pattern over the years – and had to be given the possibility of freely choosing the time and means of return as well as their final destination inside Cambodia;
- returnee convoys – there were, in total, nearly 500 by road, river, railway and air – reception centres and areas of settlement had to be protected from any sort of threat or attack;
- all those who freely opted to return to areas under Khmer Rouge control had to be permitted to do so, with UNHCR logistical support and unhindered monitoring;
- all those returning to State of Cambodia (SOC)-controlled areas should not be molested in any way on account of their reasons for leaving the country or for their stay in camps in Thailand administered by factions belonging to the former Coalition Government of Democratic Kampuchea (CGDK).

The attainment of these goals, which after the fact may appear as having been easy, was in fact fraught with danger. It would be a mistake to believe that they were all attained simply as a result of UNHCR's ability to maintain dialogue, negotiate with and secure compliance from the Khmer Rouge. In fact, as much energy had to be invested in keeping the other parties fully informed of every step taken and in securing their own cooperation. The then State of Cambodia (SOC) Party, for instance, extended full assistance in the return, registration, transit and onward transportation of those refugees wishing to settle in the Khmer Rouge area. This was to their credit and clearly indicated that, even at a time when cease-fire breaches and political violence were rampant, repatriation and the way in which it was conducted were, as all parties – including SOC – recognized, an important factor of national reconciliation. By October 1993, it had become clear that the 370,000 refugees returning from Thailand, Indonesia, Vietnam, Malaysia and other countries, who were or who could have been perceived as "opponents", "enemies", "fifth-column", "agitators" or "saboteurs", were in fact welcomed as brothers and full-fledged citizens. This was possible, thanks not least to the generosity and maturity of the Cambodian people themselves, to UNHCR/UNTAC's effective mass information campaign and to the strenuous efforts deployed by UNHCR in depoliticizing the refugee question after over ten years of punishment and exploitation of the uprooted civilian populations.

Last, but not least, the role of Prince (now King) Norodom Sihanouk deserves special mention. There is little doubt that without the personal interest he displayed since late 1991, his involvement with and overwhelming influence on the parties – including, in particular, the Khmer Rouge – and his attendance of and supportive public statements at repatriation-related working meetings and ceremonies, UNHCR would have faced even greater difficulties.

COMPATIBILITY OF TIMETABLES

The suggestion was made in early 1992 that the "humanitarian timetable" should not be made to adhere to the "political timetable". Put differently, it was felt by some that the return of refugees should not be rushed, that the populations in camps in Thailand and elsewhere should be given time to reflect and make an informed choice and that all preparations – including a lasting cease-fire and significant progress in the de-mining of agricultural land – ought to be in place before proceeding with full-scale repatriation. The Government of Thailand was also alleged to have exerted pressure on UNHCR with a view to hurrying the return of refugees.

Such views did not take into account the impatience prevailing in camps in Thailand where, by mid-1992, UNHCR was bitterly criticized by the refugees themselves for what they considered too slow a pace of return.

Moreover, humanitarian agencies cannot expect to have it both ways, as it were, calling for the solution of humanitarian problems in the context of comprehensive political settlements while at the same time claiming entitlement to a separate treatment of, and a different timetable for, those very humanitarian issues. Non-compliance with the electoral calendar would surely have put the entire peace plan in jeopardy.

Finally, UNHCR, its NGO partners and UNTAC had taken all possible precautions with a view to reducing to a minimum the risks incurred by returnees in terms of their physical security, of their legal protection, of health and mine hazards, of the state of roads and other communications infrastructure, of their children's education, etc. The outcome proved wrong all the prophecies of doom. Seeking to achieve near-perfection in reception and reintegration conditions for returnees would have been perceived as a provocation by the majority of the Cambodian population that had, in relative terms, been worse off than those living in exile benefiting from international assistance. In fact, it is to the credit of the receiving Cambodian communities — especially relatives — that returnees were by and large welcomed and supported in their readaptation to normal life and that the aid provided to them by UNHCR did not generate a rejection syndrome.

REPATRIATION, REINTEGRATION AND PROBLEMS OF INTERNAL DISPLACEMENT

As this is an evaluation of the humanitarian efforts following the Peace Agreements, it is in order to analyse the way in which, despite the successful repatriation as such, the reintegration of returnees may have been complicated by the less than full implementation of the Agreements' provisions.

Cease-fire violations

Clearly, the non-respect of the cease-fire since early 1992 — following the disturbances in Phnom Penh in preceding weeks — coupled with the failure of cantonment, disarmament and demobilization, led to a general climate of insecurity and to the emergence of areas of chronic military activity, such as Kompong Thom, certain areas of Siem Reap and Battambang Provinces. More recently, the offensives launched in August 1993 in Banteay Meanchey province by the Cambodian Armed Forces, later in the northern areas of Siem Reap and Preah Vihear Provinces and, in March–May 1994, in the eastern part of Battambang Province, by the Royal Armed Forces against Khmer Rouge strongholds, reminded the civilian population that instability was still a fact of life in parts of Cambodian territory. In fact, such fighting caused the renewed uprooting of civilians and led large numbers to again flee to Thailand, albeit for a short duration. However, low-intensity military conflict in Cambodia since the adoption of the Peace Plan did not deter the resolve of Cambodian refugees to return home. Fighting did make the return of thousands of families to their places of origin risky as a result of on-going military activity or because it rendered impossible the de-mining of areas adjacent to the conflict zone. Many of those families became, as a result, internally displaced persons, despite UNHCR's systematic attempt to find alternative solutions.

Anti-personnel mines[3]

The slow pace of de-mining of arable land in more peaceful areas was also one of the factors that made reintegration of returnees problematic. There is little doubt that a massive investment of financial and human resources is called for at the earliest possible stage of an operation of this magnitude in a war-ravaged country. If contributing countries are not prepared to make their own mine-clearance teams available, the provision of international instructors should be a top priority so as to train as many national soldiers, NGO staff and officers as swiftly as possible and reconvert them into able and relatively well-remunerated de-mining experts who, after operating under foreign supervisory teams, could fully assume the task of de-mining the land they themselves mined in the first place. In parallel with this organized and national capacity-building effort, agencies such as UNHCR, UNDP, UNICEF and WFP could join forces and pool funds with specialized non-governmental organizations to help bridge the gap. Until the Cambodian Mine Action Centre (CMAC) became operational, UN agencies and major NGOs such as Handicap International and Halo Trust in the first instance, and Norwegian People's Aid and Mine Action Group later, resorted to *ad hoc* arrangements that were certainly commendable but in many ways amateurish.

This approach is simply no longer acceptable. It is to the credit of mine-awareness and "no-go areas" campaigns that anti-personnel mines claimed comparatively few lives among returnees and resettling internally displaced persons. Although this encouraging result is another clear demonstration that a responsible approach to insecure humanitarian environments can effectively protect civilian populations, a radically different strategy is necessary. But limiting criticism to the response of the UN and other potential international actors would be unfair without recalling the primary responsibility national actors have in bringing about a peaceful environment conducive to the effective clearance and destruction of anti-personnel devices, instead of re-mining areas which had been painfully cleared.

At the international level, a coordinated effort involving governments, international organizations – including, primarily, the ICRC, the UN Secretariat, and other relevant UN programmes and specialized NGOs – and the media has, at long last, brought about some progress towards the revision and strengthening of the existing 1980 Convention on Prohibition or Restrictions on the Use of Certain Conventional Weapons and particularly of its protocols on the use of mines, booby traps and other devices. Efforts to restrict the indiscriminate use of anti-personnel devices appear futile as long as their production and export is not regulated, effectively monitored and eventually banned.

The problem of land

The lack of sufficient arable land for returning rural refugees is not only due to the continued existence of areas of active or sporadic conflict and to the

---

[3] The author was, from October 1992 to April 1993, Director *ad interim* of the newly-created Cambodian Mine Action Centre (CMAC).

related problem of landmines. The mistaken assumption by UNHCR that an average of 2.5 hectares of land could be made available to each returnee family with a rural background, coupled with lack of cooperation on the part of some authorities at the provincial, district, commune or village level, was often the source of difficulties in securing and preparing agricultural land for returnees in Cambodia. This demonstrates the problem of relationships between central and local authorities and of the limited influence that the former can exert on the latter, particularly in the case of Cambodia, where years of conflict have enhanced the autonomy and powers of provincial civilian and military governments. In the then State of Cambodia areas, where the majority of refugees were returning, Prime Minister Hun Sen and his ministers were entirely supportive of the agreed policy of providing available land free of charge to returnees with a rural background. Their ability, however, to translate that support into reality at the village level varied from province to province and from district to district. This, of course, increased the dependence of certain categories of returnees on continued food assistance and reduced their ability to attain self-sufficiency. In areas controlled by the three so-called "resistance" parties, no particular problems were encountered. In this respect UNHCR remains committed, well beyond the conclusion of the repatriation operation as such, to the identification of land and its allocation – including titles – to returnees. Renewed efforts were made in the post-electoral period with the help of the Government of the Kingdom of Cambodia.[4]

Rehabilitation and QIPs strategy

This is one of the main reasons – but certainly not the only one – why UNHCR launched with UNDP and NGOs an ambitious, albeit financially modest, Quick Impact Projects (QIPs) programme in Cambodia. The "QIPs for land" approach was often used as an incentive to greater cooperation at the village level. UNHCR had, by the end of 1994, invested over US$10 million in nearly 100 QIPs covering ten sectors of assistance. Projects were undertaken in all of the 21 provinces of Cambodia and – in the pre-elections phase – in the three areas controlled by parties abiding by the Peace Agreements. Among the projects funded were the repair or construction of tertiary roads, bridges, hospitals and dispensaries as well as schools. Hundreds of wells and ponds were dug. QIPs funded preparation of large areas of land, including the provision of rice seeds and, where appropriate, fertilizer. Vegetable seeds were also provided to tens of thousands of vulnerable families. Moreover, large quantities of fishery equipment, water jars and mosquito nets were distributed. Income-generating activities included the provision of start-up loans. Targeted assistance was also extended, through specialized NGOs, to vulnerable families, such as the elderly, female heads of households, orphans and amputees.

These joint endeavours have significantly contributed to facilitating the dignified reintegration of returnees and IDPs within their receiving

---

[4] In El Salvador, the problem of land for returnees, which (unlike Cambodia) was scarce and expensive, nearly derailed a hard-won and fragile peace settlement.

communities. Indeed, the impact of QIPs far exceeds the limited investment involved. With the experience gained in the joint UNHCR/UNDP scheme in Cambodia, it is our firm belief that rehabilitation activities of this kind are an essential consolidating ingredient in the early stages of implementing a comprehensive peace settlement, especially in countries affected by protracted warfare. The need for immediate, modest and concrete inputs in the sectors of communications, water, education, health/nutrition, shelter, community services, land preparation and crop production, sanitation, livestock, small start-up loans and assistance to vulnerable categories of persons – including war victims – is beyond dispute. Moreover, such visible and, whenever possible, labour-intensive assistance provides a tangible confirmation of international concern to uninformed populations residing in remote and often sorely affected rural areas. Last but not least, Quick Impact Projects constitute an important bridge between, on the one hand, relief assistance and, on the other, reconstruction and development aid, for which no significant cash contributions can be expected before lasting military and political stability is achieved.

It should be noted, however, that apart from the UNHCR/UNDP QIPs programme and other rehabilitation activities of UNICEF, WFP, ILO and the NGO community, which were modest by definition, UNTAC lacked – in the crucial 1992–early 1993 period – a dynamic rehabilitation policy, as well as the means to carry one out. In recognizing UNTAC's many successes, one should draw lessons from its failures. Similar comprehensive operations should in future include a rehabilitation strategy covering the entire country – in a politically impartial and even-handed manner – and all categories of vulnerable populations, commencing as early as possible after the signature of a peace agreement. Violations of the cease-fire and the consequent non-demobilization of unpaid troops, coupled with the absence of any far-reaching rehabilitation and employment scheme, led to a pervasive phenomenon of banditry. Criminality in Cambodia became as dangerous a threat to the security of the people as military activity.

CONCLUSION

An examination of a number of broader issues affecting the population as a whole, including returnees, could shed an interesting light on the Cambodian humanitarian experience and provide a fitting conclusion for this brief review.

UNTAC, like ONUSAL in El Salvador, was in many different ways a pioneering peace-making operation. More so, since it included a Human Rights Component that was expected to deliver concrete results in terms of dissemination and education, institution-building, legislative development, prevention of political violence and even penal enforcement. It is in this broader human rights and "rule of law" context that the lasting solution to humanitarian problems must be pursued. In the case of Cambodia, returnees as such were not more exposed to human rights abuses than the rest of the population. UNTAC was given the most comprehensive human rights mandate ever entrusted to a UN peace-keeping operation. A key aspect of UNTAC's human rights-monitoring role related to the treatment of minorities and other vulnerable groups, including returnees. Of particular concern were the constant racist attacks, both verbal and physical, against the Vietnamese minority in Cambodia. Regrettably, UNTAC was not able to prevent widespread anti-Vietnamese rhetoric and violence, but took successful steps to investigate and publicize such attacks, to limit their scale and whenever possible to identify the perpetrators.

Many observers of the Cambodian peace process questioned the possibility of organizing free and fair elections in the absence of respect for fundamental human rights, disarmament and the effective control of security forces, in short of a neutral and non-violent political environment. This argument was often used to criticize the "hurried" return of refugees. The answer to those legitimate doubts was, to some extent at least, given by the enthusiastic way in which Cambodians participated in the electoral campaign and by their massive turnout at polling stations in late May 1993. This, in itself, was an impressive achievement, even though electoral results would probably have been different had the environment that surrounded the run-up and the actual polling been truly neutral, which was far from being the case. The successful electoral registration of returnees – as well as the flexibility displayed by the Electoral Component in the pre-registration of those remaining in camps abroad in early 1993 – was an important factor in demonstrating the seriousness and impartiality with which UNTAC implemented its political mandate.

Lessons must also be drawn from ways in which UNTAC discharged the unprecedented "direct control" function entrusted to it by the Agreements. The vague definition of what turned out to be a "mission impossible", requiring UNTAC to exercise an unspecified trusteeship over the five key areas of defence, public security, finance, foreign affairs and information, put the UN in an unenviable position. This could well be, in future, a determining executive role for the United Nations to play in creating an effective neutral environment conducive to the peaceful resolution of internal conflicts. The UN "direct control" function which supposedly gave it actual authority during the transitional period – in conjunction with a ceremonial rather than executive Supreme National Council – was the magic formula that brought a decade of painful negotiations to a successful conclusion. However, while the Khmer Rouge invested all their hopes in UNTAC's ability to neutralize the administrative structure of the State of Cambodia, the latter deployed all its skills to prevent that from happening.

A major lesson to emerge from the UNTAC experience is that the establishment of a pluralistic and democratic society, especially in "convalescing states", is, by necessity, a tortuous, dynamic and long-term process. Hence, the unfairness of the mandate given to the UN to control, in the short-term, the uncontrollable. Suffice it to say that the Khmer Rouge problem, unresolved, continues to loom, like so many others, over the future of Cambodia.

As far as humanitarian efforts are concerned, it appears essential to the writer that a critical evaluation be carried out of the world community's performance in Southeast Asia and, particularly, in and around Cambodia. The policies pursued since 1975 in the areas of resettlement in third countries, of protection (or the lack thereof) and material assistance, be it in cross-border operations or in countries of asylum, deserves close scrutiny as we approach the end of two decades of international humanitarian involvement in Indochina. Did governments and international institutions contribute to perpetuating the outflow of Laotian and Vietnamese asylum-seekers, in particular through the level of assistance provided in first-asylum countries and their systematic resettlement? Did they do all that was in their power to protect successive waves of Cambodian refugees, ensure the neutrality of their camps and prevent their becoming the target of attacks by one party or political pawns in the hands of the other? These are only two of the many questions that must be asked and answered, in all honesty and impartiality, if the international community is to avoid repeating similar errors or omissions in on-going and future post-Cold War humanitarian crises.

23. Economics/Rehabilitation

Roger C. Lawrence[1]

INTRODUCTION

Let me begin by making some general comments on the way I see economic issues within the context of a peace-keeping operation. There are two separate ways in which economic support can advance the objectives of peace-keeping. The first is by bringing about improvement in material well-being, thereby enhancing local support for the UN operation. There is always a strong expectation from the populace that UN presence in their country will bring significant betterment to their lives. These expectations include enjoyment of human rights and participation in democratic processes. But improvement in their own material well-being is also an important aspect of these expectations. This, of course, is quite evident and obvious in the case of those who have suffered very severe degradation in their material well-being as a result of whatever situation gave rise to the need for the UN presence in the first place, and these needs are always recognized by the international community and addressed by emergency humanitarian assistance. But they extend beyond this group to involve the totality of the population in the country concerned.

A second way in which economic policies can be useful to peace-keeping is to allow external financial support to become a factor which encourages compliance by the main political actors with the political process that is being fostered by the United Nations. There are, to be sure, constraints on the linkage of economic assistance to political compliance: most humanitarian assistance cannot be so linked. Nonetheless, possibilities for such linkage exist and need to be fully utilized to promote the overall success of the UN mission.

THE NATURE AND SCOPE OF THE ECONOMIC INTERVENTION OF UNTAC

I now turn to the case of Cambodia. The first comment that needs to be made is that the nature and scope of the intervention of UNTAC in the economy of Cambodia was quite extraordinary. I will attempt to describe briefly the various interventions, which can be grouped under the five headings that follow.

---

[1] Deputy to the Secretary-General of the United Nations Conference on Trade and Development (UNCTAD), Geneva.

The exercise of direct control over finance: micro aspects

Article VI of the Paris Agreements required UNTAC to exercise direct control over finance. We understood this as requiring UNTAC to ensure that revenues of the four administrative structures were duly deposited in their respective treasuries, and that each individual disbursement from these treasuries was consistent with the Agreements: that is, with a neutral electoral environment. The central concern in this area was with respect to the SOC administrative structure. It was essential to ensure that its capacity to tax and spend did not become a means for financing the political activities of the CPP. This required us to control each act of expenditure undertaken by SOC, whether it be from the central Treasury or from provincial treasuries. As you can see, this was extremely intrusive in the operation of this administrative structure.

The exercise of direct control: macro aspects

A second dimension to the direct control over finance was its macroeconomic aspect. Here, the concern was solely with the SOC administrative structure and with the magnitude of its budget deficit, and the means through which the deficit was being financed: the large budget deficit of the State of Cambodia was being met in part by salary arrears, but mostly by currency creation. Currency creation, in turn, was the source of the high rates of price inflation which we found in Cambodia at the beginning of the mission and which continued during the first several months of the mission. Had we failed to act, it was entirely possible that we would have entered the electoral period with substantial numbers of civil servants not being paid and/or with inflation rampant. We did not wish to conduct elections in such an environment, and, more generally, reached the judgment that we had some responsibility for ensuring that a reasonably orderly economy was in place during our presence there.

Rehabilitation

A third area was rehabilitation. As you are all aware, the Declaration on the Rehabilitation and Reconstruction of Cambodia was an integral part of the Paris Agreements. The objective was to address, through external assistance, immediate and urgent needs while laying the groundwork for future reconstruction and development.

A part of rehabilitation activities was effected through direct UNTAC action. For example, where access to parts of the countryside by UNTAC military or by election officials required the repair of roads and/or bridges, this was done.

However, the bulk of the rehabilitation effort had to be financed outside the UNTAC budget, with funds raised from the donor community. UNTAC therefore proceeded to identify needs and draft an appeal for funding to meet those needs. At a donors' conference in Tokyo in mid-1992, donors pledged resources that more than met UNTAC's assessment of needs. This was an important expression of political support at a critical stage in UNTAC's mission.

Management of natural resources

When I arrived in Cambodia, I frankly did not imagine that we would be involved in the management of natural resources. However, it soon became clear that it would be quite difficult to seek assistance for rehabilitation from the donor community in circumstances in which important Cambodian resources were being used in a way not directly related to rehabilitation or the peace process. Moreover, it appeared that a substantial proportion of available natural resources might be depleted before an elected government could establish policies with regard to their exploitation.

Decisions in this area were also driven by two other considerations. One was the very keen interest of His Majesty King Sihanouk in forest preservation, and that of course must not be underestimated. The other was that restrictions on resource exploitation were believed by some to be a way of reducing the ability of the Khmer Rouge to secure financing through gem and timber sales. The result of all these considerations was the decision by the SNC to ban the export of round logs and gem stones, and to place the export of sawn timber under UNTAC control.

Human resource development and institution-building

The fifth and last area in which we intervened was in human resource development and institution-building. During the first months of the mission, we found that the conditions necessary for the effective exercise of direct control over finance did not really exist. In order to put ourselves in a position of executing our own mandate, we had to bring about certain changes in both human skills and the institutional arrangements that existed in the largest administrative structure, that is, the State of Cambodia. These activities continued throughout the mission, and in its final months were broadened to include training of members of all factions in many of the skills necessary to manage economic policy.

THE EXERCISE OF DIRECT CONTROL: HOW SUCCESSFUL WAS IT?

Let me now briefly evaluate our activities under the exercise of direct control over finance and draw some lessons from our experience. How successful was this exercise of control? I think the overall answer is that it was quite successful. But there was a wide range of outcomes in the various areas of control. These included money creation, riel expenditure, riel revenue, dollar expenditure, dollar revenue and property transfers. Let me illustrate the different outcomes by referring briefly to three areas of control, situated at the two extremes of the things we did best and the things we did less well.

Money creation

The opening months of our mission were plagued by unacceptably high rates of price inflation. During May–August 1992 inflation ran at between 10 and 20% per month. The cause of this inflation was excessive money creation by the SOC authorities. By late September–early October we were able to establish ceilings for currency creation, within the framework of an IMF monitorable programme, and effective means for monitoring adherence to these ceilings. The SOC authorities abided by these ceilings, and in fact usually held money creation well below them. Consequently, money management ceased to be a source of inflation, and we were also in a position to certify that it was not a source of finance for political activities.[2] Our intervention here was a complete success.

Budget expenditure in riel

With regard to budget expenditure denominated in riel, I believe our efforts were also highly successful. We put in place a procedure through which all payment orders directed to the Treasury had to be validated by UNTAC staff located in the Finance Ministry. These staff undertook an examination of each individual request to withdraw money from the Treasury, to ensure that the proposed expenditure was compatible with UNTAC's mandate. When our financial controllers had determined that this was the case, a stamp was fixed on the payment order, and money could then be withdrawn from the Treasury against the payment order. The control procedure just described took place in Phnom Penh at the level of central government and also in each of the provinces, which had their own treasuries and could spend within their approved budgets. Indeed, the operations in the provinces were very important because it was here that most micro-expenditure took place.

In summary, expenditure in riel was very closely controlled, both in aggregate amounts and at the micro level. The one exception to this was the military. For reasons too complex to go into here, military expenditure was controlled at the aggregate level throughout, but at the micro level only after the elections.

Finally, I should like to comment briefly on a point made by Michael Doyle in the volume that General Sanderson has distributed to you.[3] In his paper, Doyle states:

In fact, what UNTAC was supposed to control, it did not. What UNTAC seemed to control – e.g. expenditure in the Ministry of Finance of SOC – on closer examination was a mere "front" for decisions taken elsewhere. Much of the SOC administration had collapsed and effective control had slipped to provincial governors and generals, so that "controlling" ministries that themselves did not control their nominal areas of responsiblity meant very little.

While this may be fair comment on other areas of control, it misses the essence of our procedures and thus does not apply to the exercice of control over finance. It did not matter to our system of control where the actual decision to spend money came from: it did not matter whether the political power to order expenditure lay with the Ministry of Finance, with a

---

[2] There was nonetheless a brief but sharp outburst of inflation in March 1993, but this was related to political events in the run-up to the election, and had no basis in money management.

[3] Hugh Smith (ed.) (1994) *International Peace-keeping: Building on the Cambodian Experience* (Australian Defence Force Academy, Canberra), pp.79–98.

governor of a province, with the Council of Ministers, or with a general's grandmother. The point was, whatever its origin, and whoever had the authority to order spending, the order had to be reviewed and approved by our controllers before money could leave the Treasury.

Property transfers

Let me now refer briefly to the question of property transfers, because this is at the other end of the spectrum, i.e. an area in which our operation exhibited some pretty significant shortcomings. We sought to put in place mechanisms through which the privatization of the assets of the State of Cambodia would be subjected to a procedure which allowed those transactions to be completely transparent. We never sought to prohibit the sale to the private sector of state property: our objective was to ensure that the State received fair value for any sales, and that all the proceeds were duly deposited in the Treasury.

It was not until early 1993 that we were able to put forward precise and detailed procedures governing the disposition of public property. It soon became obvious, however, that we were not going to secure compliance by all administrative structures in the implementation of this procedure. We thus went to the SNC and had them adopt a resolution stating that it was the SNC's view that any property transfers taking place outside this procedure would not be recognized by the future elected Government. In this way, we put buyers on notice that deals reached without reference to our procedures might produce large losses. This worked well, in that, as far as we know, there were no further sales of state property. But it could not deter internal transfers of property from SOC to CPP, and such transfers continued, much to our embarrassment. Flagrant instances of this sort were taken up with the SOC authorities, but without concrete results. In this particular aspect of control it must be said that we were not successful.

WHY WAS THE EXERCISE OF DIRECT CONTROL OVER FINANCE RELATIVELY SUCCESSFUL?

Let me now make some comments about why the exercise of direct control over finance was generally successful.

A first point is that — as mentioned earlier — we recognized at the outset that SOC's own administrative control procedures were inadequate for our purposes. Therefore, if we wanted to exercise any kind of control over that administration, we had to move hard and fast to put in place the necessary mechanisms and procedures. Right from the start we engaged in a very intensive technical assistance effort designed to reshape procedures, train those involved, and generally make sure that the minimum requirements for the exercise of control were there. Outsiders cannot exercise control over an administration that is not in control of itself.

A second point is that we tried, to the extent possible, to politicize compliance — that is, to make it politically expedient for administrative structures to comply with our control, and politically costly for them not to comply. A good example is the case of money creation. During the first months of the mission – a period characterized by rapid inflation – my colleagues and I consistently and publicly took the view that inflation in Cambodia was the direct result of the monetary management of the SOC authorities. The SOC authorities objected to this analysis, and took the view that inflation in Cambodia was the result of the presence of UNTAC and its expenditures. We simply did not accept this line of argument and continued to insist on the role of monetary management. This eventually created an atmosphere in which the continuation of inflation in Cambodia would be politically costly to the SOC authorities, and in which it was politically expedient for them to abide by UNTAC's control – since thereafter inflation, if it persisted, could be attributed to UNTAC's management of control.

A third factor which I think explains our relative success was the extent to which we were able to develop linkages between compliance and external assistance. We did this primarily through our association with the Bretton Woods institutions – the World Bank and the International Monetary Fund (IMF). In the case of the World Bank, for example, a finding by UNTAC that the SOC administrative structure was under UNTAC financial control was a condition for disbursement written into the draft loan agreement. In addition, the Special Representative informed the SNC that there would be no disbursement of this proposed loan until UNTAC was satisfied with its exercise of direct control of finance in Cambodia. Equivalent arrangements characterized IMF activities in Cambodia. There can be no doubt that the linkage between the activities of these institutions and the exercise of control over finance by UNTAC facilitated the latter. More generally, I believe that such conditionality can be a useful tool in peace-keeping operations. Indeed, the role that can be played by conditionality associated with economic assistance is a significant unexplored issue in the area of peace-keeping.

HOW SUCCESSFUL WAS REHABILITATION?

The pace of delivery of rehabilitation assistance in Cambodia disappointed many. This is in part because the performance of donors was not everything that it could have been. But disappointment was also the result of unrealistic expectations regarding what could be accomplished. Large amounts of money were pledged for Cambodia at the Tokyo donors' conference, but not everyone appreciated the distinctions between pledges, commitments and disbursements, or was familiar with the complexity of the time-consuming procedures that had to be followed by national donor agencies to transform a pledge into a commitment, and a commitment into a disbursement. It was in fact never realistic to expect that all the monies pledged at the Tokyo conference would be disbursed during the transition period, despite efforts by many donors to accelerate their own procedures. Nonetheless, there was a distinct slowdown in the first half of 1992 in the presentation by donors of new assistance projects. Was this, as some thought, a case of donors getting cold feet because of the apparent deterioration in the peace process? Or was it a case of deliberate conditionality of the sort I referred to earlier? I will not attempt to answer this question, in part, at least, because I believe the answer would vary from donor to donor.

CONCLUDING COMMENTS

Finally, two very brief comments. Someone yesterday said that the impact of UNTAC could be measured by what happened after the mission. I believe this is right, and on this score those responsible for the exercise of control over finance can hold their heads high. The measures for expenditure control that we put in place are still being used by the Cambodian authorities, and are still fully effective. Also, macroeconomic stability continues in Cambodia: for example, the exchange rate of the riel right now is not very different from what it was in December 1992. I think that all of this speaks well for both the mission itself, the way in which the Cambodian authorities have been able to build on it, and the continued support of the Bretton Woods institutions.

Let me also comment on some staffing issues. We understood from the outset that the key people in the mission dealing with the exercise of control would have to be drawn from national governments and would have to have had extensive experience in their own national administrations in the kind of activities that we wanted to undertake in Cambodia. The first step that I took was to assemble two or three people around me who had had long experience in their own countries in the areas of budget, taxation, and customs. It was really left to those individuals to firstly come to a complete and full understanding of the administrative procedures that were in place, to conceptualize and devise the specific operational forms of the exercise of control, and to determine the skills that would be required to effect control. By and large, in the areas of customs, budget expenditure, and taxation we opted to bring in people with national administration experience. Thus, about half of our staff consisted of individuals with many years' experience in the customs administration of Australia, France and the United States, with many years' experience in budget control in Algeria and Tunisia, and with many years' experience in the internal revenue services of India and the United States, some of them at senior level. For most functions in the provinces we felt that people with general financial knowledge, sometimes coming from the UN, sometimes coming from outside the UN, would be fully satisfactory after having been trained by those with previous government experience. So we really had two levels of staff: the financial generalists and the national financial experts, and we placed them in a way that was appropriate, holding the specialized expertise in place in Phnom Penh and allowing it to be used in the provinces whenever the financial generalists who were assigned to the provinces found themselves in situations which they found hard to handle.

I mention these details in part because I noticed the following analysis in the paper prepared by General Sanderson:[4]

---

[4] *Op. cit.* n. 3, pp.15–31.

Too much was also assumed of the ability of the personnel who formed UNTAC to perform their assigned tasks. In the past, the UN has tended to rely on the international amateur rather than the trained professional ... To be very frank, many people were selected for UNTAC and elevated to positions for which they were not equipped by either training or experience.

I am not sure what part of UNTAC General Sanderson was referring to, but I wanted to assure you all that it was not that part responsible for the exercise of control over finance.

24. The Protection and Promotion of Human Rights

Dennis McNamara[1]

BACKGROUND

The provisions of the Paris Agreements on Human Rights were the most comprehensive and intrusive ever entrusted to the United Nations, not just in peace-keeping operations, but in the whole area of human rights. This was done, in part, owing to Cambodia's special history and, in part, because transitions to democracy within UN-controlled elections are essentially exercises in human rights implementation. Human rights were central to the transition, and to the move from conflict to peace in the broadest sense.

MANDATE

The mandate was essentially two-fold: firstly, to foster an environment in which human rights were respected, essentially for the purposes of free and fair elections, and secondly, in terms of the Agreements, to prevent the return to "policies and practices of the past". But Cambodia had suffered not just the atrocities of the Khmer Rouge but also authoritarianism and terrorism for decades, and had certainly never had any of the human rights standards which were spelled out in the Paris Agreements.

The authority given to UNTAC and to the Special Representative in this area was enormous. The human rights mandate was crucially linked with the disarmament provisions, with the direct administration control provisions, and with the conduct of elections. The imprecision of the Paris Agreements in some respects in this area in fact gave a flexibility which was beneficial.

It is interesting that although the implementation of the Agreements was challenged by the parties, including especially in the human rights area – and despite the criticisms that were subsequently received from a number of governments party to the Agreements – the provisions of the Agreements themselves were never seriously challenged by any government. They were certainly objected to by all Cambodian factions, the State of Cambodia and the Khmer Rouge of course, but also when we had to intervene with the other two factions, we often had the same sort of resistance and objection. The programme for human rights was essentially one involving human rights education, general oversight of human rights, investigation and, to use the words of the Agreements, corrective action.

The implementation of the human rights mandate suffered from many of the problems that were experienced also by other components. Human rights activities especially suffered from lack of resources. The Secretary-General's

---

[1] Director of External Relations, United Nations High Commissioner for Refugees, Geneva.

proposal to the Security Council allowed for ten professional staff to carry out this mandate (out of 18,000 total staff of UNTAC) on the basis that all UNTAC staff would share responsibility for human rights, and that in the field there would be no human rights staff, as UNTAC staff would take care of that. With the support of some governments, we were able to increase the staff of the component to some 15 at headquarters and one professional officer in each of the 20 provinces of Cambodia, which was vital. This was an inadequate but crucial network for human rights activities.

This is indicative perhaps of the view both within the UN and within many governments of the relative importance of human rights in general, and of human rights in peace-keeping operations in particular.

Human rights also suffered from the same delays in dispatch both of the entire UNTAC mission and of the various components of the mission, including, particularly, the Police (with which we worked very closely), the Military, and the Civil Administration Components. We suffered from this in terms of implementation. We were not fully active, as UNTAC, until September 1992, six months after the operation landed in Cambodia. That was a crucial six-month period, because during it we lost the support and the involvement of the Khmer Rouge, in particular.

We suffered also, as others, from the lack of continuity in planning. No members of the Human Rights Component were involved in the pre-UNTAC missions for the preparation of the human rights plan, and we did not have any advanced briefing or any strategy planning prior to our dispatch. We all arrived on 15 March 1992 and that was the first time we met as component Directors. Had we had advance strategy planning sessions, many of the problems that we found, including between components in that general structure, might not have occurred.

The gap between the plan and its implementors is one that also caused difficulties, particularly as we were unable to obtain any of the "travaux préparatoires" for the Paris Agreements. We had, of course, not been involved in this but we could have benefited from the analysis of what was intended in the implementation.

Still on the negative side, we dealt with an over-centralized and over-loaded UN administration. We had delays and difficulties in staff recruitment and in obtaining resources which were fundamental in carrying out our programme. In this respect, staffing of all components, and especially the leadership of the mission, was crucial. We saw generally a lack of basic human rights knowledge or background by the majority of UNTAC staff, in all components.

To counter this we endeavoured to set up training courses for our own colleagues, and particularly for the Police Component. The task was too vast — ten human rights officers could not attempt to properly brief 3,500 police and the key officers of the other components on human rights. Basic knowledge and understanding of many areas in an integrated peace-keeping operation is fundamental to avoid crucial differences in approach. We were also concerned that some staff in UNTAC who were government appointees very much reflected the fact that they came from and were returning to governments. Particularly in order to carry out a non-partisan human rights activity, it is very important that there is an international rather than a national perspective.

ACHIEVEMENTS

There were seeds sown in Cambodia in the human rights democratic area which are irreversible and which continue to flourish. Cambodia has signed more international human rights treaties than any other country in the region, as it consented to do in the Paris Agreements. The Government has signed seven international human rights treaties, and although it is not able to implement or report on them adequately, there remains an important framework for subsequent legislative and judicial reform.

All political detainees were officially released prior to our arrival, in accordance with the Agreements, and we were able to achieve some improvement of prison conditions. We provided a transitional criminal code in Cambodia, because of inadequacy of the existing legislation. It was not perfect by any means, but was a fundamental working law which we used and which should be revised. We undertook large-scale human rights education and training programmes with the Government and civil police officials. To do so we created a separate trust fund, and raised $1.5 million from donor governments for the trust fund, which enabled us to carry out training and education programmes.

In collaboration with the Information Division, we undertook large-scale mass information programmes on human rights throughout the country on radio, on television and in written form. We also had close cooperation with the electoral component, particularly in the human rights provisions of the code of conduct of the elections, where we collaborated in trying to prevent electoral violations.

During the period of UNTAC's presence in Cambodia, we recorded the killing of 440 Cambodians of ethnic Vietnamese descent, and of 633 Cambodians essentially by seemingly politically motivated acts of violence. Two hundred Cambodians were declared missing during the entire period. Fifteen UNTAC staff were killed and 67 wounded, again essentially by politically motivated acts of violence. The human rights component completed 1,300 investigations during its 18 months in Cambodia.

Acts of violence could be divided into two categories: political acts of violence by the SOC authorities against opposition parties, carried out by SOC military and police; and acts of violence by Khmer Rouge units against Cambodians of ethnic Vietnamese descent. In some cases, there were atrocities and massacres of civilians carried out on a very systematic basis by identified Khmer Rouge units. What was most concerning to many of us was that during our time in Cambodia, there was no single attempt by the authorities to take appropriate measures against those responsible for the killings and the violence, even when we had identified the perpetrators. There was no indication of any political willingness to take such actions. This situation led to the establishment, at our request, of a rather radical unit, the Special Prosecutor's Office. Though established by the Special Representative, it met with considerable opposition from many of my colleagues within UNTAC and from the authorities, in particular the SOC authorities who did not believe that this was a legitimate exercise of UNTAC's mandate.

It was essentially a last resort measure which came to fruition at the end of 1992, when Prince Sihanouk informed the Special Representative that, without attempts to curb the political violence, he would not return to Phnom Penh. In January 1993, the Office of the Special Prosecutor was established although, owing to official and internal opposition, UNTAC in fact only arrested three alleged perpetrators. Due to the non-functioning and political control of the judicial system in Cambodia, it was not possible to arrange a trial of those arrested. The detainees were eventually turned over to the authorities on the termination of UNTAC's mandate.

Apart from respect for a free press and the free expression aspects which were key parts of UNTAC's activities, two notable achievements were the authority given to the UN Centre for Human Rights to have, for the first time, an operational presence outside Geneva, and the nomination of a Special Representative provided for in the Agreements, to monitor human rights in Cambodia. In fact, within the Commission of Human Rights, a number of governments resisted the mandate of the Special Representative on human rights. The result was that we had a Special Representative without the full authority of the mandate as initially envisaged in the Paris Agreements. The Centre for Human Rights has finally been established in Cambodia, again after considerable delay.

FAILURES AND WEAKNESSES

Violations of human rights continue in Cambodia, according to the report by the Special Representative and other human rights observers monitoring the situation. The lack of accountability for official action continues essentially because of the non-existence of a functioning, independent judicial system and the failure to disarm the factions.

One question which needs to be clarified is the confusion which exists both within the UN and with some governments as to exactly what human rights they wish to have protected in these operations. When the mandate was drawn up, we essentially did not touch economic, social and cultural rights at all; we tried to function within existing political and civil boundaries. The lack of an effective enforcement mechanism in the face of non-cooperation by the key factions made this extremely difficult.

Potential conflict between the human rights and the political objectives of the mission were fundamental. The conflict between diplomacy and confrontation in which human rights are involved is not easily resolved. Lack of clear policy guidelines on human rights issues from both New York and from Geneva were noteworthy. Fundamentally, the failure to disarm the factions and the failure or lack of any effective control of the national security apparatus were among the main problems.

Another important aspect was the unwillingness of the Cambodian factions, after elections, to allow UNTAC a proper role in the Constitution-drafting process. The provisions of the Paris Agreements on the Constitution are clear, and some of those provisions have not been incorporated. It was very clear, post-election, that UNTAC's input was not particularly welcome. The Special Representative for Human Rights has pointed out that the new Constitution, for example, excludes any protection for Cambodians of ethnic Vietnamese origin. The inability (or unwillingness) of UNTAC to have more influence on the Constitution-drafting process was a failure in this respect.

In the post-UNTAC situation, there was a failure by the international community, particularly governments, as well as the UN, to give proper priority to, and investment in, institution-building in Cambodia. In a society which lacks all the basic institutions in terms of a functioning and trained judiciary, a functioning police force, or civil redress, there was a lack of priority given to the institution-building aspect. Without such a functioning system, the immediate response to political problems is the resort to military means, and that is what may well continue to happen in Cambodia. This is a field where the international community by and large has failed to invest properly.

SOME LESSONS FOR THE FUTURE

The human rights activities of UNTAC have had a mixed success: some things were achieved, and continue; others were not even seriously begun. In the process, many valuable lessons were learned, and it is regrettable that the international system, including the UN, did little to benefit from them. As the first fully operational peace-keeping Human Rights Component, there was much of value which might have helped to avoid many of the mistakes subsequently repeated in Rwanda and elsewhere.

25. UNTAC's Information/Education Programme

Timothy M. Carney[1]

MANDATE

The vital, central role of information received early and complete recognition. The two documents which provide the mandate for UNTAC treat information imaginatively. The Paris Agreements themselves deal with two basic aspects of information. The first is in Article 6 which puts the field, and the word "field" rather than just "Ministry" is operative, among the five areas under the direct control of UNTAC. The Agreements further deal with the notion of control of the "field of information" in Annex 1. That Annex also elaborates on the importance of UNTAC information in its treatment of the Electoral Component. The relevant sections stress the requirement for both voter education and ensuring fair access to the media for all political parties.

The UN Secretary-General's 19 February 1992 report cites information more or less explicitly in a dozen paragraphs. The role of information in fostering the goals of the Human Rights Component, of the Civilian Police and, of course, of both the Civil Administration and Electoral Components all receive mention. Paragraph 27 specifically notes that "establishment of a radio broadcast and print facilities ... may be foreseen". The choice of the subjunctive is a lesson to us all. Neither subjunctive nor conditional modes suffice to make clear the vital need for anything. And a subsequent paragraph noting that radio is the most efficient method to convey the UNTAC message proved, as we shall see, inadequate.

More intriguing is one of the final paragraphs which notes that the object of radio programming is to "establish and maintain UNTAC's credibility and thus to enhance its effectiveness", regarded as a "key element enabling the success of missions of this type". The Information/Education Division (INFO/ED) took that mandate at its word and ran with it.

STRUCTURE AND OPERATIONS

At its height, INFO/ED had a staff of 150, with about 45 international staff from 16 nations and a budget of US$7 million. INFO/ED was not a component but rather a "division" of the Office of the Special Representative of the Secretary-General. The head of the Division was formally "Advisor on Information to the SRSG".

My becoming Advisor on Information resulted from an 11 February interview with Mr Akashi. We discussed the secrecy of the ballot and the

---

[1] Deputy Assistant Secretary of State for South Asia Bureau, Washington DC.

vital need to ensure that Cambodians understood that secrecy. I broached an idea that had been gestating for some months, to the effect that secrecy must include not only the individual's own ballot, but that his village must be insulated as well by counting the ballots at a central point and not releasing results for individual polling places. The electoral law subsequently incorporated this notion.

An analysis unit made up of academic specialists on Cambodia who had field experience there and who spoke and read Khmer seemed a vital element of any information and education effort. After consulting with colleagues and friends in Cambodian studies, as of 31 March, a number of faxes and telephone calls had gained commitments from half a dozen to come on board. It took the Field Operations Division another six months to bring the last one into the country. The unit provided the necessary expertise to vet the factions' public statements and broadcasts and to explain Cambodia to senior staff. Its role in assessing UNTAC's image and credibility proved vital, resulting in several focused, confidential memoranda to senior colleagues about areas that needed their attention. Analysis staff played the vital role in Civil Administration Control Teams which Mr Benny Widyono has mentioned. During the actual election, staffers moved to key provinces, attached to the Civil Administration Provincial Director for the purpose of serving the electoral requirements.

The other three Units covered Control, Dissemination and Production. The Control Unit matched journalists and Cambodian academic specialists with diplomats and managers in an effort to achieve a synthesis that would meet the need to assess, for example, "fair comment" in the Cambodian context. The Dissemination Unit ensured that the radio, video and print output got to the UNTAC provincial offices for use in mobile video broadcasts and with provincial radio and TV stations. The production staff numbered over 100 and included a TV studio that produced an hour of TV a day at its height; and a print operation for banners, posters, handbills and comic-book educational skits and dialogues. Finally, the Production Unit passed the target of nine hours of new radio broadcast material daily in mid-April 1992, and went "live" for 15 hours a day on 12 May 1992, continuing until Radio UNTAC went off-air on 22 September.

RADIO VOICE

Considerable prior thought and planning had gone into the information effort. The Department of Information produced a mid-February paper on a possible radio facility. It argued for an FM network to cover all of Cambodia — a notion fatally flawed by the need to have multiple transmitters which would have been vulnerable to sabotage or simple theft.

Some concern in Washington centred on the possibility that the UN would "gold plate" the UNTAC operation. Thus, as of early 1992, a radio broadcast facility seemed excessive. But it took only a few days on the ground with exposure to the SOC media and to the rather more specifically targeted Democratic Kampuchea Radio, to convince all of the senior UNTAC staff and all of the Expanded Permanent Five representatives that the mission must have its own station.

In the interim, exploration with USIA in early March 1992 centred on the use of the Voice of America Royal Thai Government transmitter which broadcast from Bangkok on medium wave (AM) with a strength of one million watts, literally the "mother of all AM radio stations". A meeting at the Thai Foreign Ministry with then spokesman Sakthip Krairiksh followed that with colleagues in Washington. Preliminary results included a willingness by USIA to offer broadcast time, but only in the small hours of the morning. The effort came to fruition only after the SRSG wrote directly to the head of USIA and gained American agreement to UNTAC use of prime time, something which the Thais had readily offered. I signed for UNTAC in a July 1992 ceremony in Bangkok and Radio UNTAC was on the air from Bangkok on 31 July, supplementing the broadcasts of tapes given to the radio stations of the four factions. The Khmer Rouge never played a single one of our programme tapes.

Unfortunately the UN delayed its own broadcast effort. The Secretary-General himself doubted the necessity for a broadcast facility and told the senior staff during his April 1992 visit that he believed broadcasts on factions' transmitters and from neighbouring countries' facilities should suffice. It took three months to change his mind, a delay which the UN tendering and procurement process compounded. The first draft radio tender looked so unlikely of rapid completion that the SRSG authorized INFO/ED to negotiate with the SOC to acquire the use of an antique transmitter made surplus by completion of the Russian Federation transmitter project. Mr Akashi himself successfully finished the negotiations that resulted in UNTAC's beginning broadcasts in November 1992 from the old vacuum tube transmitter that served as a base facility until the end of the mission.

DIRECT CONTROL

Among the worthwhile prior planning documents was a UNESCO paper which included an idea for a consultative body on the media, readily adapted when INFO/ED decided to form a Working Group of all faction and independent media to discuss guidelines for the media. That Working Group responded to the distinction between areas requiring consensus, the principle on which subcommittees operating in the SNC framework operated, and bodies engaged in the five fields over which UNTAC had direct control. Even in the latter case, developing guidelines demanded the participation and acceptance of the results by all the players. For INFO/ED this proved ultimately vital when even the SOC became recalcitrant in accepting direct control in the wake of the Khmer Rouge refusal to join in Phase Two. Until the SRSG established directives relating to the election period itself, the "media guidelines" which the Media Working Group elaborated were the only documents UNTAC information control staff could cite that had all-party (except DK) acceptance. This proved particularly important in dealing with cases of defamation and the resulting right of reply and in arguing successfully for the importation of equipment to ensure a plurality of media. Both concepts figure prominently in the guidelines.

Control, however, never succeeded in realizing the goal of fair access to the media. Rather, UNTAC used its radio station and TV studio to give the electorate enough information about the political parties and then the political parties produced electoral programming to balance SOC's failure to grant fair access. This party information effort went forward in tandem with imaginative programming to assure voters that their vote would be secret and that the secrecy of the ballot was their shield against intimidation.

The electoral campaign itself marked a toughening of the direct control effort as the Division sent letters to media which defamed political opponents; refused to let two parties make radio tapes which included material that verged on racial hatred; ordered a particularly egregious newspaper offender to publish a letter from the Director of INFO/ED declaring the daily's treatment of FUNCINPEC defamatory; and asked the SOC authorities to justify use of their media for CPP advertising by showing receipts to confirm paid use of the state media.

LESSONS LEARNED

Seven lessons come from the Information/Education experience in Cambodia.

Radio

A UN mission in general must have it own voice. UNOMOZ would seem to have failed to understand this reality. The Field Operation Division (FOD) was notably deficient in answering this need for adequate transmitters for the UNOSOM II station in Mogadishu.

Mandate

Interpreting the mandate – more specifically, interpreting the implementation of a given mandate – demands flexibility. Historically the UN has been a "strict constructionist" concerning mandates. That is not adequate for modern operations. At the same time, a mandate cannot be realized without consensus on its measures of implementation by the concerned parties, as the media guidelines demonstrated in the Cambodia case.

Analysis

A politically knowledgeable analytical element, best based in the SRSG's office, is indispensable to avoid elementary mistakes in dealing with the host culture, and ensuring real-time understanding of public positions in nations where UN languages are not widely used. Mr Akashi took this lesson to heart and recruited a Yugoslav specialist to be part of his staff in former Yugoslavia.

Procurement/personnel

FOD, unsurprisingly, was desperately slow and inadequate in the Cambodia case. On the procurement side, even expanding purchasing authority in the mission area to US$500,000 proved inadequate for radio or TV. On the personnel side, the new idea of a UN reserve could partly address the problem of UN cronyism, as well as limiting the scope for Permanent Representatives to parachute their favourites into missions. This would also help realize the new developing "can-do" ethos of UN mission staff, a needed replacement for the historically rooted and, in the Cambodia case, still too common impulse of staff "to be" rather than "to do": that is, to be a D-2 or P-5 rather than to do a job that could subject a staff member to criticism and limit advancement.

Media themes

Regular meetings, about every six weeks with the SRSG, enabled a check on the direction of themes and for suggestion of new ones. The exclusive broadcast in Khmer usefully limited second-guessing and potential micro-management, as no senior or mid-level expertise in the language existed outside the INFO/ED Division. The down-side was a doubt among colleagues that the division was doing much of anything. Translation and screening of selected TV productions aimed to redress such ignorance.

Content

Timely, accurate and, above all, transparent programming as censorship-free as possible vitally ensured UNTAC credibility and built its audience. At the same time, a very careful political vetting of drafts, translations and final broadcasts by Khmer-speaking international staff ensured its political appropriateness on the basis of the Khmer-language text of the Paris Agreements.

Training

UN reporters who had reported on UNGA and UNSC sessions proved inadequate for the mix of news and features for Radio UNTAC. Needed aspects of training include elementary journalism, as well as the mechanics of radio and TV production.

26. Election-Monitoring: Preparation and Conduct

Professor Reginald Austin[1]

THE OBJECTIVES OF THE PARIS AGREEMENTS AND UNTAC

The Paris Agreements of 1991 for a "Comprehensive Political Settlement of the Cambodia Conflict" sought in essence to:

- "maintain, preserve and defend the sovereignty, independence, territorial integrity and inviolability, neutrality and national unity of Cambodia";
- "restore and maintain peace in Cambodia, and promote national reconciliation"; and
- "ensure the exercise of the right of self-determination of the Cambodian people through free and fair elections".

These objectives demonstrate a remarkable consistency with the priorities set out in the UN Charter, reaffirming as they did the conviction that state sovereignty is not only the basis of world order but is also inextricably linked with peace and democracy. Until the early 1990s the consistent and uniform implementation of the democracy and peace aspects of this formula was made impossible by the fundamental Cold War contradictions on the meaning of "democracy". With the collapse of the Soviet Union, a critical new consensus emerged, making it clear that democracy was understood to be based upon political pluralism and free and fair elections which would provide legitimate government. Where necessary, this electoral process could also ensure peace by replacing armed contest with political competition.

In Cambodia, the transformation from war to peace, from totalitarian to democratic government, was to be achieved by a dramatic and unprecedented degree of international intervention in the military, civil administration and especially the electoral affairs of "sovereign" Cambodia.

The instrument of intervention was to be the United Nations, in the form of the UN Transitional Authority in Cambodia (UNTAC).

THE BACKGROUND

To understand the extraordinary phenomenon of the intervention agreed to under the Paris Agreements, one needs to recall, briefly, the background.

Cambodia and its people are a classical victim of a combination of colonialism, undemocratic and idiosyncratic national leadership and the careless, cynical and brutal intervention which typified the Cold War era. From the 1960s, it suffered the consistent and growing ravages of internal and external war. Despite its attempts to maintain neutrality and non-alignment

---

[1] Legal and Constitutional Affairs Division, Commonwealth Secretariat, London.

in the bitter Indo-Chinese war, it was engulfed by its own corruption and the irresponsible power of others, in that maelstrom of mutual destruction. This came first as a "side-show" to the US–Vietnam war, then as a bizarre mix of extreme inhumanity, chauvinism and perverse Maoism of the Khmer Rouge Pol Pot regime, succeeded by its "eviction" by a Vietnamese "blitzkrieg" and culminating in the extraordinary collapse of the country into four territorially-based factions. This drastic situation was then compounded by the grotesque alignment of the "West", the ASEAN states and China with the three "resistance" factions (the Royalist FUNCINPEC, the republican KPNLF and the Khmer Rouge) on the one side, and the more predictable support of the Soviets and Vietnam for the ex-Khmer Rouge cadres of the CPP occupying/governing 80% of the country as the State of Cambodia (SOC).

Thus, by the late 1980s Cambodian sovereignty, like its infrastructure and any pretence of order, was almost totally shattered. The country was heavily armed and littered with millions of landmines. The only demographic certainty was the 350,000-odd refugees on the Thai border. All civil documentation had been destroyed, villages' and people's names had been changed, maps were unreliable, and everyone, civilian and soldiers alike, was the surviving victim of decades of savagery, intolerance, arbitrary authoritarianism and, for most young Khmer, quite literally, a lifetime of inhumanity in a fundamentally uncivil, undemocratic society.

It is remarkable that it was possible to develop any plan at all to deal with this prototypical "failed state". However, the combination of the Soviets' awareness of impending collapse, the non-Soviets' sense that an opportunity for radical change was at hand, and the sudden realization among the four factions that these, their sponsors, were serious about ending the supplies of arms and money, concentrated their combined minds amazingly. From self-destruction they moved their focus to self-determination as a solution. Their problem was that no faction would trust any other, or any combination of themselves to "hold the ring" during the transformation process from war to peace and through to democracy.

THE SNC AND UNTAC

The dilemma was resolved by a combination of Cambodian and international inventiveness and political will. The Cambodian key lay in the remarkable personality and survivability of Prince Norodom Sihanouk, the former King, Non-Aligned Movement champion, enemy and then ally of the republicans, the Khmer Rouge, the SOC and patriot *extraordinaire*. The remnants of Cambodian unity and identity were recognized to be symbolized in him by all four factions. This provided the basis for the creation of a critical legal fiction in late 1990 during the Paris conference process, namely the establishment of a Supreme National Council (the SNC). This body of 12, presided over by Prince Sihanouk, would represent both the "resistance" factions and the SOC incumbent in Phnom Penh. The Paris Agreements recognized it as "the unique legitimate body and source of authority in which, throughout the transitional period, the sovereignty, independence and unity of Cambodia are enshrined". Because of the continuing impasse between the factions, the real role of Prince Sihanouk was to maintain the deadlock and the balance of violence within reasonable limits, while UNTAC would "exercise the powers necessary to ensure the implementation of [the Paris] Agreements", including those relating to "the organization and conduct of free and fair elections and the relevant aspects of the administration of Cambodia".

In effect, while the SNC would provide the pretence of continued sovereignty, UNTAC was authorized by the Paris Agreement and the Security Council to secure, by its military and civilian presence, a cease-fire and demobilization plus a "neutral political environment" throughout Cambodia. In this "transformed" environment UNTAC would set up and operate an electoral machine to register voters, provide for multi-party organization, enable them to campaign, provide a secret ballot to voters and guarantee a proper and secure count. Thus it would deliver a Constituent Assembly resulting from a free and fair election. This Assembly would create a constitution based upon liberal principles set out in the Agreements and become a government to lead Cambodia on an irreversible course to democracy, stability and reconstruction with the UNTAC-certified endorsement of its voters and the recognition of the entire international community.

The novel civilian dimension of UNTAC, captured perfectly in the two words of its title "Transitional Authority", marked a decisive departure from earlier UN peace-keeping or electoral supervisory roles. The degree of intervention involved would have been unthinkable before UNTAC; its significance is that now, after Somalia, Rwanda, Liberia (and Haiti?), it may be indicative of future demands for UN intervention. The UNTAC operation and its outcome may also have revealed more clearly whether an even deeper and longer commitment will be necessary if the international community seriously believes that the establishment of democracy and stability are legitimate objectives and UN intervention the appropriate instrument in a post-Cold War world.

THE UNTAC STRUCTURE

Following the establishment of UNAMIC in November 1991, UNTAC arrived in Phnom Penh on 15 March 1992. Under the overall management of the Secretary-General's Special Representative, UNTAC consisted of several functional components. These were as follows.

The Military Component

This Component consisted of a Headquarters and initially battalions from Bangladesh, Bulgaria, France, Ghana, India, Malaysia, the Netherlands, Pakistan and Uruguay, plus two Indonesian battalions. These were joined in 1993 by a Japanese contingent of peace-keepers. Engineering, planning, communications, logistics and other military specialist units were also provided by, *inter alia*, Canada, China, Australia, New Zealand, Namibia and

Thailand. An elite group of Military Liaison Officers, operating as cease-fire monitors on a more or less individual basis, included officers, generally colonels, from other states including Member States of the Security Council.

The Civil Administration Component

This was made up of specialists recruited from governments or intergovernmental agencies. Its mandate was the direct supervision and control of the factions' administrations in the fields of Foreign Affairs, National Defence, Finance, Public Security, and Information. In fact Information control and supervision was undertaken by a Unit, headed by Tim Carney from the US State Department, set up in the Special Representative's office, as was the Finance Unit headed by Roger Lawrence of UNCTAD. The inability of the UN to identify and recruit appropriate and sufficient staff for this substantial task – virtually the shadow Government of a country in chaos – was a major difficulty for UNTAC. Its complexity and scope were clearly insufficiently appreciated by those who proposed and planned this aspect of the operation. One consequence of this shortcoming was that this UNTAC task, which should have brought supervision to all four "existing administrative structures" in Cambodia, was in fact visited exclusively upon the (admittedly dominant) structures of the SOC, first in Phnom Penh and, eventually, in its 20 other provincial capitals, but not on the other factions and, most notably, never upon the Khmer Rouge.

The UN Civil Police Component (CIVPOL)

CIVPOL was, with the Military and Electoral Components, the most ubiquitous UNTAC presence in Cambodia. Unlike the military, which was deployed in strictly national battalions under their own Sector Commanders reporting to General Sanderson, CIVPOL units were all multi-national, under the most senior officer among them. This was not the best arrangement for discipline and efficiency. Their (vast) task was "to ensure that law and order are maintained effectively and impartially, and that human rights and fundamental freedoms are fully protected". In a country where SOC's long-standing paramilitary (and enormous) secret police forces were never disbanded and the factions' armies never disarmed or cantoned, these objectives were, unsurprisingly, never achieved, despite the 3500 CIVPOL strength (eventually) deployed.

The Human Rights Component was something of an afterthought in the Paris Agreements

This was reflected in the provisions made for it under the Security Council's resolutions. Originally staffed only nominally and, despite the energetic efforts of its UNHCR-seconded head, Dennis McNamara, it remained under-resourced. More important, it lacked the necessary legal authority to monitor, much less redress, the widespread human rights violations in Cambodia during the mission.

The Refugee Repatriation Component

The UNHCR had been "in the field" for many years, dealing with Cambodian refugees, most of them in Thailand. Apart from the international legal and political aspects of the problem, the Paris Agreements themselves contained specific obligations regarding the return of refugees and their participation in the elections. The efficiency with which repatriation and resettlement was achieved, even in areas which remained dominated by the non-cooperating Khmer Rouge, was dramatic proof of the excellent capacity of the UNHCR in the field and the high quality of its staff and leadership.

The Rehabilitation and Reconstruction Component was created to respond to Annex 4 of the Paris Agreements containing the Declaration on the Rehabilitation and Reconstruction of Cambodia

This "requested" the Secretary-General of the UN "to help coordinate the programme guided by a person appointed for this purpose". The scheme was somewhat vague, envisaging its funding from donors and its direction from the Cambodians. The request for "a" person appears to have been taken almost literally by the UN, which appointed as Director of the component a former UNDP official of long standing, Berndt Bernander, without any staff beyond a secretary. After a couple of months the Component was subsumed into the office of the Finance Unit. Consequently, a minimum of rehabilitation was achieved during the UNTAC period. This was partly for reasons of limited resources. More important, it was politically impossible to pursue serious rehabilitation in the 80% of Cambodia controlled by SOC (where most of the destroyed infrastructure lay), without vehement objections from the "resistance" factions, especially the Khmer Rouge, and the danger of a loss of UNTAC's "neutrality". As a result, the existence of a totally ineffective UNTAC component also cost the UN some credibility and provoked some cynicism. More careful analysis and advance thinking in this issue, by both the parties to the Agreements and within the UN, might have avoided such problems.

The Administration was essentially the UN's own overall service management and delivery system for the mission

It dealt with the gigantic challenge of creating, out of less than nothing, the physical infrastructure. Offices, vehicles, fuel, furniture, materials, boats, aircraft, air navigation, warehouses, electricity supply, telephones, water, food, internal security, health and welfare, personnel recruitment and management and, where necessary, roads and any other basic or sophisticated needs of the mission which might arise, was Administration's mandate. All of this, the creation of the semblance of an up-and-running modern state, it was expected to deliver, operationalise and then extract, within 18 months. Little wonder that it failed to satisfy all the demands and expectations of it. It was headed by a senior officer of the Field Operations Division at the UNHQs, Hocine Medili, and remained, at all times, severely understaffed. This meant, from the particular point of view of the Electoral Component, that it was not able to deliver, through its Movecon Unit, the critical logistic capacity required by an election machine. In addition, the UN administrative procedures, bred in the process-oriented institutions of New York HQ, were totally inappropriate to the more result-oriented demands of the field-based electoral activities. Even in well-established, smooth-running, national electoral systems there is every reason to allow the electoral management to develop and run its own independent logistical, procurement and planning capacity. This applies *a fortiori* in *ad hoc* mission conditions where everything, at all stages, is operated on a crisis-management basis. This lesson was in fact learned and applied during the UNTAC mission. The Electoral Component evolved a *modus vivendi* by adopting (a) turn-key arrangements with private contractors for the procurement and delivery of electoral equipment for polling, and (b) engaging with the Military Component in joint planning of the logistical needs, for supplying and operating voting stations and counting centres, and relying for logistics almost exclusively on the UNTAC military.

The Electoral Component

The Component was recruited essentially from without the UN system. Its specifically electoral specialization involved drawing heavily upon expertise from countries with strong professional, permanent and independent Electoral Commissions, primarily Australia, Canada and India. Bangladesh, Pakistan and Zimbabwe, whence the author was recruited, were also drawn upon quite significantly. The Electoral Component was expected to create a credible and effective electoral service throughout Cambodia. This would establish and service the setting up of an effective electoral presence in all 170 districts and 21 provinces; assessing the essential material and logistical needs for staffing and materials for recruiting and training for registration; informing and motivating the population to register; ensuring the effective participation of political parties in registration, campaigning, voting and counting observation; establishing a computer-based registration system; conducting a campaign of voter education and awareness of political pluralism; convincing everybody that the electoral machine would be fair and the vote absolutely secret; ensuring a logistic capacity to deliver and return, first registration and then voting; equipment, materials and staff; planning and setting convenient and effective registration points and voting stations; recruiting, training and deploying its own international staff (70 provisional and some 460 district officers) as well as national officers (800 for registration and 50,000 for polling), and finally some 1000 international observers for the voting and counting, and ultimately surveying, establishing and equipping counting stations.

In this context special mention must be made of the role of the 460-odd District Electoral Supervisors, provided by the UN Volunteer Service. These volunteers, many of them recruited for development rather than electoral work, were crucial to the establishment of electoral credibility among the Khmer people. By their committed and constant "presence" in their districts, available to the voter on a 24-hour basis, they brought the election to life as an identifiable human reality in Cambodia. All of this electoral activity was envisaged, and initially planned, on the assumption that a cease-fire, combined with 70% disarmament and demobilization, would have been established. It was also assumed that the supervision and control of the Civil Administration would, in association with the work of the CIVPOL and the Human Rights Components, have created a "neutral political environment". In this context the "existing administrations" would not be able to use their civil powers "to directly influence the outcome of the elections", and "human rights and fundamental freedoms would be fully protected". This would mean that voters were protected from any intimidation or harassment which could undermine the freeness and fairness of the election, so that these impediments to a credible election would have been removed.

THE REALITIES

The reality was totally different. The election was, at all stages, conducted while war conditions prevailed everywhere. (It must be stated, however, that UNTAC was not initially the target of more than rhetorical and threatened violence.) The environment in all zones was physically hostile to and dangerous for the political opponents of the locally incumbent administration. This danger was absolute in Khmer Rouge zones, where no registration, campaigning or voting was possible. It was a serious problem in the CPP, SOC-administered zones, especially during the registration, campaigning and post-voting periods, but significantly less so during the polling itself. Normal electoral conditions were theoretically provided in the KPNLF and FUNCINPEC zones, but because of their proximity to the Khmer Rouge, CPP candidates did not dare penetrate those areas on the whole and even the "resistance" parties kept strictly within their small areas of control.

UNTAC: SOME ELECTORAL PROBLEMS AND SOLUTIONS

Security

By 30 June 1992 the cease-fire was expected to be in place and cantonment was due to commence. In fact fighting continued, especially between the NADK (the Khmer Rouge Military) and CPAF, the army of the SOC. In addition NADK acts of terrorism, primarily against Cambodians of Vietnamese origin, commenced. There were also occasional "kidnappings" of UNTAC Liaison Officers by the NADK. Nevertheless, preparations for registration continued, and by this stage the electoral infrastructure, at least in its human form, namely the 460-odd District Electoral Officers (DEOs), was in place in most parts. Only Preah Vihear, on the Northern Cambodia/Thai/Laos border, had not been properly deployed.

By December 1992 the security situation had deteriorated. At this point critical decisions had to be made, by both the UNTAC and the Security Council. In essence the two basic conditions for the fulfilment of the Paris process had failed: there was no cease-fire, no real cantonment nor demobilization. The Khmer Rouge's refusal of these, as well as its refusal to endorse the electoral law or participate in the election, had led to reciprocal military action by the SOC, which, together with FUNCINPEC and KPNLF, had formally committed themselves to the election. Most observers and the media predicted a blood-bath and disaster if UNTAC proceeded. It was argued that UNTAC should "cut its losses" and leave.

Despite those negative circumstances, there were still reasons for optimism. Such "peace election" transitional processes are typically risky and problematical. The electoral process often creates a "window of opportunity", because even the factions' soldiers, who often oppose it for fear of its transforming and pacifying consequences, may find it difficult to totally confront it. It is after all an expression of the people's will, and political movements (even if totally militarized) must take this into account. This was still true in Cambodia.

By December 1992 the NADK had still not attacked the totally vulnerable and virtually unprotected UNTAC civilian and electoral presence. Indeed there was some evidence of NADK soldiers registering as voters. More important and specific was the fact that, by this time, some five million Khmers had registered, despite threats, uncertainty and allegations of UNTAC's pro-Vietnam bias from the KR. There was now a totally new "party" to the Paris Agreements process: the Cambodian people. This made it virtually impossible for UNTAC to withdraw from the election and abandon them. Not surprisingly, the Security Council gave its support to continuing the mission. UNTAC was to stay and conduct an election for the Constituent Assembly.

One vital adjustment, in the interests of security, went with this Security Council decision: the Military Component would not (as planned) be reduced. It would retain its strength, provided originally to guard the cantoned and disarmed troops, to carry out the somewhat different task of guarding the election. This was a considerably extended exercise, since the election machine by definition seeks to reach out to every voter, rather than restrict itself to secure and convenient areas. But the UNTAC forces were given no augmented armament or equipment, or new rules of engagement. To help carry out its new task the military redeployed into sectors which matched the civil and electoral system more conveniently. This created a vital new relationship between Sector Commanders and Provincial Electoral Officers (PEOs) which was to provide an important improvement in communications and management for the election. It meant that critical electoral/security problems would be resolved where they could best be dealt with — at the sectoral level and not at HQ in Phnom Penh. Decentralization was the basic managerial policy of the Electoral Component.

Legal problems

The ability to carry out all the electoral tasks: planning, education, training, conscientisation, credible presence, registration, logistics, voting and counting, necessarily involved a tightly arranged sequence, with rigid lead times. Delay was thus a constant worry and a problem for the election process. It occurred first with recruitment and deployment of the basic electoral staff who were needed to assess, plan and set up the various aspects of the component, i.e. the Operations and Computer Unit, the Education and Training Unit, the Complaints, Compliance and Enforcement Unit and the Electoral Administration Unit. But the most frustrating and extensive delay was the delay in the finalization of the electoral law. This was drafted in New York in January 1992, by a team of three, who were eventually to be the Director and Senior Deputy Director of the UNTAC Electoral Component and the Legal Advisor to the Special Representative. After consultations, the law was presented, on April 1 1992, to the SNC for consideration. It was only passed, by the authority vested in the Special Representative, on 12 August 1992. This meant that four full months of electoral preparations were badly destabilised and deadlines undermined. In particular nothing in the way of manuals or regulations could be finalized until the law and its various consequences were certain.

The reason for the delay was UNTAC's understandable desire to allow the Cambodians to make representations and become more clearly the "owners" of the law. In the event, the KR rejected any association with the law and the other two "resistance" factions accepted it reluctantly as "80% satisfactory". Only the SOC found it unobjectionable. Both FUNCINPEC and the KPNLF, despite the interminable discussions before its adoption, continued to revisit and advocate their original objections well into the election campaign.

Their "problem" was not so much with the law as with the Paris Agreements which they themselves had ratified. They wished, contrary to the clear provisions of Paris, to exclude all non-Khmers, on a purely racial basis, from the franchise. This was also fundamentally contrary to the basic principles of the UN Charter. It was all the more absurd for being pressed for at precisely the time when South Africa was in the final stages of abandoning apartheid and the Bosnian Serbs were commencing their "ethnic cleansing" practices in former Yugoslavia. It would be impossible in a "document-cleansed" country to trace anyone's ancestry authoritatively and objectively. Nevertheless, the dialogue continued for four months. The racial franchise demand was eventually refused.

Other sources of delay included other attempts to amend the Paris Agreements with respect to the registration of voters, by extending it to Cambodians in foreign countries. This was eventually refused, although it was conceded that foreign polling stations would be provided in three locations abroad.

In September 1992, a proposal emerged demanding an additional election: for a President of Cambodia as well as for the Constituent Assembly. This was fundamentally contradictory to the entire idea of the Constituent Assembly, since it would have conceded, in advance, that the Head of State would be a President and would furthermore have identified that President before the Constitution itself was finalized. The proposition was essentially an interest of Prince Norodom Sihanouk's, supported by those who wished to please him. Eventually (in January 1993) it was energetically rejected by the Prince himself, on the stated ground that it had been criticized, for constitutional reasons, by the Australian Foreign Minister, Gareth Evans. Until this time UNTAC's practice of seeking to compromise with these "political considerations" promoted uncertainty and forced the Electoral

Component to dangerously postpone final procurement and other preparatory electoral activities.

Ultimately the electoral law emerged much as it had been drafted but, due essentially to the important uncertainty, at a considerable cost in the quality of electoral management, staff workloads and overall service.

Another problem involved the law and a typical practical electoral problem. It demonstrates the critical importance of absolute attention to detail in elections. The electoral law had provided that each political party would be able to place its own seal on each ballot box. The specifications provided by the Component to the manufacturers were wrong on this detail, and the boxes, as supplied, did not have space for these party seals. As was possible under the electoral law, the rule was then amended retroactively to exclude this requirement. One party, the CPP, objected on the grounds that other parties would tamper with the boxes and thus create serious doubts among the CPP supporters as to the credibility of the results. These could only be removed by the party itself proving that their own seal had been untouched. This unfortunate error in specifications, though it did not reduce the essential security of the boxes, which rested fundamentally on the integrity and independence of the neutral and constant guardians of the boxes — UNTAC — fuelled the paranoia of the CCP and its doubts (not uncommon in such elections) about the impartiality of the election supervisors. These doubts are usually connected with the simple fact that losing suddenly dawns on previously confident parties as a real possibility. The trauma of this is even greater when it dawns upon a party such as the CPP, which had held undisputed and total power for 13 years.

In Cambodia their fears were deepened by certain political decisions taken by UNTAC relating to essentially electoral management issues. These were based on a policy of "balanced favours" or "equal time" neutrality, rather than a strict "rule of law" neutrality, which treats all parties the same, whatever the political difficulties this might create. The phenomenon of interference can face national electoral managements when governing parties are inclined to use their authority (if the management is not absolutely independent) for what such government sees as "good" political reasons.

Political decisions on electoral matters

As indicated above, the Cambodian factions did not embrace the spirit of electoral tolerance and accept a neutral environment. They used their power whenever possible to influence the election. It was difficult for UNTAC, consistent with its determination to conduct the election in spite of this military and political reality, to maintain a consistent policy and apply the law rather than political expediency. Such resort to expediency meant that the credibility of the election suffered, as it does in any election where political manoeuvres are adopted rather than the consistent application of pre-ordained and published law. These are examples:

- The CPP, although committed to the election, was the major culprit with regard to the harassment of its opponents, probably because it had the power. One area of consistent breach of the code of conduct was with regard to freedom of movement and association. It was deadly dangerous for the opposition to move in or through SOC-controlled areas. Consequently, FUNCINPEC, the main "opposition" in the campaign, decided to use aircraft. Abusing its administrative powers over civil aviation, the SOC, in particular Minister Prince Chakrapong, prohibited them from flying. UNTAC had the power, given to the Special Representative, to act against such breaches, including the power to remove such officials. However, it was considered politically dangerous to use this legal power. Consequently, UNTAC resorted to a subterfuge. It gave FUNCINPEC leaders free lifts in its own UN helicopters to critical electoral rallies in SOC areas. This was seen by the CPP as a "favour" and not an action based on a rule of law.

- At an SNC meeting a few weeks before the election, the FUNCINPEC leader complained that polling booths would not, as in France, be enclosed by curtains. If curtains were not provided, FUNCINPEC threatened to join the Khmer Rouge boycott. This was a serious threat at this late stage in the process. The Special Representative, though advised in a rapid, whispered "consultation", that it would be virtually impossible to implement this, judged that it would be too dangerous not to concede the request, and curtains on each booth were promised. The CPP again pointed out that the law did not provide for this and objected. It was seen as another "favour" by UNTAC, and SOC's sense of bias grew. In fact, the curtains having been purchased (in their thousands of metres) were delivered during the last, most pressurized, pre-polling period and were, almost everywhere, not fitted to the booths. Because it was the successful party, FUNCINPEC did not complain. Had it lost, it might well have elevated this "illegal" promise into the major source of its failure at the polls and an "irregularity" which put the free and fair election in doubt. Since FUNCINPEC was the party most likely to prefer an election to continued war, it may have been better to have acted on the established rules, to have refused the request, and to have called its bluff.
- The worsening security situation as polling approached created a serious problem for both the Electoral and Military Components. Their priorities were virtually the opposites of one another. The electoral officials needed to extend the service to all voters, even those in dangerous or difficult areas. Security officials needed to shorten lines of communication and concentrate their limited forces as much as possible. Eventually a compromise was reached at the level of each Sector Commander and PEO. The number of polling stations was reduced from the 2200 agreed between electoral and military planners in February 1993, to about 1600 in May 1993.
- In addition, rather than posting guards each night at each polling station to protect ballots, the military decided that the ballots would be moved each night to "safe havens" and each morning back to the polling stations. This contributed to another practical problem for the electoral component, in that the seals on the boxes, specified and manufactured on the assumption that each box would move once (empty) to the polling

station and once (full) to the counting centre, was now required to withstand the test of multiple movements. Furthermore, these would be made by soldiers rather than election officers, over bad roads and in hurried helicopter trips. The result of the additional movements was that in some cases ballot boxes opened and spilt their contents. This was connected with a further political decision.

At about 9 p.m. on Friday 21 May 1993, 30 hours before polling was to commence, the Special Representative ended a tense meeting with the CPP/SOC leaders. It was now their turn to threaten to boycott the election and to expect that "equal time" favours would be extended to them as they had been to FUNCINPEC. The combination of the CPP's growing suspicion (real or deliberately created) that UNTAC favoured the opposition, plus the recent creation of "safe havens" and the plan to move ballot boxes there from polling stations, where their party agents would have been stationed, combined with the fact that the ballot boxes would not be sealed by their own party seal, had convinced them (or as they put it "their supporters") that UNTAC could not be trusted. They thus questioned the central thesis of the Paris Agreements and the basis of international electoral observation and supervision: that the best guarantee of a free and fair election in Cambodia lay in the fact that it would be run exclusively in all the critical areas, by absolutely reliable, neutral, independent international civil servants. By the UN!

The initial CPP "line" was that the integrity of the election under the new arrangements would be challenged not by them, since they expected to win, but by the losers, the opposition. Only when it was pointed out that the opposition had openly and clearly accepted the arrangements, and had raised no questions about them, did the CPP's position change to suggesting that the danger was that their supporters might doubt the result and cause problems.

To overcome this suspicion of the UN the CPP demanded the right (again) to apply their own seals. This was physically impossible and was refused. They added a new demand: that their own party agents should be admitted into the "safe havens", to guard or at least supervise the UN guardians. Electoral officials at the meeting were hastily consulted and indicated that it would be dangerous to insert an entirely new set of procedures into the electoral management on the ground (especially involving, as it would, not electoral officials, but soldiers). It would also be extremely difficult to ensure uniform and effective communication of this late and substantial procedural change to the military officers and electoral officials. Furthermore (and most important) the party leaders and party agents of the other parties, who had not been at the meeting, would be even more difficult to inform of the new system. The "favour" to the CPP would not be enjoyed by all parties in practice. Despite these dangers, and given UNTAC's earlier "favours" to the "opposition", it was virtually impossible to avoid granting this "equal time" concession to the CPP, or to ignore the boycott threat.

The outcome was that the communication of the new procedure was extremely uneven or ineffective, and the promise — like the earlier "curtains concession" — was not delivered uniformly and became the source of bitter controversy at many "safe havens" at the end of the first day of polling. The refusal of access by some military officers became another "proof" of UNTAC bias and irregularity in the eyes of the CPP. Ultimately it was used as a justification for their rejection of the FUNCINPEC victory in the election and a carefully stage-managed secession by CPP hard-liners. The essential result of this was that a "political adjustment" of the election result was achieved by the CPP: instead of its becoming the parliamentary opposition, it became part of a government of national unity. This may have been inevitable, given the continued imbalance of power and the continued mobilization of the CPAF, plus the need for a two-thirds majority to adopt the Constitution. What was unfortunate, and avoidable, was that the legitimacy of the election and the Assembly was put into question when, as a device to enable the CPP to cover its act of gross intimidation with the pretence of a legitimate complaint as to the propriety of the election, UNTAC agreed to set up an inquiry into the "irregularities". This was despite its own earlier declaration (endorsed by a Security Council resolution) that the election had been "free and fair".

CONCLUSION

One comes back to a basic question which the UN Cambodian mission raised, and which other missions since then have also posed: is the international community, and especially the Security Council, really aware of what they are aiming to get the UN and its officials to do in such peace-keeping, peace-making, democratizing acts of intervention? UNTAC proved, in spite of the serious risks it took, that an election could be held in an imperfect situation and that political sleight-of-hand could keep "all the balls in the air" for long enough to deliver an assembly and a government before a rapid UN withdrawal. But was that a proper solution, or was it a cynical gesture which some might now be tempted to compare with the establishment of "safe havens" in former Yugoslavia? Much of the criticism such questions generate is heaped on the UN and its officials, who are faced with impossible or unrealistic choices by inadequately considered Security Council responses to such situations. UNTAC proved that dedication and hard work can achieve a great deal, and that the UN and its objectives still inspires confidence in people who need help, as well as commitment by those prepared to assist others. But this invaluable instrument and its interventionary potential must be more critically evaluated in the context of the new realities, or else it could be discredited and lost.

27. A Legal Perspective on UNTAC – An Overview

Vishakan Krishnadasan[1]

OUTLINE OF DUTIES AND RESPONSIBILITIES

As a Legal Adviser of the United Nations Transitional Authority in Cambodia (UNTAC), I advised the Special Representative of the Secretary-General of the United Nations (SRSG), the DSRSG, the Force Commander and the Directors of the Electoral, Civil Administration, Human Rights, Rehabilitation and Reconstruction, and Repatriation Components, the Director of the Information Division and the Commissioner of Civilian Police on all legal aspects of UNTAC's activities and responsibilities in the fulfilment of UNTAC's mandate in Cambodia.

In particular, I undertook the preparation of the electoral law of Cambodia, the statutes relating to the Cambodian Mine Action Center (CMAC), the National Heritage Protection Authority in Cambodia (NHPAC) and the transitional criminal procedure and penal code for Cambodia and provided assistance to the drafting of the Constitution of Cambodia.

I was also the Chairman of the Technical Assistance Committee on Territorial Boundaries and on Immigration and Foreign Residents. At the request of the SRSG, I conducted negotiations on various aspects of the Agreements on a Comprehensive Political Settlement of the Cambodia Conflict with the Secretariat of the Supreme National Council and officials of the existing administrative structures, including the question of the presence of foreign forces in Cambodia and the powers of arrest and detention by UNTAC within the territory of Cambodia. In the closing stages of UNTAC's mandate, I served as the Chairman of the Special Representative's Electoral Advisory Committee, which was directed to inquire and report on the complaints raised by the Cambodian People's Party relating to the conduct of the polling and counting in the Cambodian election held in May/June 1993. The Advisory Committee reported its findings to the SRSG and transmitted a copy to the Cambodian People's Party. Under my supervision and control, the Legal Office advised the UNTAC Administration on all legal aspects of UNTAC's operations in Cambodia, including contracts, the necessary procedures and regulations governing UNTAC's operations, and the training of Cambodian law officers. In exercising these functions, I maintained coordination with the United Nations Office of Legal Affairs in New York, and directed and supervised an office of ten personnel, who included six lawyers.

---

[1] Former Legal Adviser, United Nations Transitional Authority in Cambodia, Phnom Penh.

LOAN AGREEMENT BETWEEN CAMBODIA AND THE ASIAN DEVELOPMENT BANK (ADB), IN RESPECT OF A LOAN IN THE AMOUNT OF SDR 46,917,000 FOR A SPECIAL REHABILITATION ASSISTANCE PROJECT

Pursuant to Sections 9.01 and 9.02 of the ADB's Special Operations Loan Regulations a legal opinion was prepared in this regard at the request of HRH Prince Norodom Sihanouk, Head of State and President of the SNC.

The legal opinion dealt in particular with some of the issues that have been touched upon at this conference, namely those relating to the powers of the SNC, the extent to which the sovereign capacity of the SNC was limited by the delegation of authority to UNTAC under Article 6 of the Agreement on a Comprehensive Political Settlement of the Cambodia Conflict (the Agreement), the SNC's decision-making procedures and the powers of the Head of State and President of the SNC to bind Cambodia.

After an examination of the circumstances relating to the establishment of the SNC in Jakarta on 10 September 1990, the joint statement issued thereat, the relevant provisions of the Paris Agreements and obligations of the parties thereunder and the support expressed by the United Nations for the accords, it was opined that under international law the SNC was the sole source of authority in which the sovereignty of Cambodia was enshrined throughout the transitional period and that during such period the SNC was fully empowered to represent Cambodia externally.

Consideration was given to whether the delegation by the SNC to the United Nations under Article 6 of the Agreement of "all powers necessary to ensure the implementation of this Agreement as described in Annex 1", including that of direct control over the existing administrative structures in the area of foreign affairs, national defence, finance, public security and information, limited the sovereign capacity of the SNC *qua* SNC (namely without the participation of UNTAC) to authorize the loan agreement.

An examination of Annex 1 to the Agreement, read in conjunction with Article 6 (and the practice over the past months), revealed that the principal objective of the powers exercised by UNTAC, including direct control, was to ensure a neutral political environment conducive to free and fair elections in Cambodia and the strict neutrality of the Cambodian bodies responsible for the areas subject to direct control. Thus UNTAC control for particular purposes, such as finance, did not deprive the SNC of the normal incidence of sovereignty during the transitional period. In the field of finance, UNTAC's mandate under the Agreement could not be interpreted to include the authority to approve long-term foreign loans on behalf of Cambodia. UNTAC's control in this regard would, in the main, be confined to matters related to the implementation of the loan agreement. It was to be noted that the UNTAC letter of endorsement to the ADB stated that "UNTAC will provide full cooperation in the implementation of the loan and sub-projects financed through the loan during the transitional period".

SNC decision-making procedure

The decision-making procedures of the SNC *qua* SNC was next examined, bearing in mind that such procedures could be held to constitute "an internal law" of fundamental importance, manifest violation of which could affect the authority to execute the loan agreement. The SNC confirmation letter to the ADB stated that "The loan negotiated has been duly approved by the Supreme National Council of Cambodia (with nevertheless a reservation from one faction)". Whether or not the approval qualified by a reservation constituted a decision by consensus or by the SNC President taking fully into account the views expressed in the SNC, and whether or not it was considered necessary to apply the decision-making procedures of the SNC *qua* SNC or those in Annex 1, Section A of the Agreement as applying not only to the resolution of all issues between SNC and UNTAC but also, *mutatis mutandis*, to the decision-making procedures within SNC itself, it was opined in either case that the SNC confirmation letter constituted satisfactory evidence that all the necessary action had been taken to authorize the execution and delivery of the loan agreement on behalf of Cambodia.

HEAD OF STATE AND PRESIDENT OF SNC

Annex 1, Section A, sub-paragraphs (c) and (d) of paragraph 2 of the Agreement refers to HRH Prince Norodom Sihanouk as "the legitimate representative of Cambodian Sovereignty". Official documents also reveal that the four Cambodian parties had "... solemnly and officially declared in writing" on behalf of the Cambodian people and nation "that HRH Prince Norodom Sihanouk has never ceased to be the legal and legitimate Head of State of Cambodia of the whole of Cambodia ... consequently ... HRH Prince Norodom Sihanouk ... takes henceforth the official title of Head of State of Cambodia and President of the Supreme National Council of Cambodia, until such time when a new Head of State of Cambodia is elected by universal suffrage".

Article 7, sub-paragraph (a) of paragraph 2 of the Vienna Convention on the Law of Treaties embodies a well-established rule of international law that a head of state is considered as representing his state for the purpose of all acts relating to the conclusion of a treaty. The practice followed by the SNC even before the entering into force of the Agreement showed that the implementation and the external manifestation of the decisions taken collectively by the SNC had always been entrusted to HRH Prince Norodom Sihanouk. Thus, as evidenced also by past practice, it was opined that the bank might rely on the authority of HRH Prince Norodom Sihanouk, as Head of State and President of the SNC, to bind Cambodia by his execution of the loan agreement.

CONSISTENCY OF LOAN AGREEMENT WITH THE PARIS AGREEMENTS

The rehabilitation programme contemplated in the loan agreement is consistent with and falls within the scope of the Paris Agreements, in particular the Declaration on the Rehabilitation and Reconstruction of Cambodia. Based on the foregoing, it was opined that the loan agreement had been duly authorized by and executed and delivered on behalf of Cambodia and was legally binding upon Cambodia in accordance with its terms.

Foreign forces and the obligations of UNTAC in the context of the Agreement

A working paper was distributed on the above subject at the working session of the SNC on 2 July 1992 and a revised working paper was discussed in depth with representatives of the four Cambodian parties from 20 to 22 January 1992. The paper sought (a) to define the scope of the term "foreign forces" under the Agreement, and (b) to provide a framework for UNTAC to investigate the presence of foreign forces in order to ensure their withdrawal and non-return.

This question assumed a particular significance because the Party of Democratic Kampuchea (PDK) stated that such withdrawal and non-return was one of the principal preconditions for complying with the peace process. The provisions which may be examined in this regard are Articles 8 and 10, Annex 1, section C, paragraph 1(a) and Annex 2, Articles VI, VII and X.

Scope of the term "foreign forces"

The true meaning of the term has to be arrived at by taking into account the consequences which normally and reasonably flow from the relevant text, namely the relevant articles in their entirety. Forces may be said to constitute a group of (armed) persons assembled for collective action and belonging to another country. Although "foreign forces" are not defined in the Agreement, it was noted that under Annex 2, Article 1, paragraph 2, "forces" belonging to the Cambodian parties "are agreed to include all regular, provincial, district, para-military and other auxiliary forces". If this definition was analogously applied, *mutatis mutandis*, to "foreign forces", such forces might be said to include regular (army), paramilitary (supplementing the strictly military) and auxiliary (subsidiary or subordinate) forces; additionally "foreign forces" would include (military) advisers and military personnel as stated in Article 8 of the Agreement and Annex I, section C, paragraph 1(a). This definition also derives support from the fact that the verification and withdrawal from Cambodia and the non-return of "foreign forces" is the task of the military component of UNTAC. It also appeared, taking into consideration Article 10 of the Agreement and Annex 2, Article VII, which relate to the cessation of all outside military assistance to all Cambodian parties, that the term "foreign forces" would include those who entered Cambodia after the entry into force of the Agreement.

Thus, by examining the relevant textual provisions and by analogously applying the definition of "forces" belonging to the Cambodian parties, the "foreign forces" to be subject to UNTAC investigation would include foreign regular, paramilitary and auxiliary forces, (military) advisers and military personnel remaining in Cambodia upon the entry into force of the Agreement and "foreign forces" who entered Cambodia thereafter. Any such person or group of persons now residing in Cambodia, be he/she a member of the military or a civilian, will be subject to withdrawal and non-return. Accordingly, as approved by the SNC at its meeting on 20 October 1992, any such person who:

- on or before 23 October 1991 was in Cambodia and remained in Cambodia thereafter;
- withdrew from Cambodia on or after 23 October 1991 and returned thereafter;
- entered Cambodia *de novo* after entry into force of the Agreement,

would be considered to fall within the term "foreign forces" under the Agreement.

Proposed investigatory framework

The proposed investigatory framework sought to extend the procedures specified in Annex 2, Articles VI and VII of the Agreement by providing for UNTAC acceptance of observers from each of the four Cambodian parties to be at the check-points and also to be attached to the mobile investigation teams set up by UNTAC. Provision was also made for the strategic investigation teams (SITs) set up by the Military Component to accept observers from each of the Cambodian parties to assist in their task.

In addition to the procedures for withdrawal and cessation of outside military assistance under the Agreement, UNTAC was to inform the states whose nationals had been identified as "foreign forces" and request their cooperation with regard to the withdrawal of such nationals. In practice the efforts of the SITs were hampered by the lack of cooperation from the Cambodian parties; if such cooperation had been forthcoming this issue could have been substantially resolved.

Notwithstanding Security Council resolution 810 of 8 March 1993, neither SOC nor the Government of Vietnam were prepared to fulfil their obligations concerning either the three persons identified on 1 March 1993 or the four persons identified shortly thereafter as "foreign forces".

OFFICE OF THE SPECIAL PROSECUTOR

The establishment of this Office was proposed by the Human Rights Component in response to the increasingly serious violations of human rights by officials of the SOC and the PDK throughout the months of November and December 1992. In many instances the existing administrative authorities either refused to conduct investigations or expressed the view that they did not have the capacity to either investigate or prosecute such matters. Despite UNTAC investigations over these matters which implicated and identified officials of the SOC and the NADK (PDK), UNTAC had not succeeded in taking corrective action against any official for human rights violations. The framework provided by the transitional criminal law adopted by the SNC on 10 September 1992 was also inoperative, due not only to the threat of interference faced by the state-appointed prosecutors but also to the physical danger they faced should they seek to institute penal action against the will of the relevant existing administrative structure.

The Office of the Special Prosecutor was established on 6 January 1993 by a directive from the Special Representative with power to arrest, detain and prosecute persons accused of serious human rights violations, particularly of officials, police or military officers of existing administrative structures. UNTAC's powers were to be exercised within the transitional criminal law. UNTAC also sets up a detention facility for the detention of persons they had arrested under the Special Representative's directive (only four persons were arrested). When it became clear that the SOC judiciary was not independent of the executive and legislative authorities of SOC – that the SOC authorities were unwilling to make a court available for prosecution to take place – no further matters were brought before SOC courts by the Special Prosecutor.

As a result, the Special Representative issued a second directive on 3 February 1993 which effectively removed UNTAC detainees from the jurisdiction of the SOC courts. UNTAC was authorized to detain suspects until such courts become available. The legal basis for the establishment of the Office of the Special Prosecutor was sought to be founded on Articles 6 and 16 and Sections B and E of Annex 1 of the Agreement. Notwithstanding the radical need at the time for effective corrective action for human rights violations, the question was whether the establishment of such an office was within the mandate of UNTAC under the Agreement. An examination of the relevant provisions of the Agreement in accordance with the general rules of treaty interpretation, and more particularly the provisions of Articles 31(1) and 31(3)(b) of the Vienna Convention on the Law of Treaties, would indicate, in the view of the writer, that such establishment was *ultra vires* the mandate of UNTAC under the Agreement.

Consideration was also given to the fact that if prosecutions were to proceed before the courts, the possibility existed that a defence counsel would question the powers of the Special Representative to establish such an office under the Agreement and a court would rule on it. Thus a court of one administrative structure could possibly interpret the power of the Special Representative under the Agreement. Should it be deemed essential to proceed with the establishment of the Office it was opined that a valid legal basis could be predicated upon SNC approval by consensus or, failing consensus, by a decision of the President of the SNC and, thereafter, the endorsement to the Security Council in consultation with the other signatories of the Agreement. Be that as it may, cognisance of the establishment of the Office was taken by the Secretary-General in his third progress report on UNTAC to the Security Council on 25 January 1993. Predictably, the SOC Minister of Justice was clearly of the view that the establishment of the Office and directives relating thereto were *ultra vires* the mandate of the UNTAC under the Agreement.

After intensive and somewhat tortuous negotiations with the SOC authorities, amendments were made to the transitional criminal law to incorporate the two UNTAC directives into Cambodian law. These amendments were adopted by a decision of the President of the SNC on 20 March 1993 over the objections of the SOC. The amendment remained a dead letter, in that attempts to locate a competent court met with no success and the detainees languished in the detention facility for the remainder of UNTAC's mandate in Cambodia. It was clear, therefore, notwithstanding the subsequent legitimization of an act that was possibly *ultra vires*, that UNTAC was unable to discharge its responsibilities effectively with regard to serious violations of human rights by officials of the existing administrative structures.

The prevention of such human rights violations, or at least the amelioration thereof, and subjecting such violations to the due process of law, would necessitate the granting of the requisite authority and resources to any future UN peace-keeping operation in having to contend with similar circumstances.

THE POSSIBILITY THAT THE FRANCHISE UNDER THE ELECTORAL LAW WAS AT VARIANCE WITH THE FRANCHISE PROVISIONS IN THE AGREEMENT

Under Annex 3, paragraph 4 to the Agreement, every person, whether or not he/she is a Cambodian citizen, will be eligible to vote in the election, provided that the criteria of age 18, birth in Cambodia or being a child of a person born in Cambodia, are satisfied. Paragraph 4 is structured *de facto* on the *jus soli* principle that one's nationality is that of the country in which one was born. Accordingly, Article 15 of the draft electoral law submitted by UNTAC to the SNC on 1 April 1992 reflected the meaning of this paragraph. The formula contained therein was possibly intended to overcome the disagreements between the SOC and the other parties over the status of the Vietnamese settlers in Cambodia. While a settler born in Vietnam to parents born there lacked electoral rights, those born in Cambodia or whose parents were born there might vote.

When the draft law was considered by the SNC, the NADK, FUNCINPEC and KPNLF were for the introduction of a franchise based on citizenship. In an effort to break a seeming deadlock, a re-examination of the relevant provisions was undertaken. To the Legal Adviser the question at issue was whether an alternative interpretation might in good faith be given to Annex 3, paragraph 4, in the context of the Agreement as a whole in the light of its object and purpose. Viewing the terms of the Agreement it was noted that there were several references to "All Cambodians", "the Cambodian people", "all Cambodian citizens" and "all Cambodian refugees and displaced persons" in the relevant provisions relating to their right to participate in the electoral process.

If these references are read in their context and taken in conjunction, and also if the *ejusdem generis* doctrine is applied, the words "Every person" in

Annex 3, paragraph 4 may in good faith be construed as referring to the right of "All Cambodians including ... Cambodian refugees and displaced persons ... to take part in the electoral process" as stipulated.

The specific reference to the right of all Cambodian citizens to undertake activities that would promote and protect human rights and fundamental freedoms in the Paris Agreements, the references in the Preamble and Article 12 of the Agreement to ensuring "the exercise of the right to self-determination of the Cambodian people through free and fair elections" and "the right to determine their own [the Cambodian people's] political future through a free and fair election of a constituent assembly", respectively, also lend credence to this interpretation, which is to some extent predicated upon *jus sanguinis*, the principle that one's nationality is that of one's natural parents. It may also be noted that under the Covenant on Civil and Political Rights to which Cambodia is a party "the right and the opportunity to vote and be elected at genuine periodic elections" is limited to every citizen (Article 25(b)).

It was opined that the alternative interpretation provided was consistent with the relevant provisions of the Vienna Convention on the Law of Treaties and the principles of customary international law relating to treaty interpretation. If this alternative interpretation was accepted, it would not be necessary to substantially amend Annex 3, paragraph 4 of the Agreement. Such acceptance would have accommodated what was then thought to be the unanimous view of the President of the SNC and all four Cambodian parties. It would, of course have been necessary to provide agreed criteria with regard to Cambodian citizenship or being a Cambodian person.

Subsequently, however, this unanimity was lacking. An examination was also undertaken of former Cambodian laws on the subject, especially because at one SNC meeting in a rare, though short-lived, display of unanimity, all the parties and the President of the SNC were in agreement that the relevant 1954 kram no. 913 on citizenship could apply. The relevant kram stated, *inter alia*, that to be a citizen, a person generally had to be born in Cambodia to parents born in Cambodia, or the child (wherever born) of such a person.

The revised draft electoral law was an effort to meet the concerns expressed by the Cambodian parties that the franchise be restricted to "Cambodian persons". It was predicated on an alternative interpretation, that the text of the Agreement should be interpreted as giving the right to register to every "Cambodian person" – who is of or over the age of 18 years or will attain that age during the registration period – defined as follows:

(a) a person born in Cambodia, at least one of whose parents was born in Cambodia; or
(b) a person, wherever born, at least one of whose parents is or was a Cambodian person within the meaning of paragraph (a) above.

Thus a person born outside Cambodia, one of whose parents and a grandparent from the same side of the family who were born in Cambodia, was eligible to vote. It will be noted that the revised draft contained some elements of the 1954 Cambodian law.

The electoral law, though opposed by the NADK, was adopted by the SNC in accordance with its decision-making procedures, whereby the Special Representative took fully into account the views expressed in the SNC.

Subsequent efforts to extend the franchise to the so-called Khmer-Krom residents in Cambodia, that is ethnic Cambodian born, or with a parent born, in southern Vietnam (as proposed by FUNCINPEC and KPNLF/BLDP and supported by the President of the SNC) were rejected by the Secretary-General of the UN, who concluded that the extension of the franchise on purely ethnic grounds to persons who were not born in Cambodia would not be consistent with the letter and spirit of the Agreement. It may be noted that a further concession, clearly not in keeping with the Agreement but which took account of an important political reality, was also made in an additional amendment to the franchise provisions, whereby a "Cambodian person" should mean "a person wherever born who is a member of the SNC"!

THE ELECTORAL ADVISORY COMMITTEE

Article 45 of the electoral law established the Special Representative's Electoral Advisory Committee in accordance with the Agreement to ensure the prevention and control of irregularities. Although formally established, it was neither staffed nor motivated as designed. As stated by the Chief Electoral Officer in his report on the evaluation of the election, the Committee was provided for in the electoral law to fill the legal vacuum arising from the probable inadequacy of the legal system in Cambodia. The proposed Committee was not a court, but its make-up was designed to give it an independent, quasi-judicial identity, and an aura of neutrality. Its non-functioning led to the Electoral Component's Complaints, Compliance and Enforcement Unit becoming involved in the actual policing and sanctioning of political parties.

The members of the Committee were appointed on 22 June 1994 and on 24 June 1994 the Special Representative referred to the Committee, for inquiry and report, the complaints raised by the CPP relating to the conduct of the polling and counting in the Cambodian election, held in May/June 1993. It may be noted that the referral to the Committee was after the Special Representative had issued a statement at an SNC meeting on 10 June on behalf of the Secretary-General of the UN that the election as a whole had been free and fair. The Security Council endorsed the results of the election on 15 June 1993. Although the belated functioning of the Committee may have been timeous politically (namely, to facilitate the acceptance of the outcome of the election by the CPP), it called into question the determination already made that the election had been free and fair.

The Special Representative's Electoral Advisory Committee, having examined the allegations of the CPP in relation to questions of access, security of ballot material, polling procedures, counting procedures, and electoral law offences, found that the irregularities complained of related, in essence to:

(a) allegations which could not be substantiated due to lack of further and better particulars;
(b) complaints acknowledged by UNTAC but where prompt remedial action was taken; and
(c) instances where UNTAC displayed a lack due care and attention in the performance of its functions.

In considering the above irregularities, proven and unproven, the Committee placed the Cambodian electoral process within the experience of organizing and conducting elections elsewhere, where imperfections were not unknown.

The Committee also had regard to the climate of violence, intimidation and harassment that had prevailed in the run-up to the election, and which resulted in an election that was conducted in an atmosphere that was not susceptible to the full control of UNTAC. Such circumstances necessitated special security measures being taken by UNTAC. One such measure, the provision of safe havens, contributed to the occurrence of some of the proven irregularities, namely, broken seals and locks, and access to "safe havens".

Notwithstanding the proven irregularities, the Committee's inquiry revealed that no evidence had been presented to indicate that these irregularities had been deliberate acts intended to affect the electoral chances of a particular political party, or that the scope of such irregularities would have been sufficient to question the validity of the results.

It would be fair to say, therefore, that the extent of such irregularities would have been vastly reduced if the election had been conducted in a more peaceful climate. The Committee noted that the Cambodian election was observed by a large number of national and international bodies, apart from a sizeable number of the media, none of whom had any hesitation in declaring that the election had met with established standards for this process and was a clear expression of the will of the Cambodian people. It is to be noted that 4,267,192 Cambodians, representing 89.56% of the country's registered voters, turned up to vote. The Committee concluded that the conduct of the polling and counting in the election held in Cambodia from 23 to 28 May 1993 was free and fair. If, as is possible, the Cambodian model will be used as a reference for elections organized and conducted by the UN under similar circumstances in the future, it is essential that such a committee be constituted early on in the electoral process to ensure the effective exercise of its functions.

THE CAMBODIAN MINE ACTION CENTRE

Pursuant to its mandate under the Agreement, which included assistance with clearing mines and undertaking training programmes in mine-clearance and a mine-awareness programme among the Cambodian people, UNTAC proposed to the SNC the establishment of CMAC. On 10 June 1992, the SNC established CMAC and a Governing Council to oversee its activities and adopted statutes for these purposes. CMAC is perhaps unique in that it is possibly the first instance of a UN body, namely UNTAC, controlling the functioning and management of a national institution.

The 14-member Governing Council was composed and appointed in such a manner that UNTAC control was ensured at all times. The Director and Treasurer of CMAC were also members of the Council and were appointed by the Vice-President of the Council, who was the Special Representative. CMAC's Management Committee of 11 members was appointed by the Governing Council and included, additionally, the CMAC Director and Treasurer. Thus UNTAC control was also ensured at the management level, notwithstanding that the Chairman and Co-Chairman of the Management Committee were appointed by HRH Prince Norodom Sihanouk, the President of the Governing Council, after consultation with the Vice-President.

While CMAC possessed full juridical authority and had capacity to do and perform all acts and things which were necessary for or are incidental to the furtherance of its purpose, UN participation in the Governing Council or in CMAC (proper) was not to be deemed a waiver of the privileges and immunities accorded to UN officials under the relevant UN and Specialized Agencies Conventions, the IDEA Privilege and Immunities Agreement, and the Agreement between the SNC and the UN on the Status of UNTAC. Thus to all intents and purposes, in this regard, CMAC, a Cambodian institution, was treated *pari passu* as a UN agency in Cambodia, albeit under Cambodian law.

While the Governing Council's existence terminated at the end of UNTAC's mandate, the existence of CMAC was extended beyond the mandate period, prior to the termination of the UNTAC mandate, by a decision of the Governing Council. It is understood that CMAC has now become a statutory agency of the Cambodian Government.

THE CAMBODIAN CONSTITUTION

At the request of the SNC, and especially its President HRH Prince Norodom Sihanouk, UNTAC facilitated debate on a future constitution among Cambodians by holding three seminars on a new Constitution for Cambodia.

The seminars were convened by the Director of the Electoral Component and the Legal Adviser and sought to identify and discuss relevant constitutional issues, determining their urgency and importance as well as identifying the immediate tasks of the Constituent Assembly. They provided a forum for debate and exchange of views and ideas among the Cambodian parties contesting the Constituent Assembly elections. There were participants from all 20 political parties contesting the elections and from Cambodian non-governmental organizations.

Ambassador Tan Boon Teik's paper on "Drafting the New Constitution" will provide further elaboration on the specific themes discussed at the seminars, with international specially invited or UNTAC experts acting as resource persons or mediating the debate among the Cambodians. In response to an invitation from the Acting President of the Constituent Assembly for technical comments from UNTAC on the draft Constitution, assistance was provided to the Cambodian Constituent Assembly in the drafting on the Constitution of Cambodia.

While paying full regard to the sovereign right of the Constituent Assembly to draft and adopt the Constitution, UNTAC's observations related in particular to the principles for a new constitution for Cambodia stipulated in Annex 5 of the Agreement. Specific observations were made in relation to the special measures required to assure the protection of human rights, the establishment of an independent judiciary, the recognition and respect for the relevant international human rights instruments and several other chapters of the draft Constitution including the National Assembly, the Constitutional Council, the Government and the Transitional Provisions.

While several of the observations appear to have been seriously considered and incorporated, it may be noted that, as yet, the Cambodian Constitution contains no provision prohibiting the retroactive application of criminal law, as required by Annex 5 of the Agreement.

TECHNICAL ADVISORY COMMITTEES TO STUDY THE QUESTIONS RELATING TO THE TERRITORIAL BOUNDARIES OF CAMBODIA AND TO FOREIGN RESIDENTS AND IMMIGRANTS

Both Committees were set up, as subsidiary bodies of the SNC, with a view to facilitating the task of the future Cambodian Government in these all-important areas. What was significant in the discussions leading to the establishment of these Committees was the remarkable lack of dissent between the Cambodian parties when considering these issues of national importance.

The terms of reference of the TAC on Territorial Boundaries was adopted by all-party consensus at the SNC on 10 February 1993. The Committee was charged under the chairmanship of UNTAC with the task of verifying the territorial boundaries of Cambodia as internationally recognized before 18 March 1970. The work of the Committee was thus to be focused on showing, cartographically, on the basis of available information and fieldwork, the pre-1970 territorial boundaries of Cambodia and ascertaining, to what extent, the location of the existing boundary markers correspond or do not correspond to the said boundaries. The exercise, therefore, was to be limited to information-gathering and verification, and did not extend to the delineation or demarcation of Cambodian national boundaries, which was to be the task of the newly elected Government of Cambodia. UNTAC was to assist the TAC.

In furtherance of UNTAC's assistance to the TAC, two UN cartographers conducted research in the Cartotheque Institut Géographique National in Paris. On the basis of their initial findings UNTAC was able to provide important technical information to the Constituent Assembly on Cambodian maps which was directly relevant to Article 2 of the Cambodian draft Constitution. This information was duly incorporated in Article 2 of the Cambodian Constitution.

The genesis for a TAC on Foreign Residents and Immigrants lay in a proposal by Mr Khieu Samphan of the PDK. The terms of reference were adopted at an SNC meeting in February 1993. The Committee was charged under the chairmanship of UNTAC to undertake the following mandate:

(a) to collect, receive and examine all relevant information relating to foreign residents and immigrants in Cambodia, including a review of the past and current legislation and treaties as well as procedures applied by the existing administrative structures;
(b) to study matters relating to the acquisition of citizenship by foreign residents and immigrants, including past and current legislation and the procedures whereby such citizenship is obtained; and
(c) to present its findings and recommendations to SNC.

Regrettably, ensuing events, including the run-up to the elections, prevented the Committee from carrying out its functions.

28. Drafting the Cambodian Constitution

Ambassador Tan Boon Teik[1]

The first consideration of all newly independent nations is the drafting of a constitution. All regimes on assuming power, however, and whatever the means of securing such power, first want to create the aura of a new era dawning upon the people. Such an event cannot be more aptly announced then by the promulgation of a new supreme charter, often containing high-sounding principles of government to ensure democracy in its most acceptable and updated version. The new constitution will therefore accord any new government that has arisen out of revolution or conflict the legitimacy such a government needs.

So it is with the Kingdom of Cambodia in the drafting of its rather unusual number of constitutions, which date from 1947–1989. The most recent Constitution, that of 1993, cannot be viewed so cynically, however. The parties to the Paris Agreements were well aware of the importance of a constitution in establishing a firm basis for the future of the country.

The genesis of the present Constitution is to be found in the Paris Agreements which set up UNTAC. Indeed, you will find the basics of the sort of constitution that was being proposed in Annex 5 to the Paris Agreements. Five principles have been specifically mentioned:

(a) Constitution to be the supreme law;
(b) a declaration of fundamental human rights – no retroactive criminal law, and courts to adjudicate and enforce;
(c) independence and neutrality and national unity;
(d) a liberal democracy based on pluralism;
(e) an independent judiciary.

The importance of two of the five principles cannot be overemphasized, viz. human rights and an independent judiciary. These, it was and is expected, will form the corner-stones for law and order for a future democratic Cambodia. They were particularly needed, if only because of the horrendous upheavals of the last decade. For example, the 1989 Constitution had in effect rendered the Supreme Court quite subservient to the executive and legislature. The concept of the doctrine of separation of powers was unknown. The Council of State was given powers to establish courts of law with special jurisdiction and powers. The Public Prosecutor had overriding powers in exercising a supervisory jurisdiction over the courts. In short, even as recently as 1989, the concept of an independent judiciary was alien to Cambodia.

Like all modern constitutions, therefore, the new Constitution was to be

---

[1] Ambassador of Singapore to Hungary, Austria and the Slovak Republic, Singapore.

promulgated by a Constituent Assembly whose sole purpose was to enact a constitution. But in the case of Cambodia, the assembly elected to enact the Constitution was to continue in existence and transform itself into a National Assembly, once it became *functus officio qua* Constituent Assembly.

UNTAC was given the task of ensuring an election process that would not only have the participation of as many of the main political parties as possible, but also would ensure that elections were conducted in as fair and open a manner as to truly reflect the wishes and aspirations of the electorate. This particular task was, despite the doubts of observers local and foreign, a truly successful achievement of UNTAC.

Besides the myriad of components with military and civil responsibilities, there was one to see to the conduct of elections. This Component, led by Professor Austin, was also given the added task of attempting to educate the electorate as to the importance of the whole exercise. Austin was chosen because of his experience in Zimbabwe, where he was professor in the law school. In discharging this particular responsibility, Austin was to organize seminars for members of parties registered as viable contestants by UNTAC. They included a large cross-section of the Cambodian elite, comprising a fair number of exiles from America and France who had returned to take part in the elections while at the same time retaining their foreign affiliations. I met a professor from Toulouse who taught constitutional law as a subject, and he gave me a copy of their suggested draft. It was based on the French Fourth Republic which de Gaulle had inspired, but included quite a few provisions from the American Constitution. The draft was most comprehensive and some of the provisions are in the new Constitution.

Besides myself and Professor Chai-Anan, there was Professor Jenner from Brussels, who was asked to give the Continental dimension in the conduct of these seminars. We had two separate visits to Phnom Penh in late January 1993 and April 1993, when we conducted a number of sessions. They were all very well attended, with a fair number of returnees – most of whom were rather pessimistic about the whole effort and presaging chaos after the departure of UNTAC. Despite reports of shootings at night, the conditions in Phnom Penh then were quite conducive to studies in the law being enacted. One weekend I discovered we were not the only ones interested in the electoral process in Cambodia. There was a seminar being conducted by a joint group of Americans representing the US Democratic and Republican parties. They appeared to be imparting to their audience the American system of government and the conduct of elections in the US and their practical aspects. Like us, they were emphasizing the need to keep separate the three branches of government.

All the sessions of our seminars were well attended and represented. The Khmer Rouge were egregious in their absence. I was impressed with the number of well-known persons, who included General Intan, You Hockrey and Say Bory (who later took part in actually drafting the Constitution). The Drafting Committee of the Constitution was approved by the Constituent Assembly at its very first Plenary Session on 30 June 1993.

Before the actual seminar began, Professor Chai-Anan and I visited the offices of some of the parties that had registered as would-be candidates. The meetings with the party officials were instructive, in that they disclosed their keenness to restore the economy of the country and a genuine feeling that liberal democracy was preferable to anything they had experienced. Previously, the Paris Agreements had been widely read and digested. UNTAC was there to assist in the attainment of the objective they were about to embark upon – great were the hopes pinned on UNTAC. At the same time, the fact that the returnees were there only for a limited time – some alone, with their families abroad – clearly showed their fears for the immediate future. Among the parties visited was one that owed their allegiance to Lon Borer. Another, a group that called themselves Le Parti ADD (Action pour la Démocratie et pour le Développement) had a most comprehensive draft constitution ready.

We visited the ruling party's HQ and those of FUNCINPEC and the Bhuddist Party led by Son Sanh. Professor Chai-Anan's father had been a well-known figure and had been Thailand's Ambassador to Phnom Penh during the days immediately before Lon Nol assumed office. He was remembered by nearly all the persons we had met. As the conversations were all in Thai, my impressions were necessarily secondhand – some of the parties had no idea of their aims and objectives if they formed the government, but the main ones were quite keyed up. The one main central objective was to end the guerrilla war waged by the Khmer Rouge and to seek aid and foreign investments to sustain the economy. They were all too conscious of the temporary nature of the then current sense of well-being and apparent affluence, brought about principally by the presence of UNTAC. The Constitution was seen as a first step toward economic resuscitation and also as a means of firmly establishing a system of law and order throughout the land.

In the elections organized by UNTAC with all the backing of legitimacy via the Paris Agreements, they saw real hopes of founding a system of government, but were also aware of its limitations in regard to law enforcement. UNTAC's attempts to set up a system of criminal courts and a prosecutorial service had not been successful, but the general atmosphere of hope and confidence in the future built up by UNTAC's ubiquitous white vehicles and blue berets did much to provide a sense of public order prevailing in the Phnom Penh and the country as a whole. I travelled as far as the centre of the country, and far south to Kampot and the Gulf of Thailand, in the comparative ease and comfort of a local merchant's Land Rover.

THE SEMINARS

We discussed at some length the separation of powers in the first visit. As to the general framework of the Constitution, we had discussed the desirability of having a strong government with ample powers to administer within the terms of the five principles in Annex 5, as these were not exhaustive. To enshrine human rights clauses in the Constitution would not be a sufficient safeguard if the Constitution itself had given the ruling party or Prime Minister or Cabinet powers that were untrammelled. Obviously, a balance had to be struck. There could be no better way of resolving the problem than by examining other constitutions in the region. Their own was the obvious first choice, while Singapore's interested quite a few parties. Our success was itself a recommendation. I warned them that the most important part of the whole exercise lay in the implementation. Therefore the new Government must be returned with a strong enough partner; it was recognized even at this stage that with the proliferation of parties registered, a coalition was the most probable outcome. The encouraging part of the seminar was the keenness shown by all — though some were obviously not taking it all in, because of language difficulties, despite the presence of simultaneous translators, French, English and Khmer. The UN Information/Education office had provided funds to interpret these sessions for the attendees, who presumably would go back to educate their cadres. I was touched when, before left, I was presented with a copy of my lectures translated into the Khmer language.

The next series of seminars was just a couple of months before the elections, and we could feel a sense of urgency again. There were those with dire forebodings. I was told that on 8 May there would be real fireworks by the Khmer Rouge here in the heart of Phnom Penh. The next day, there were reports of shootings; one UN official was killed at a road block by a government soldier. His car had sailed on past the barrier with the UN flag prominently displayed. The next incident was near the UNHQ where the seminar was being held!

THE PRESENT CONSTITUTION

Although it might be presumptuous to claim that the seminars had any effect in shaping the present Constitution, there are some provisions that would lend support to such a claim. Though not unlike the Constitution that preceded it in its references to the portions that are autochthonous, it has safeguards for the protection of human rights adequately set out. These have been balanced by provisions to ensure public order and security. Naturally, in view of their recent past, the whole of Chapter III, which sets out rights and obligations, in effect leans towards individual freedoms, no capital punishment, physical abuse, nor ill treatment (inhuman punishment). Corresponding duties spelt out had been discussed at our seminars, but no one had discussed the obligation toward one's parents — children to take care of their elderly parents, Article 47, part of their tradition to do so. The desirability of having an ombudsman was discussed. One had to appreciate the recent past history of Cambodia indeed, since its independence from the French in 1947, to realize the attractions of such an institution. The realization that implementation of these ideas would be difficult did not seem to dissuade participants like Say Bory from repeating the need for such an office. I suppose this faction did have these views recognized by the provision Article 9 which in effect gives the King a role not too dissimilar. The King, under Article 9 of the present Cambodian Constitution, is to be the final arbiter in the faithful execution of public powers. Conceivably he would, in that role, be the ombudsman, Acts of malfeasance, improper exercise of discretionary powers and excess of jurisdiction in the exercise of powers by officials, could at least in theory be brought to his attention for redress.

I had spent a portion of my time at the Seminar on State Succession and am glad to note in Article 55 a reference to treaties and the rejection of an unqualified acceptance of the principle of *pacta sunt servanda*, yet it would be hard to say for sure that so-called unequal treaties will not be honoured. The article provides for the annulment of treaties incompatible with the independence, sovereignty or neutrality or national unity of Cambodia. The most one can say is that it provides for an acceptance of the clean-slate theory, which had also been discussed. The response to this suggestion had provoked much support as being quite the natural consequence of attaining independence.

The chapter on the economy is new to Cambodia, and – a natural result after the command structure that had prevailed during the Communist regime – is the desire of the people to ensure a departure from one of the worst aspects of authoritarianism and collectivization. The 1989 Constitution had referred to the natural economy as consisting of the state economy, joining state-private and private economy with emphasis on the important role of the state economy in issuing guiding principles for the development of the collective economy – in short, a command structure in the economy.

THE LEGISLATURE

At our seminars, a bicameral legislature had been widely canvassed. I spoke against such a set-up. It could be a hindrance, especially when laws had to be passed quickly to attain the essential legal framework for resuscitating the organs of government and to administer law and order.

I am therefore glad to note that in the present Constitution there is only one National Assembly, no upper house. The number of assemblymen is set at a minimum of 120. This again is new, in that such a minimum is not in previous constitutions of Cambodia, but it is in strict compliance with the requirements of Annex 3 to the Paris Agreements. Also, the minimum age for voting is set at 18. Those qualified to stand as candidates for election must be 25 years old.

Obviously the Constituent Assembly did not think that the country could afford the luxury of a second talking shop, when there was so much to be done – basic infrastructure to be established before Cambodia could begin to attract the investments it so sorely needed. All the legal framework for these plans will have to be worked out with experience gained elsewhere in the region. They were particularly keen to learn from Singapore's success story.

The problems associated with building an administrative machinery for Cambodia occupied the minds of the attendees in the seminar. With practically all its former civil service removed by the Khmer Rouge, the establishment of an efficient, corruption-free civil service was recognized as an essential first step. The Constitution had to provide for the system of appointments to the civil service – in short, a Public Service Commission. I would have thought that this would have been provided for, but it is conspicuous by its absence. I must admit that the seminars could have been structured to emphasize the importance of this topic instead of focusing on the separation of powers.

THE JUDICIARY

The separation of powers is recognized, with a special chapter ensuring the independence of the judiciary. Although there were provisions in previous constitutions on the judiciary, the present provisions are rather more tightly drafted to ensure its independence in specific terms. Again I would like to think that points flowed from the sessions we had. At the same time, recognition of the separate functions of a Public Prosecutor has been mentioned, in particular the prosecutorial discretion *vide* Article 112.

In place of the Second Chamber of the previous Constitution, there are provisions for a Constitutional Council and the National Congress. These are extra-parliamentary organs of state which have their origins in the French system. They approximate the *Conseil d'Etat* and the referendum mechanisms of the peculiarly Continental systems.

On the whole, I would judge that the role played by UNTAC in helping shape the present Constitution has been useful – not only as regards the legal form, but also the more important basis for the establishment of a modern-day government of the people of Cambodia responsible to the electorate and for safeguarding human rights. It was an almost *ad hoc* setting up of a resource base to conduct these constitutional seminars but, given the short space of time, I would like to think we achieved our purpose.

They could have been better organized, but I rather suspect, with all the problems encountered by UNTAC, these seminars could not have had much priority. The second session was better organized; we had more resource persons for language and communication facilities.

To those who are quick to cavil at UNTAC's efforts in this regard, it might be pertinent to note that UNTAC's mandate did not cover Constitution-making. This was a task that was specifically (and quite rightly, in my opinion) accorded to the Constituent Assembly.

29. Perspective from the Department of Peace-Keeping Operations (DPKO)

Hisako Shimura[1]

UNTAC IN THE CONTEXT OF RECENT DEVELOPMENTS IN PEACE-KEEPING

Let me first say that we, in DPKO, are very much conscious of most, if not all, of the concerns and criticisms about UNTAC that have been brought to our attention during the course of this conference. We share those concerns and are trying to make the best of our experience of UNTAC, in order to improve our performance in the future. Instead of trying to address these specific issues, however, let me try to put some of the successes and failures, strengths and shortcomings of UNTAC in a somewhat broader context. In DPKO we are dealing with 17 operations at present. Perhaps we have the advantage of looking at UNTAC in the context of these other operations and of recent trends and developments in peace-keeping. In doing so, I hope some light can be shed on the specific issues that have been raised as well.

As mentioned by many speakers, peace-keeping operations have undergone an enormous transformation and evolution in the last several years. Any appropriate and fair assessment of UNTAC must keep in mind the fact that, in many ways, UNTAC was the first, or the most extreme, example of these changes that have been affecting us. There is a certain amount of confusion as to whether or not UNTAC was still the largest operation ever mounted up to that time. I think the confusion arises from the fact that in earlier years we only recorded the number of military personnel, whereas today, because the civilian staff, including civilian police, play an important part, we also include the number of those personnel. So, if we applied the same standards, I believe ONUC, the operation in Congo, comes out sightly larger than UNTAC. But, there is no question that UNTAC was, in any case, one of the two largest UN operations established up to that time. Of course, it has been surpassed by UNPROFOR and UNOSOM since. There is also no question that, including these more recent operations, UNTAC is the most complex, most comprehensive operation in terms of its mandate, its tasks and its structure. We can consider UNTAC to have been the first major comprehensive and multi-dimensional operation planned and established since the Cold War ended. It is also one of the few operations and the only major operation the UN has undertaken in Asia. Many of these characteristics of UNTAC being "the first" or "the most" or "the only" have affected its performance and its record. At the same time, I think we should also carefully keep in mind in any assessment that UNTAC was

---

[1] Director, United Nations Europe/Latin America Division, UN Department of Peace-Keeping Operations, New York.

clearly planned to be a Chapter VI operation, a traditional peace-keeping operation in terms of use of force, consent of the parties, and so one, and not as a Chapter VII operation, which we have subsequently attempted in UNPROFOR and UNOSOM. And even with the serious obstacles arising from the non-cooperation of the Khmer Rouge, there was never any question, never any doubt that it should continue as a Chapter VI operation. There were many suggestions even from within UNTAC's ranks that the Chapter VII approach should be adopted. But General Sanderson recommended, with the full support of Mr Akashi, that UNTAC should continue as a Chapter VI operation. This was fully supported by all concerned departments at the UN Headquarters, the Secretary-General and all members of the Security Council.

IN PLANNING AND PREPARATION, AND LATER IN IMPLEMENTATION, UNTAC FACED SPECIAL CHALLENGES, ISSUES AND DIFFICULTIES OF BREAKING NEW GROUND

I would like to deal with certain features of UNTAC in which it faced special challenges, issues, and difficulties because it was the "first" or the "most" in many ways, and it was a ground-breaker in the field of peace-keeping operations. One aspect of this has already been stated: UNTAC was given the broadest, most complex and comprehensive mandate and objectives of all peace-keeping operations. The determination of the mandate of an operation is of course up to the Member States of the Security Council, but I shall simply mention that the comprehensiveness of the UNTAC operation was probably possible only because it was planned and established precisely at that time – not before, not after.

UNTAC was a post-Cold War operation, created at a time when the belief in the potential of UN peace-keeping operations was perhaps at its greatest. This was fortunate in many ways because, at least in this operation, the planners cast their sights very widely and considered and incorporated many aspects, which the various speakers have addressed before me. Some may think that it was too ambitious an objective, others may think that there were important gaps. But this was certainly a very audacious undertaking and the complexity of its mandate and its composition in many ways reinforced each other and strengthened the chance of success. In order to accomplish such an ambitious mandate, enormous resources are needed. The 16,000-strong military component was then second only to ONUC, and the 3600 strong civilian police component was the largest ever. There were also a significant number of other civilian personnel and the variety of their tasks and the expertise required were equally unprecedented.

Although, in the case of UNTAC, we were more fortunate than in many other recent experiences in being given the resources to enable us to accomplish the mandate, a great deal of effort was needed in searching for new sources of contribution – new contributing governments, new expertise, etc. It was a challenge to secure the large number of military and civilian police, many from first-time contributors. But a particular difficulty was encountered in the case of civilian personnel. In traditional peace-keeping operations, the core of the manpower was military, and there was a relatively small number of civilian personnel in an advisory or support capacity. This was not the case in UNTAC. In the earlier operations, because the bulk of the operation – the military personnel – served for six months, the few civilians were normally provided from among the serving Secretariat staff, in order to provide the continuity and the "UN-ness" to the operation. Because UNTAC was the first major departure from this pattern, we were not as quick in realizing the nature of the new demands and the attempt was made in the initial stages to search for the needed personnel within the UN family, i.e. the Secretariat and the various specialized agencies. Another factor was the financial constraints. In fact, there was a specific instruction from the highest level that we should search within, and not to go, in the first instance, outside or to governments to obtain the necessary civilian expert personnel. It soon became obvious, however, that this would not do, because we did not have either the number or the range of expertise required by UNTAC, and we later began to approach governments to give us their experts, on secondment. This was a part of the reasons for the delay in recruitment and deployment of the civilian personnel of UNTAC, particularly in the Civil Administration Component.

Another first was the role of the Permanent Five (P5). Because of the pre-eminent role the P5 have played in many recent operations, we may have already forgotten that this is a very new phenomenon. In the 40 years of traditional peace-keeping, a practice had developed of not, as a rule, calling upon P5 members to provide personnel. The reasons for this are well-known. There were of course exceptions. France was involved in UNIFIL and UNTSO, and the United Kingdom in UNFICYP. In fact, the United States and the then Soviet Union provided a small number of observers to UNTSO, but this was always considered to be an exception. After the end of the Cold War, we felt that the inhibition of shielding peace-keeping operations from major power rivalries was no longer applicable, and embraced the involvement of these powers. I think some of the later examples may have given some of us pause about the benefits of the involvement of major powers. There are of course benefits – in fact a necessity – in peace-keeping operations, today and in the future, for active major powers' involvement, but we have also come to realize that there can be certain drawbacks. In the case of UNTAC, a happy balance was struck as regards the role of major powers. It has already been recognized that in the political process leading up to the Paris Agreements, the major powers played an important and beneficial role, along with regional powers such as ASEAN and a number of others. At the stage of implementation, as well, all five major powers were involved; it was only the second time that all of them were simultaneously participating in a given peace-keeping operation. But their participation was by and large not overwhelming. France provided a large battalion, China provided an engineering battalion, the United Kingdom another specialized unit, but the United States and the Russian Federation provided less than 50 observers each. One might say that the major powers indicated their support to the operation, without overwhelming the operation.

Another area in which UNTAC's status as a first had an impact is the relationship between the mission in the field, particularly the leadership of the mission – the Special Representative and the Force Commander – on the one hand, and the UN Headquarters in New York – the Secretary-General and DPKO – on the other. Again, in earlier traditional peace-keeping operations, there emerged a tradition and a practice for UN Headquarters to keep a rather close rein over decision-making affecting peace-keeping missions in the field. I think this was largely due to the fact that those were fairly straightforward operations. At the same time, while those operations relied largely on military personnel and were headed by a military officer, they were also considered to be essentially political operations. Military personnel were used in a way that was entirely different from the use of national armed forces. This led to the practice and tradition that these operations had to be closely guided by Headquarters. And when we had an entirely different kind of operation in UNTAC – large, complex and headed by a civilian chief – which could not possibly be micromanaged by New York, New York was somewhat slow to realize that change had taken place. We have now come to realize this. One of the major issues over which UNTAC and UN Headquarters often disagreed was to what extent the Paris Agreements should be scrupulously observed or not, and whether they should be interpreted with some flexibility. UNTAC operated with considerable flexibility and a decentralized decision-making, quite understandably. New York tended to take a more strict constructionist approach regarding the Paris Agreements, and tried to keep decision-making in its hands, often to the detriment of the effectiveness of the operation. Now, there is a greater awareness of this new situation and a need for a new relationship between New York and the field.

MANY ISSUES AND DIFFICULTIES THAT ARE INHERENT IN PLANNING AND MANAGING UN PEACE-KEEPING OPERATIONS WERE ACCENTUATED IN UNTAC'S CASE

There were also many issues and difficulties which were inherent in the planning and management of any UN peace-keeping operations which affected UNTAC. Because of its complexity, these difficulties tended to be magnified and accentuated. For example, many speakers have referred to the need for better planning. In fact, UNTAC has been one of the better planned operations in recent experience. I remember in early 1989, Mr Ahmed, the then Special Representative, judged that the negotiations had reached the stage where close coordination between his office and the then Office for Special Political Affairs, the predecessor of DPKO, was necessary. We met frequently and began to make contingency planning. But there are also limits to any planning, particularly in the case of peace-keeping operations. For example, it was not until after the Paris Agreements were signed in October 1991 that the parties, the factions in Cambodia, finally agreed to give us more or less accurate numbers of their respective troops and their deployment; without that vital information, accurate planning could not have been done before then. Also, it was only after the signing of the Paris Agreements, even though the UN had sent a number of reconnaissance missions before then, that the last group of reconnaissance missions could be dispatched and bring back the important information on which the final plan could be made. It requires no elaboration that the fact that the UN does not have a standing army or force, and that each and every peace-keeping operation has to be planned and executed from scratch, is a great drawback in terms of efficiency, rapid deployment, etc. At the same time, once a political decision has been made by the Security Council to establish a peace-keeping operation, there is a great pressure to do so as quickly as possible and this leads sometimes to less than optimum use of resources and less than appropriate decisions.

Although, as I said, UNTAC was more fortunate than other recent operations in essentially being given the resources to organize the kind of operations that the mandate required, this did not apply to the support structure at Headquarters in New York, essentially, DPKO and also FOD (which at that time was within the Department of Administration and Management). When UNTAC planning was at its height, the DPKO had only about a dozen political affairs officers and about half a dozen military officers dealing at that time with some ten peace-keeping operations. There was not yet a unit or staff dedicated to planning new operations. Again, this was because UNTAC was one of the first major operations ushering in this great deluge of peace-keeping operations which has followed, and headquarters had not yet had an opportunity to catch up with this explosion of tasks and responsibilities.

The slow and cumbersome legislative and budgetary procedures which affect the UN, including the establishment of peace-keeping operations, is also fairly well-known. After the Security Council approves an operation, the budget is prepared and has to go through the ACABQ, the Fifth Committee and the General Assembly, normally taking at least several weeks. And until the budget is approved, theoretically, the Secretary-General has no authority to spend one cent. In UNTAC's case, of course, this was partially compensated by the expedient of getting a US$200 million advance commitment authority. But this was only a commitment authority, not cash, and the cash problem was very much a hindrance in mounting UNTAC. It should also be noted that peace-keeping operations are guided by the established UN administrative and financial rules and regulations. This is quite understandable and proper, because we handle monies provided by the Member States and they have to be managed prudently. However, these rules and regulations, which were designed for much more static regular operations of the UN, now also govern the needs of peace-keeping operations. These are much larger problems, which cannot be resolved by DPKO alone, and we need the support of Member States in adjusting the support structure in the Secretariat to enable it to meet the expanding responsibilities.

30. UNITAR's Program of Correspondence Instruction (POCI) in Peace-Keeping Operations

Dr Harvey J. Langholtz[1]

BACKGROUND

Throughout most of the last 40 years the UN peace-keeping force has been well under 10,000 personnel, and the UN has relied on a small number of nations to contribute troops to conduct traditional peace-keeping operations. Each nation trained its own personnel to different standards and there was no centralized method to provide common training. The superpowers were infrequently involved and, with some notable exceptions, UN peace-keeping operations were intended to consist of unarmed or lightly armed observers monitoring an established cease-fire at the request of both parties to a conflict.

This picture changed dramatically with the end of the Cold War and efforts are now underway in all facets of UN peace-keeping to cope with expanding demands. As of the summer of 1994, UN peace-keeping operations were staffed by 70,000 personnel from 70 nations, and individual peace-keepers were being called upon to function together on missions as diverse as humanitarian relief and military enforcement.

It is widely recognized that the training facilities designed to meet the needs of a small population of traditional peace-keepers during the Cold War lack the capacity to serve today's expanded population of peace-keepers, and also lack the capability to cover the widening scope and complexity of today's missions – peace enforcement; humanitarian operations; civilian police; and others.

The call for the strengthening of UN peace-keeping training has come from many sources, and the concept of developing self-paced training modules to be distributed to UN peace-keepers has been discussed in many fora: the UN Special Committee for Peace-Keeping Operations included the topic in the 1993 and 1994 conclusions and recommendations; the Contact Group for Peace-Keeping included the topic during its July 1992 meetings; the Stimson Center's recent report included the idea; the recent Vienna meeting on peace-keeping training contained it; US presidential decision directive 25 supported the initiative; and the General Assembly addressed the problem in the fall of 1993 in the omnibus peace-keeping resolution, agenda item 87, A/48/648. While the exact wording of these sources may vary in detail, they consistently reach the same conclusion: there is a need to provide common UN-approved training to support interoperability, a

---

[1] Director, UNITAR Programme of Correspondence Instruction in Peace-Keeping Operations (POCI), New York.

common understanding of UN procedures, and standardized levels of performance.

But training can be expensive, and the UN and Member States must have the ability to provide standard training to a large population of UN personnel on short notice at a low per-student cost. This training must be carefully managed so as to be affordable to personnel of all nations.

LOW-COST TRAINING THROUGH CORRESPONDENCE COURSES

Many alternatives have been put forward to deliver training to UN peace-keepers. Each is designed to fill a specific need and reach a recognized population of students. One of the approaches discussed was the development of a series of self-paced training modules – correspondence courses – that would be provided to individual peace-keepers and would cover various aspects of peace-keeping.

The correspondence-course concept has been put forward by US military personnel, and personnel from other nations, accustomed to using correspondence courses as an efficient method to deliver standard training on a variety of topics to a large population of soldiers and sailors. Each of the United States uniformed services maintains its own correspondence school to serve the training needs of its own members: the US Army operates the Army Institute for Professional Development (IPD) in Fort Eustis, Va.; and the US Navy, Air Force, Marine Corps, and Coast Guard each maintain their own correspondence schools. The Netherlands has its own military correspondence school, and the Norwegian Armed Forces Correspondence School already has its own course on peace-keeping. Each of the military institutions functions as an independent administrative command, geographically separated from resident training schools, and operating in close coordination with the personnel and training organs of its parent service. The US Army IPD currently has 250,000 students enrolled world-wide in 1200 different subcourses covering Army topics, and the other military correspondence schools carry enrolments commensurate with the size of their service population. The cost of these operations will vary with the complexity of the course and the number of students, but generally is in the range of $50 per enrolment.

IMPLEMENTING A SOLUTION AND THE DEVELOPMENT OF UNITAR'S PROGRAM OF CORRESPONDENCE INSTRUCTION

The initial planning and early implementation have taken place to establish UNITAR's Program of Correspondence Instruction in Peace-Keeping Operations (POCI). POCI has been designed to function as envisioned by those who introduced the idea in the UN Special Committee on Peace-Keeping Operations. POCI will produce a series of exportable self-paced training modules. Material will be economically produced and the program will be financially self-supporting based on small per-student enrolment fees.

Planning meetings have been held with the UN Department of Peace-Keeping Operations (DPKO) and Assistant Secretary-General Iqbal Riza, and letters in support of the program have been exchanged between the US mission to the UN and Under-Secretary-General Kofi Annan. The DPKO Training Unit has been kept well informed, has shaped organizational development, has proposed course titles for development, and has reviewed course outlines and course drafts. A meeting of 13 interested nations was held and a general approach was adopted. An international faculty of 14 experienced peace-keepers, representing 10 nations, is at work drafting ten courses. The first course has been revised following DPKO review, portions of several other courses have been received, and additional material is expected soon. Progress to this date has not required any funding, but as course authors complete their drafts there will be a need for funding to equip POCI with the capability to prepare camera-ready copy, print an initial inventory, publicize the availability of training material, and ship courses to students.

GOALS AND METHODOLOGY

Self-paced training modules

POCI will develop self-paced training modules to be delivered to individual peace-keepers *in situ* world-wide, in support of UN peace-keeping missions. These courses will provide students from all nations with standard UN-approved training that supports accepted UN doctrine. Each course will cover a different topic and will include readings, study material, and tests. POCI will be coordinated from the UN in New York, a nominal per-student enrolment fee will be charged, nations will support the program in proportion to the number of students they have enrolled, and the program will strive to be financially self-supporting, with enrolment fees covering all operating expenses.

Language, media and delivery

Training material may be developed and made available in any of the six official languages of the UN, or other languages based on need and forecast enrolments; however, the first courses are being written in English and a cost analysis will be completed before courses are translated into other languages. The ten courses currently under development all use print media and book format. Future courses may incorporate video, audio, or other media as appropriate, depending on cost, availability, target students, and suitability of the content of the course. POCI will maintain the capacity to provide UN-approved standardized training at short notice to small or large numbers of peace-keepers anywhere in the world, and permit the UN to react quickly when trained personnel are urgently needed.

Two categories of courses currently under development

As discussed above, POCI's first course has been completed, and nine additional courses are currently being developed by experts who are internationally recognized in various aspect of peace-keeping and UN military operations. POCI courses will fall into two general categories: topical, and mission-specific.

Topical courses

Each topical course will cover an important aspect of peace-keeping:
- the history of peace-keeping;
- humanitarian operations;
- logistical support of peace-keeping operations;
- peace-keeping on the ground;
- the management of traditional peace-keeping operations;
- the law of war as pertaining to peace-keeping operations;
- convoys and escorts;
- de-mining; and
- civilian police.

Mission-specific courses

The mission-specific courses will deal with the larger peace-keeping missions and will familiarize potential UN peace-keepers with their mission prior to deployment. These courses will cover two areas. The first area will be the genesis and background to the dispute, and will include the social, political, and ethnic issues that may have contributed to the conflict. The second area will be the nature of the United Nations intervention and the organization of the mission. This section will include:

- the Security Council Resolution establishing the mission as well as the organization of the UN force;
- command, control, and communication;
- rules of engagement;
- status of forces;
- transportation; and
- other topics relating to the actual operation of the mission.

The Annex to this paper provides additional information on both topical and mission-specific courses under development.

Target students, course length and exams

POCI courses are being written for officers and enlisted personnel of the armed forces of member nations, but enrolments from other populations are anticipated. The courses may vary in length but will normally be no more than about half of an upper division undergraduate course – no more than 300 pages, or 40 hours of reading. Each course will contain no more than 15–20 lessons of less than two hours each, with a 20-question self-quiz at the end of each lesson, with answers provided. In addition to the self-quizzes, each course will have a 50-question end-of-course examination. Students will submit their completed end-of-course examinations to POCI for grading, passing will be 75%, and POCI will issue a certificate of completion to the student to certify mastery of the material. Course authors will draft two separate end-of-course examinations to permit first-time failures to have a second opportunity to pass.

Course authors, course content and remuneration

Course authors will submit a brief course outline to POCI before drafting begins, and both the course outline and final draft will be subject to editorial and content review by POCI or DPKO. Existing UN documents or texts (e.g. *The Blue Helmets, Resolutions of the Security Council,* or *Standard Operating Procedures*) may be used as study material, or course authors may choose to draft the entire manuscript themselves. POCI courses will never appear to establish policy or doctrine and will teach only recognized UN procedures. Course authors will draft the course manuscript and submit a computer-readable file to POCI. POCI will be responsible for the layout of text and the printing of the material. Course authors will be compensated 15% of tuition received, but this may vary with courses and authors depending on individual circumstances and the regulations of Member States.

Printing and shipping: US Army cooperation with POCI

The US mission to the UN has corresponded with the US Army, endorsing the POCI concept, and requesting direct technical support for the project. The Directors of the UN's POCI and the US Army's IPD have met several times and come to an agreement that IPD would be prepared to print and distribute POCI material on a cost-reimbursable basis. Additionally, the Directors informally agreed that IPD could provide office space to be occupied by a POCI project officer. An MOU is currently being circulated for review and approval. Both parties recognize the UN will be responsible for the content, all materials will clearly appear to be from the UN, and the IPD will only function as a contract printer and shipper. All contact with the student will be through the UN in New York, not the US Army in Virginia.

DPKO review of material

The Department of Peace-Keeping Operations will have the opportunity to review course content and direct that modifications be made at four points in the development process: (1) the selection of the title and author; (2) the author's submission of a course outline; (3) the author's submission of the manuscript; and (4) any time after a course has been placed in circulation.

Financial self-sufficiency

It is POCI's goal to become financially self-sufficient. Once course development and printing have been completed, operating expenses will be covered by student tuition – an approach that has proven successful for organizations similar to POCI. During the early stages of development, POCI will be faced with initial start-up costs associated with course writing, printing, publicity, and distribution. Actual operating expenses and revenues will vary with the number of student enrolments, but will be structured to expand or contract, based on the number of enrolments.

THE START-UP OF POCI

POCI is completing the planning phase and entering the implementation phase. The blueprint for the organization is in place and POCI is prepared to commence staffing, print the now-ready first course, and continue production of subsequent courses as they are completed by course authors. It is important that POCI be established in phases to permit carefully managed growth and expansion, based on the number of enrolments.

First phase: a small liaison office for printing

The initial step in implementation will be the establishment of a liaison office to coordinate printing with the US Army IPD in Fort Eustis, Va. It will be the objective of this office to commence operation, and serve a limited number of students – up to perhaps 2000 – during the early stages of growth. Initially, this office will be staffed by one full-time program manager who will receive direction from the Director of POCI and be responsible for developing and implementing the functions and procedures outlined in the Annex.

CONCLUSIONS

There have been many calls for the development of correspondence courses to train UN peace-keepers. This training method is recognized as a low-cost way to provide standard training to large numbers of students who are geographically distributed, and who require rapid delivery of material covering a wide variety of topics. The foundation for POCI is in place, the organizational concept has been widely accepted, one course has been completed and others are in draft. POCI is in the process of identifying resources needed to support the initial printing of courses, and is scheduled to commence operations during the winter of 1994–95.

ANNEX: OUTLINE OF COURSES

History of peace-keeping

Description

Part I: A history of peace-keeping from 1948 to 1988. The United Nations Charter, characteristics of peace-keeping and peace-making. Background, establishment, military and civilian operations, financial aspects, and lessons learned from each United Nations peace-keeping mission.
Part II: A history of peace-keeping from 1988 to the present. The 1988 Nobel Peace Prize; The end of the Cold War; Chapter VI, VI 1/2, VII of the UN

Charter. The evolution from peace-keeping to peace-enforcement and other UN actions, Agenda For Peace, UNPROFOR, UNTAC, UNOSOM. Lessons learned from recent United Nations missions.

Course status

First draft submitted and under review by POCI.

Course authors

Mr F.T. Liu of the International Peace Academy and Dr David Cox of Queens College, Kingston, Ontario.

Peace-keeping on the ground: the management of traditional peace-keeping operations

Description

A how-to course outlining how to command, control, lead, manage and operate peace-keeping operations. Management, logistics, organisation, the goal of a peace-keeping operation, rules of engagement, communications, legal authority and legal restrictions, security, civil matters. Strategy and tactics.

Target students

Mid-grade and senior military officers and civilian administrators.

Course status

General Indar Rikhye, course author. General Rikhye retired from the Army of India after serving as Chief of Staff of the UN Emergency Force in Gaza, Chief Military Adviser to the UN Secretary-General, and UN Force Commander.

Front-line peace-keeping

Description

A how-to course. Frontline strategy and tactics. The goal of peace-keeping operations, negotiations, how to run a check-point, surveillance, communications, responsibilities of peace-keepers, handling civilians, handling terrorists, security of peace-keepers.

Target students

Front-line enlisted personnel.

Primary text

United Nations Peace-Keeping Training Manual.

Course status

Lt.-Col. Lars Andersson, Army of Sweden, course author.

United Nations peace-keeping operations: logistical support

Description

How UN peace-keeping operations are supported. Functional areas of logistical operations, responsibilities, sources, command and control, logistics principles, force logistical support, planning phases, financial arrangements and reimbursement, property and inventory control, cost accounting. What the donor nation is responsible for, and what the UN is responsible for.

Target students

UN logistics officers and donor nation logistics officers.

Primary text

United Nations Logistics Support of Peace-Keeping Operations: Lt.-Col. Grimm of US Army.

Course status

First draft submitted by POCI to UN Assistant Secretary-General Riza for review at his request. Comments received from DPKO training unit and revisions completed. Course is complete and ready for circulation.

Humanitarian operations and disaster relief

Description

UN response to disasters, responsibility, disaster relief operations, refugees, refugee housing, refugee security, children, sovereignty, medical/health issues, protecting a civilian population during a war. Steps to handling an emergency: needs assessment, implementing arrangements and personnel, supplies and logistics, site selection, health, food and nutrition, water, sanitation, social services and education, fieldlevel management.

Target students

UN peace-keeping personnel, UNHCR, others.

Primary text

UNHCR Handbook for Emergencies.

Course status

Development pends identification of course author.

The law of war as pertains to peace-keeping

Description

The legal aspects of war as pertaining to UN peace-keeping operations. The Geneva Convention, Status of Forces Agreements.

Target students

Mid-grade and senior officers.

Course status

Lt.-Col. Juhani Loikkanen, Army of Finland, course author.

Escort and convoy operations

Description

How to conduct convoy operations. Concept, control, types of convoys, environment, dynamics, humanitarian operations, the responsibilities of those being convoyed.

Target students

All.

Course status

Capt. Jeffery McCoon, US Army, course author. Course outline submitted to DPKO and comments received.

De-mining

Description

How to conduct de-mining operations. Mine identification, establishment of corridors, the protection of civilians, the disarming and disposing of mines.

Target students

All.

Course status

Pends identification of course author.

Civilian police

Description

The establishment of a civilian police force as a transition from peace-enforcement to self-governing civil society. The establishment of local law, arrest procedures, courts, incarceration, civil rights of the accused.

Target students

Potential civilian police or military police conducting civilian operations.

Course status

Under discussion with DPKO CIVPOL.

Mission-specific courses

Description

The mission-specific courses will deal with the larger peace-keeping missions and will familiarise potential UN peace-keepers with their mission prior to deployment. These courses will cover two areas. The first area will be the genesis and background to the dispute, and will include the social, political, and ethnic issues that may have contributed to the conflict. Also included will be the geography and weather of the region, and customs and culture of the population. The second area will be the nature of the United Nations intervention and the organisation of the mission. This section will include the Security Council resolution establishing the mission as well as the organisation of the UN force; command, control, and communication; rules of engagement; status of forces; transportation; and other topics relating to the actual operation of the mission.

Target students

Officers, civilians, and senior enlisted posted to the missions.

Primary text

To be based on each mission's SOP and other references as appropriate.

Course status

Mission-specific courses currently under development:
- UNOSOM, Brigadier General Asif Duraiz nominated by Pakistan as course author;
- UNPROFOR, Col. Richard Gray of the Army of New Zealand, and Lt.-Col. Miguel Moreno of the Army of Argentina: Drafts submitted and under review by POCI;
- UNTSO, Lt.-Col. Richard Dobbie of the Army of Australia: course outline submitted, reviewed and returned to author;
- ONUMOZ, Mr Mwenya Lwatula, Zambia;
- ONUSAL, Lt.-Col. Luis Alejandre and Major Pedro Galan, Army of Spain, course authors.

31. A French Perspective on Peace-Keeping

Lieutenant-Colonel Xavier Guérin[1]

In order to be able to cope with the numerous post-Cold War conflicts, the UN was led to increase considerably the number of its interventions in favour of peace. The volume of forces involved in operations conducted in support of a peace process (peace-keeping or peace-making) keeps growing. This evolution gives an increased importance to the training of troops designated to take part in these ever more complex operations.

PRINCIPLES

Combat training is the essential part of the general training required for the troops involved in peace-keeping operations

The specific education for peace-keeping operations must be seen only as marginal and complementary. It should never become so predominant that one may be entitled to speak about forces that are "specialized" in peace-keeping, especially with the new context – which has now prevailed for the last three years – in which these operations are conducted and in which France has acquired a certain amount of experience.[2]

MAIN FEATURES

Education for peace-keeping operations takes on various forms

Education for peace-keeping is individual and/or collective, permanent and/or occasional, general and/or specific. It concerns officers, NCOs and soldiers and all statutory categories of personnel: professionals on active duty as well as reservists serving under contract, in either the Army, the Navy, the Air Force, the Gendarmerie or the support services.

Education for peace-keeping operations covers various subjects

In the classical military field, there are courses in command, control, communication and information, tactics and support. In addition, instruction in other fields includes international humanitarian law, knowledge of the mission environment (history, geography, ethnic, cultural, religious and linguistic aspects), knowledge of the UN and its procedures and of regional organizations liable to get involved in a peace-keeping operation decided by

---

[1] Head of Studies on Peace-Keeping Operations, French Army, Paris.
[2] A total of almost 30,000 French officers, NCOs and soldiers have now served in former Yugoslavia, Somalia and Cambodia.

the UN (CSCE, WEU, NATO, etc.), knowledge of the media world and of the NGOs. Obviously, according to the level of responsibility and specialization of the personnel involved, one or another particular subject will be emphasized. However, all personnel are given general information on all subjects, as it is considered that any soldier involved in such an operation might have to carry out highly diversified missions. Therefore, it appears that versatility is necessary at all level. This concerns mostly officers and some senior NCOs. This education is part of a normal military career (short or long) and is given during each of its major phases in the form of a specific training included in the overall training programmes.

Education for peace-keeping operations is permanent

- Basic training (at platoon level): Military Academy, platoon leaders course.
- Unit commanders training (company level): combat team commanders course.
- Staff officers training: Staff School (Majors and Lieutenant-Colonels).
- Senior officers: Joint Staff College (Lieutenant-Colonels), Advanced Military Studies Institute (Colonels).

Education for peace-keeping operations must be adapted to circumstances

A specific education is systematically given to all personnel and units designated for a given peace-keeping operation during the months or weeks before they are actually committed in the theatre of operations. This education takes into account the specifics of the commitment: country, population, terrain, etc.

CONCLUSION

To sum up, education for peace-keeping operations:

- is mainly based on classical combat training;
- does not exclusively concern a few "specialists" in the units; on the contrary, all personnel are concerned;
- is part of the permanent military training of personnel;
- is the object of contingency measures taken for units designated for a given mission to be carried out in a specific theatre.

ANNEX 1   TRAINING OF UN OBSERVERS

Officers to serve as UN observers are trained in Strasbourg and Paris, under the responsibility of the General Staff. The course is two weeks long. One week (in Strasbourg) is devoted to language training and familiarization with UN procedures, the second one (in Paris) being devoted to the study of the observer's responsibilities and the various theatres of operation. Language training consists mainly of a refresher course in English. However, officers designated to serve with UNTSO, MINURSO and UNIKOM who already have a fairly good knowledge of the English language are given a basic training in Arabic. Every year, a total of about 200 observers from the Army, the Air Force, the Navy or the Gendarmerie are trained. Some of these officers get their language training from a joint training centre at Rochefort. There, they take so-called "immersion" courses, during which they spend their entire day in a completely foreign environment.

ANNEX 2 TACTICAL TRAINING FOR PEACE-KEEPING OPERATIONS

Officers and NCOs of operational units (infantry, armour, artillery or engineers), from platoon leader to battalion commander level, take a two-week course in the Infantry School in Montpellier. During this course, besides language training, they are given additional information about their future zone of action and are taught technical procedures and tactics specifically related to peace-keeping operations (interposition, escort, negotiating, etc.)

The technique of negotiation is certainly the most specific of the few specific peace-keeping techniques. It must be taught carefully, bearing in the mind some broad principles:

- learn to listen and ascertain;
- do not negotiate everything, everywhere, ever at any price; negotiate only what is useful and when and where it is useful for the implementation of the mandate;
- the use of arms; opening fire is the alternative if the negotiation system fails.

ANNEX 3 LOGISTIC SUPPORT TRAINING

Officers who will be given logistic or transit responsibilities either in a staff position or in a unit take a two-week course in the Transport School at Tours. The course, which includes language training, makes them familiar with the UN logistic structure and the current UN procedures. They also learn how to operate the ADP systems which will be at their disposal. There, as in the Infantry School, officers who have recently taken part in peace-keeping operations are often called to brief the students on their own experience.

ANNEX 4 COLLECTIVE TRAINING OF THE UNITS

A unit designated to take part in a peace-keeping operation (from battalion to brigade level) systematically spends about three weeks in a training camp prior to its departure. Gradual exercises are conducted, starting at platoon level up to battalion level with scenarios corresponding to the reality of the future theatre of operations.

During their stay, the members of the unit will be given additional information on the theatre[3] and will be familiarized with peace-keeping techniques. In fact, these are few. The main concern of the officers and NCOs is to make their soldiers sensitive to the risks of life in a dangerous environment and to obtain a perfect discipline of fire from them, since using their weapons is authorized only for self-defence, which sounds like an easy concept but is in fact extremely difficult to apply in day-to-day reality.

In any case, the best "soldier of peace" will always be one who is best prepared for war, since any peace-keeping operation may easily become a peace-enforcing operation requiring the use of combat techniques and tactics for which the troops will fortunately have been trained. Or, even if the PKO force need not go as far as that extremely difficult shift of mission, at least it may have to launch more forceful actions. It must be prepared, trained and equipped so as to be able to undertake those dynamic actions.

ANNEX 5   UN STAFF PROCEDURES TRAINING

Officers to serve in a UN staff take a two-week course in the Staff School at Compiègne. They are given additional information on their future area of engagement and are made familiar with the UN procedures and modes of action. According to the future assignment of the officer, emphasis is placed either on operational or logistic techniques. Also, both the Joint Staff College and the Advanced Military Studies Institute include the UN as one of the subjects to be studied by their students.

---

[3] In principle, officers and NCOs have already taken the course at Montpellier or Tours.

32. Cambodia Today

Benny Widyono[1]

THE COUP ATTEMPT AND ITS AFTERMATH

The failed coup attempt of 2 July 1994 epitomizes the latest in a series of tumultuous events sparked by the reconquest by the NADK of Pailin and their hot pursuit of fleeing RCAF troops stopping just short of Battambang. This followed the King's gloomy press conference predicting catastrophe for Cambodia and blaming both the DK and the Royal Government for misbehaving, his premature departure to Beijing, the failed reconciliation talks in Pyongyang and Phnom Penh, the King's bombshell interview with the *Far East Economic Review* in which he proposed to come back to Phnom Penh and appoint four deputy premiers including Khieu Samphan, the equally unprecedented letter from Mr Hun Sen to the King, the declarations of the CPP against rumour-mongers, the debate on the bill outlawing the DK, and finally the attempted *coup d'état* and the successful quelling of this attempt. These continued shock waves underscore the fact that there is still some unfinished business which needs to be settled one year after the elections.

To use a United Nations term which is in vogue now, Cambodia is a country in transition from Communism to democracy, with all the attendant problems this brings with it. This explains the almost diametrically opposed perceptions which came out in the open in yesterday morning's discussions and which is characteristic of all discussions in Phnom Penh these days. On the one hand, there are the prophets of gloom and doom who predict imminent collapse, on the other there are optimists who point to the many clear signs of recovery and slow but sure progress in rehabilitation and development. One day everything seems to go the right way and then another day, it seems like everything is about to fall apart. Visiting a supermarket like Lucky in Phnom Penh, these days, we feel as if we were in Bangkok: shoppers, 70% of them Khmer members of the newly-emerging middle class, buy such items like dog food and muesli or pancake mix. Then, travelling to Siem Reap, we see machine guns guarding the temple. Cambodia today is a picture of contrasts and that is why it continues to fascinate and mesmerize all of us gathered around this table and that is why, thankfully, there is no donor fatigue in Cambodia. Economically, Cambodia is ready to be sucked into the maelstrom of dynamic growth characteristic of ASEAN and beyond. Let us look at these many faces of Cambodia today.

The coup attempt was a blessing in disguise. It cleared the air by flushing out into the open the simmering tensions caused by some CPP elements, and an unknown number of supporters, who are still sulking at the failure of the

---

[1] Secretary-General's Representative in Cambodia, Phnom Penh.

secessionist move last year and are still blaming UNTAC for the "irregularities of the elections". The CPP, in a declaration on 23 June, just one week before the coup, followed by the declaration of Chea Sim at the 43rd anniversary of the founding of the Communist Party (now CPP) on 28 June – just three days before the coup – praised the magnanimity of CPP in doing everything possible for the sake of democracy and national reconstruction by setting aside the irregularities of the elections.

The declaration also issued a stern warning against a group of individuals, merchants of bad news, who spread rumours and wrong information to spoil public opinion, to destabilize political opinion and to destroy the achievements of the comprehensive political solution and the Constitution. It further explained that those rumours were clearly directed against the CPP and its leaders. This strong stand in support of democracy and the Constitution is quite clearly implemented by Co-premier Hun Sen and was used by him, in cooperation with Prince Ranariddh, to swiftly quell the coup attempt.

The coup plotters, on the other hand, obviously wanted to turn the clock back and revert to the days when they had absolute power. They had no desire to uphold the results of last year's elections, but they wanted to complete last year's unfinished business of the secession. They planned to arrest the Co-premiers and establish a provisional government pending new elections for parliament and a president. They rallied police forces from Prey Veng and other provinces "to fight the Khmer Rouge who have infiltrated Phnom Penh in large numbers to destroy the National Assembly and the legitimate government in order to form a new government with the inclusion of the KR."

What they did not count on was Co-premiers Hun Sen and Prince Ranariddh's dogged determination to make their coalition government work. Today, the cooperation between the Co-premiers, which Hun Sen emphasized in his letter, is a reality. At a briefing to diplomats in the aftermath of the coup, Mr Hun Sen did warn that the many troops whom the coup leaders were able to muster was an indication that if the DK was actually brought into the government, it would be easy to rally troops to stage a coup!

This brings out the problem which was discussed yesterday afternoon: should the KR be brought into the Government or not? As late as the negotiations, there were still hopes for bringing the KR back on the basis of the King's three plus two formula, which will bring the KR into the Government in return for a cease-fire and incorporation of DK troops and territory into mainstream Cambodia. The King, in his famous interview, warned that we must be patient and talk. He was not in favour of outlawing the Khmer Rouge and of renewed warfare.

Although Mr Hun Sen dealt with the coup attempt swiftly and efficiently, there seems to be little news regarding the investigations of coup suspects and their possible trial, except for the 14 hapless Thais. As the investigations are not yet complete, newspapers were warned not to create false rumours, in the interest of national security. Newspapers which talk about the coup too openly are stifled and one editor is still in jail.

PREPARATIONS FOR RENEWED FIGHTING

If the failed coup attempt was a plus factor in clearing some of the unhealthy atmosphere in Phnom Penh, the Royal Government of Cambodia (RGC) can now concentrate on economic rehabilitation and on the other major problem: how to deal with the DK. Let us discuss the latter first in the context of yesterday's discussions. The outlawed bill, finally signed by Mr Chea Sim on behalf of His Majesty the King, provided little relief, at least in the short run, from feverish efforts to prepare for renewed warfare on both sides. It was greeted by a proclamation of a provisional government of national salvation by the DK, headquartered in Preah Vihear Province. As brought out in yesterday's discussions, the picture in the north and northwestern provinces is a stark contrast to the one in the capital. In Battambang, government troops are now back on Route 10 making progress towards Pailin. In Siem Reap, reportedly there is a heavy concentration of troops in Samrong. The deputy governor stated to us that they want to defend Samrong at all costs. The NADK is reported to move only in small groups in both provinces. At the same time, it is generally believed that despite the alarm signals, particularly from the foreign media, which were sounded when Pailin and An Long Veng fell to the NADK, no provincial seat is in imminent danger of falling into their hands. On 5 May the KR issued a declaration of war and singled out Somdej Krom Preah for having betrayed them.

At the end of the month, the attack on the train in Kamphot province by about 50 guerrillas was the biggest story after a lull in fighting. When the Khmer Rouge were ousted from their house in Phnom Penh, they threatened renewed warfare, this time including the south. Three westerners, a Briton, a Frenchman and an Australian, were reportedly among those captured and not yet released at the time of writing. Three Vietnamese train passengers, however, were reportedly killed. All 200 passengers were robbed of all their valuables and 30 Khmers are still held captive. Meanwhile, there were strong indications that the three hostages captured a few months ago near the southern town of Sihanoukville were presumed dead.

Apart from the chronic problems of bad discipline, disorganization and corruption, the RCAF seems to be faced with three acute problems: (a) a lack of ammunition, (b) a lack of funds and (c) an apparent shortage of troops.

The lack of ammunition is now reaching crisis proportions. Prior to 1990, the then Soviet Union supplied the CPAF with ammunition for Soviet-made AK47s. Since then, the supply has dried up and the RCAF has been sending missions with a shopping list trying to obtain ammunition, helicopters and sophisticated arms, apparently to no avail. Western powers and some ASEAN countries, at the recently concluded ASEAN meetings in Bangkok, seem to agree that administrative reform and training should precede the granting of lethal aid; otherwise such aid might fall into the hands of the NADK. Thailand is vigorously opposed to the granting of lethal aid. China has also come out against the US giving military aid, stressing that the Cambodian problem is an internal problem which is best left to the Cambodians to solve under the leadership of His Majesty the King. The DK radio strongly opposed military aid to the "puppets" and threatened that it, too, would be compelled to purchase weapons or seek military assistance. The main problem, it seems, is lack of suitable ammunition for the predominantly Soviet arms that are in use. Recently, in conjunction with the ASEAN Regional Forum on Security, Western countries as well as some ASEAN countries expressed support for giving arms to the RCAF. However, they all seem to agree that training and administrative reform must precede the provision of arms. In desperation, the RCAF is now trying to purchase ammunition. For this and other war purchases, it needs money.

The Royal Government's decision to allow the Ministry of Defence to be in sole control of logging concessions and revenues, bypassing the control over such revenues by the Ministry of Finance and other ministries, created quite an uproar in the international donor community. This decision violates a policy framework agreement between the IMF and the Government of last February promising the centralization of revenue disbursement as a condition for international assistance to reconstruct Cambodia. The Government clarified, however, that the decree only affects some logs which were felled by the Khmer Rouge and which must be exported in order to prevent their rotting. For other concessions, the old law in which revenue is controlled by the Ministry of Finance still prevails.

The apparent shortage of troops has led to forced conscription. Although on paper the RCAF has about 130,000 troops, in actual fact it is difficult to find these troops as most of them are phantoms. Meanwhile, Chief of Staff General Ke Kim Yan stressed that the Government is engaged in trying to demobilize part of the 130,000 strong army as part of the reform process. He denied any recruitment policy taking place. However, local militia, the backbone of village defence, needs to be replenished. Apparently some irregularities took place in certain districts in this recruitment drive. UNHCR and human rights associations have reported some evidence of forced recruitment, which might threaten the next rice harvests; young boys are forcibly taken from paddy fields or from their homes to fight on the front.

HUMAN RIGHTS ISSUES BEING HIGHLIGHTED

Human rights issues were highlighted by the visits of the High Commissioner on Human Rights USG Jose Ayala Lasso and Justice Kirby, the former for two days and the latter for three weeks. Mr Kirby, who is here for the third time since January, is positive about the country's progress. Mr Ayala Lasso was also pleasantly surprised at the openness of the government ministers in describing their shortcomings in human rights affairs. Indeed, there is a perceptible relaxation in the atmosphere in Phnom Penh since the coup attempt. After all, the coup leaders controlled the dreaded security system, at least up to a point.

The two visitors concentrated on issues related to the plight of ethnic Vietnamese at the border; the continued operation of the dreaded Chue Khmau secret prison in Battambang and other illegal prisons and the general conditions of prisons; the predicament of journalists who dare to oppose government policy or to publish accusations in the aftermath of the coup; an improvement in the judiciary system; and the question of de-mining. A report is being written for presentation to the General Assembly.

ECONOMIC PICTURE BRIGHTENS

If the political picture continues to be murky, the economy, as Ambassador Imagawa pointed out yesterday, shows bright spots here and there which give hope for the future. Although the political uncertainty of April/May caused a jump in the inflation rate and the flight of foreign currency, the coup attempt barely sent a ripple through the economy. Indeed, economically speaking, the situation remains solid. The inflation rate for 1994, at 13.4%, while higher than expected, is a far cry from the triple digit figures of recent years. The riel shows remarkable stability at 2,500 riel per dollar. Fluctuations of the riel during the pre-election period brought the rate at one point to 6,500 per dollar. The IMF has shown its confidence by announcing an increase in Cambodia's funding quota from SDR 25 million to SDR 65 million. In early May it also approved an enhanced structural adjustment facility worth US$120 million with an interest rate of 0.5%. This facility puts Cambodia in the category of economies in transition, an advantage. The success of the Finance Minister, Sam Rainsey, has attracted international attention and won him respect and admiration. What is little known is that his success can be attributed, in no small measure, to the success of the financial controls introduced by Roger Lawrence, whose team is now still in place as advisers to the Minister. In fact, this area is one in which UNTAC was clearly successful and should be studied in more detail for future operations.

UNTAC is gradually being replaced by UNDP and some ten agencies, as well as the IMF, the World Bank and the Asian Development Bank, who are all disbursing aid pledged at the ICORC meetings. Key areas for foreign aid have been identified as basic infrastructure, the agricultural sector and education and human resources training. Almost every day, new agreements for aid with bilateral and multi-lateral donors are being signed. Mr Nay Htun's visit coincided with the completion and approval of the Cambodia country programme which will be presented to the UNDP Executive Board in October for final approval. Private investors, more cautious as they are investing their own money, are still reeling from the KR offensive in April/May. New projects, mostly in the service sector such as apartment buildings, stores, banks and trading companies, are opening up almost on a daily basis. The Government has declared three growth poles for development: Siem Reap, Phnom Penh and Sihanoukville. Tourism is still depressed but is also slowly coming back. Last week, the morning flights to Siem Reap were fully booked with tourists, mainly from Europe.

FOREIGN POLICY TAKING OFF

ASEAN welcomed Cambodia's intention to join the regional grouping. In its final statement, ASEAN fully supports the Royal Government of Cambodia and condemns the coup attempt and the proclamation of the provisional government by the DK. The overseas visits by Cambodian leaders and the foreign ministers have brought back pledges of support and assistance.

33. UNTAC: A Flawed Paradigm/Success

Ken Berry[1]

Despite having ultimately achieved its principal objective of organizing and bringing the Cambodian elections to a successful conclusion, UNTAC nevertheless had a number of flaws, both major and minor, in its implementation. Hindsight does not, however, always provide a reliable or useful lens through which to view past events. Some of the lessons to be drawn from UNTAC are, moreover, Cambodia-specific, and it would be misguided to apply them blindly to other operations.

Nevertheless, there were clearly a number of things which went both right and wrong in the Cambodian operation, from which useful lessons can be drawn for future peace-keeping operations. Some may appear obvious, but since the same mistakes seem constantly to be made, the lessons bear repeating:

- The first condition for a successful PKO is the need for a conceptually sound and appropriately detailed peace plan. The Paris Agreements were a complex blueprint which, however, may have been overly ambitious in some respects, and which had important lacunae.
- The second condition, more honoured in the breach than in the observance, in the case of UNTAC, is the early deployment of adequate planning and oversight resources soon after the parties to a conflict have reached agreement, so as to maintain and build confidence.
- The third basic condition is the establishment of clear and achievable operational goals, not least to avoid unrealistic or ill-founded expectations of the UN as peace-keeper.
- The fourth condition for a successful PKO is the need for support of the parties to the conflict. In Cambodia, Khmer Rouge non-compliance, and the less than full compliance of the other parties, affected every aspect of the UNTAC operation.
- The fifth condition is the need for an appropriate level of external support for the operation.

Operational inflexibility shown by UNHQ on major and minor aspects of UNTAC's implementation underlined the need for reform in the Secretariat. The apparent lack of an effective mechanism whereby the UN can draw the necessary lessons from operations such as UNTAC, and guard corporate memory, should be covered in this reform.

There is clear potential for training courses, to ensure that civilian and military personnel used in UN operations have a common level of expertise. UN personnel should also be trained in basic principles of human rights.

---

[1] Senior Member, Personal Staff of Australian Foreign Minister, Canberra.

Justice packages may increasingly be an important element of UN operations in countries in which the basic infrastructure of law and order has broken down. Short and long-term training for local officials would be an important part of such packages. For Australia, Cambodia also demonstrated the value of middle power diplomacy and the potential for regional initiatives to point the way for the UN and complement future efforts to resolve conflicts:

Planning is an unnatural process. It is much more fun to do something. The nicest thing about not planning is that failure comes as a complete surprise, rather than being preceded by a period of worry and depression.

Sir Harvey Jones

INTRODUCTION

Amongst recent peace-keeping operations, UNTAC stands out as a rare example of one which largely lived up to its major objectives. Despite continuing problems of internal insecurity in Cambodia, and the expectations of elements of the international media who evidently thought that a fully functioning democracy can be created overnight, the international community can be rightfully proud of its achievements.

There is, however, an understandable human tendency — and a dangerous one — to remember only the successes, while burying the failures. There is thus a corresponding dangerous tendency to automatically use an operation which has been broadly categorized as successful as a paradigm for future operations. What should be borne in mind is that UNTAC was in fact a flawed success, and exposed a number of aspects of the UN system which either did not work or were simply no longer suited to conditions in the post-Cold War world and the types of complex operations the UN is now called upon to undertake. The recurrence in UNTAC of many of the problems which had already surfaced in previous UN operations shows that the lessons of the past have not been heeded, and that there is apparently no system in place to maintain corporate memory, much less act on it.

The fact that none of the areas of UNHQ most directly involved in planning and implementing UNTAC have sought to analyse, or, if they have, sought to publish or otherwise make available, the material to interested donor governments is an important lacuna and lesson in itself. It must, of course, be acknowledged that those offices and agencies all have their hands full at the moment with a variety of international crises. But it is nevertheless the case that even a fairly brief analysis of UNTAC's mistakes, supplemented, of course, by the political will to undertake the reforms necessary to avoid their repetition, would have been useful in the establishment and implementation of UN operations that have followed. Certainly there must come a point (which some would argue has already arrived) when the patience of donor governments expected to supply the human and material resources necessary to face the world's crises runs out in the face of the UN's inefficient use of those resources. A conference such as this is therefore extremely valuable in cataloguing the pluses and minuses of an operation such as UNTAC. But at the same time, we all need to be careful, and thus selective, when considering the situation with the benefit of hindsight.

There are two main categories into which an analysis of such an operation might be notionally divided: firstly, there are the "macro" or general lessons to be drawn, which pertain to the broader, geopolitical considerations affecting a decision to go into an operation and when to end it; and secondly, there are the "micro" or specific, internal lessons relating to the circumstances unique to each operation which can be learned from the day-to-day implementation of a mandate.

Many of the "macro" lessons have an ongoing relevance. The danger with the "micro" lessons, however, lies in trying to use them as a template in circumstances which are significantly different from those in which they were learnt. Within the constraints of a paper such as this, it would in any case be impossible to attempt to catalogue all the "micro" mistakes which may have been made during and even in the period leading up to UNTAC: that was the purpose of earlier sessions of this conference. This paper will thus concentrate on the "macro" lessons, while referring to illustrative "micro" lessons along the way.

THE "MACRO" LESSONS

From Australia's viewpoint as a central player in the various Cambodian peace negotiations over the past decade, one of the broader "geopolitical" lessons to be learned from the Cambodian experience has been the vindication of middle-power diplomacy — that is, effective coalition-building conducted by a country such as Australia, which is not a superpower or even a major power, with like-minded countries to achieve a selected, realistic goal. Our coalition-building in this case meant working from the outset with Indonesia and the other ASEANs, all five Permanent Members of the UN Security Council (the P5), Vietnam and the four Cambodian factions themselves. The fact that Australia came to the process without the political or other baggage normally associated with superpower or major power status meant that the various central parties were more prepared to listen and be less suspicious of our proposals.

In a similar way, Cambodia also demonstrated that a regional initiative can successfully show the way to the United Nations, rather than the other way around. In this case, while the Cambodia problem was not susceptible of a wholly regional solution and ultimately, inevitably had to depend on P5 support, nevertheless finding a solution to the Cambodia conflict reinforced the view put by Senator Evans in his recent book, *Cooperating for Peace*,[2] that in certain circumstances, "regional efforts and regional solutions are likely to become increasingly important in the international repertoire of conflict resolution and avoidance". However, as has been all too tragically demonstrated in Somalia, Rwanda and Bosnia-Herzegovina, more is required than just oral or moral support.

---

[2] Gareth Evans (1993) *Cooperating for Peace* (Allen and Unwin, Sydney) pp.29–33, 76–79.

While still on the regional dimension, the degree of consultation and cooperation amongst the countries of the Asia Pacific region, which ultimately led to the Paris Agreements, was in itself an important confidence-building measure, showing that similar cooperation on other security issues might be similarly productive. It is no exaggeration to say that the successful outcome of the Cambodian process was an important element in the creation of the ASEAN Regional Forum, which had its first formal ministerial-level meeting in Bangkok on 27 July.

UNTAC AS A MODEL FOR FUTURE PEACE-KEEPING OPERATIONS

The operation in Cambodia was arguably the United Nations' most complex, though not its largest, to date. The operation called for 15,900 military personnel, 3600 civilian police and 1020 civil administration personnel from more than 30 countries. Australia contributed the Force Commander; nearly 500 military communicators; ten civilian police; a 30-member movement control unit; a number of civilian personnel; and, during the elections, nearly 70 International Polling Station Officers and six Blackhawk helicopters and their crews.

UNTAC's mandate went far beyond that of traditional peace-keeping, and included comprehensive efforts towards institution-building and social reconstruction as integral parts of a peace-building package designed to secure a lasting end to armed conflict and a genuine transition to democracy. To this end, UNTAC was endowed with significant electoral, civil administration, police, human rights, repatriation, rehabilitation and reconstruction functions. To the extent that some of these peace-building objectives have not yet been achieved, it must be acknowledged that the Paris Agreements have still some way to go before we can make an overall assessment of their success.

Nevertheless, it is fair to say that UNTAC achieved its primary objective of organizing and conducting free and fair elections so that the Cambodian people could express their collective will – and reassume some control over their future – in a genuine act of self-determination. UNTAC also succeeded in removing the Cambodian conflict as a source of regional tension; Vietnam has entered into more productive relations regionally and internationally; external patrons have largely withdrawn material support for the various political groupings, thereby at least reducing the possibility of a destructive civil war continuing endlessly; more than 365,000 displaced Cambodians from the Thai border were successfully repatriated; Cambodia has assumed its rightful place in the community of nations – albeit while still facing many of the problems common to other poor, developing countries (including a continuing insurgency); and the process of reconstruction has at least begun.

As has already been made clear, however, there were at the same time a number of serious flaws in the UNTAC operation: tardy deployment of some central elements undermined the aims of the mission from the outset; civil administration control over the key areas of government was late in coming and by no means fully achieved, which gave the Khmer Rouge a facile excuse for not cooperating, which in turn meant that a neutral political environment was never really established; the civilian police element was, with some exceptions, ineffective; and effective prosecution of human rights abuses proved impossible.

If one is still seeking for paradigms, it can at least be argued that five basic conditions for an effective peace-keeping operation may be derived from the Cambodian operation. The list is not necessarily exclusive.

The first is a conceptually sound and appropriately detailed peace plan. The UNTAC peace-keeping operation was itself the outcome of a successful – if protracted – peace-making exercise conducted over a number of years, bringing together a wide group of countries as well as the internal players, and producing a very complex peace blueprint, the Paris Agreements, signed on 23 October 1991.

The essence of the Peace Plan – and its distinguishing feature from other UN operations – was for the United Nations itself (and not the warring parties, who could not agree on interim power-sharing arrangements) to assume responsibility for the internal administration of Cambodia during its transition to elected government. The Australian initiative of late 1989 was an amalgam of a number of earlier ideas, and subsequently refined and developed by the P5 working with the Co-chairmen of the Paris International Conference on Cambodia. As already noted, the fact that the ideas had been re-packaged and sold by a middle power such as Australia, and the coincidence of its timing with a number of other factors, gave the plan greater chances for success than its predecessors.

Although some of the plan's assumptions – especially about military demobilization – were undermined by Khmer Rouge intransigence, it also proved, for the most part, sufficiently detailed and robust in practice to give effective guidance and support to UNTAC and the international community throughout the evolution of the operation. There were, of course, some significant exceptions, including lack of clear direction on the role and operation of the SNC, and on what should happen in the event of non-compliance by one or more of the parties. Equally, however, it could be argued that the agreements would never have been concluded if these issues had been covered in any detail or at all.

The second condition is early deployment of adequate resources as soon as possible after the parties to the conflict have reached agreement, so as to build and maintain the confidence not only of the parties but, often more importantly, of the local population as well, thus enabling the effective implementation of the PKO's mandate. The UN operation in Cambodia unfortunately showed that this basic rule is more honoured in the breach than in the observance. While the period between the signing of the Paris Agreements in October 1991 and the arrival in Cambodia of the first UNTAC elements in mid-April 1992 was five months, it was another five to six months before UNTAC was fully operational, particularly in the all-important Civil Administration Component.

In part, the delays in UNTAC's deployment were due to, or aggravated by, inadequate planning and preparation caused by deficiencies in the work of the UN Advance Mission in Cambodia (UNAMIC), which was deployed in November 1991. It must also, however, be acknowledged that UNAMIC cannot wholly be blamed, being in itself the victim of insufficient preparedness to react to the pace of developments on the part of UNHQ in New York.

The slow and labyrinthine process for budget approvals, even for the most clearly essential items, remained a serious problem for the duration of UNTAC, and highlighted the need for reforms both in ACABQ/Fifth Committee and UNHQ procedures. This also illustrates the need for the Secretary-General to consider further structural changes in the Secretariat to meet the increasing demands being put on it and as a means of improving the administration of peace-keeping operations. The view of many of those who have implemented the various elements of the UNTAC operation is that multi-dimensional peace-keeping requires a new or, in some cases, revamped planning structure in the Secretariat, with new or enlarged planning units dedicated to military and political affairs, human rights, electoral, police and administration. These sorts of changes, some of which are already occurring, have staffing and financial implications, although there might be scope for the better deployment of existing Secretariat personnel and resources. The alternative is the continuation of *ad hoc* planning for multi-dimensional and multi-billion dollar operations.

At the very least, more flexibility needs to be shown, in particular giving operation commanders (civilian and military), who after all are best aware of the complicated conditions on the ground and most immediately concerned with speedy reactions, greater direct authority over funds allocations. A cogent example of the point was the delay of well over a year in the establishment of the important UNTAC civilian radio station, caused by UNHQ's excessively ponderous tender processes. In the meantime, the propaganda of two of the factions, who controlled their own transmitters, was broadcast essentially without challenge.

That being said, however, we should also collectively bear in mind the need for efficient spending of the always-scarce funds once they are made available. As already noted, it is not the purpose of this paper to give a litany of individual examples of inefficient expenditure such as too many vehicles of one type, or not enough of another; too few computers, arriving too late; the high cost of supplying water to UN personnel all over Cambodia; radios of insufficient range. But it is nevertheless useful to cite examples if they point to fundamental flaws in the preparation and planning processes for PKOs generally.

Some units of the UNTAC military component, for instance, arrived with equipment which was either old (and thus requiring more spare parts/replacements to be held in reserve or procured) or totally inappropriate (e.g. electrical equipment running on 110V, and not UNTAC's 220V, thus necessitating the purchase of extra generators). There were also complaints about engineering support arriving too late in-country (often with inappropriate equipment), and delays in the creation of an efficient logistics chain.

While some of these examples may sound picayune in comparison to the scale of the task facing UNTAC, it can nevertheless be argued that they were symptomatic of central planning defects which, unless addressed, will adversely affect other operations. They clearly demonstrate the need for more direction or guidance to be given to donor countries to ensure greater uniformity (and utility) of the equipment national units bring with them. Use of check-lists or, ideally, appointment of a "Force Inspector-General" to oversee standards, could be a start. Consideration might also be given to such things as the greater use of engineering units from the region in which the operation is taking place, in order to ensure speedy deployment. Joint regional training centres in certain useful specialities deployed in most UN operations these days (e.g. UNMOs, CIVPOL, information) might also be a way of ensuring minimum uniform standards.

Another essential part of adequate preparation is the early designation of senior staff – both civilian and military – and their rapid involvement in the planning of the operation. In the case of UNTAC, the UN Secretary-General's Special Representative was only appointed in January 1992; the Force Commander in December 1991; the Police Commissioner and the Civil Administration and Human Rights Directors in March 1992. UNTAC subsequently suffered from a lack of both continuity and institutional memory, due largely to the even later appointment of many of its subsidiary staff and the subsequent rapid – and often arbitrarily timed – rotation out of many of them.

The final judgment must be that these cumulative delays were critical in that they cut into the tight (and equally tightly funded) timetable outlined in the Paris Agreements, and affected UNTAC's credibility in the eyes of the Cambodian people (not to mention some donor and other countries).

The United Nations and Member States must also ensure that they provide the best qualified, professional and well-disciplined personnel in order to maintain the credibility of the operation. There should be an obligation on the part of the contributing countries to meet the criteria set by the United Nations for personnel, and a right by the UN to reject unsuitable or unqualified personnel at the donor's expense. Pre-deployment training to a common UN standard, when this is lacking, should also be regarded as essential. At the very least, efforts should be made to ensure commonality of language used by UN personnel in particular areas, something which did not always occur in UNTAC and which completely undermined any utility those personnel might otherwise have had.

UNTAC's 21,000 personnel ranged from highly qualified professionals to those who were incompetent and, in some cases, a menace to their colleagues and the Cambodian population. Unfortunately, there were far too many instances of personnel in the latter category not being rejected, possibly for fear of offending contributing counties or simply because there were no alternative personnel available. Worse for morale within UNTAC was the appointment (or even "promotion") of such personnel to more comfortable jobs, simply to get rid of them from sensitive areas. Moreover, the unacceptable behaviour of some military personnel caused resentment and alienated Cambodians. For future operations it is essential that a code of conduct be established for UN personnel.

The third basic condition for ensuring an effective peace-keeping operation is the establishment of clear and achievable goals, not least to avoid unrealistic or ill-founded expectations of the UN's role as peace-keeper. In Cambodia, there were serious weaknesses in the actual implementation of what was in many ways the most innovative single element of the Paris Agreements – the civil administration function. This was largely due to the mandate being overly ambitious and in some respects clearly not achievable, given the United Nations' stretched resources and the situation in Cambodia, where years of armed struggle had caused enormous damage both to the population and to the basic infrastructure of the country.

UNTAC's failure to take rapid and, in some cases, adequate control of the key areas of the civil administrations of the factions – particularly that of the State of Cambodia (SOC), which was the largest and really the only effective one – and to initiate corrective action when necessary, meant that UNTAC was unable to deal effectively with corruption and with the continuing SOC intimidation of political figures from other parties during the election period.

It also served up on a silver platter spurious justification for the decision of the Party of Democratic Kampuchea – the Khmer Rouge – not to comply with key provisions of the Paris Agreements, including the cantonment, disarmament and demobilization process, claiming that the UN itself was not implementing another essential element of the settlement. This in turn meant that the elections could not be held in a strictly neutral political environment. While there can be endless, and probably fruitless, debate over whether the KR would ever have complied with the Paris Agreements, it must be acknowledged that it should not have been the UN which gave them such a tailor-made excuse in the first place.

The situation of the civil service in Cambodia is, moreover, still far from ideal, with factionalism rife and many instances of discrimination in favour of former SOC civil servants and against those of FUNCINPEC or the KPLNF. There is clearly scope, in the context of assistance to Cambodia in its nation-building effort, for training courses designed not only to improve the efficiency of individuals but also to imbue them with loyalty to the government of the day, rather than to specific parties.

The fourth condition essential for a successful PKO illustrated by the operation in Cambodia is the need for support of the parties to the conflict. As mentioned above, the non-compliance of the Khmer Rouge with key provisions of the Paris Agreements, and the less than full compliance of the other parties, affected every aspect of the UNTAC operation.

When the Khmer Rouge effectively withdrew from the process, the options open to the United Nations were, firstly, to change the peace-keeping mandate to one of peace enforcement; secondly, to soldier on in a peace-keeping role, re-emphasizing the peace-making functions, at the risk of both physical danger to the peace-keeping force and of the peace process becoming bogged down indefinitely; or thirdly, to withdraw, which would have meant abandoning the advances that were being made in returning Cambodia to the community of nations.

Cambodia (as things turned out) is a successful example of soldiering on. The UN Secretary-General rightly decided to continue on to the elections, even though UNTAC had to compromise in a number of important areas and risked the operation failing altogether, as happened in Angola. The elections had to be held without a central element of the Paris Agreements in place, namely cantonment and demobilization of the factional armed forces, effectively leaving two of largest armed forces still in place. UN military forces as a result had to spend most of their time protecting the voter registration process, rather than on other aspects of the Agreements set down for them.

As is well known, there were some advocates, including from within the UNTAC military component, who would have preferred conversion of the mandate to one of peace-enforcement. It was Australia's view that a mid-stream change of this kind was likely to cause major problems for the troop-contributing countries. And despite the number of troops already deployed, it had to be recognized that an enforcement operation probably also faced an uncertain outcome. After all, over 300,000 well-trained Vietnamese troops had not succeeded, in their ten years within Cambodia, in eradicating the Khmer Rouge.

The fifth condition for a successful PKO is an appropriate kind of external support for the operation. As Cambodia showed, in a peace-keeping operation which is premised upon the agreement and compliance of various parties, particularly warring internal parties, the support of external players, who had been involved previously in supporting one side or another in the conflict, is essential to ensure that the operation can be carried through. One reason for the success of holding the elections in Cambodia was that the external backers of the various factions pressed their clients not to return to violence.

Stepping back much further to the origins of the peace process itself, it would do us all well to remember that although there was a distinct and tragic Cambodian dimension to the problem, the main issues really had little to do with Cambodia. They were, rather, geopolitical, and it was only with developments such as the Gorbachev "Initiative" of 28 July 1986 that individual members of the P5 began to see Cambodia no longer as an excuse to keep apart, but as a good reason to get together on the wider issues, and that real movement forward on Cambodia became possible. On top of that was the fact that the countries in what became known as the Core Group or "Expanded P5", maintained a commitment to Cambodia's future within the international community, and were also useful in focusing and maintaining pressure and persuasion on the Cambodian factions to comply with the terms of the Paris Agreements.

OTHER SPECIFIC LESSONS

Human rights

I have already mentioned the problems caused by the late and incomplete implementation of the civil administration aspect of UNTAC's mandate. A related lesson from the Cambodian experience which the international community should bear in mind for future operations is that of situations where the observance of human rights is critical to the comprehensive settlement of a conflict — and this is arguably so in most operations. It now seems clear that the Paris Agreements should have included specific measures for, initially, providing a temporary substitute for, and subsequently building, a functioning criminal justice system as part of the transitional period and post-conflict peace-building exercise, as the rule of law, and the institutions needed to support it, had clearly broken down in Cambodia.

It is worth noting that Australia's original elaboration of the main elements of a comprehensive Cambodian settlement, the so-called "Red Book",[3] recognized and sought to deal with the problem in a manner which would not have been labour-intensive. But our view did not prevail. The point is simply that if a peace-keeping force is given a mandate to guard against human rights violations but there is no functioning system to bring violators to justice — even those who violate others' right to life — then not only is the UN force's mandate to that extent unachievable, but its whole operation is likely to have diminished credibility, both locally and internationally.

A necessary and obvious corollary is that all UN troops and police should also receive training in basic human rights if they are to teach by example while in the country concerned. Again, the behaviour of some UN personnel in Cambodia demonstrated clearly that they had little concept of the most elementary principles of human rights. Equally, there is a clear role in this respect for suitably structured and coordinated training courses — both short and long-term — for nationals of the country in which the UN operation is taking place.

Budget support

Another lacuna which was both serious at the time and may still be having negative effects, was the question that arose after the elections and the installation of the provisional Government, that of the payment of the wages of the Cambodian troops and police (and, for that matter, the civil service). The factional administrations had effectively emptied their treasuries to pay for their electoral campaigns, and there was the real danger of the military and police taking matters into their own hands and/or turning to banditry to survive. As it was, the immediate problem was resolved by the cobbling together of an arrangement for budget support, based initially on the remnants of the 1991 trust fund set up by a few countries to get action underway more rapidly on the UN's preparations. But whether with the benefit of hindsight or not, it is arguable that the situation was one which should have been foreseen.

The formation and effective training of the Royal Cambodian Armed Forces (RCAF) is still, of course, a contentious issue. It was one which was recognized by the parties when drafting the Paris Agreements, but it was decided then that it was a matter more properly left to the sovereign Cambodian Government when it was installed. Pay (or lack of it) is also still a

---

[3] "Cambodia: an Australian Peace Proposal" (Working Papers prepared for the Informal Meeting on Cambodia, Jakarta, 26–28 February 1990), Australian Government Publishing Service, Canberra, (1990), pp.17–18, 35–36.

central problem affecting morale, encouraging corruption, and to an extent even perpetuating the factionalism of the formal armies now comprising the RCAF, correspondingly setting back efforts to form a unified force.

Although it might have been *realpolitik* which dictated this lacuna in the Paris Agreements, it is nevertheless a curious result that the international community should devote such considerable resources to the reconstruction and rehabilitation of Cambodia, while effectively ignoring one of the principal institutions on which the country's future security and stability clearly depends. Military assistance is not ruled out by Agreement III on Cambodian neutrality. The drafting was quite careful on this point, as there was no wider agreement on specific references to building a new national army. Indeed, there is a duty on the signatories – and even the UN – under Article 5 of that Agreement to take action to prevent or suppress the sort of massive violations of human rights which might be expected should the Khmer Rouge ever succeed in retaking power. To date, however, only a handful of states have shown any willingness to extend military assistance to Cambodia. It is nevertheless a start which is to be encouraged if we do not want to be confronted with the need for an UNTAC II, or the greater shame of refusing to create such an operation.

CONCLUSION

Despite the problems, the United Nations succeeded in giving back to the Cambodian people some hope for the future, and despite anything else, this is something in which we can all take some pride, while at the same time recognizing our share in the responsibility for ensuring that aspiration is realized.

Looking back over the past five years, I would be less than honest if I did not admit that there were occasional bouts of gloom in the Australian Government about the achingly and sometimes frustratingly slow pace of the peace process, and the many alarms and excursions which accompanied it along the way. The international media were – and still are – looking for a bad news story. This was shown clearly when, after the first marvelous day of voting in May 1993, more than half of the nearly 2000 journalists accredited to cover the elections left Cambodia because there were not the Khmer Rouge attacks they had been predicting with various degrees of relish. Some journalists, of course, had taken their doom and gloom to the point of suggesting that the whole peace plan was only some sinister international plot by Australia and others to actually return the Khmer Rouge to power!

But at the end of the day, all of us around the world involved in the process kept our nerve and showed that the international community could, if it put its collective mind and energy to it, cooperate successfully for peace. It was a far from perfect operation, but when one compares it to other such exercises around the world today, we did not do so badly. The Cambodian people certainly seem to be prepared to make that assessment. The trick now, though, will be to translate the lessons we learned in Cambodia into useful guidelines which can be applied in other parts of the world where the problems seem just as intractable as they did in Cambodia for more than 20 years. But as I noted at the outset, the danger lies in trying to apply any of the lessons too rigidly, and I would repeat that it is in that spirit that I have proffered these comments.

A final lesson, though, which all of us would do well to bear in mind, can be summed up in an expression that is common to many languages: prevention is better than cure. In terms of resource outlay, it can be shown convincingly that preventive diplomacy can be significantly more cost-effective than either peace-keeping or peace-enforcement.[4] In terms of preventing human suffering, however, the savings might be immeasurable.

---

[4] *Cooperating for Peace*, op. cit n. 2, p.177.

34. UNTAC: A Paradigm for Future UN Peace-Keeping Operations?

John Pace[1]

I would like to try to answer the following question, which has been repeatedly put forth during this meeting: can (or should) UNTAC be considered as a paradigm for future United Nations peace-keeping operations? I will limit my contribution to the human rights aspects of the operation. My answer will be: yes, if the word "paradigm" is taken in the meaning of "example"; no, if it is taken in the meaning of "prototype". That is to say, that we can certainly learn from the UNTAC experience and adopt it as a starting point for future operations, but we should not merely reproduce it *in toto*, because it can be improved.

Human rights concerns were certainly taken into consideration by the drafters of the Paris Agreements and by the governments and factions participating in the peace negotiations for Cambodia. As a result, specific provisions were included in the text of the Agreements, with a view to ensuring guarantees of respect for human rights during as well as after the transitional period (UNTAC monitoring and promotional mandate; provision, in Annex V, for human rights principles to be included in the Constitution; post-election role of the Commission on Human Rights). However, human rights did not occupy the place they should have within UNTAC planning and operation.

It should by now be seen as a truism that a successful transition to democracy requires the establishment of solid national institutions to ensure long-term and continuing protection of human rights and fundamental freedoms under the rule of law. Monitoring and investigating human rights violations, although essential, is not enough to lay the foundations for a State and a society able – and bound – to prevent violations and assure redress where they occur. Rather, this implicitly requires the establishment of a legal framework in conformity with international human rights norms; of institutions, such as the judiciary, able to ensure the redress of human rights violations; and the creation of a certain level of awareness of human rights within the civil society to ensure sustained support to democratic institutions and a continuing, well-articulated and domestic demand for protection of human rights. Hence, the importance of integrating human rights in the peace-keeping process since the beginning should be self-evident. Human rights, if they are set as the foundation for government, become an essential condition for that government, and can be perceived as a constructive force instead of as a threat or hindrance to effective governance.

---

[1] Chief, Advisory Services Branch, United Nations Centre for Human Rights, Geneva.

The substantive basis for the process described above is provided by the internationally recognised human rights norms, to be translated into national legislation and adjusted to the "particularities" of each specific situation in which the UN operation has to work. It is not the business of the Organisation to "sell" the system of one country or another in its nation-building activities.

The Centre for Human Rights, which is now part of the newly-established Office of the High Commissioner for Human Rights, has developed, through its programme of technical cooperation and other mandated activities, a specific expertise in this field, which can certainly be used to improve the planning, implementation and follow-up of future United Nations peace-keeping operations. The Centre has over the years developed an institutional capacity in a number of areas crucial to the successful implementation of United Nations peace-keeping operations, which themselves increasingly entail specific human rights mandates.

As a result of its involvement in high-level international negotiations on human rights issues, the Centre is the only body within the United Nations where the true international common denominator on human rights can be ascertained, and it houses the only institutional memory on the tools that have been agreed to and applied by the international community in regard to human rights. Thanks to this, the Centre is therefore in an ideal position to provide substantive advice on the human rights elements during settlement negotiations and the planning and implementation of United Nations operations.

Since 1955, through its Programme of Advisory Services and Technical Assistance in the Field of Human Rights, the Centre has carried out activities aimed at strengthening democracy and respect for human rights, focusing on the following areas: constitutional assistance, electoral assistance, legislative reform and development, national human rights institutions, judges, magistrates and lawyers, police and security forces, the military, prisons, treaty reporting, national plans of action for human rights, curriculum development and teacher training, support to NGOs and civil society, the mass media, public information and documentation, needs assessments and evaluations. The ultimate objective of technical assistance activities is to translate internationally agreed human rights norms into state practice. In this regard, the Centre's long-standing involvement in the setting of human rights standards and their adoption by Member States into binding international instruments, as well as the monitoring of the application of these standards at the national level, places it in a unique position to incorporate international standards into domestic law and practice in a manner which takes into account and reflects the local needs, aspirations and historical and cultural realities of the recipient country.

I would like to emphasise, in this connection, the Centre's involvement in Cambodia, which is the first example, in the history of the United Nations, of follow-up to a peace-keeping operation in the field of human rights. The Cambodia case also provides an example of how the institutional expertise of the Centre can be effectively exploited in these operations. The Centre established an office in Cambodia immediately after the expiry of UNTAC's mandate, and elaborated a wide-ranging programme of activities aimed at supporting and strengthening the newly established Cambodian democratic institutions. The Centre's programme focuses on:

- building national institutions and legal structures for human rights and democracy, which includes assisting the Cambodian authorities in establishing a legal framework ensuring respect for human rights and providing mechanisms for redress of violations;
- securing a system for the administration of justice consistent with international standards;
- strengthening civil society, including through non-governmental organisations;
- raising awareness of human rights and encouraging popular support for democratic reforms and institutions.

The programme covers, therefore, all the areas which have been identified above as essential to a successful transition to democracy. I would like to add that a number of these activities could have been initiated already during a pre-electoral period, had the Centre been associated more closely to the UNTAC operation. The building of infrastructures for the protection of human rights should be integrated into any United Nations peace-keeping operation, and should not be left for attention only at the conclusion of such operations. The Centre will most likely be involved in a similar experience in El Salvador, in the post-ONUSAL phase.

The fundamental importance of integrating human rights considerations in United Nations peace-keeping operations leads me to stress the need for providing the staff assigned to these operations with adequate training in human rights. This applies equally to the Military, Civilian Police, Electoral and Civil Administration Components. The various functions to which these components can be assigned within each specific peace-keeping operation are all likely to have an impact on human rights. In addition, there is a clear need, which has been repeatedly identified both within and outside the United Nations system, to sensitise United Nations peace-keepers to their responsibility to abide by international human rights standards and to exhibit the highest standards of behaviour.

In this connection, I would like to stress that the Centre has recently provided human rights training to the Civilian Police Component of the United Nations Operation in Mozambique (ONUMOZ), and is currently discussing with the Department for Peace-Keeping Operations ways to institutionalise this kind of training in future United Nations operations.

35. UN Peace-Keeping Operations in the Future

Ambassador Hisashi Owada[1]

At the outset, I would like to express my appreciation to the distinguished participants of this symposium for their candid discussion of the lessons we might draw from our experience with UNTAC. I deem it a privilege to have this opportunity to share with you my own thoughts as to how United Nations peace-keeping operations might be conducted in the future, based on the views and suggestions of those directly involved in such activities, both in the field and at headquarters.

UN peace-keeping operations have a long history. In recent years, however, they have undergone drastic modifications to cope with the diverse international and regional conflicts that have erupted since the end of the Cold War. Permit me to comment on several ways in which recent UN peace-keeping operations have been modified.

First of all, their mandates have become more complex and comprehensive. An operation is no longer expected simply to maintain a cease-fire. Its mandate may now include a broad range of activities such as election-monitoring, de-mining, refugee repatriation, troop demobilization, protection of human rights, and support for national reconstruction. In other words, UN peace-keeping operations are increasingly expected to assist in nation-building. The UN effort in Cambodia was a prime example of this new type of peace-keeping operation.

Secondly, peace-keeping operations have become larger and, as a result, more costly. UNTAC and UNOSOM II each deployed more than 20,000 personnel, and UNPROFOR more than 30,000. The cost of each of these operations came to over US$1 billion. As might be expected, these large-scale operations have placed a tremendous financial burden on the Organization. But they have also raised the question as to whether the UN is in fact capable – in terms of expertise, equipment, and general preparedness – of meeting the demands that are being made of it. Thus the two most urgent issues facing UN Member States today relate to financing and organizational reform.

Thirdly, peace-keeping operations are being given the additional task of protecting humanitarian assistance activities in countries where there is civil war and where the central authority has collapsed. The concept of peace enforcement as proposed by the Secretary-General was first introduced in UNOSOM. Discussions continue as to the feasibility of peace-enforcement measures and the necessary conditions for their inclusion in future peace-keeping operations.

The fourth change which merits our attention is that of preventive deployment. This new peace-keeping mechanism has already been put into

---

[1] Ambassador, Permanent Representative of Japan to the United Nations, New York.

practice in the former Yugoslavian republic of Macedonia, and a General Assembly resolution has affirmed its validity. I believe it is important that we explore the applicability of preventive deployment in other situations, and consider how it might be further developed and made readily available as a pre-emptive measure wherever there is a potential conflict.

Finally, I wish to note the growing weight of the civilian component in peace-keeping operations. As UN peace-keeping operations have become more comprehensive, the role of civilian personnel – particularly in the fields of election-monitoring, security, administration, and humanitarian aid – has grown more important. The mobilization and training of such personnel, and their deployment in the field in an integrated manner, demand careful study. It is also necessary that further efforts be made to guarantee their safety.

In the light of the changing nature of UN peace-keeping operations, many discussions have been held both within and outside the UN to improve their effectiveness and efficiency, as well as to increase the confidence which Member States have in such operations. I am encouraged that these discussions have been conducted in a very forward-looking and constructive manner, and would like at this time to underscore a number of points that have been raised in the course of these talks.

In planning and preparing a peace-keeping operation, we must bear in mind that every international conflict is unique, shaped by the historical, ethnic, and social experiences of the disputing parties, and that peace-keeping requirements are different for each conflict. Therefore, when the Security Council decides to launch a peace-keeping operation, its decision should be based upon accurate and thorough information regarding the nature and prognosis of the conflict. The dispatch of a UN fact-finding mission to the site of a conflict at an early stage has proved to be productive in this regard. I believe this is a function of the UN Secretariat that should be enhanced.

A peace-keeping operation should have an achievable objective, and its mandate and duration should be clearly and precisely defined. It must be conducted as effectively as possible, with the limited financial and human resources that are available and within a reasonable period of time. It might be useful to introduce a "sunset clause", to avoid the undue prolongation of deployment.

The command and control structure of the UN should be consolidated in the field and at headquarters so as to better integrate troops, and immediate steps should be taken to improve coordination between the military and humanitarian and other civilian aspects of peace-keeping operations. This is especially important in view of the increasing role played by the civilian component.

We have learned the painful lesson that without the understanding and support of the people in the host country, a peace-keeping operation cannot achieve its objectives. It is a sad irony that those who have dedicated themselves to restoring peace and stability in a nation have sometimes been misunderstood and even rejected by the very people they were trying to help. The success of the radio broadcasting strategy pursued in Cambodia suggests that a more pro-active approach to public information on peace-keeping operations can be effective. Therefore I would like to suggest that in order to gain public understanding, well-designed communications networks should be established and staffed with competent personnel who are in close contact with the populations they are meant to reach. I might mention in this regard that the Government of Japan has donated audio-visual equipment to the United Nations operation in Mozambique to be used to teach the people of that country about the electoral process.

I am pleased to note the arrangement that is now in place whereby some 70,000 personnel from approximately 30 countries are available for peace-keeping operations on a standby basis. In view of the growing importance of the civilian component in peace-keeping activities, I believe it would be useful to likewise establish a standby force of civilian personnel which Member States could provide upon the urgent request of the United Nations.

In order to increase the confidence of Member States in the Security Council, it is necessary to enhance the transparency of the Council's decision-making process. Toward this end, informal and frequent consultations among the Secretariat, countries that contribute troops and financing, and Security Council members should be held on a regular basis. Indeed, unless such efforts are made, the Council will not enjoy the full and necessary support of contributing countries in launching a new peace-keeping operation. I am pleased to note that this concept of consultation has been put into practice recently.

The training of peace-keepers is also of great importance, particularly since the troops that participate in UN peace-keeping operations come from many different countries and cultural backgrounds, and thus reflect a range of attitudes and experiences. Although it might not be possible to unite these different troops under a common ideological banner, it is nevertheless necessary that they recognize minimal and common rules of peace-keeping activities. The establishment of peace-keeping training centers or training courses for cadres of troops could enhance the UN command and control function in the field and foster a "UN culture" among the troops of the various Member States. These training efforts might also serve to enlighten the public and enhance popular support for UN activities.

The safety of personnel engaged in peace-keeping is a serious issue, and one that could affect the future of UN peace-keeping operations. Having considered the discussions held in the Security Council and the General Assembly, as well as the report issued by the Secretary-General last August on this subject, I would like to offer two suggestions:

- Firstly, I believe renewed efforts should be made to achieve a degree of integration and accountability among various bodies to ensure the security of UN personnel. Toward this end, the activities of the Office of Security Coordinator at UN Headquarters should be strengthened and expert staff recruited to assist the Security Coordinator and his designated officials in the field.
- Secondly, I would strongly urge that whenever the Security Council contemplates launching a peace-keeping operation it take into considera-tion the safety of the personnel involved. Moreover, it is the responsibility of the Secretariat to inform the members of the Council

as to whether the Secretary-General has been given sufficient means and resources to protect the lives of those who are engaged in the peace-keeping operation in question.

Based on the foregoing discussion, I would like to comment on four issues, all of which are important as we consider the future of UN peace-keeping operations.

First of all, peace-keeping operations should be prepared and implemented in a well-designed and comprehensive manner, with the objective of achieving a political settlement. The traditional peace-keeping operation, deployed to prevent the recurrence or escalation of a conflict by intervening between disputing parties, has a better chance of bringing about a durable peace if it is conducted as part of a broader political effort for the restoration of peace and national reconstruction. The Cambodian operation is a case in point; the secret of its success lay in its comprehensive and multi-faceted approach. Because the situation in Cambodia was extremely complex, it would have been futile to have simply deployed a traditional peace-keeping force there. Intense diplomatic efforts were first necessary to bring about a degree of national reconciliation, which was consolidated with the Paris Agreements. Japan, together with other like-minded countries, played a decisive role in those efforts, which were pursued in close coordination with the Permanent Members of the Security Council. Under the Paris Agreements, a framework was established for efforts to restore peace in Cambodia. UNTAC was then launched with a mandate that included a wide range of tasks, from the organization and conduct of elections to civil administration. Involving some 22,000 personnel, it was the costliest operation in the history of the United Nations. But equally important were the parallel and concerted diplomatic efforts to create a political environment that would be conducive to durable peace, as well as the provision of economic assistance for the rehabilitation and reconstruction of the war-torn nation. I believe this well-planned operation will serve as a model for future UN efforts.

Secondly, I would like to touch upon the element of "peace-enforcement" as provided for in Chapter VII of the UN Charter. In the aftermath of the ill-fated operation in Somalia, we are faced with the choice of either scrapping this mechanism, or retaining it as an essential aspect of future peace-keeping operations. On the one hand, we have learned that when the authority of a central government has completely collapsed and competing factions within the country are engaging in acts of violence, a peace-keeping force is required to ensure that humanitarian assistance is delivered to those for whom it is destined. Under those special circumstances the concept of peace-enforcement would seem to have a certain validity. At the same time, however, the experience in Somalia has taught the Security Council to be cautious in invoking the provisions of Chapter VII for launching a peace-keeping operation for this purpose. Any enforcement action must be thoroughly planned, and the time-tested principle of impartiality must be carefully weighed against the need for taking any action containing an element of enforcement, so that the peace-keepers themselves may not become victim to the conflict. My views are consistent with those of the

Commission of Inquiry established to investigate the armed attacks on UNOSOM II. In its report issued last June it stated:

The United Nations should refrain from undertaking further peace-enforcement actions within the internal conflicts of states. If the United Nations decides nevertheless to undertake [an] enforcement operation, the mandate should be limited to specific objectives and the use of force would be applied as the ultimate means after all peaceful remedies have been exhausted.

Thirdly, I wish to emphasize the importance of preventive diplomacy. The deployment of UN troops in the former Yugoslavian republic of Macedonia has been successful in preventing the conflict in the former Yugoslavia from spilling across the border and in enhancing Macedonia's sense of security. I am of the view that this mechanism should be more fully utilized in situations that are likely to threaten international peace and security. And as I indicated earlier, sending UN investigation missions to areas where there is the danger of a conflict erupting can be extremely useful in the context of preventive diplomacy.

Furthermore, we should continue to explore the effectiveness of economic and humanitarian assistance in defusing situations that could lead to conflict. I believe it would be helpful if the United Nations closely monitored even subtle changes in politically volatile regions, and if neighboring countries were requested to provide up-to-date information on these regions.

Lastly, what is probably the most critical issue for UN peace-keeping efforts is that of securing adequate financing. Although it has been said many times, it bears repeating that Member States must recognize this problem as their collective responsibility, and pay their assessed contributions in full and on time. At the same time, we must continue to encourage the Secretariat to improve its administrative and budgetary management of the operations as well as to strengthen the system of audit and inspection in order to ensure accountability and enhance the mechanism of financial control. Before considering the Secretary-General's proposal that Member States be assessed for a third of the total estimated costs of an operation as soon as it is approved by the Secretary-General, as well as his proposal to raise the ceiling of the Peace-Keeping Reserve Fund from US$150 million to US$800 million – a sum equivalent to about four months' expenditures under the 1993 peace-keeping budget – Member States should first thoroughly scrutinize the present system of planning, budgeting and administration and consider ways of streamlining it. Moreover, the Reserve Fund should be fully funded at its present level, before we consider raising its ceiling.

It is all too clear that the present budgeting for only a few months' financing at a time of each operation separately is a piecemeal approach, and this is partly responsible for operations being inadequately planned and poorly administered. At this time, when UN peace-keeping operations play an ever greater role in world affairs, and account for an ever-greater share of the UN budget, it is absolutely essential that the Organization should improve its planning, budgetary and management system. In fact, I believe it is necessary to develop a new system that will place financial control of an operation in the hands of Member States and at the same time ensure that the operation is efficiently implemented.

Part III

Annexes

Annex 1: List of Conference Participants

Resource Persons

USG Rafeeuddin Ahmed, *Associate Administrator, UNDP, New York*
Professor Reginald Austin, *Legal and Constitutional Affairs Division, Commonwealth Secretariat, London*
Ms Sylvie Bermann, *Counsellor, Permanent Mission of France to the United Nations, New York*
Mr Ken Berry, *Senior Member, Personal Staff of Australian Foreign Minister, Canberra*
Mr Timothy Carney, *Deputy Assistant Secretary of State for South Asia Bureau, Washington DC*
Dr Hrach Gregorian, *Director, Education and Training, United State Institute of Peace (USIP), Washington DC*
Lieutenant-Colonel Xavier Guérin, *Head of Studies on Peace-Keeping Operations, Recruitment Section, HQ, Paris*
Ambassador Yukio Imagawa, *Ambassador Extraordinary and Plenipotentiary of Japan in Cambodia, Phnom Penh*
Professor S. Jayakumar, *Minister for Foreign Affairs and for Law, Singapore*
Mr Khieu Kanharith, *Secretary of State, Ministry of Information, Phnom Penh*
Ambassador Ataul Karim, *Director of Political Affairs Division, UNOSOM II, Mogadishu*
Mr Takahisa Kawakami, *Assistant Director, United Nations Policy Division, Ministry of Foreign Affairs, Tokyo*
Mr Vishakan Krishnadasan, *Former Legal Adviser, UNTAC, Phnom Penh*
Dr Harvey Langholtz, *Director, UNITAR's Program of Correspondence Instruction in Peace-Keeping Operations (POCI), New York*
Mr Roger Lawrence, *Deputy to the Secretary-General, UNCTAD, Geneva*
Mr Dennis McNamara, *Director of External Relations, UNHCR, Geneva*
Dr Steve Pieczenik, *Consultant, United State Institute of Peace (USIP), Washington DC*
Brigadier-General Klaas Roos, *Deputy Commandant, The Netherlands Royal Marechaussee, The Hague*
Lieutenant-General John Sanderson, *Commander, Australian Joint Forces, Canberra*
Ms Hisako Shimura, *Director, United Nations Europe/Latin America Division, Department of Peace-Keeping Operations (DPKO), New York*
HRH Prince Sirirath Sisowath, *Ambassador, Permanent Representative of the Kingdom of Cambodia to the UN, New York*
Ambassador Nana Sutresna, *Ambassador-at-Large, Head Executive Assistant to the NAM Chairman, Jakarta*
Ambassador Tan Boon Teik, *Ambassador of Singapore to Hungary, Austria and the Slovak Republic, Singapore*

Ms Tan Lian Choo, *Senior Correspondent, The Straits Times, Singapore*
Ambassador Tan Zainal Abidin Sulong, *Chairman, Malaysian Industrial Development Authority, Kuala Lumpur*
Mr Benny Widyono, *Secretary-General's Representative in Cambodia, Phnom Penh*

Participants

Brunei

Senior Superintendent Hj. A.R. bin Hj. Md. Jaafar, *Deputy Director of Operations, Royal Brunei Police*
Lieutenant Colonel Hj. R. bin Hj. Kampong, *Director of Intelligence and Security, Ministry of Defence*

India

D.P. Srivastava, *Director (UNP), Ministry of External Affairs, New Delhi*

Indonesia

Dr Hassan Wirayuda, *Director, International Organisations, Department of Foreign Affairs*
Colonel (Inf) Aqlani Maza, *Operations Assistant, Military Regional Command, Palembang, Southern Sumatra*

Japan

Mr Nobuhiro Fukuoka, *Deputy Director, International Peace Co-operation HQ, Prime Minister's Office*
Colonel Fukui Yusuke

Malaysia

Ambassador N. Parameswaran, *Under-Secretary, International Organisations Division, Ministry of Foreign Affairs*
Major General Dato' Jelani Asmawi, *Ministry of Defence*

The Philippines

Mrs Minda C. Cruz, *Director, Division for Political, International Security and Legal Matters, UNIO*
Colonel Gliberio E. Suwa, *GHQ, AFP, Camp Aquinaldo*

Singapore

LTC Michael Lim Teck Huat, *Head Joint Operations Planning Branch, Ministry of Defence*
Mr Hirubalan Vp, *Deputy Director, Ministry of Defence*
Senior Assistant Commissioner Chua Chin Kiat, *Director of Operations, Police Headquarters*

Thailand

Mr Asda Jayanama, *Director General, Department of International Organisations*
Lieutenant General Sanan Kajornkian Am, *Joint Operations Centre, Supreme Command*

USA

Mr Frank Jannuzi, *Analyst, Bureau of Intelligence and Research, US Department of State, Washington DC*

Vietnam

Mr Ngyuen Duy Hung, *Deputy to the Director, Department of Southeast and Pacific Asia, Ministry of Foreign Affairs*
Colonel Nguyen Duc Khiem

Observers

Pg. Hjh Masrainah bte Pg. Hj. Ahmad, *Acting Director of Economy, Ministry of Foreign Affairs, Brunei*
Stephen Fuller, *Representative, The Asia Foundation, Kuala Lumpur*
Damien Healy, *Deputy to Lieutenant General John Sanderson, Australian Defence Force, Canberra*
John Pace, *Chief, Advisory Services Branch, Centre for Human Rights, Geneva*
Takeo Uchida, *Senior Academic Officer, UN University, Tokyo*

Co-Chairs

Dr Marcel A. Boisard, *Acting Executive Director, UNITAR, Geneva*
Ambassador Tommy Koh, *Director, IPS, Singapore*
Ambassador Hisashi Owada, *Permanent Representative of Japan to the United Nations, New York*

Rapporteurs

Ms Nassrine Azimi, *Deputy to the Acting Executive Director, UNITAR, Geneva*
Mr Mark Hong, *Director of Directorate IV, Ministry of Foreign Affairs, Singapore*

Annex 2: Agenda of the Conference

Tuesday, 2 August

8.30–9.00	**Registration**
9.00–9.15	**Keynote address**

Professor S. Jayakumar, Minister for Foreign Affairs and for Law, Singapore
Messages from the United Nations Secretary-General and President, United Nations General Assembly

9.15–9.45	**Introductory statements by Conference Co-Chairs**

Ambassador Tommy Koh, Director, IPS
Ambassador Hisashi Owada, Permanent Representative of Japan to the UN
Dr Marcel A. Boisard, Acting Executive Director, UNITAR

9.45–10.00	Coffee
10.00–12.30	**SESSION I**
10.00–10.40	**Crafting the Paris Agreements**

Ambassador Yukio Imagawa, Japan's Ambassador to Phnom Penh
Ms Sylvie Bermann, Counsellor, Permanent Mission of France to the UN, New York

10.40–11.20	**UN's role in bringing about peace in Cambodia**

USG Rafeeuddin Ahmed, Associate Administrator, UNDP
Mr Khieu Kanharith, Secretary of State, Ministry of Information, Cambodia

11.20–11.50	*Key discussants*

Mr Mark Hong, Director (Directorate IV)
Dr Hrach Gregorian, United States Institute of Peace (USIP)

11.50–12.30	General discussion
14.00–17.30	**SESSION II**
14.00–14.20	**Lessons: exercising the Transitional Authority**
	Mr Takahisa Kawakami, Assistant Director, UN Policy Division, Ministry of Foreign Affairs, Japan
14.20–14.50	*Key discussants*
	Ms Tan Lian Choo, Senior Correspondent (Former Bangkok Correspondent), *The Straits Times*, Singapore
	Dr Steve Pieczenick, United States Institute of Peace (USIP)
14.50–15.20	General discussion
15.20–15.40	Tea
15.40–16.00	**ASEAN's role**
	Ambassador Tan Sri Datuk Zainul Abidin Sulong, Chairman, Malaysian Industrial Development Authority, Malaysia
16.00–16.20	**The Cambodian perspective**
	HRH Prince Sisowath Sirirath, Cambodia's Permanent Representative to the UN
16.20–16.35	*Key discussant*
	Ambassador Nana Sutresna, Ambassador-at-Large, Head Executive Assistant to the NAM Chairman, Indonesia
16.35–17.30	General discussion

Wednesday, 3 August

9.00–13.00	**SESSION III: UNTAC COMPONENTS**
9.00–9.20	**Introductory statements and an overview of the operation**
	Ambassador Ataul Karim, Former Head of Mission, UNAMIC and Former Senior Political Adviser, UNTAC

Annex 2: Agenda of the Conference

9.20–9.40	**Role of the military**
	Lieutenant-General John Sanderson, Former Force Commander, Military Component, UNTAC
9.40–10.00	**Civilian police**
	Brigadier-General Klaas Roos, Former Commissioner, Civilian Police Component, UNTAC
10.00–10.10	General discussion
10.10–10.25	Coffee
10.25–10.45	**Refugees and displaced persons' reintegration**
	Mr Dennis McNamara, on behalf of Mr Sergio Vieira de Mello, Director, Policy Planning and Operations, UNHCR
10.45–11.05	**Economics/rehabilitation**
	Mr Roger Lawrence, Former Economic and Financial Advisor to SRSG, and Director, Rehabilitation Component, UNTAC
11.05–11.15	General discussion
11.15–11.35	**Protection of human rights**
	Mr Dennis McNamara, Former Director, Human Rights Component, UNTAC
11.35–11.55	**Information/education**
	Mr Tim Carney, Former Director, Information Division, UNTAC
11.55–12.15	**Election-monitoring: preparation and conduct**
	Professor Reginald Austin, Former Director, Electoral Component, UNTAC
12.15–12.25	**A legal perspective on UNTAC – an overview**
	Mr Vishakan Krishnadasan, Former Legal Adviser, UNTAC
12.25–13.00	General discussion
14.20–17.30	**SESSION III (Continued)**

14.20–14.40	**Drafting a new constitution** Ambassador Tan Boon Teik, Ambassador to Austria, the Czech Republic and Hungary, Singapore, Former Attorney-General, Singapore
14.40–15.00	**Perspectives from the Department of Peace-Keeping Operations on the management of UNTAC** Ms Hisako Shimura, Director, Department of Peace-Keeping Operations, UN
15.00–15.30	*Key discussants* Dr Harvey Langholtz, Director, UNITAR Training Program of Correspondence Instruction in Peace-keeping (POCI) Lieutenant-Colonel Xavier Guérin, Head of Studies on Peace-Keeping Operations, HQ, Paris
15.30–15.50	**Inputs and update on current follow-up to UNTAC** Mr Benny Widyono, Secretary-General's Representative in Cambodia
15.50–16.00	*Key discussants* Mr Khieu Kanharith Ambassador Yukio Imagawa
16.00–16.30	Tea
16.30–17.30	General discussion

Thursday, 4 August

9.00–10.40	**SESSION IV: UNTAC AS A PARADIGM?**
9.00–9.20	Mr Ken Berry, Assistant Secretary, Department of Foreign Affairs and Trade, Australia, Senior Advisor to Senator Gareth Evans, Australia
9.20–10.40	*Discussion/Review/Next steps/Key discussants* Ms Hisako Shimura Professor Reginald Austin Lieutenant-General John Sanderson
10.40–11.00	Coffee

11.00–11.20	**The future of peace-keeping**
	Ambassador Hisashi Owada
11.20–12.00	**Summing up – closure of conference**
	Ambassador Tommy Koh
	Dr Marcel A. Boisard

P.D.O.

PRESS
Embassy
46
London S

Modern
KUWAIT

PRESS OFFICE
Embassy of The State of Kuwait
46 Queen's Gate
London SW7

Modern
KUWAIT

David Sapsted

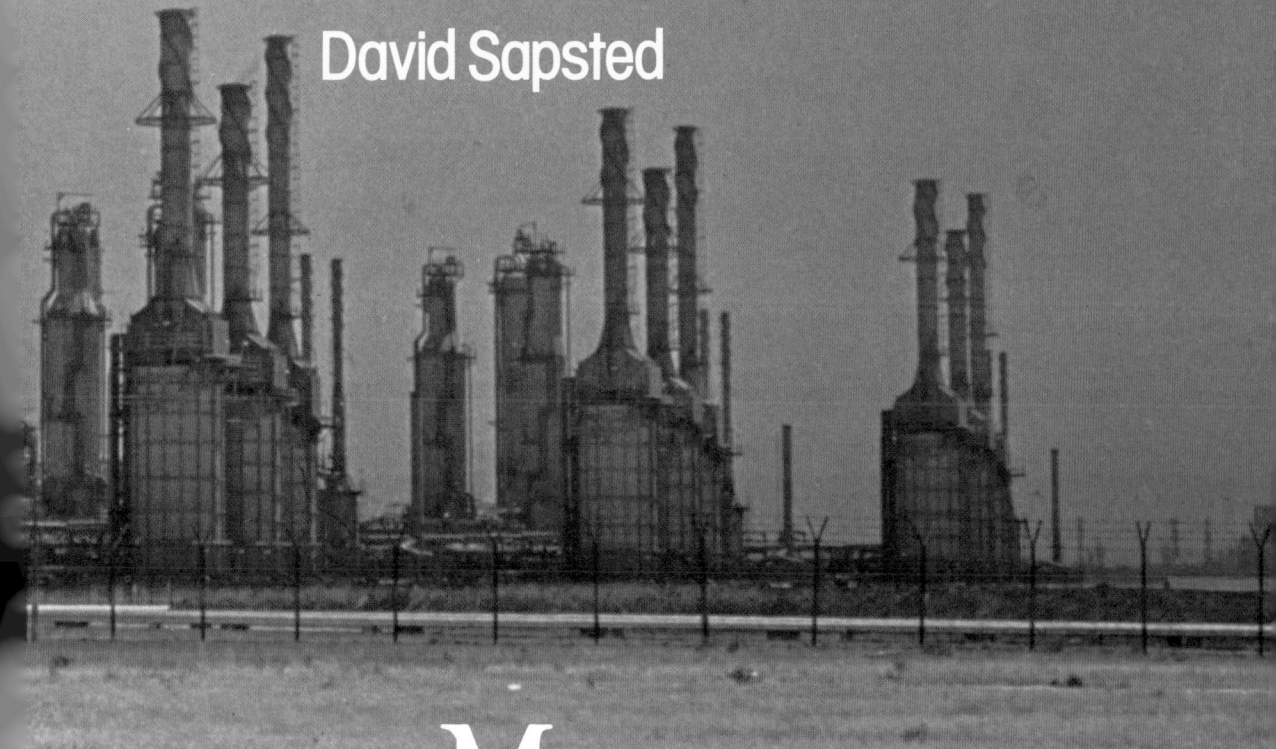

M

... reproduced or ... permission.

Associated co... , Dublin, Hong Kong, Johannesburg, Lagos, Manzini, Melbo... k, Singapore, Tokyo, Washington and Zaria

Phototypeset in Great Britain by Filmtype ...vices Limited, Scarborough
Printed in Great Britain by Sackville Press Billericay Ltd

British Library Cataloguing in Publication Data
Sapsted, David
  Modern Kuwait.
  1. Kuwait
  I. Title
  953'.67'05   D5247.K8

  ISBN 0-333-31098-5

The photograph on p.73 is reproduced by
permission of Bruce Coleman Ltd.

Contents

Introduction   1

The People   5
The Country   33
The Government   77
Public Services   87
The Oil   127
Trade, Commerce and Industry   157
The Future   179

Index   184

PRESS OFFICE
Embassy of The State of Kuwait
46 Queen's Gate
London SW7

Introduction

Kuwait ... the place the oil comes from. But what else? Ask an outsider and the likely response will be a glazed look or a fantastic tale of petrodollar extravagance or some hazy yarn steeped in the legends of *The Arabian Nights*. Unfortunately myth, misconception and sheer ignorance tend to obscure the view of this Arabian Gulf State. While many people may know that it enjoys the highest per capita incomes (in terms of GNP) in the world, few realize how this wealth is used, either nationally or internationally.

Kuwait has achieved in a generation the sort of progress that many nations struggle to achieve in a century. Of course, it has had the oil-generated means to get on with the job, and its transformation must be viewed in the context of size: a population of little more than a million does not present the problems of scale encountered in larger, more populous states.

But the story of Kuwait is no less remarkable for that. During the past three decades monuments to progress abound – in industry, social services, housing, transport, education and many other spheres. And this growth has been paralleled by the development of the Kuwaitis themselves. Skills in management, government, commerce and technology have been steadily acquired, and though the process is far from over, there now seems to be an underlying confidence and maturity in the Kuwaitis' approach to the future.

The aim of this book is not only to show what the nation and its people have achieved in the past and are trying to achieve during the 1980s, but also to explain the reasons why. To understand that, it is necessary to understand the elements which shaped the nation, its history, religion and culture. Arabism, the values of a tribal society and the influences of developed nations are undeniably important ingredients, as is the awareness of responsibilities to developing countries and to sister states on the Arabian Peninsula, perhaps the most strategically important group of nations in the world.

Oil, inevitably, permeates the story. The development of the oil industry is described separately, but that oil provides the money for growth, that it brings with it not only benefits but far-ranging responsibilities, and that it is not going to last for ever, are factors which together or singly have a direct bearing on so much that has happened recently in Kuwait.

Internal political stability has been the silent partner in the country's development. For more than two hundred years, Kuwait has experienced continuous rule by members of the Al-Sabah dynasty.

In size, Kuwait amounts to 17,820 square kilometres. It is wedged in the north-west of the Arabian Gulf and shares its borders with Saudi Arabia and Iraq. Inside these borders live 1.35 million people. The main population concentration centres on Kuwait City, the capital, and the surrounding urban sprawl on the south shore of Kuwait Bay, one of the finest natural refuges for shipping in the Gulf. Modern highways link the city to other communities, most notably the oil and industrial complexes around Ahmadi in the south and the historical farming oasis at Jahra in the north. Much of the rest of the country consists of desert scrubland – steppes virtually barren but for the pools of black gold beneath the surface.

And then there is the sea, which in effect is Kuwait's *raison d'être*. Long before the discovery of oil, the Gulf provided Kuwait with its wealth, its food and its principal ties with the rest of the world. It remains the essential artery through which the nation's lifeblood flows.

A great deal has happened in Kuwait's past and even more is happening in its present; the future cannot be predicted. But let us begin this book with a look at what the current Amir, Sheikh Jaber Al-Ahmad, has described as the most important of the state's natural resources: not its oil, but its people.

The People

The Kuwaitis have been renowned for their skill in making and handling boats since the middle of the eighteenth century — a skill which led in turn to their success as merchants and, later, businessmen.

Kuwait society often comes across to the outsider as a paradox, in which relentless drive towards modernity goes hand in hand with attitudes which remain staunchly traditionalist — a place where innate conservatism rubs shoulders with radical change. Some observers tend to dismiss this as a simple case of a people being unable to keep pace with the speed with which the trappings of modern society have overtaken it. Give the Kuwaitis time, they say, and they will catch up. Such a view not only does a disservice to the Kuwaitis but also ignores what this Gulf nation is striving to achieve: namely, the establishment of the benefits of wealth in a setting compatible with traditional values.

Certainly there have been dramatic changes in recent years, yet the combination of Islamic principle and Arab pragmatism has endured as the basis for government, business and private life. Outside influences have been keenly felt and ideas from abroad have been freely imported alongside the cars, radios and refrigerators. But the aim has always been to accommodate them within a framework which Kuwaitis find acceptable.

This does not mean that society and its attitudes have not changed. They have. But the Islamic–Arab–Kuwaiti cornerstone of the nation has remained unshaken.

There are many examples of the apparent paradox, but it may be enough to cite just one. It is a fact that of the 10,000 or so students at Kuwait University, more than half are female – and this in a country which less than twenty years ago could not muster up one Kuwaiti woman with a degree. It is also true that Kuwaiti women are today playing an increasingly important part in areas of work calling for a high degree of professionalism. Yet a survey among female students revealed negligible support for any Western-inspired changes in the traditional role of women.

Who are the Kuwaitis? Their history as a nation goes back not much more than two hundred years, but their roots as a people stretch back over countless centuries. The desert environment and the sea have played vital parts in moulding their character, but both of these pale into insignificance compared with the influence of their faith.

Islam

Islam is the last of the world's great religions: it has the second largest number of adherents (estimates vary widely at somewhere between 550 and 800 million-plus) and is arguably the most vibrant religious force in the world today. Followers of Islam regard it as a synthesis of the faiths that have gone before; they accept Christians and Jews as 'people of the book' but maintain that the final word of God was made known through the angel Gabriel to Mohammed who, in turn, revealed it through Islam's only miracle, the Holy Koran. Mohammed himself is considered the last and greatest representative of a series of prophets which included Adam, Noah, Moses and Jesus Christ.

One aspect of Islam of enormous importance to Kuwait – an overwhelmingly Moslem country – is that the faith combines both the spiritual and temporal sides of life. It seeks

Near the busy shopping centre at Salmiyah, the Abdullah Gulum Ashkanani Mosque with its intricate decoration is one of the few in Kuwait to boast four minarets.

to determine not only a person's relationship with God but also his or her relationship with society. This has given rise to such concepts as the Islamic nation, Islamic law and to institutions regulating secular life. Kuwait has opted for a legal system based on Moslem principle and implemented through a mainly French-inspired code. Hanging is retained as the death penalty for such crimes as murder but there have been few executions in recent years. Kuwait's crime rate is one of the lowest anywhere in the world.

It is impossible to say exactly when the tribesmen inhabiting the desert which is today's Kuwait first became converted to Islam. Certainly, it could not have been long after the death of the Prophet in Mecca in A.D. 632, for by 714 the Islamic Empire had spread as far as Spain in the west and Central Asia and India in the east.

From then on, the religious allegiance of the Arabian Peninsula was never in doubt. When the early settlers came to the shores of Kuwait Bay in 1710 they set about building a society based on Islamic concepts, particularly the Five Pillars: the profession of faith ('There is no God but Allah and Mohammed is His Messenger'); the five daily prayers; Zakat (the giving of alms); fasting during Ramadhan, the ninth month of the Islamic Calendar; and the holy pilgrimage to Mecca which every Moslem should make at least once in his life.

A vivid account of the influence of Islam on the everyday life of the nation is contained in *Kuwait – Prospect and Reality*, a book by Zahra Freeth and Victor Winstone, published in London:

> Kuwait before the days of Oil was a Moslem State barely touched by outside influences. It formed a God-fearing community for whom religion coloured practically every thought and action of life. The observance of the five daily prayers was never a meaningless formality; it was homage paid to a watchful and ever-present God who punished those who flouted His laws. Similarly, the fast of Ramadhan was an exercise in self-denial by which men proved their personal devotion. Because of the lunar calendar, the month of Ramadhan occurs at varying times by the Western calendar (each year it falls a little earlier). This means that there will be times when the period of fast has to be observed in the heat of summer. Since August shade temperatures average 112 degrees Fahrenheit [44°C] and even a drink of water is forbidden in the hours of daylight, the fast at such times is a severe hardship.
>
> There were few comforts in the average Kuwaiti family's daily life in those days and no protection against sickness or epidemics. For both bedouin and townspeople, life was full of uncertainties and in the natural hazards of the wilderness and the oceans, all were conscious of man's helplessness and the need for a protecting God. Favourable conditions – good rainfall and pasture, or fair sailing winds and a good trading profit, or the natural joys of family life

such as the birth of children – were always seen as manifestations of God's bounty. Gratitude for His beneficence was constantly on their lips, but complaint never. When disaster or distress came their way, they accepted it fatalistically, especially the bedouin whose control over their emotions was absolute. They believed that though Allah had a propensity to mercy, He had fore-ordained their lives.

Theft, dishonesty or crimes of violence were rare in old Kuwait town and when such offences occurred in the desert there were well-established rules for compensation in money or blood. There can have been few societies where the accepted moral code was more universally observed and it was recognised by everybody that the code was God's rather than man's. An evil-doer was by definition 'one who does not fear God' or one who neither fasts nor prays. The pilgrimage to Mecca was everybody's ultimate ambition and many of those who spoke of it afterwards did so in a way that showed it had been a genuine source of strength and inspiration.

The influence of Islam is not so evident today, although it remains an extremely potent force. Despite the fact that Kuwait now has about four hundred mosques, weekly prayer meetings on Fridays (the Moslem day of rest) are usually full to overflowing. Observance of Ramadhan also appears widespread, and even non-Moslems are expected to refrain from eating, drinking and smoking in public during daylight hours. Some subtle changes may be noticed these days, however: while the faithful still observe the fast during the day, food sales during Ramadhan are now actually higher than during the rest of the year as the newly affluent enjoy night-time feasts with their families and friends. This is not a situation peculiar to Kuwait, and there have been calls throughout the Arab world in recent years for people to observe not only the letter but the spirit of the faith. The fact that the fast falls during the hottest summer months at the moment also encourages people to take holidays abroad during Ramadhan, and Kuwait can seem an empty place during the holy month.

Despite this, there can be no mistaking the continuing Islamic allegiance of the nation. Roadsides are often littered with buses, trucks and taxis while their drivers and passengers pray towards Mecca at the prescribed times, and the *haj*, the pilgrimage to the holiest of Moslem cities, remains the goal of every follower. In a typical year more than 10,000 pilgrims leave Kuwait, either in convoys of buses and trucks or by special flights to Jeddah. Countless thousands of others from Iraq, Iran and further afield pass through Kuwait on their way to Mecca, and the Government provides a wide range of services to ensure the comfort, health and well-being of its own and foreign pilgrims, many of whom spend nights in special transit camps. Each year a mobile hospital unit is equipped by the Ministry of Public Health to tend the sick on their way to and at the holy sites.

One thing noticeable both on the *haj* and in other aspects of the country's religious life is the age of the participants: the young appear to find as much attraction and comfort in their religion as older generations. Religious instruction occupies a place of paramount importance in the curricula of state schools. It is not just in schools, though, that Islamic influences are evident – they permeate newspapers and magazines, while religious programmes are nightly and not unpopular features of Kuwait television. The Ministry of Awqaf and Religious Affairs makes its voice heard in numerous ways, arranging seminars and research into religious matters, organizing the importation and translation of religious texts, publishing magazines for adults and children, and running Koran reading classes and a college for religious instruction. The ministry also handles *Awqaf*: questions of religious endowment. The Government as a whole conducts its business within the framework of Islamic principle and is liable to adopt policies compatible with, if not entirely dictated by, the faith.

Parking can be a headache at Friday services at one of the country's largest mosques, the Fahad Al Salem Mosque in Salmiyah.

Visitors to Kuwait notice the Islamic influence in more obvious ways, not least in the absence of alcohol; pork, too, is unavailable. Women are not expected to appear on public beaches in anything less than everyday clothing (the position of women in modern Kuwait society will be dealt with later in this chapter).

Generally, there is little which could be described as oppressive about Islam in Kuwait: it is part of the people's make-up and contributes to their lifestyles and philosophies. All they ask of outsiders is that they do not offend the faith of the vast majority. Religious freedom is guaranteed under the constitution, and there is a fine Catholic cathedral and an Evangelical church in Kuwait City as well as a multi-denominational Protestant church at Ahmadi.

Of Merchants and Mariners

Important though religion has been in shaping society in Kuwait, some strictly local influences have also played their part over the centuries. Most of these influences stem from either the desert or the sea, and it was the sea that turned the Kuwaitis into some of the Gulf's leading merchants.

It all began in about 1710, when drought forced a group of tribesmen and their families to travel from the Arabian interior in search of new pastures. Stories handed down the generations have it that their journey was long and hard until they came to a large, sweeping bay where they found a supply of sweet water. They settled on the site of what is today's Kuwait City on the south shore, the name Kuwait probably being derived from *kut*, Arabic for fort – the actual fort was either built by the settlers or the ruins of one put up by the Portuguese to protect old trade routes. The foundations of the nation were laid by those early families which included the Al-Sabahs, modern rulers of Kuwait, the Al-Khalifas, now the ruling family in Bahrain, and several others

At the end of a day's fishing, a traditional Kuwaiti-built dhow ties up at one of the small harbours along the southern shore of Kuwait Bay.

whose descendants are today prominent in the business and commercial life of the nation.

Expansion of the small community must have been rapid, for by 1764 the Danish explorer Karsten Niebuhr estimated the population at 10,000. He was the first to record the extent of the Kuwaitis' new-found involvement in fishing and pearling, an industry which at the time was employing more than 800 boats, the gracious wooden dhows which are still built and used in Kuwait. The influx of newcomers to the prospering community increased in 1776 when, after the occupation of Basra by Persian forces, many merchants moved headquarters to the staunchly independent state. They were joined by the British East India Company which began sending its mail from India to Kuwait, and from there to Aleppo by the renowned 'Desert Express', camel caravans which could do the journey in two to three weeks.

It was, however, to the sea that most of the townspeople turned. Arabs had been famous as sailors for many centuries,

Fishermen mend their nets as they always have – squatting on the seashore and using both hands and feet to get on with the job.

and Basra had long been a prosperous port. The establishment of the Kuwait community must have been followed by an immediate recognition of the opportunities offered by Kuwait Bay with its splendid shelter and long, gently shelving shore ideal for building boats. A pattern soon evolved in which there were three distinct types of seafaring activity. First there were the smaller boats which were used for fishing, as lighters to bring ashore cargo from British India ships in the bay, and – in the case of the larger vessels – for meeting Kuwait's increasing need for fresh water from the Shatt Al-Arab.

The largest of the boats, the ocean-going *boums*, were the special pride of the Kuwaitis. These were used for the annual *safar*, or trading voyage, which lasted for six to eight months and covered thousands of miles at sea. The boats, some of them up to 300 tons, would leave the bay in early autumn, often heading to Iraq to collect dates. They would then follow one of the traditional trade routes, going to India to collect wood, or to Aden for salt, cloth and oil before heading down the African coast as far as Zanzibar where they would pick up mangrove poles for house roofing. The expertise displayed by the captains and sailors on these voyages was fantastic, fathers handing down to sons their knowledge of navigation, currents, winds and weather. In the Indian Ocean they navigated with almost intuitive accuracy by the stars, while on the run back along the East African coast they would be required to short-haul and show the sort of skilled seamanship for which they became famed. During the *safar* entire families were often deprived of every male over the age of ten, and there were wild scenes of rejoicing when the sailors came safely home... or grief when days turned into weeks and a *boum* did not return.

Yet if the *safar* was a tough, demanding way of life, it could not compare with the daily rigours of Kuwait's other principal seafaring activity: pearling. Until the late 1920s, pearling was Kuwait's most important trade and the Gulf was supplying the world with the finest pearls. At the turn of the

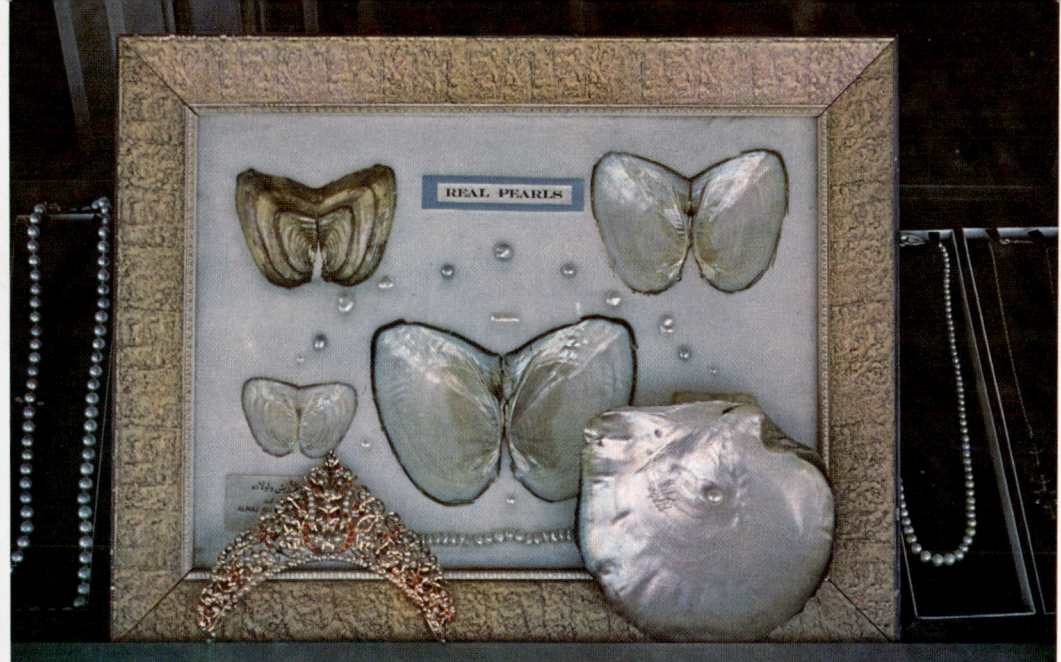

Reflections of the past in a display of the Gulf pearls which represented the backbone of Kuwait's economic life until the late 1920s.

century the number of crews and divers from Kuwait totalled about 15,000 men, and as the town itself could not supply such a large force, people would leave the desert pastures each year to try their luck in diving for pearls. They would crowd on boats varying in length from 30 to 60 feet (9-18 metres) and holding up to 200 men, and would then head for the traditional pearling grounds some 160 kilometres to the south. The season lasted from mid-May to mid-September, the hottest time of the year, and the divers would work from sunrise to sunset, the day's haul of oysters being opened in front of the entire complement in the evening. The diver worked for a share in the profits and drew no wages. Consequently, if there were no profits, he would be obliged to dive for the same skipper the following season to wipe out the debt. It was a vicious circle which tied divers to one particular captain for years on end – if they lived that long. Many succumbed to sickness and fatal cramps, others fell victim to sharks. The divers' health was often ruined by descending too quickly to depths of 12 metres where they would prise oysters loose with knives, or by eating too little in an effort to ward off cramp. There can have been few more rigorous or dangerous ways of earning a living, and it is a heritage the Kuwaitis do not forget.

The emergence of the Japanese cultured pearl and the worldwide economic collapse of 1929 sounded the death-knell of the Kuwait pearling industry, but even so there were few families which did not have some sort of stake in pearling even as late as the 1930s.

As seafaring activities grew over the years, so did land-based support. Not only did shipbuilders and chandlers flourish, but so also did the merchants and agents handling the increasing number of goods for the expanding community. That, in turn, led to the beginnings of service industries and a great many other activities which are reflected today in Kuwait's wide range of businesses.

Special mention deserves to be made of the men who actually made the sailing vessels, and there can be few finer testimonies to their work than that of a visitor to Kuwait who described at the beginning of this century a scene which must have been unchanged for more than a hundred years.

> Along nearly the whole length of the front [of Kuwait Bay], the sloping beach was lined with boats, among them vessels in all stages of construction. By the roadside stood steel capstans and wooden water tanks and everywhere there were masts and spars and piles of timber. Where the road was wide enough, the white sails would be spread out on the ground for the sail-makers to sew. On every side one could see the industry and craftsmanship and sheer hard labour which had gone into making and maintaining Kuwait as the finest boat-building port in the Gulf. The boats which took shape there were marvels of the carpenter's art, made with primitive, traditional tools but shaped into lines so functionally graceful they were a delight to the eye.

These boats still live on in the small harbours along that same stretch of shore on the south side of the bay, although today construction is restricted to Doha, on a northern headland. They were the boats which brought the first taste of wealth to Kuwait, just as it was the sea which shaped the distinctive character of today's Kuwaitis.

At Doha on a headland jutting out into the north side of Kuwait Bay, the traditional dhow-building skills – little changed for more than two hundred years – are preserved in the hands of dedicated craftsmen.

Culture and the Arts

Although the social history of Kuwait cannot be traced to the earliest days of civilization, the cultural heritage of the early nomadic life survives. It has been enriched by the seafaring legacy of the pearlers and the merchants, and while the Kuwaitis cannot lay claim to any fine old buildings or institutions, their links with the past remain very much alive in their songs, dances and music. Open-air public performances by one of the fifteen permanent folk troupes are guaranteed to attract massive crowds of spectators.

These troupes come under the auspices of the Association of Artists, which has permanent headquarters in Kuwait City and through which the Ministry of Social Affairs and Labour funnels generous financial support. Each of the men's groups has a hardcore of a dozen or so 'masters', but at a performance the number of participants can swell to a hundred or more as enthusiastic (and, usually, accomplished) amateurs join in.

The most frequently seen and popular dance is the *ardah* which dates back countless centuries to bedouin celebrations of victory in battle – although it is not so much war-like as expressing a satisfaction and joy of life. The form of the dance is common to most of Arab art, with the emphasis on straight lines. In the middle of the dancing area is a flag, but the dancers – all males, carrying swords or rifles – never actually form a circle around it: they move to and fro to the incessant beatings of traditional goatskin drums and tambourines. It is difficult even for a Westerner not to be induced into a state of semi-hypnosis by the beat and the chants – little wonder that Kuwaiti men are seldom able to resist the urge to join in.

One of the most sensational dances for women is the *freasah* or colt dance. Like the *ardah*, it marks victory in battle and centres around a dummy horse. The women make much the same movements as the men in the *ardah*, and are actually dressed in male clothing, the point of the dance being to recall the achievements of the many Arab wives and sisters who donned men's clothes and rode into battle with their loved ones. The most attractive of the women's dances however is the one traditionally performed at weddings – one of the rare occasions when young women were allowed to display their beautiful long black hair in front of men. For this dance the girls dress in splendid, richly coloured dresses embroidered in gold; they wave their heads in time to the music, and often sing as well.

Song, indeed, is never far away in Kuwait. The long-retired pearl divers have a special centre in Kuwait City where they meet to talk, sing and dance, handing on their experiences and unique culture to younger generations. Much of the music remains centred on the drum, tambourine and *rabbaba*, a single-stringed instrument with a sound box covered by goatskin. The dances and songs themselves may date back as far as the third century A.D., yet the music itself is constantly evolving and developing. In the words of a folklore specialist at Kuwait Museum: 'It is not just a question of preserving old customs. It is a continuous process, constantly being added to ... an expression of originality in the people.' The Ministry of Education makes a determined effort to keep the tradition alive among the young by ensuring that children learn all about folk art at school. It appears to need little encouraging, for singing, dancing and music are among the most popular items on the curriculum.

Islam represents an important part of the cultural heritage, the Holy Koran remaining not only the unquestioned word of Allah (God) as revealed to Mohammed but also the greatest literary achievement known to the Arab world. Poetry continues to be a widely practised art in Kuwait. The Ministry of Information has a team of academics working on ancient manuscripts with the aim of preserving and analysing them; the fruits of their labour are being published in a huge, multi-volume project.

Modern efforts in various fields of the arts find ready support from the Government. The National Council for Culture, the Arts and Letters has been established to pursue an active policy of encouraging talent locally and exposing Kuwait to art-forms from abroad – anything from traditional Oriental work to the paintings of Andy Warhol. Financial support goes to Kuwaiti painters and writers, enabling them to develop their skills without the associated worries of money and regular employment. Theatres are being built, and artists, writers and performers are given grants to show their work overseas at exhibitions and festivals. It would scarcely be realistic to expect a nation the size of Kuwait to make a major impact on the international arts scene, particularly as serious excursions into such fields have occurred only in the past few years. Nevertheless, there has been one notable achievement: the success of the first full-length motion picture made in Kuwait. A young Kuwaiti director took his own script and Kuwaiti actors and technicians and made a film about life during the pearling days. The film, entitled *The Cruel Sea*, went on to win a host of awards, including the International Critics' Award for the Best Film at the Venice Film Festival – a remarkable feat in a country with no previous experience in movies.

A young Kuwaiti sculptor practises his art at a centre which receives generous help from the Government.

Kuwaitis in their traditional summer dishdashas meet after a day's work at one of the open-air cafés near the old port.

Society Today

Clothes, it is said, make the man. Not so in Kuwait, where virtually every indigenous male adult will opt for summer dress consisting of sandals, the traditional white robe (*dishdasha*) and a white head cloth (*guttra*) held in place by a black cord. A sure way to tell that winter is arriving is by the sudden change to shoes, *dishdashas* made of dark suiting material, and heavier quality *guttras*. Arabian men have dressed in a similar way for countless centuries, and the arrival of modern living conditions and Western influences appears to have made little impact on the preferred and proven style. It tends to be that way in more than one aspect of life in today's Kuwait.

While the houses the Kuwaitis live in may be filled with the latest electronic gadgetry, while their buildings may be futuristic in design and the cars they drive may be the latest that Detroit or Europe or Japan has to offer, the typically Arabian lifestyle endures to a greater or lesser extent.

Of all the misconceptions about Arab life, none stands out more than the misunderstanding over the role of women. It is true that a Moslem may have up to four wives, but it is also true that polygamy in Kuwait today is very much the exception. In any case, the Koran stipulates that if a man fears he would not be able to be absolutely fair in the treatment of his wives, then he must have only one. The typical Kuwaiti family is much like any other: husband, wife and children (admittedly, the more children the better). The family unit is all-important, and the birth of a son continues to be a more momentous event than that of a daughter. Most Kuwaiti marriages are still arranged by the parents, which may seem curious to Western minds but which appears to work as successfully as any other match-making device. And while Kuwait remains a predominantly patriarchal society, male-dominated outside the bounds of domestic life, the progress made by women in recent years has been startling.

Islam regards men and women as equals, but with different roles. The coming of oil and the subsequent increases in educational and employment opportunities have dramatically increased the scope of this role for women, and they now occupy important positions in government service, education, commerce and the professions. Yet this has come about without any radical alteration in traditional attitudes, the women themselves seeming set on achieving their goals within the boundaries of Islamic thought and custom.

Segregation of the sexes remains a feature of daily life. State schools are single-sex, and although Kuwait University is coeducational it has a separate college for women. There are all-male social gathering places (*diwania*) where the men meet in the evening to drink bitter Arabic coffee, while in many homes there is a room in which the womenfolk

The ceremonial robes of young Kuwaiti women, richly embroidered with gold, add a splash of colour to performances of traditional songs and dances.

congregate. And at cinemas, restaurants, sports arenas and other public places there are usually areas reserved solely for women or for families. At most modern social gatherings, however, men and women mix freely.

If anything, the Kuwaiti male tends to put a woman on a pedestal rather than subject her to his will. It was, after all, the Prophet who said: 'Paradise is under the feet of mothers.'

The hours for work and play differ in Arabia from many other, less warm areas. Because of the scorching summer heat, traditional working hours are between 7 a.m. and noon and from roughly 4 p.m. to 7 p.m. The siesta enabled people to sleep through the hottest part of the day, and many commercial offices still observe these hours despite the advent of air-conditioning. Many of the newer industries, however, observe a five-day week, the 7 a.m. to 4 p.m. routine only interrupted by an hour for a midday meal. Government business tends to start around 7 a.m. and finishes at lunchtime. Most businesses and shops work at least a five-and-a-half-day week, stores usually opening about 10 a.m. or later and not shutting until about 9 p.m. These unorthodox hours and the fact that Friday is the weekly day of rest can make life confusing and complicated for businessmen visiting the Middle East for the first time.

Life in general seems to be lived at a more leisurely pace in Kuwait than elsewhere, which is no doubt due in large part to the heat. Many of the old desert customs survive, and although modern Kuwaitis are often urbane and intelligent, the desert still has its allure for them. There are no longer great numbers of bedouin living off the land, but an annual exodus from the towns takes place in early spring as Kuwaitis take their families and friends to live in tents in the greening desert for a weekend, a week or more.

At Play

What do Kuwaitis like to do when it is 49 degrees centigrade in the shade and there is precious little shade to be found? Go ice-skating, of course. That, at least, is the current craze

24

The Olympic-sized ice rink was opened in 1979 and has since proved one of the major leisure attractions in a country more used to warmer-weather sports.

following the completion in 1979 of the nation's first ice rink. Or, rather, two ice rinks – one Olympic-sized arena for men and another smaller version for women and families. Skating facilities are among the latest items to be added to the already lengthy list of sporting and leisure amenities. Unquestionably, the sporting life has arrived in Kuwait with a vengeance.

The subject of leisure has been taken seriously in the past decade, with the construction of everything from sports centres to beach clubs. In a country where people have both the time and the money to devote to leisure activities, it could be no other way.

For centuries, the prime sporting activity centred on the desert: falconry, hunting and horse or camel racing. These still take place (much to the consternation of conservationists, who are understandably concerned by modern hunting techniques), but they have been joined by pursuits as diverse as they are many.

Soccer is today's number one spectator sport in Kuwait. The Kuwaitis have been four times winners of the Gulf Cup and won the Asian Cup in 1980, and have spent vast amounts of money in increasing the number of grass pitches enclosed in modern stadia. The policy of importing Euro-

Horses have always played an important part in the life of the desert, although pure-bred Arabs like this one are now kept for breeding and racing.

pean and South American coaches to develop club sides and train the national team has paid rich dividends, although Kuwait's poor performance in the 1978 Asian Games caused something of a shake-up which led to the country embarking on a scheme to build a new, younger team. The pool of players is not exactly large: there are only about 1500 Kuwaitis of all ages playing football under the auspices of Kuwait Football Association, although untold hundreds of other players take part in various expatriate competitions. Kuwait's soccer reputation, however, is among the best of any developing country, and the national side came within an ace of qualifying for the 1978 World Cup Finals.

The clubs being built are not simply devoted to football but include a range of facilities from swimming pools to squash courts. Track and field athletics have not really caught on, the heat acting as a deterrent, but there are some keen distance runners and Kuwait's only medal at the last Asian Games came from a shot putter.

With such fine beaches and warm, clear water, it is hardly surprising that much of the nation's leisure time should be concentrated on, in, under or bordering the Arabian Gulf. Sailing is increasing in popularity, while powerboats fairly swarm over coastal waters at weekends. Fishing, too, is immensely popular, and newer pastimes such as water skiing and sub-aqua swimming are attracting large groups of adherents. The arrival of sea clubs run by the government-initiated Touristic Enterprises Company has opened the way for ordinary men, women and children to get club membership and facilities at reasonable cost. Previously, such facilities were restricted to exclusive haunts like the privately run Gazelle Club, just north of Fahaheel on the coast, or to clubs organized by companies for their employees.

Oil companies, Kuwait Oil Company in particular, were the first to introduce comprehensive recreational facilities and still offer some of the finest in the country. In addition to its own Families' Beach Club (an organization which has seen considerable expansion in recent years), KOC has two clubs for different grades of employee – senior staff joining the Hubara Club and other personnel the Unity Club – which have everything from swimming pools and tennis courts to restaurants and cinemas. Set among the trees of Ahmadi, they are more like large country clubs than sporting clubs, although they support a variety of teams playing squash, soccer, cricket, hockey, tennis and many other games. In addition, KOC has opened more than a dozen different clubs and societies specializing in such activities as amateur dramatics, music, riding, clay pigeon shooting, rugby football, natural history, sailing and power boating.

Against the backdrop of high-rise apartments along the south shore of Kuwait Bay, a sailing boat heads for the marina at Ras Salmiyah.

The annual leisure jamboree is the Summer Recreation Programme organized by the Government and featuring weeks of entertainment, including appearances by international artists – from the much-loved Bolshoi Ballet to pop groups. Performances by Kuwaiti, Gulf and other Arab musicians and performers are always high on the agenda, while for children there are many more active events including beach and sports competitions. There are film shows, exhibitions, firework displays and open-air entertainments for all ages. Some events are free, for others a nominal entrance fee is charged. The programme, which runs for several weeks each year, is traditionally opened with an impressive parade and ceremony at a sports stadium.

Not everyone stays in Kuwait during the summer, however. Many Kuwaitis travel to the European capitals and cities of North America to escape the blistering heat of July and August. Efforts are being made to increase the appeal of stay-at-home vacations – a large holiday chalet complex is being built on Failaka Island, for instance, and a plan to build a Kuwaiti version of Disneyland on the north shore of the bay could come to fruition in the early eighties. The development of beaches and beach clubs should help, too, although the Kuwaitis are not attempting to create an international resort centre. Rather they aim to cater for the local population, as well as making the leisure hours more enjoyable for the thousands of business visitors who pour into the country each year.

One form of entertainment that is very much alive and well is the cinema. It is not uncommon for every seat in every cinema (including the nation's single drive-in) to be sold out on any given night. Statistics show that up to five million tickets are bought in a year, representing about four visits to the cinema by every man, woman and child in the country. The programmes available range from the latest American and European films to Arab and Indian movies, non-Arabic productions always having sub-titles. Foreign television programmes are similarly dubbed, and the opening of

Two ever-popular sources of entertainment: the Salmiyah cinema (top) which nightly attracts full houses to its screenings of films from all over the world, and (bottom) one of the sea clubs run by the Touristic Enterprises Company which has done much to increase facilities for all sorts of water sports.

Kuwait's second colour TV channel in 1978 gave this nation of inveterate viewers a far wider selection of programmes.

Yet, for all the innovations, the old pastimes remain. The *diwania*, the social gathering places where men get together to discuss every sort of issue and topic, remain as well patronized as ever. Falconry is an ancient skill which still attracts wealthy enthusiasts, many of whom belong to the Hunting and Equestrian Club which is also doing much to foster show jumping. There is a race-course where fine Arabian stallions vie for cash prizes (betting is proscribed under Islam), and fleet-footed camels from the stables of the rich also make a few public appearances.

And, as we have seen, Kuwait has every conceivable modern sporting facility; there is even a golf course – a little unusual, perhaps, stuck in the middle of a desert, but no more so than an Olympic-standard ice rink. One comes to accept the unusual and incongruous in Kuwait.

Certainly, there is no reason these days for any Kuwaiti to feel at a loose end during his or her leisure time.

The Country

The Al-Jahra Gate, now preserved as a national monument and one of the few reminders of the mudbrick wall which once surrounded Kuwait City.

Kuwait is easy to describe in general terms: desert. It rises gently from the blueness of the Gulf in an east–west direction, and it can be flat or rolling, desolate and lifeless or, at times, alive with vegetation and animal life. But it remains inexorably, defiantly, desert. Man has made his impact with roads, buildings and industries and there are plans to make long-term changes by turning large, inhospitable tracts into arable land. Yet all such efforts, beneficial as they may be to the lot of the human race, can only scratch the surface of the ageless desert.

Researchers at Kuwait University have for convenience split the country into four sections: the coastal dunes, the salt marsh and saline depressions around Kuwait Bay, the sparsely vegetated desert plateau in the west, and the desert plain with patches of coarse grasses littering the sand which occupies the vast bulk of the country. All of it is mostly flat or gently undulating although there are rare rock outcrops, wadis in the north-west and, running along the north shore of the bay, the Zor Hills – a geological fault where an uplift has broken the plain and left an impressive scar. These hills are much favoured by naturalists, picnickers and motor-cyclists, the varying interests of the three groups not always proving compatible.

The main concentration of population is in Kuwait City and the urban sprawl around the bay to the headland at Salmiyah. There has also been considerable development in the traditional farming area of Jahra, at the Kuwait Oil Company town of Ahmadi, and at southerly coastal towns such as Fahaheel (near the oil complexes and the Shuaiba Industrial Area) and Fintas. In the past twenty years these areas, which had changed little in the previous millennium, have been transformed by every imaginable convenience and service.

However, the desert remains the dominant feature of the landscape as inevitably as the climate dictates lifestyle. Despite the appearance of air-conditioning in practically every home, office, shop and car, the heat of summer is one of those facts of life in Kuwait which determines everything from architecture to the hours that people work. And it does get hot: sometimes as high as 50 degrees centigrade in the shade, and regularly 45°C during peak summer. Apart from anything else, this results in Kuwaitis gulping down more soft drinks than virtually any other people in the world barring their Arabian neighbours. Meteorologists put some definite limits on the Kuwait summer: it runs, they say, from 21 May to 4 November, the really scorching weather occurring in July and August. Between September and early November the mercury gradually falls to the mid-30s, although a marked increase in humidity can make it the most uncomfortable period of the year. A month of pleasantly warm days and cool nights follows before the onset of winter, defined as between 6 December and 15 February, when there is a remarkable drop in temperature with an average daily maximum of between about 7 and 14°C. There are cold north-westerly winds and, in January particularly, the night thermometer can drop to freezing and there may be frost. The minimum temperature so far recorded was at Kuwait International Airport on 20 January 1964, when it was −4°C.

What little rainfall there is occurs between November and May, the annual total rarely amounting to four inches. The spring and early summer can be extremely pleasant except for the dust-storms or *taus* which descend like a suffocating orange fog.

The small amount of rainfall poses obvious problems. Although there are reservoirs of sweet water underground, almost all drinking water has to be obtained by distillation, the end-product being mixed with chemicals and quantities of brackish water to ensure the presence of desirable trace elements. Plans to bring in potable water by pipeline from the Shatt Al-Arab are under way between the respective Ministries of Electricity and Water of Kuwait and Iraq.

The amount of rainfall also determines whether or not the desert will put on its green mantle in the winter and early spring period. Downpours in the last quarter of the year can transform the steppes into lush areas covered with plants and flowers – as many as 400 species of flora have been recorded by amateur naturalists from the Ahmadi Natural History Group. Many of the species originate in Europe, while a lesser number come from Africa; the seeds may lie dormant for several years if there is not sufficient rainfall. A few seasons of plentiful plant-life will lead to an increase in the number of grazing animals which, in turn, leads to problems during dry years. In recent times there has been a decrease in some types of vegetation because of the over-pasturing of sheep, goats and camels.

Although most of Kuwait's population today lives in the towns, the bedouin still exist, living their lives much the same as ever in low black tents in the desert. Their numbers have declined as more and more take up government offers of jobs and housing, but the nomadic, ascetic lifestyle of the bedu and their animals remains. Strangely perhaps, the ownership of camels appears to have increased in recent years as many townsfolk rediscover the pleasures to be had from these durable pieces of evolution, even if their contact with them is restricted to occasional weekend visits.

Off the coast of Kuwait is a group of islands, the largest of which, Bubiyan, is uninhabited and no more than an extension of the desert plain lying close to the north-east shore. Some of the small southern islands, particularly Kobbar, get regular visits from boat-owners, but the only thriving island community is on Failaka in the mouth of Kuwait Bay. And it is on Failaka that the nation can trace links to the dim and distant days of the beginnings of civilized man.

The Dilmun Connection

Although Kuwait can trace its roots as a nation for little more than two centuries, excavations on Failaka Island have uncovered some fascinating links with ancient civilizations stretching back more than four thousand years. Indeed, finds at Failaka indicate that the island was the focal point of a flourishing community between 3000 and 1200 B.C. and that it was once part of the 'lost nation' of Dilmun, which is now generally accepted as being centred on Bahrain. The Failaka discoveries have added weight to theories that the Gulf formed an early civilization contemporary with those of Mesopotamia and India, and have shed new light on our understanding of the earliest days of civilization.

It was in 1958 that an archaeological expedition from Denmark first started digging at Failaka and uncovered evidence to connect the island with Bahrain and the Dilmun civilization dating from around 2800 B.C. While the entire story has yet to be pieced together, it seems possible that Failaka existed as a holy island at least four thousand years ago. The finds surpassed all expectations: they include red brick similar to that found in excavations in Mesopotamia, glazed pottery like other pieces unearthed in Bahrain, the ruins of a temple as Greek as the Parthenon, and the remains of houses, workshops and fortifications.

The Failaka link with the time of Alexander the Great has been clearly established, but the Dilmun connection remains tantalizingly vague. This civilization came to the fore about 2800 years before the birth of Christ and dominated trade routes between Mesopotamia and ancient communities of the Indus valley. Certainly, Failaka – some 400 kilometres from Bahrain – was in the area of Dilmun influence, and discoveries of intriguing stone seals, similar to some found in Mesopotamia, lead archaeologists to believe that there must have been trade links and perhaps political alliances between the Failakans and the Sumerians. The seals date from the old bronze age (3000 to 2100 B.C.), which would make Failaka younger than the 5000-year-old Dilmun site at Bahrain but still a vital part of the history of this, one of the world's earliest communities. Further excavations may yield more light on the role and importance of Failaka but, for the moment, there is a gap in the story between the early civilizations and that established during the time of Greek influence.

An account of Alexander the Great's campaigns written several hundred years after Alexander's death in 323 B.C. gave an account of the voyage of a Greek naval commander who sailed up the Gulf before heading for what is now Pakistan. He is said to have called at two islands; the one near the Euphrates, called Ikaros by Alexander, housed a shrine to Artemis. This was undoubtedly Failaka, for the remains of a temple to Artemis have been unearthed on the island in the last twenty years, and the name Ikaros was found engraved on a stone tablet. It appears that a Greek-sponsored community, complete with its own fortifications, was established there, and extensive remains of a township built along Seleucid lines have been found (the Seleucid empire covered almost all the land-mass from the Nile through to India after the death of Alexander). A rich hoard of silver coins, one bearing a head resembling King Antiochus who ruled the empire from 223 to 187 B.C., has been uncovered on Failaka. In addition, some inscribed with the mail mark of Alexander were found, but these were probably produced some time after his death.

The discovery of a brick-built workshop complete with a kiln for firing terracotta figures indicates that an advanced community flourished on Failaka in the third century B.C. Much speculation surrounds this community: it is believed to have been abandoned following raids by pirates, and later rebuilt; the first of Alexander's forces probably arrived in about 320 B.C. Excavation of the temple produced a stone bearing a message from the second Seleucid ruler to the island inhabitants, and other finds included remains of Greek statues, stones and coins. It is likely that there is still a great deal more to be found, and excavations continue on the island site close to the modern ferry terminal.

Eventually, with the rise of Rome, the Greek colony disappeared and the name of Ikaros fell into disuse. Only in the past couple of decades, when Failaka has become popular as a leisure resort for mainlanders, has the exciting past of the island begun to be rediscovered. Important questions still beg to be answered, not least of them concerning two statues found on Failaka and bearing the inscription of Inzak, the god of Dilmun. Is it possible that Failaka was a holy island of the old community and housed a temple to Inzak pre-dating by some two thousand years the one to Artemis?

Let us hope that more light will soon be shed on this most interesting ancient site.

Kuwait City

Clumps of tower cranes still dominate the Kuwait City skyline as a reminder that the recession which hit hard in many Gulf states in 1976-7 left Kuwait, with its more broadly based economy, relatively unscathed. Although construction activity fell off for a time, a series of major developments is currently under way. These buildings will change the face of the capital over the next few years – and it will not be for the first time. Old Kuwait City all but disappeared in the fifties and sixties when the Government encouraged land purchase as a means of transferring some of the national wealth into the hands of the Kuwaiti people. The results came in the form of high-density, medium-rise buildings which, although now jaded, still dominate much of the downtown area and commercial district.

Kuwait is a land of contrasts, and the City is no exception: four-storey buildings crammed into the main shopping streets back on to yawning spaces of sand, hitherto used only as parking lots for the thousands of cars which daily pour into the city. Times are changing, however, with new, more attractive and better planned buildings going up in both the public and private sectors. Multi-storey car parks are becoming more common, too, as one answer to a problem which is

Fahad Al Salem Street, one of the main thoroughfares in downtown Kuwait City and the home of many commercial enterprises.

inevitable in a country of this size trying to cope with some 600,000 vehicles on its roads. But cars are not the only things crowding in on Kuwait City. The Buchanan Report, named after the firm of British consultants which compiled it some fifteen years ago, estimated that by the year 2000 the city centre would accommodate 95,000 workers and 80,000 residents. Those figures have now almost been reached, twenty years ahead of schedule!

Even so, the high density of the buildings means that the city does not give the impression of being crowded, except on the wide, modern thoroughfares which criss-cross it. Certainly, the new buildings being erected in and around the centre belie the scarcity of space: the Ministry of Information complex, set amid lawns and fountains, is an obvious example, and other government buildings now in the throes of construction will heighten the illusion of spaciousness.

Two of the more modern faces of Kuwait: shops and boutiques (below) in Salmiyah, selling goods from all over the world, and (right) residential flats in Dasman Square, not far from the city centre and the Amir's palace.

Among the latest additions is the new National Assembly going up along the shores of the bay; tasteful additions to the Seif Palace, including a new Ministry of Foreign Affairs headquarters, are under way; and a ministries' complex near the historic Shamiya Gate is the centre of much activity.

Outside the Green Belt strip of parkland which loops around the city centre are the tenement blocks which house expatriate communities; some of these are pleasant and modern, but others are crowded and look older than their ten or twenty years. There are also Kuwaiti areas containing some fine houses with well-tended lawns and gardens – something to marvel at in a country where natural water resources are scarce.

Plans for further expansion of the city and its environs are limited by geography. Kuwait City has grown up around the southern side of the bay, with traditional growth occurring along the shore to the headland at Ras Salmiyah and then in an arc back to the industrial and port area of Shuweikh. This land forms a virtual peninsula, its landward boundaries marked by a succession of ring roads. The Sixth Ring Road represents the limit of expansion so far, and it is likely that the city's urban sprawl will be contained within this area for the foreseeable future.

Apart from the actual city centre, the main shopping and residential areas are based on Salmiyah, a district usually chosen by Western expatriates working outside the oil sector, and Hawalli, once a village quite separate from Kuwait City but now, like Salmiyah, part of the expanding conurbation. In these and other areas nearer the centre, the various groups of expatriates live in vast stretches of apartment blocks.

One of the capital's most impressive sights can be seen along Arabian Gulf Street, which follows the southern sweep of the bay from Ras Salmiyah into the city centre. The final stretch of the six-lane (and, for part of the way, eight-lane) highway was completed in 1979, since when the road has become one of the main commuter arteries, relieving the burden of other main roads which emanate from the centre like spokes from a wheel and which are bisected by a succession of ring roads. Along Arabian Gulf Street stands the most prominent of Kuwait's landmarks, the Kuwait Towers, situated on a small headland near the Dasman Palace, home of the Amir Sheikh Jaber Al-Ahmad. The towers were built in the mid-seventies and became fully operational in 1979. The imposing structures, the tallest topping the 180-metre mark, were designed to be not only aesthetically impressive but also functional, two of the three towers serving as water reservoirs. There are also viewing galleries, a restaurant, lounge, cafeteria, banqueting hall and an indoor garden. The Towers capture the essence of modern Kuwait in a design which embraces both the space age and the lasting values of Islamic society.

Arabian Gulf Street has other spots worth lingering over, in particular the string of dhow harbours along the front just south-east of the city centre. Here you can see at close range the incredible skills of the men who made, and still make, these remarkable wooden craft. They remain in use for

The most notable of all the country's landmarks, the Kuwait Towers, serve a practical purpose: the two larger spheres were designed as water reservoirs.

Luxury residential complexes, complete with their own shops, on Arabian Gulf Street, the main commuter highway running along the bay from Salmiyah to the City.

fishing, trade and lightering, with sail mostly giving way to diesel engines.

The main dhow harbour lies behind the Seif Palace, the elegant administrative headquarters of the Amir on the site where Mubarak the Great declared himself ruler of Kuwait in 1896. It was Mubarak who ordered the construction of the first stage of the existing complex, and part of the yellow brick *serai* or government building still stands to the west of the present palace. This, the former office of the ruler, is next to what is now the Council of Ministers' building which faces the main palace across an enclosed grass courtyard. Construction of the new Seif Palace began in the early sixties and, from the start, it was envisaged as a pleasant building of basically uncomplicated, orthodox design which would fit in with the older parts. Both inside and out it is elegant but simple, with facilities which include the Amir's office, administrative rooms, a VIP reception hall where diplomats present their credentials and visiting Heads of State are received, and a conference room. But the most important part as far as the Kuwaitis are concerned is the main ceremonial hall, a vast room where the Amir meets his people to hear their complaints and problems or, on certain holidays, to receive the wishes of the many thousands who line up to shake his hand.

Work started on additions to the palace in 1978-9 and will include a new library and Ministry of Foreign Affairs. These will, however, continue to be overshadowed by the Seif Palace's best-known feature, the gold-domed clocktower which serves as a daily reminder to motorists bunched along Arabian Gulf Street that they are early or, more commonly, late for work. There is also an inscription over the main palace gate which reads (roughly translated): 'If others could

have retained the seat of power, it would never have reached you.' The words are Mubarak the Great's and, though they lose something in the translation, they remain a call to the nation's leaders to tackle their tasks with humility and fairness.

Traditional Kuwaiti cafés are strung along the seashore, the menfolk meeting there in the evenings, sitting outside in their white *dishdashas* during hot weather to chat and drink Arabic coffee or Kuwaiti tea. On the other side of Gulf Street are many different types of buildings: modern, luxury apartment blocks and large, individually designed houses and, closer to the city, some fine examples of traditional dwellings. Entrance to the latter can normally only be gained through large doors, invariably of heavy wood studded with iron – truly works of art in themselves. Along the boulevard are other interesting buildings, not least the former headquarters of the British Political Agent. This fine, terraced building was given to Colonel H.R.P. Dickson, the last agent before Independence, as a mark of appreciation by the Amir. Colonel Dickson was the author of some of the most authoritative books on the desert, bedouin and early life in Kuwait, and his widow, herself a pioneer in the study of the nation's flora and fauna, still lives in the house. The Saudi Arabian, British and American embassies are also located on the highway, although it is Istiqlal Street, running roughly parallel to Arabian Gulf Street, which has deservedly earned the nickname 'Street of Embassies'.

At the end of the street nearest the port of Shuweikh stands the Marriott Hotel, one of an increasing number of luxury hotels being built in Kuwait. Strictly speaking, the Marriott was not built: a former cruise liner, it was already converted into a hotel before being towed into Kuwaiti waters in 1978 for its final berthing in concrete. It opened early in the spring of 1979, a few months after a 200-room extension opened at the Sheraton Hotel. For several years the Sheraton, situated close to the city centre, and the Hilton Hotel, close to the Towers on Arabian Gulf Street, dominated the luxury

In a pleasant blend of the old and the new, the Seif Palace near the old dhow harbour serves as the administrative headquarters of the Amir and the council of ministers.

accommodation market in Kuwait. Until recently the only other hotel listed by the Government in the luxury class was the Messilah Beach Hotel, which can hold 600 people in chalet-type accommodation overlooking a private beach, swimming pools, shops and so on. Most of the short-stay businessmen went to the Hilton or Sheraton, however, because these were considerably closer to the city centre. With occupancy rates running for much of the year at 100 per cent, both hotels were encouraged to plan extensions. An epidemic of hotel building then began. First the Marriott; next the Regency, with room for 700 guests, not far from Fahd Al-Salem Street; and on the way, a Holiday Inn near the airport and a luxury complex near Ras Salmiyah. There are other, smaller hotels in the downtown area, including several

The individual architecture of the homes of the more prosperous Kuwaitis brightens residential areas near the City reserved for the native population.

The construction boom of the sixties and seventies continues apace in the eighties, particularly in the building of complexes of offices, stores and much-needed car parks.

in the first-class category which offer comfortable accommodation at prices which are somewhat more reasonable than the extremely high rates charged at luxury hotels. Kuwait, of course, has one of the highest costs of living in the world as well as the highest level of income.

The Government keeps the hotel industry under careful review through specialists at the Ministry of Commerce and Industry. It also has a 49 per cent stake in the Kuwait Hotels Company (the remaining stock being in the hands of private Kuwaiti shareholders) which owns the Hilton, but does not manage the hotel, and manages the Messilah Beach and the

first-class Sahara Hotel, but does not own them. The company, which made a humble start in 1962, is also in charge of the catering side of the nation's sea clubs, themselves managed by the Touristic Enterprises Company, and manages the Royal Kensington Hotel in London. As if all this were not enough, it has a 15 per cent share in the 1000-room Ramses Hilton going up on the banks of the Nile in Cairo; a 49 per cent stake in the Khartoum Hilton; interests in hotels in Saudi Arabia, Dubai, Morocco and Tunisia; and a 47 per cent partnership in a British firm managing hotels. The Kuwait Hotels Company is currently completing its own resort complex on wide beaches at Dba'iyyah, south of Kuwait City. It will offer villa and chalet accommodation, a private club, swimming pools and a wide range of other facilities.

Most companies have offices in Kuwait City, even Kuwait Oil Company officially listing its main office in one of the commercial centres although in fact all administrative, executive and operational divisions are headquartered at Ahmadi. Kuwait National Petroleum Company, on the other hand, has a prestige building close to the banking area and, large though this building is, has taken two overspill floors in a modern complex with offices, shops and car parks not far away. The tallest building in the city is the Telecommunications Centre, with its huge antenna tower representing the focal point of Kuwait's links with the rest of the world. The restriction on the height of buildings in the capital has been lifted in the past few years, evidence of which can be seen in ever-rising blocks of offices, most notably the Kuwait Airways Corporation (KAC) building. The new Ministry of Information centre also has an administration tower shooting fourteen floors above street level.

Yet for all the new shopping complexes, office developments and government buildings, the old Middle East flavour can still be found, especially in the charmingly ramshackle *souk* (market) where open-fronted stores sell everything from antique Persian carpets to high-quality

A carpet seller shows his wares in the souk, *the old bazaar in Kuwait City where retailing, Arabian-style, goes on in much the same way as it has done since the days of Aladdin.*

stereo systems. It is a place of real character: here you may find bedouin women squatting on the ground selling traditional dress and make-up; an alley where falconers from all over the Gulf meet to buy trained birds of prey; a fish market to which dozens of species are brought direct from the nearby dhow harbours; fresh fruit and vegetables from all over the Middle East, many of them exotic and unknown to outsiders' eyes; hand-crafted musical instruments, camel hair rugs, open cafés... so much. Not surprisingly, the place is a planners' nightmare, and schemes are periodically put forward to pull down the web of streets and wooden shops and replace them with a modern covered complex made of brick and stainless steel. Many hope fervently that it will never happen.

What gives Kuwait City its real character, however, is the multitude of mosques: old, mudbrick ones little changed in style from the traditional buildings which have dotted the Arabian Peninsula since shortly after Mohammed's death; more recent ones which reflect architectural styles from all over the world of Islam; and modern, sometimes startling ones of futuristic design. The mosques with their inevitable minarets monopolize the sense of sight – they are everywhere to be seen, with new ones going up all the time – and sound – the noise of modern living means that the muezzin or crier must now use a loudspeaker system to call the faithful to prayer five times a day, whereas before he would shout across the rooftops from the balcony running around the top of the minaret.

The mosques no longer fulfil their earlier roles as places of political and community meetings, as educational institutions and even as courts, but they retain their prominence in the everyday lives of people great and small. Obviously they are still at the heart of religious observance, particularly on Fridays when services fill them to overflowing. But more important, the mosques serve as a constant and visible reminder of the nation's commitment to religion as a way of life.

It is this commitment which echoes through so many aspects of modern Kuwait City and, indeed, through the country as a whole.

Town and Country

While Kuwait City remains the hub of government and commercial activity, it has been obvious for some time that it cannot continue to grow indefinitely. A review of the Buchanan master plan suggests that the City and its suburbs can only hold about 1.5 million people, a limit now accepted by Kuwait Municipality, the urban planning authority. As a result, planners have turned elsewhere in a bid to find suitable sites to accommodate a population which, according to some estimates, could reach 2.75 million by the year 2000.

The traditional pattern of development has been towards the south. From the Messilah Beach roundabout at the limit of the city's suburbs, a six-lane highway runs parallel to the coast past Fintas, Fahaheel, the oil installations, the Shuaiba Industrial Area and port, and various housing developments until, just past Mina Abdullah, it becomes a two-lane road running to the Saudi border. The majority of urban housing development has occurred on either side of this highway between the roundabout and Fahaheel, and the one-time sleepy village of Fintas is now being developed as an urban centre as a stop-gap measure to relieve the pressure on Kuwait City. More ambitious plans are called for, however, and the Government is currently considering an idea to build a completely new town miles from the metropolis. The most favoured site is Subiya, about 100 kilometres round the bay from the city – that is, to the north, which would help to balance the traditional southern bias. Such a town would have to house about half a million people, and to be a success it would also have to be largely self-sufficient, which would mean moving certain government services, businesses and industries there. Not only would this be a considerable task in itself, but the necessary infrastructure for successful development would have to be built up from scratch.

Until forty years ago Kuwait consisted of little more than a concentration of population around the City and scattered communities at such places as Jahra, the northern oasis which had become the home of the nation's market gardening 'industry'. Then came oil – or, more specifically, Kuwait Oil Company, which started to build a township on a slab of inhospitable desert near the fast-developing Burgan oilfield in the south, some five kilometres inland from Fahaheel. Nissen huts were put up first, soon to be followed by an airfield. Next came the bricks and mortar: an administrative headquarters, a few houses, a mosque and a Protestant church, then more houses, paved streets, a hospital, school and clubs. And trees. Plenty of trees. The town of Ahmadi, named after Sheikh Ahmad, the first ruler of the oil era, grew from virtually nothing to a busy, bustling centre in a few hectic years between 1946 and 1949 and, in so doing, established the southern tilt for development which has never been altered. Today, Ahmadi retains its reputation as the most attractive place to live in Kuwait, with its abundance of greenery in pleasant, well-established residential areas. It deserves its nickname of the 'Green City', with a golf course, cricket pitches and a baseball diamond that are legacies of earlier Western ownership of KOC. But today the Kuwaiti *dishdasha* predominates among the residents – evidence of the remarkable rise of the indigenous population to positions of responsibility in the oil industry. Ahmadi, however, remains the home of most Western expatriates still employed by KOC, as well as other Arab personnel.

Although some high-density housing has been erected around the town, particularly near the industrial support area of East Ahmadi, the Green City itself has growth limitations. This has led to considerable high-rise building activity nearby at Fahaheel which, in turn, has led to the creation of service industries. More jobs came to the area with the expansion of the KOC terminal at Mina Al-Ahmadi and the establishment of what was then the Aminoil terminal at Mina Abdullah. Development became virtually self-perpetuating, accelerated still more by the transformation of a stretch of empty coast at Shuaiba into an industrial area. Fahaheel today is crammed with houses and apartment blocks, a recent shopping and office precinct near the long-established fish market and *souk* area lending a degree of elegance to an otherwise haphazard pattern of development. The community is longer than it is wide simply because building is squeezed between the Fahaheel road and the shores of the Gulf. Building is going on all along this strip from Fahaheel to Fintas, and on the other side of the road there are Kuwaiti residential areas, a massive hospital to serve the district, and showpiece housing estates for people with limited incomes.

This ribbon development has come as an inevitable consequence of the oil and industrial development in the southern part of Kuwait, but it has not been repeated elsewhere. Jahra has broadened out somewhat, but between it and the outskirts of Kuwait City there has been comparatively little building, and away from the coastal strip there has been no residential development whatsoever. Indeed, the country's interior is practically devoid of human life except for the remaining tribesmen and personnel at military installations and outlying oil stations.

On the historically important island of Failaka there exists a small but stable community. The old part of the fishing town still looks as Kuwait City must have looked forty years ago, with low, square mudbrick houses hugging each other along narrow dirt streets. Until the seventies the only way to reach Failaka was by dhow from the City; now fast modern ferries ply the route every hour from a terminal at Ras Salmiyah, and the island has become a popular spot for day-trippers as well as a fashionable place for holiday homes. The first phase of a vacation complex being built by the Touristic Enterprises Company is nearing completion, and will eventually include 300 chalets, a hotel, restaurant, swimming pools, supermarket and public beach.

A community that has changed little over the past two hundred years is Doha, located on a spur of land jutting into the north side of the bay. Here the primary occupation is boat-building, and craftsmen still carry out their work with skills unequalled in the Gulf. Even the establishment of a container depot nearby seems to have had little effect on families who can trace their way of life back to the very earliest days of the nation.

There are other scattered communities in Kuwait but until (and if) the northern strategy becomes a reality, the main thrust of activity will remain concentrated on the City and the southern coastal strip. And as the sea is never far away, the municipality has been putting no small amount of effort into improving the shore itself. Public beaches with all amenities have been made out of some uninspiring stretches of sand, the best example being at Ras Salmiyah where there are now

seafront gardens, ample parking, paved walkways and restaurants with the tables set along concrete jetties leading into the sea. There has also been an intensive programme to construct a string of eleven sea clubs along the coast from Kuwait City to Fahaheel, as well as the completion in 1979 of four new public beaches on the stretch between Messilah Beach and Fintas. Beyond Fahaheel, the main feature of the shore is the seemingly endless line of chalets built by Kuwaitis for weekends. Although very pleasant for the people who own them, these remote second homes have closed vast stretches of beautiful beach to the public, and there remains some question as to the legality of this.

One of the favourite haunts of European and American expatriates is the so-called Green House beach at a distant southerly spot near the site of Kuwait's brand-new naval base. Its remoteness enables Western women to go in for the sort of skimpy beachwear that is rarely seen anywhere else in

Large-scale construction of a promenade, gardens, car parks and cafés has changed the face of the shoreline at Ras Salmiyah, now one of the most popular public beaches in Kuwait.

Kuwait except in private clubs. For those who care to follow the road even further towards the Saudi border, there are some excellent beaches around the creek south of Getty Oil Terminal but, again, private development has made access difficult in many parts.

Perhaps the most ambitious plan for beach development concerns the sweep of Kuwait Bay running parallel with Arabian Gulf Street. This highway was built mainly on reclaimed land, and Gulf Dredging Company, partially state-owned, has put forward plans to turn the area into a beach resort that would give the southern side of the bay a whole new look.

On the Road

In 1960 there were 33,000 vehicles on Kuwait's roads. By 1979 the number had jumped to over half a million, and estimates for the eighties put the rate of annual increase at around 40,000 vehicles. This situation gives Kuwait the doubtful distinction of having traffic densities similar to those of Tokyo and Los Angeles, with all the attendant problems of traffic jams and rush-hour congestion. In a way though the state has been fortunate, because the wholesale reconstruction of the past couple of decades has enabled modern roads to be built as an integral part of development plans. Except in the heart of Kuwait City most streets run straight and true, and although a road system that seemed adequate in the sixties has been somewhat overtaken by events at the dawn of the eighties, it does provide the framework for expansion and modification. Besides, Kuwait is blessed with the wide open spaces which facilitate major road-building plans without the problem of knocking down buildings and homes – except, once again, in the inner city area.

The completion of Arabian Gulf Street along the southern shore of the bay has relieved the load on the other, dual-carriageway arteries leading to the city, but the burgeoning number of vehicles has meant that the road-builders have only been able – at best – to maintain the status quo rather than ease the situation. Hopes are high at the moment, however, that the current programme of freeway construction will improve links throughout the country and that alterations to urban highways will speed the journey to and from the city. What to do in the city centre itself is a problem which remains to be solved.

One snag with the urban highways has been the roundabouts which, while adequate to meet the needs of ten years ago, are now choked every morning with commuters' cars and, more often than not, in late afternoon with shoppers' cars. Traffic lights at major junctions with ring roads also proved to be a problem and so, starting in 1978 and continuing through 1979, the first flyovers were built, one being completed every two months. As if by magic traffic began to flow swiftly and smoothly over notorious bottlenecks, particularly around the Shuweikh Industrial Area and along the Fourth Ring Road, one of the principal highways which by-passes the city and links roads to the south and north.

Passenger vehicles are not the only cause of the problem, for Kuwait is a nation without a train system (although plans for a goods line have been drawn up) and so all material arriving at the docks or airport has to be delivered by road. Much of the remainder is imported directly by truck, road transport accounting for between 20 and 36 per cent of Kuwait's annual imports in the past decade. This brought an invasion of heavy goods vehicles from near and far – food, fresh fruit and vegetables from other Arab states and Mediterranean countries, high technology from Europe, and a great deal more besides. In 1975 a hardtop road was built running south to the Saudi Arabian border, and a highway is already under construction as a four-lane expressway. Similarly, the Jahra road running north to Iraq bears the brunt of the HGV onslaught and has had to be partially reconstructed. A third highway running west from Jahra to Saudi Arabia completes the list of established roads leading out of the country.

Driving the orange and white street taxis is a reserved occupation for Kuwaitis or bedouin tribesmen who are discovering a new lifestyle in the cities.

The eighties will bring the fruition of grandiose plans to construct a network of freeways to relieve commuter traffic on city streets, to improve communications between the city and such spots as the Ahmadi oil region and airport, and to accommodate the increasing amount of commercial traffic. The first phase of the system should soon be open, with 6.5 kilometres of eight-lane freeway connecting the outskirts of Kuwait City to the Fifth Ring Road, an enormous flyover being built on the site of the Shaab roundabout, formerly one of the largest and most congested of all the gyratory systems. Kuwait Municipality, which devised the freeway scheme, intends that in a few years the new routes will run from near the city centre to Ahmadi; will form a loop round dormitory and industrial areas; will link the brand-new airport with other super-fast highways; and will eventually run all the way north to the Iraq border. Undoubtedly the new system will be fast, and planners reckon that the absence of traffic lights, intersections and turn-arounds on the freeways will make them safer than the nation's other multi-lane roads.

Another problem which the municipality has had to tackle on existing roads arises from the increasing size and axle loads of commercial vehicles – much of the work on the Jahra road has been necessitated through damage done to the surface by heavier and heavier trucks. Discussions on load and size regulations have been under way for some years, and there are also plans afoot to regulate commercial routes and introduce parking restrictions. Finding suitable aggregates for the actual road surfaces has not been easy, either. The Ministry of Public Works has been striving for years to get the right blend for roads built on sand which have to take heavy loads and which must cope with temperatures that not only vary greatly according to season but also rise and fall suddenly. The situation is scarcely helped by downpours of winter rain causing erosion and subsidence.

Yet all the work seems to be paying off. Despite the problems, Kuwait can point to an excellent road system, most of it following the north–south pattern of develop-

Roundabouts and crossroads, adequate to meet the demands of ten years ago, are now being replaced by an elaborate series of flyovers in a bid

60

to beat the daily rush-hour crush.

ment, the one notable exception being the westerly route to Saudi Arabia. The bulk of the building has occurred in recent years and the prospect of a freeway system in the eighties will give the country one of the Middle East's finest networks of roads. Even then, it will probably still be a good idea to dodge Kuwait City during the rush-hour.

The Land and the Sea

'The economic importance of agriculture in Kuwait has so far been very limited. The contribution of this sector to domestic output does not exceed 0.04 per cent. Reasons for this marginal role ... are to be found in deficiencies of soil, scarcity of irrigation water, climatic conditions and the limited supply of manpower trained in agricultural skills.' Thus, in a nutshell, the Ministry of Planning's annual statistical abstract sums up Kuwait's farming endeavours. Yet despite this apparently discouraging situation a considerable amount of effort and experimentation is being aimed at improving the nation's performance within the inherent limits of desert agriculture.

There have been some surprising advances: Kuwait now produces almost half of the fresh vegetables consumed domestically, along with 41 per cent of the milk, 34 per cent of the poultry and 18 per cent of the eggs. Not that this comes near the record of the fishing industry which catches enough to meet 99 per cent of consumption, the outstanding one per cent being accountable to a few people's penchant for smoked salmon and other imported delicacies.

Keeping with the figures, the Central Statistical Office estimates the total cultivable area at 18,000 donums (1800 hectares), more than half of them occupied by vegetables and crops. Another 1000 or so donums are taken up by orchards and timber. There are well over 500 agricultural holdings including 313 specializing in vegetables, 86 in poultry and 40 in dairy herds. The major crops are tomatoes, radishes, melons and cucumbers, while clover is grown on a fairly large scale as animal feed. The underground water, which is the main source of irrigation, is pumped from deep wells and has a salinity range of between 0.3 and 1.1 per cent. There is also an incidental date industry which grew up following a drop in production in Iraq, traditional supplier of dates to Kuwait. Householders started growing date palms and from this a small-scale industry developed which currently satisfies about half of the local demand.

Beehives on the Experimental Farm just outside Kuwait City. Though the primary purpose of the farm is experimental, food produced here makes a useful contribution to the supply available.

Jahra is the traditional farming centre, although these days there are various concentrations scattered around the country, including a flourishing cluster of smallholdings as far south as Wafra near the Saudi border. The agricultural department of the Ministry of Public Works gives the farmers ample financial support to purchase land, equipment, seed and feed, contributing up to two-thirds of the cost. The department provides farmers with an active advisory service on soil analysis and the sort of crops that are likely to grow well; it also distributes pamphlets giving details of new techniques applicable to the harsh Kuwait environment.

But the department's most important tool in developing agriculture comes in the shape of the Experimental Farm. This has made a massive impact on Kuwait farming in the past decade and could make an even bigger one in the years to come. Current work at the farm, near Kuwait City, concentrates on hydroponics – a method by which plants grow on a gravel bed fed with carefully controlled solutions of water and fertilizers – and on the use of cloches and other coverings to protect the plants and encourage growth. The crammed fields at the Experimental Farm make their own contribution to the food supply, the crops going for sale at local markets; there are also some prime sheep and cattle kept under careful observation to see which ones best adapt to Kuwait conditions.

In an experiment carried out under the agricultural department's direction, an area approaching 1000 hectares has been set aside far away in the desert, to see whether treated sewage water can be used successfully for crop irrigation. Work is also going on to develop new strains of plants capable of taking to the local soil, which is 90 per cent sand, and of surviving the scorching heat of summer or the frosts of winter, or both. The brackish water also presents problems – many species simply cannot survive on it – while such hazards as dust storms and the dreaded red spider are never far away. Nevertheless, the department's experiments have already paid some handsome dividends in helping

Hydroponics – growing plants with liquid nutrients rather than in soil – is being closely studied at the Experimental Farm. Here a healthy crop of tomatoes can be seen.

farmers to get the most out of their soil. For the future, there is the hope of new irrigation methods plus the possibility of new crop strains: the signs are promising, for example, that a unique, specially developed potato will prove viable, thus further broadening the range of local vegetables.

Work is also going on at the Kuwait Institute for Scientific Research (KISR) which could have long-term ramifications. The institute was originally started by the Japanese-owned Arabian Oil Company as part of the agreement for an offshore oil concession. It was taken over by the Government in 1973 and today employs scientists and technicians from Kuwait, Japan, Europe and elsewhere. Its early brief included the development of agriculture in the desert, and at the moment it is co-operating with the Experimental Farm in developing a revolutionary greenhouse which uses solar energy for heat control.

Shrimping has always been a steady industry in Kuwait, and the old methods continue while research goes on to provide new ways of breeding and rearing a greater supply.

The KISR is also active in the field of aquaculture. Its marine biology and fisheries division, which has headquarters at Ras Salmiyah, is pioneering the way in fish farming in the Gulf. The division is currently working on three major projects: shrimp culture, fish culture and micro-organism studies, particularly the development of marine yeast as feed. The large Gulf shrimp (*Penaeus semisulcatus*) tastes and looks as good as the best found anywhere, and at the KISR station up to 20 million young shrimps a year are developed from the eggs of captured females and released into the open sea. Although the mothers produce 'only' about 50,000 eggs in captivity compared with 200,000 in the sea, the youngsters' chances of survival are far higher: recently, one of the five large tanks at the station notched up a survival rate of an incredible 53 per cent. One of the scientists' tasks is to discover how this was achieved. Another is to determine how far released shrimps roam in the open sea – there is, after all, little point in rearing shrimp if they are to be released and caught somewhere else. The problem with keeping them in captivity is that Kuwait does not have the natural small bays and inlets which have proved ideal in established fish-farming areas. There are also difficulties in getting shrimp to mate in controlled conditions, the females which are used at the moment all having had their eggs fertilized in the open sea. In terms of fish, KISR is concentrating on the most popular of all Kuwait varieties, the 'hamoor' or brown-spotted grouper, as well as black sea bream and grey mullet. The survival rate of hamoor has already been increased from 0.1 per cent to about 5 per cent.

The Arabian Gulf undoubtedly needs all the help it can get as far as fish stocks are concerned. The population explosion all along the Gulf coast has led to serious over-fishing, while industrial development has given rise to pollution worries, especially at the northern end of the Gulf where the water change is minimal. Much of the fishing activity still takes place from dhows, although many fishermen meet the needs of local markets with small, fast boats dashing among concentrations of fishing pots. The shrimp dhows usually unload at the small harbours near the seafront and sell their catches directly on the quayside.

Large-scale commercial fishing comes under the banner of United Fisheries of Kuwait, which has more than 150 vessels including factory ships operating in the Gulf, Red Sea, the Indian Ocean, the Atlantic Ocean and further afield still. The company has become one of the largest and most important of its kind in the world, and it is also playing its part in assisting the development of fishing industries in emerging nations. The company's haul of shrimps alone places it at the very top of the fishing league, and its fleet includes 500-ton stern and side trawlers. In addition to its Kuwait slipway, it has others on an island near Australia and another in Nigeria; its modern shrimp and fish-processing plant in Shuaiba handles over 100 tonnes of produce daily and includes a plant making animal feed from shrimp and fish waste. The United Fisheries' 3000-plus personnel handle exports to such prime markets as the United States, Europe and Japan.

What of the chunk of water immediately off Kuwait's shores? The bottom consists mainly of fine silt and sand brought down from the Shatt Al-Arab, the confluence of the Tigris and Euphrates, with a few reefs and coral islands offshore. The marine life is a splendid diversity of sharks, rays and 300-odd species of other fish, all deriving from Indo-Pacific varieties. There are also at least two species of highly venomous sea snakes (which, fortunately, are not aggressive) and many dolphins which frequently play around the larger boats. Kuwait's pollution controls are better than most but, regrettably, industrialization elsewhere has led to a considerable rise in pollution off the nation's coast. In 1978 the Kuwaitis hosted a conference of Gulf nations in an effort to get international action to save the sea from the sort of predicament encountered in parts of the Mediterranean. Action is unquestionably needed if one of the country's most important natural assets is to be protected from further damage.

At the end of a day's fishing there is always much to do: the catch to be sold on the quayside or sent to market, and the nets to be inspected and maybe mended before tomorrow's trip.

Life in the Wild

Much has happened to Kuwait's wildlife since the coming of oil, not all of it good, but far from all of it bad. Increases in horticulture and agriculture have led to many varied species adopting Kuwait as either their permanent home or stopping-off place during migration; on the other hand, modern hunting methods have taken a terrible toll of some traditional birds and animals. The saddest loss must be that of the desert gazelle, which roamed wild in the state for centuries but has not now be seen since about 1958. Similarly, the magnificent hubara bustard has been hunted to the edge of extinction, although a few were recorded in 1978 – the first to be spotted for several years.

There exists in Kuwait a general indifference to the fate of virtually all forms of wildlife, and even the newcomers survive despite, rather than because of, man's efforts. The serious study of flora and fauna remains at a low level: the only active professional bodies are those at the Kuwait Institute for Scientific Research and Kuwait University. It is the amateur, however, who has made the most significant contributions to understanding life in the wild. The Ahmadi Natural History Group, an organization affiliated to Kuwait Oil Company, provides the vast bulk of the information available. This incredibly active group was started about thirty years ago and its membership remains overwhelmingly Western expatriates – a situation the organization has been striving to change for years, but with little success. It now holds exhaustive records on practically every species to be found in Kuwait.

Birds provide some of the most spectacular examples of visiting wildlife, none more so than the birds of prey which call in during migration. So far, more than 30 types have been positively identified. Considerable excitement was generated in 1978 by the first sighting of a golden eagle. Ospreys are commonly seen, as are the splendid steppe eagles with their great wingspans which rest and hunt in the Zor Hills during migratory flights from the USSR. Then there are the honey buzzards, imperial eagles, peregrine falcons, lesser kestrels, sparrowhawks... in short, some of the world's most splendid birds. Amateur ornithologists from the Natural History Group are currently preparing a book on Kuwait's birds; it will be full of exciting discoveries as well as some bitter disappointments, none more so than the one concerning the fate of the first eagle owl's nest ever found in the country. This rare bird decided to settle in Kuwait in the late seventies, but just days after naturalists had tracked down its home to the Wadi Al-Batin, someone destroyed the nest and stole the eggs. Similar sad tales exist: a pair of black storks, again the first seen in Kuwait, were spotted minutes before being blasted out of a tree by shotgun-toting youths who left the corpses to rot on the ground. Unfortunately, the balance has been tilted heavily in man's favour, because most hunting is undertaken no longer as a necessary means of adding to the food supply but, rather, for the dubious pleasure of killing things. The disastrous effects of man and gun make naturalists cautious about the chances of survival of some species – notably the sand grouse which has disappeared once already but, for no apparent reason, has staged a comeback in recent years.

Despite the absence of protected areas or sanctuaries, the benefits of a changing environment have helped to counteract the detrimental effects of hunting. Growing urbanization, more parks and more farming have led to a greater number of birds being attracted by the consequent increases in supplies of water, vegetation and allied food supplies (insects and so on). The town of Ahmadi with its extensive greenery, for example, has become a refuge for birds of both desert and sea, where domestic cats are the sole predators. In Kuwait City swallows, martins and swifts rub feathers with such ubiquitous colleagues as pigeons and sparrows. Starlings rest over in the City during winter although, for reasons unknown, decline to fly the few extra kilometres to Ahmadi.

In addition to the urban and cultivated areas, five types of habitat offer their own appeal to various species: inland water and reed beds; flattish open desert; hills, waddies and gullies; beaches and surrounding areas; and saltmarshes and mudflats. It is on the last, at the end of Kuwait Bay, that a huge range of water birds can be spotted, including flamingos which, though migratory, can be seen during every month of the year. The number of visiting birds far exceeds the number of breeding ones and there are, of course, a few accidental visitors – the golden eagle is one probable example and the spur-winged plover most certainly is, only one ever being sighted and that twenty years ago. New discoveries are being made every year, and the list now stretches to as many as 300 species.

The most numerous members of the animal kingdom are the insects and, once again, many owe their presence to man-made changes. The largest and most spectacular butterfly, the Asian swallowtail, only survives because citrus trees on which the larva feed have been imported. Kuwait's 16 species of butterfly come either from Europe or from India and Asia, the former tending to be present in the winter while the latter come into their own in summer. There are also some 150 species of moth, plus many dragonfly attracted from the north by supplies of fresh water. Less welcome are the three species of locust although, contrary to popular belief, these live mainly solitary lives and if numbers are kept low do not become gregarious or form a migratory swarm. It has been several years since the last small swarm in Kuwait, and it is felt that locusts no longer present a menace.

As well as the billions of insects there are spiders – including various camel spiders which, for their size, have the most powerful jaws of any creature – and, of course, scorpions. Of the two types in Kuwait the black scorpion is the larger, growing to 10 or 12 centimetres, while the less common, yellow-green variety is more dangerous. Being primarily nocturnal, scorpions are rarely encountered by visitors to the desert, and although their bite can be extremely painful and cause considerable swelling, it is not regarded as fatal even to a child.

Flamingos, although only stopping off in Kuwait as migrants, can be seen all year round in groups large and small on the mudflats at the end of Kuwait Bay. Altogether, about 300 species of birds can be spotted in Kuwait, the vast bulk of them on annual north–south migratory routes.

Other unfriendly desert inhabitants are poisonous snakes, including two types of viper and the Arabian rear-fanged snake. Among other, non-poisonous varieties are the sand-boa, a member of the boa constrictor family, and the sand snake. These mainly restrict their activities to darkness, and the most commonly seen reptiles are the lizards, 17 species having been identified in a three-year study of reptiles conducted by the Ahmadi Natural History Group in conjunction with experts from the British Museum. The most splendid example is the rare monitor which grows up to 120 centimetres and, though not aggressive by nature, will bite if challenged. The largest of the more common reptiles is the dhub or spiny-tailed lizard which grows up to 90 centimetres in length and was previously a delicacy of the bedouin table. As lizards depend on outside heat for body warmth, the dhub changes colour dramatically according to season – dark brown in winter to attract maximum heat and bright yellow for the opposite reason in summer.

There are not many wild mammals in Kuwait, although two types of common fox, both very similar, are known to exist. Usually inhabiting geological faults, they are more lightly built than their European relatives and their ears are spectacularly larger, a feature shared by the hedgehog which has become a feature of many Ahmadi gardens. The jerboa can sometimes be seen in the desert despite its skittishness, while bats, particularly the date bat, are fairly common if not numerous. As already mentioned, the desert gazelle, the largest of the land-based mammals, has disappeared from the Kuwait wilderness and is now only to be found in Kuwait Zoo, a fairly small zoo due to be replaced by a grander affair in the eighties. The biggest animal now to be seen (though only occasionally) is the common European wolf, which is not resident but sometimes enters northern Kuwait on night-time hunting forays. There is speculation that the northern part of the country might also yield a form of wildcat, and that the fennec – a small fox found only in Arabia and North Africa and, arguably, one of the most appealing members of the animal kingdom anywhere – may also be present. Studying wildlife in the desert terrain is particularly difficult, and because of the heat most creatures stay under shelter until dusk. Consequently, a great many questions remain to be answered.

The desert flora are not so shy, however, and after the winter rains as many as 400 species of plants and flowers cover the desert in a carpet of colour. Many of them can be found in Europe and a lesser number in Africa, a fact explained simply by geography, for there is less desert between Kuwait and Europe than there is between Kuwait and Africa. Researchers at Kuwait University have divided the area into four eco-systems each supporting its own types of plant. Interesting work has also been conducted by two men, one from the Ministry of Public Health and the other from the Ministry of Agriculture, into the medicinal properties of native Kuwaiti plants. For centuries these were used by tribesmen to treat anything from headaches to snake bites, from colds to diabetes. This initial study has opened the way to further research – why, for example, would certain thorns, taken by humans as a tonic, prove fatal to sheep?

Sheep and goats are the dominant life-forms in the desert, large herds grazing on the lush vegetation in spring or on coarse, hardy grasses during the remainder of the year. And then there are the camels, those supreme survivors whose role as ships of the desert has been usurped by articulated lorries trundling across modern highways, but whose place in the hearts and minds of the people remains constant. As already observed, there has been something of a return to camel ownership as a form of status symbol, and to a limited extent camels still serve the remaining bedouin in their traditional roles. The single-humped dromedary is *the* Arabian camel and today's stock is little changed from the animals which once roamed wild. The camel is still regarded, incidentally, as something of a man's animal: in the unwritten code of the bedu, milking the camels was one of the few domestic chores an adult male would perform.

The Government

One of the most impressive of the ministry buildings is the Ministry of Information complex, opened in 1978. The picture shows the main administrative building; television and radio centres are on either side.

Government in Kuwait has traditionally been a matter of consensus. In many respects it is still that way, although the real decision-making power is vested in the Amir, in conjuction with the Heir Apparent and Prime Minister, and the Council of Ministers. There is a constitution, the most important provisions of which guarantee freedom of religion and worship, of individual liberty and the press. Independence of the judiciary is also assured, as is the abolition of discrimination on the grounds of race, language and social origin. There is also provision for the establishment of a National Assembly, its members to be elected by a ballot of all Kuwaiti male adults.

In a nationwide address given in 1978 Sheikh Jaber Al-Ahmad said: 'Our affairs have always been conducted by mutual consultation which has become a basic characteristic of our rule devotedly kept by successive generations of our people. Thus democracy has been a long-standing, inherent quality of our character as Kuwaitis.'

There is, undoubtedly, a history of consultation between rulers and the people. It exists at many levels, including informal meetings between ruler and subjects at *diwania*, and at regular sessions at the Seif Palace where the people come to discuss their problems or get action on complaints. The small size of the population has traditionally enabled the ruler to keep a finger on the pulse of the nation, but with the recent huge increase in population the task has become that much more difficult. More formal channels have been set up – ministries, advisers, and so on – but Sheikh Jaber Al-Ahmad remains a staunch advocate of direct contact.

Government ministries have responsibilities which include housing, education, foreign affairs, defence, the interior, transport and communications, finance, public health, social affairs and labour, public works, justice, *Awqaf* (religious endowment) and Islamic affairs, commerce and industry, electricity and water, information and, of course, oil. For the purpose of administration, the country is divided into four parts: the City, the Hawalli area, Ahmadi and Jahra.

The Money

The 1978–9 budget caused disappointment in some circles when the Ministry of Finance announced a 2.3 per cent cut in total spending. But the Government is adamant that runaway spending must be curbed and the level of surplus maintained. A successful battle has been fought since 1977 to reduce inflation, and ministries have recently been told to keep costs down and to steer away from prestige projects. With a population increasing at a rate of 5.5 per cent a year through births and immigration, the cash is needed to meet demands in such fields as health, housing, education, roads, electricity and water. Industry has also been getting more money in a bid to underwrite the nation's future, although the Government has been careful not to plump for labour-intensive concerns requiring more foreign labour.

Each year, 10 per cent of government revenue goes automatically to the Reserve Fund for Future Generations, a fund intended to benefit coming generations of Kuwaitis who miss out on the oil era. In 1977–8 the state's surplus amounted to KD 971 million, a drop from the KD 1279 million recorded the previous year (KD 270 million of this went into the Fund for Future Generations while the remainder was held by the State General Reserve). For 1978–9, the surplus was estimated at only KD 310 million, although this turned out to be gross underestimation – the previous year, the actual surplus was more than three times greater than the estimate and, for 1978–9, Kuwait received the bonus of substantial oil price rises and an increase in demand because of the absence of Iranian oil. Revenue for 1978–9 had originally been estimated at about KD 2.3 billion, a figure which did not include income from investment, likely to be around KD 400 million – a nice boost for the reserve funds.

Recurrent expenditure, which almost doubled between 1974 and 1975, has to a large extent levelled out in recent years while development spending has risen more swiftly, increasing from KD 128 million for 1973–4 to KD 480 million for 1977–8. The figure of KD 390 million for expenditure in 1978–9 always looked likely to be exceeded because of the peaks reached in hospital and house-building programmes. Spending has been helped by the drop in inflation (from about 25 per cent in 1977 to 10 per cent two years later), the Ministry of Finance employing a stiff fiscal policy and the Central Bank of Kuwait doing its best to control money supply, an effort now being co-ordinated with the ministry. Spending though has obviously increased, and the most recent set of complete figures shows that the total amount of ordinary, development and property acquisition expenditure in 1977–8 stood at KD 1538 million, excluding a KD 50 million contribution to the Kuwait Fund for Arab Economic Development.

Virtually all state revenue is derived from oil and related products. There is a 4 per cent import duty imposed on non-essential goods but there are no internal taxes. It is possible, however, that an idea to introduce some sort of tax on companies will receive greater attention in coming years.

It is difficult to gain an accurate idea of the state's assets: the total certainly stood at more than 30 billion dollars at the start of 1978 and subsequent developments must have increased it substantially. The Reserve Fund for Future Generations, established in 1976 with KD 850 million, is sacrosanct: nobody may touch the ever-increasing capital and interest for twenty-five years. The remainder comes under the State General Reserve and includes commercial investments in the industrialized nations and the Arab world. The Ministry of Finance and the Kuwait Investment Office, attached to the Kuwait Embassy in London, handle much of the money, but a large amount is handled by Kuwaiti investment companies, in particular by Kuwait Investment Company (50 per cent government-owned); the Kuwaiti Foreign Trading, Contracting and Investment Company, which is 85 per cent government-owned and which handles many of the investments in Arab and developing nations; and the Kuwait International Investment Company, a privately owned merchant bank and holding company. The investments tend to be well spread, and among the best known are the nation's 14 per cent share in Daimler Benz, land ownership along the Champs Elysées, and development of a luxury island resort in South Carolina. The United States is the most popular place for investments, the recent sufferings of the dollar having little relevance to long-term investments, while Britain is one of the favourite spots for property, short-term and equity investment. Kuwait's reserves, however, are spread throughout the world: in South America, Europe, the Far East, Africa and, of course, the Arab world. In addition to government funds, there is also a vast private investment, the size of which it is impossible to estimate.

The oil reserves underpin all this activity and could continue to do so for another seventy years or more. Such a lifespan depends on the production of crude oil hovering around the prescribed conservation level of 1.5 million barrels a day – such a rate not only gives the petroleum reserves the prospect of a long and happy life but also provides enough annual revenue in the state coffers to meet existing expenditure and development plans. And it also provides a healthy annual surplus to enable Kuwait to invest for its present and its future.

Foreign Affairs

Financial strength and large oil reserves have thrust Kuwait into the limelight on the international stage. Its response to the challenge has been to develop a constructive foreign policy aiming for the maximum possible co-operation among Arab and other developing nations. The policy, naturally, remains as flexible as the changing world demands, but there are certain concepts which the Government holds sacred. The most obvious concerns the state of Israel and the occupation of the Palestinian homeland by Zionists. Kuwait's Minister of Foreign Affairs said at the United Nations in 1977: 'Peace will not be established in the Middle East unless the people of Palestine exercise their right to self-determination and an independent Palestinian State is established for them. Likewise, peace will not be restored to the area unless Israel withdraws from all occupied territories.' Like other Arab countries, Kuwait opposed Egyptian initiatives, and in 1979 broke off diplomatic relations with Cairo and suspended economic assistance. When there are so many displaced Palestinians living in countries such as Kuwait, a solution to the problem looks as far away as ever – the situation being complicated by the fact that Arab Jerusalem, a holy city of Moslems as well as Jews and Christians, was annexed by the Israelis in 1967.

It is not only the occupation of Palestine which concerns the Kuwaitis. Unity of approach among sister Gulf States is a high priority, as is their opposition to world dominance by super-power blocs. The nation, although avowedly opposed to Communism, maintains good relations at both political and commercial levels with most governments, the sixty-plus diplomatic missions in the country including those of the USA, USSR and China. The closest ties are obviously those with Saudi Arabia, the Coastal Gulf States and other Arab countries. But the vast amounts of aid freely given to developing nations around the world have won Kuwait many friends and admirers in the international arena.

Kuwait achieved full independence in 1961, and became a member of the United Nations in 1963; during 1978 and 1979 it was a member of the Security Council. The country joined the Arab League in 1961 and, although the league has experienced many ups and downs since being formed in 1945, Kuwait remains committed to the organization's goal: 'to strengthen and consolidate the ties which bind all Arab countries and to direct them towards the welfare of the Arab world, to improve its conditions, to ensure its future and to realize its hopes and aspirations.' Kuwait's horizons, though, extend beyond the Arab world, and its concerns include big-power hegemony in international affairs and the attitude of the developed nations in the apparently futile North–South dialogue. Kuwait is anxious to see industrialized nations share their technological expertise with developing countries and has been agitating for international action to improve agricultural techniques. 'What the world needs,' the Foreign Minister says, 'is not guns but better standards of living and eradication of the evils of poverty, illiteracy and disease.'

The state is active in more than twenty international organizations and agencies, but it is its part in just one group that attracts most attention: OPEC, the Organization of Petroleum Exporting Countries. Kuwait was a founder member of the organization (along with Saudi Arabia, Iraq, Iran and Venezuela) when it was formed in 1960 to deal with the effects of outside influences on oil prices and, consequently, on the economies of the producing countries. It was not until 1973 that OPEC realized its own strength, when members tripled the price of a barrel of marker crude. The Minister of Oil has reiterated his belief that the unity of OPEC will be retained in years to come despite the efforts of importing nations to divide the group. Unquestionably, Kuwait will continue to work for this unity during the testing times of the eighties. A second oil organization in which Kuwait is active is the Organization of Arab Petroleum Exporting Countries (OAPEC), which has its headquarters in Kuwait City and which was founded in 1968 by Saudi Arabia, Libya and Kuwait. Today it has nine members, and its main aim is to promote technical co-operation among Arab oil producers and also to establish pan-Arab petroleum ventures. The Arab Maritime Petroleum Transport Company (also with headquarters in Kuwait) and the Arab Shipbuilding and Repair Yard in Bahrain are two companies founded and funded by OAPEC members.

Apart from oil affairs, international diplomacy is handled by the Ministry of Foreign Affairs which has new premises under construction on the sea front near the Seif Palace.

A Helping Hand

An international survey concluded that Kuwait's aid programme was based on a 'genuine moral wish to help others'. Indeed, the nation's track-record as a giver of aid has won it unstinting admiration the world over: its no-strings-attached assistance amounts annually to 11 per cent of the total income from oil. Much of the assistance is disbursed through bilateral agreements or international financial organizations in which Kuwait has long been a prime mover, but the best known of aid institutions remains the Kuwait Fund or, more properly, the Kuwait Fund for Arab Economic Development (KFAED). Britain's *Financial Times* described the organization thus:

> Established shortly after Kuwait became independent, it quickly laid down standards of management and objectivity which the second generation of funds has tried to emulate. Despite the complexity of the task of assessing projects, the Kuwait Fund has a reputation for fast work and can process projects faster than many Western aid organisations.

State-funded but politically independent, the Kuwait Fund is free to give assistance purely on the basis of need. Since 1974, it has also been free to give aid to non-Arab countries, and between January 1975 and the middle of 1978 some 29 per cent of the money disbursed went to Asian countries, 16 per cent to African states and a little over half to Arab nations. Average annual disbursements between 1977 and 1979 amounted to KD 51 million on commitments of KD 121 million – in 1975–6 record-breaking disbursements of KD 160 million were chalked up. Most of the money to African and Asian nations went on infrastructure: power projects took up about half, agriculture 22 per cent, industrial development 16 per cent and transport and communications 8 per cent. The very first Kuwait Fund loan was paid to Sudan in March 1962: more than $24 million for a railway project with interest set at 4 per cent, the whole repayable over 15.7 years with a 3.7-year period of grace. Up to the time when non-Arab countries became eligible, KFAED aid was extended to dozens of projects ranging from Suez Canal expansion and oil pipeline construction to agricultural, industrial and utilities developments in fourteen Arab countries. The first non-Arab countries to benefit were Malayasia and Rwanda in 1975 and, since then, receiving countries include India, Pakistan, Bangladesh, the Philippines, Thailand, Sri Lanka, Burundi, Mali, Ghana, Indonesia and many others. The fund does not usually supply technical support, but because of shortcomings in administrative set-ups it has sent teams to various countries to advise on projects, most recently in North and South Yemen and the Comoros. The efficiency, generosity and fairness of the Kuwait Fund has earned the nation many friends – paradoxically, more than it probably would have done had it been a politically inspired organization bent on doing just that. When a US Treasury Secretary visited Kuwait, he described the country's aid record as outstanding; in all probability he was thinking primarily of KFAED, although in fact the fund is but one of the channels through which financial assistance is directed.

Considerable amounts of money are given by direct bilateral aid, though these figures are usually kept secret. Kuwait, Saudi Arabia and the Libyan Jamahiriya are the biggest contributors to the Arab Fund for Economic and Social Development which was the first proposed by Kuwait and now has its headquarters there. Its main aims are to support inter-Arab and social welfare projects, while the General Authority for the Arabian Gulf and South Arabian States finances and in many cases runs more than a hundred schools, several teacher training colleges, 10 hospitals, 20 health clinics, and one university (in North Yemen) on the peninsula. Its budget is entirely met by the Kuwait Government and its board chaired by the Minister of Foreign Affairs.

Kuwait has contributed hundreds of millions of dollars to the International Monetary Fund's oil facility and to the World Bank's bond portfolio, as well as making donations to the 'third window' facility. Straightforward cash donations have regularly been given to the UN Emergency Assistance Fund and to various relief organizations including the Relief and Works Agency for Palestinian Refugees. The nation also eases the plight of homeless Palestinians through contributions to the Palestine Liberation Organization. Financial support is lent to the Rome-based Food and Agricultural Organization and the International Fund for Agricultural Development – Kuwait is also in the position to boost cash donations with tons of fertilizer from its petrochemical industry. Another development fund, the Arab Bank for Economic Development in Africa, has seen Kuwait along with Saudi Arabia, Qatar and the United Arab Emirates pledge extra capital in recent years, the fund being devoted to using Arab money and technical assistance to support projects in developing black African states.

In any given year, Kuwait commits itself to well over a billion dollars in foreign aid. It is a staggering sum for a nation of little more than a million people, yet it serves as continuing proof of the state's awareness that oil confers not only benefits but responsibilities as well.

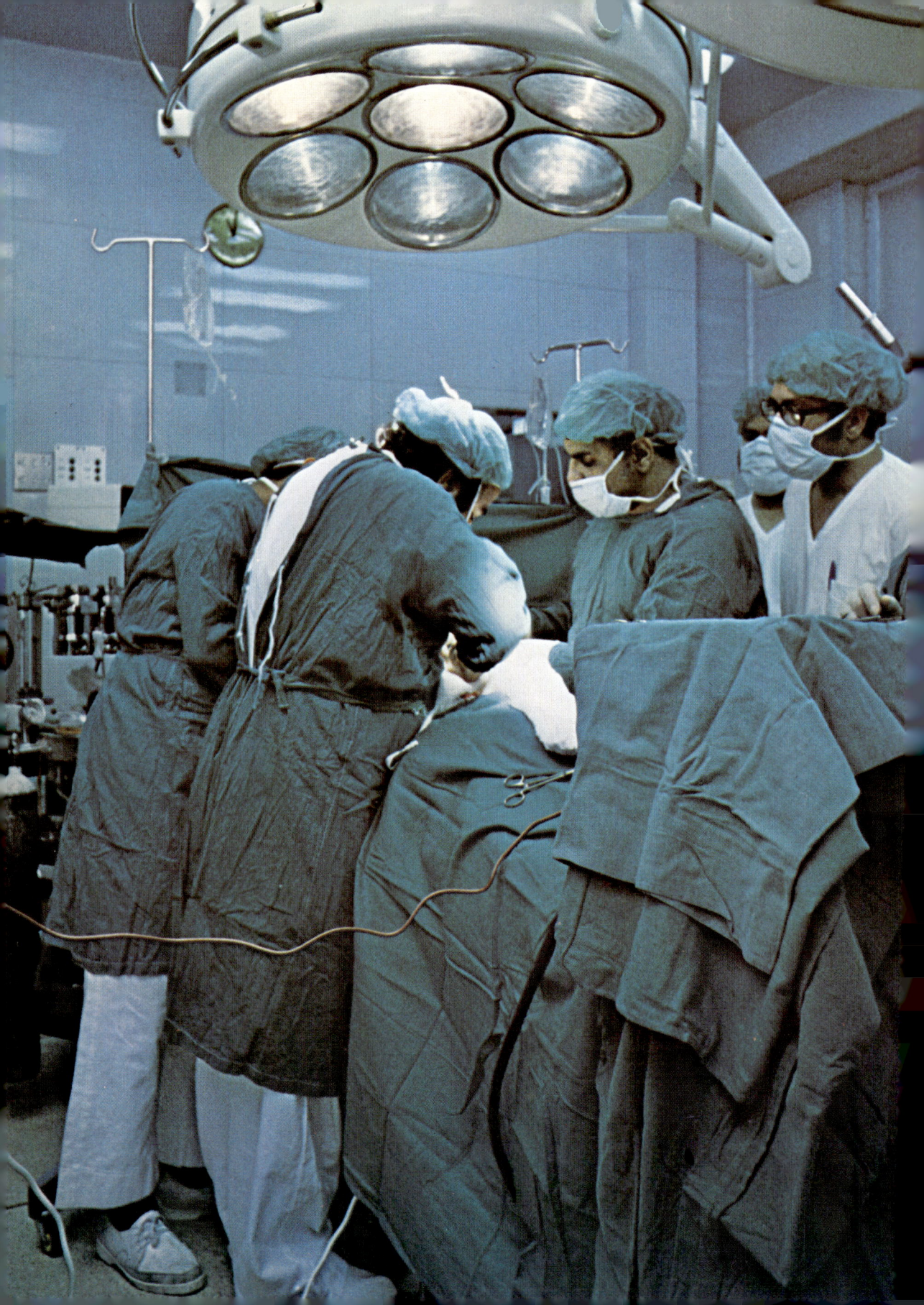

Public Services

An operating theatre at the Al-Sabah Hospital, one of the largest and most modern in the Middle East, where treatment – as in all public hospitals in Kuwait – is free to both citizens and visitors alike.

The population of Kuwait is increasing at a rate of 5.5 per cent a year, the Kuwaiti birthrate alone accounting for a 3.5 per cent rise. Just to keep pace with this, one of the world's fastest-growing populations, would mean the annual expansion of services on a large scale. But Kuwait is attempting to achieve more. Yet again this has meant virtually starting from scratch. It cannot be over-emphasized that forty years ago the visitor would have found few of the amenities that today's generation takes for granted. There was only one small hospital, no electricity until 1934, no radio, no television – not, in fact, much of anything. The picture today is dramatically different.

In such matters as health, education and public housing, the record speaks for itself. But there are other areas in which developments do not receive the credit they deserve. Public transport in Kuwait, for instance, comes in for a lot of criticism – as it does in most places – yet for all its faults it has been built up from nothing to a position where it provides reasonably reliable and cheap transport for thousands.

Overall, the services provided by the state must rank among the very best offered by developing nations, even oil-rich ones.

Spending on services continues to grow, and the benefits can be seen everywhere. The return on such a massive investment, however, can scarcely be matched by the record achieved by the nation's schools.

Education

Not surprisingly, Kuwait's top budget priority is education, currently gobbling up about a tenth of national expenditure. It is – as with so much else – an investment in the future. Young Kuwaitis are guaranteed free education from the day they enter kindergarten to the day they graduate from university. And 'free' in Kuwait means exactly that: not only are there no tuition fees, but the cost of text books and even clothing is completely met by the state. The benefits can be seen in the vastly increased reserve of expertise which Kuwait has at its fingertips today, a situation which even fifteen years ago would have seemed impossible.

As we have seen, those past fifteen years have had a profound, almost revolutionary effect on many aspects of life in Kuwait. But in a country where, until recently, illiteracy was almost accepted as the norm, it is education that provides the most staggering example of change.

The roots go back to 1911, when a group of merchants chipped in to open the first proper school. Before that, a typically Arabian system existed, whereby the few whose parents could afford it would visit the home of a teacher to learn how to read the Holy Koran, occasionally with a bit of arithmetic thrown in. The pattern began to change in 1911 with the opening of the Mubarakiyah School, which was primarily designed to produce a handful of youngsters suited to life as clerks. The syllabus of arithmetic and correspondence was expanded in 1930 to include history, geography and drawing, but the school was forced to close down the following year because of the recession which had

Kuwaiti schoolgirls take part in a keep-fit class against a background dominated by one of the country's many mosques

hit the pearling industry. In 1936 a new education system was begun and, with the arrival of teachers from Palestine, it was extended the following year to include girls for the first time. In 1937, 620 boys and 140 girls were in strictly segregated schools. And then came the oil which was to change the whole future of the nation. By 1949, the number of students in public schools stood at 4665; thirty years later the figure easily topped the quarter million mark, with a further 60,000 youngsters attending the various private schools built to meet the requirements of specific expatriate groups. Government expenditure amounted to about KD 130 million, with KD 40 million going towards university education.

Perhaps the most impressive aspect of the system is the way it has kept pace with the burgeoning population. The total of students enrolling at government schools has been increasing at a rate of more than 7 per cent each year, yet the number of schools and classrooms has kept pace. In fact, the pupil–teacher ratio has fallen consistently from more than 30 to 1 in the forties to about 10 to 1 by the late seventies, and less than 10 to 1 in secondary schools. The number of school buildings

It is said that the Arabs write more poetry than the rest of the world put together, and in the extensive library (below) of a secondary school Kuwaiti youngsters have the opportunity to enjoy this and many other literary forms. And for the science-minded, the schools provide comprehensive laboratory facilities (right).

of all types has soared: in 1970–1 there were 210 kindergartens, primary, intermediate and secondary schools; by 1978–9 there were 437 and that year the Ministry of Education announced plans to build still more.

The proportion of girls in both public and private schools averages slightly less than 50 per cent, a remarkable change from a few years ago. The schools themselves are invariably bright and modern, often possessing their own mosques, theatres and libraries in addition to the normal range of classrooms, laboratories and sports facilities. Youngsters enter the system early, the aim being to give a comprehensive education from kindergarten age right through to young adulthood. Standards have steadily improved, a fact reflected by the growing number of universities abroad which will accept Kuwaiti students at high school graduation diploma level even for such demanding faculties as medicine. But the

The main administration building at Kuwait University – an institution which began with a handful of students less than twenty years ago and now has more than 10,000 enrolled ... and the expansion programme still goes relentlessly on.

need for Kuwaitis to go overseas for university education has diminished in recent years with the growth of Kuwait University. Until the mid sixties, the young man or woman seeking a degree was obliged to go abroad, often to Arab universities such as the American University at Beirut, or to the United States or Great Britain. Because of the high standards, the range of specialist courses and the opportunities for advanced studies, several hundred Kuwaitis still attend English-language universities overseas, but the development of Kuwait's own higher education system has enabled a vast number of students to receive degrees without leaving the country.

The university was founded in 1966, with 418 students and fewer than 150 teachers, administrators and other staff. Today there are more than 17,000 students, more than half of them girls, and within a few years a new campus should be

completed at Shuweikh at an estimated cost of KD 400 million. By then, enrolment will probably have surpassed the optimum figure of 20,000 students, many of whom will be from other Gulf states and, to a lesser extent, other parts of the Arab world. At the time of writing, the faculties are scattered over several campuses around Kuwait City, but this has not stopped the university blazing a new approach to higher education. As the Rector said to me: 'I believe that Kuwait University should not stick to the classical role of universities, simply teaching and research, but it should extend its services to Kuwait society through community projects and training programmes. We must get away from the concept of an ivory tower.' The philosophy has led to considerable community involvement, with courses devised to bring maximum contact and communication between students and society. The university has started a Community Service Centre: this offers people of all ages the opportunity to learn anything from foreign languages to business administration (and much else) in a series of night-time courses currently catering for 1500 people. No formal educational qualifications are needed and most courses are over-subscribed.

The university began with only one faculty, which combined both science and the arts. This was soon divided, and the science faculty now boasts departments dealing with mathematics, chemistry, zoology, physics, botany and geology. The faculty of arts and education traditionally attracts the largest number of students and covers such fields as Arabic and English language and literature, history, geography, philosophy, psychology, education and sociology, and social sciences. The first graduates from the faculty of law and *shari'a* (Islamic law) emerged in 1971. The faculty of commerce, economics and political science awards degrees in economics, political science, administrative sciences, accountancy and economics, statistics, insurance and computers. The inauguration of the faculty of engineering and petroleum in 1975 was of considerable importance in view of the

There is plenty of opportunity for learning new skills in Kuwait: the young men (above) are making ceramics, while the girls are attending a manicure and hairdressing class.

demand for mechanical, electrical and civil engineers in Kuwait, and discussions are under way which will lead to a new department being opened for petroleum as well as chemical engineers. The last faculty to be established – medicine – became a reality in the academic year of 1977–8, admission being restricted to those who particularly distinguished themselves in secondary education. The period of study is seven years to be followed by a three-year training period in hospitals. The advent of this faculty should ease the situation in a country where there is no shortage of hospitals and medical facilities but where doctors and other staff have always had to be imported. The faculties are co-educational, although there exists a separate college for women where studies in the arts can be pursued by girls from families who are still adamant that there should be segregation of the sexes. The range of disciplines offered by the college has decreased in recent years because of the difficulties in running a string of courses parallel to but entirely separate from those of the main campus.

About 60 per cent of the university students are Kuwaitis although, in total, around 25 nationalities are represented, many from Arab countries but quite a few from further afield. Several of the courses are conducted in English and, in the case of law, in French. Students in engineering, for example, spend the first year studying English as it is the language of high technology. This is not an ideal situation but it is likely to remain unchanged for several years. The courses themselves are geared to local and regional needs, students becoming actively involved in projects which will be of material help to Kuwait, in either scientific or social fields.

There are, however, certain reservations about the university system. Some Arab educationists feel that oil-rich states have gone 'degree mad' – that the kudos of getting a university education is paramount where, in many cases, vocational courses would be more appropriate. But Kuwait seems to be aware of the problem, for an increasing amount

Youths at a welding class – one of many vocational courses now being run in Kuwait to meet the widespread need for skilled workers without having to resort to expatriate labour.

of vocational education is being introduced. A range of commercial, industrial, religious and teacher-training institutions has been built, while many companies – particularly the oil companies – have extensive programmes to train and develop employees from the level of field workers right through to upper management positions.

Other groups requiring special facilities are not ignored: Kuwait can be justifiably proud of its educational programmes for the handicapped, who unquestionably enjoy the highest standards of care available anywhere in the world. Similarly, there has been a determined onslaught on illiteracy, with the establishment of nationwide centres offering adults the opportunity of learning to read and write. Tens of thousands have taken advantage of the scheme, and although it seems unlikely that illiteracy will be completely eradicated for many years to come, the programme, coupled with the availability of free education for all youngsters, has had a dramatic effect in a nation where, only thirty years ago, literacy was the exception rather than the rule.

In all spheres of education the most modern teaching aids and techniques are used. The new university will have the most up-to-date computer network (which other bodies, government and commercial, will be able to plug into); there is an abundance of audio-visual aids at every level; and the Special Institute for the Handicapped has an impressive range of facilities and equipment. Applied research receives generous government funds, and Kuwaiti students who travel abroad for special courses or higher education get state sponsorship which amply covers their needs.

Progress in education has been truly amazing and today's system is geared to producing competent and qualified Kuwaitis who, without outside help, will spearhead the nation's drive into the next century.

Health

At one time, it was not a good idea to fall sick in Kuwait. Until 1949 there was just one hospital in the country, and even more recently than that the standards of care and treatment on offer were suspect. Today, thanks to an ambitious government programme, the nation can claim some of the finest medical facilities, one of the best ratios of hospital beds to total population, and specialist treatment previously available only abroad. A wide range of health services is provided, for the most part entirely free, to everyone resident in the state. All of which does not mean that such services in Kuwait are devoid of problems, but it does mean that the nation has gone a long way towards providing the best possible.

More attention has been directed towards the provision of health services than anything else with the possible exception of education. Some hard lessons have been learnt on the way: one is that it is not enough to provide well-equipped hospitals without the necessary administrative and organizational support or, indeed, medical service infrastructure to back up the buildings and the doctors.

The need to set up a health service virtually from scratch has proved a monumental task, further compounded by the rapid increase in population. The health services have boldly answered the challenge: in 1979 alone, six new hospitals were either completed or in the final throes of completion. This programme and the renovation of an existing hospital will add some 3000 beds to the total of about 5000 already available to the public. There is also a well-established private sector with eight smaller hospitals and clinics offering almost 500 beds and a range of specialist treatment. These facilities are closely monitored and controlled to make sure that they conform to state standards.

Modern medicine did not arrive in Kuwait until 1911 when Dr Stanley Mylrea opened the American Mission Hospital. The nation's own health service got off the ground in 1936 with one doctor, one pharmacist and a free health clinic. Work started on the Amiri Hospital (on the sea front close to the heart of Kuwait City) in 1940 but because of a shortage of building materials at the time it was not completed until 1949 when the ruler, the late Sheikh Ahmad, officially opened the premises. At that time the number of doctors in government service totalled four. Today there are over 1500 with another 250 in the private sector. The Amiri Hospital still exists, although it is much changed from the original which was knocked down in 1978 when work started on the new, 500-bed complex. The hospital never actually closed its doors to the public, as prefabricated emergency wards were erected before demolition of the old buildings began.

The late forties marked the real start of intensive activity to establish public health services, with plans being laid for the construction of facilities in a variety of medical fields. It was during this time, incidentally, that a patient suffering from appendicitis was admitted to hospital – the first case ever recorded in Kuwait of an illness which has since proved one of the most common.

A hospital for the mentally sick opened in 1949. Now known as the Nervous and Psychological Disorders Hospital, it has been completely rebuilt and offers treatment to some 300 in-patients. The Amiri was expanded in 1950 with an X-ray department and ophthalmic unit, and a dental section was added a year later. In the following year, a TB sanitorium was opened which admitted male patients, a women's sanitorium starting up in 1953 at temporary premises in Shuweikh. These facilities were superseded in 1959 by a custom-built complex providing the most advanced treatment, and since then the incidence of tuberculosis in the state has been dramatically reduced. The sanatorium has a main three-storey building and a new annexe set in a huge garden overlooking the sea, and the equipment includes a chest-surgery set in addition to facilities for thoracoplasty and minor heart and lung operations. A special clinic for vocational training has been constructed next to the main building, and there is also a school, a dispensary, a dental clinic and laboratories.

Smallpox too has been brought under control and even, it is hoped, eradicated. The last large-scale epidemic in Kuwait occurred in 1932 when an estimated 4000 people died in just ten days. One of the earliest contributions made by the fledgeling preventive medicine service was to introduce a state-wide inoculation programme in 1952.

Another important development of the fifties came in the form of a centre affording care to mothers and infants. The centres are now spread throughout the country, and expectant mothers pay regular visits from the second month of pregnancy. Complete post-natal services are available, both at the centres and at the maternity hospital which was opened in 1961; this has two wards of 50 beds for mothers and a further 200 beds for women who are sick. When it was built, the hospital was the first in the Middle East to include a vacuum extractor, and the high level of care has been progressively increased through the intervening years of expansion.

In 1962 the opening of an infectious diseases hospital was outshone by a ceremony to mark the start of operations (in every sense) at the Al-Sabah Hospital, one of the largest and best equipped in the Middle East. Occupying an area of more than 400,000 square metres, the Al-Sabah has three main buildings with 700 beds, plus residential buildings with apartments for doctors and nurses. There is also a lecture hall which seats 750 people, workshops, garages, servants' quarters and even a helicopter pad for bringing patients from Failaka Island or remote desert areas. The hospital itself has seven principal operating theatres and two annexes, all equipped with the most modern surgical equipment, and there are X-ray departments, a radiotherapy division for cancer sufferers, laboratories, pharmaceutical stores, incubators for premature babies, a vast laundry, independent power and water plants, and a central-heating and air-

conditioning system serving every ward and department. The Al-Sabah Hospital remains the jewel in the Ministry of Health's crown, although it is currently the subject of a major renovation scheme.

In fact, the Al-Sabah has been overtaken in size by the Mubarak the Great Hospital, construction on which started in the late seventies and which, when fully operational, will have more than 1000 beds. The hospital, located on the Fourth Ring Road close to the densely populated suburbs of Hawalli and Salmiyah, has two main hospital buildings, each with eight floors, plus more than 20 large buildings of one or two storeys for out-patients, services and nurses' accommodation. One of the most impressive aspects of the site however is the mosque, which is open to both patients and visitors. A 500-bed hospital has also been opened near Fahaheel; there is a 500-bed military hospital at Sulaibikhat; the new Amiri has been designed to accommodate 390 in-patients; and three others are going up around Kuwait City. In addition to the Al-Sabah, the public hospital at Sulaibikhat has also been earmarked for renovation. The 3000 beds thus

The main building of Al-Sabah Hospital, opened in 1962, has recently undergone a major refit to maintain the hospital's reputation as one of the best in the Gulf.

added to the public health service will require a total staff estimated at almost 10,000. And therein lies a problem. Although it has not proved difficult in the past to find nurses or junior doctors to come to Kuwait, the necessity of importing virtually all medical staff poses obvious problems. The effects of the university's new medical faculty will not be felt for some years, and many senior doctors and administrators are reluctant to leave career structures in their native countries despite the lure of high, tax-free incomes. There is a worldwide shortage of qualified medical staff, and Kuwait's insistence that outsiders must have a working knowledge of English further limits the field. The Government is making strenuous efforts to entice more qualified personnel to the country; apart from the salaries, one big thing in Kuwait's favour is the standard of facilities and equipment it can put at the disposal of staff.

The size of the country means that the hiring of certain specialists on a full-time basis cannot be justified: there are simply not enough cases of a number of rare illnesses and ailments to keep a qualified man fully occupied. To overcome this problem some foreign specialists visit Kuwait for a limited period each year, while in other cases Kuwaitis go abroad for treatment, their expenses usually being met by the Government. There has in any case been a trend for wealthy Kuwaitis to seek private treatment overseas – there is even a

The Mubarak the Great Hospital, the largest of three new hospitals completed recently, stands at the junction of the Fahaheel highway and the Fourth Ring Road, close to the densely populated suburbs of Salmiyah and Hawalli.

Overleaf: Modern equipment in the radiology room of the Al-Sabah Hospital.

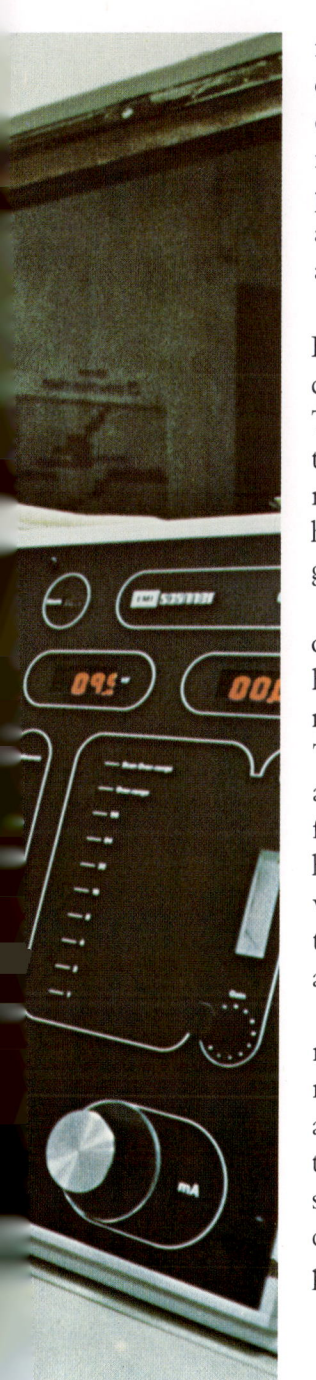

full-time medical attaché at the London Embassy taking care of the needs of some 1500 people who annually visit private clinics in the United Kingdom. The expansion and improvement of local services is designed to obviate the need for this: plans have been made, for example, for the construction of advanced facilities to treat diseases such as polio, and kidney and eye centres are also planned.

Community health care has long been a feature of life in Kuwait. The Government has built over 50 clinics staffed by doctors and nurses at a string of suburban shopping centres. These are matched by a similar number of dental clinics, and there is also a series of mother-and-child and preventive medicine clinics. In addition there are several hundred school health clinics, and a special clinic has recently been opened to give family planning advice.

Private treatment is far from cheap in Kuwait: the one exception used to be Southwell Hospital, one of the first hospitals built in Kuwait and designed specifically to meet the needs of Kuwait Oil Company employees and their families. The standards and facilities there have always been regarded as among the best in the country and are currently being further improved by the Government, which took over the hospital (and changed its name to Ahmadi Hospital) along with the assets of the oil company as a whole in 1974–5. Now the impressive complex is state-owned and open to the public as well as KOC employees.

For the future, Kuwait is committed to constant improvement of its medical services – the determination and the money are there to ensure that the nation maintains its place among the leaders in the provision of such care. Although there may be short-term staffing problems, the situation should ease in the late eighties when the first crop of qualified doctors from Kuwait University's school of medicine start pacing the wards.

Housing

A recent survey by an international business publication concluded: 'The Kuwaiti seems to consider the basic right of citizenship to be, not the right to vote, but the right to a government-provided house.' The state has been supplying its citizens with homes ever since redevelopment started in Kuwait City centre and tenants were moved out from old homes earmarked for demolition into new houses built on plots provided by the Government. Particular emphasis has been placed on finding accommodation for low-income groups and for desert dwellers, and a total of almost 18,000 homes for people with limited incomes is expected to have been made available between 1975 and 1980 (the total for

The need to provide modern, permanent homes for families with limited incomes has led to a massive public housing effort in the state.

1979 alone was 12,000). The National Housing Authority is committed to the construction of 5800 low-income units a year, which typically comprise a flat-roofed, two-storey building with its own high-walled garden or yard. Usually there are seven rooms in addition to the kitchen, garage and bathrooms and, for all this, a family pays only between $2\frac{1}{2}$ and 5 per cent of its income. Furthermore, the family will eventually own the house if, over a minimum of ten years, it has paid in rent the government-estimated cost of construction – a figure which is normally a fraction of the real cost.

The encouragement of home ownership has not been restricted to the poorer elements of society: Kuwaitis deemed to be in the average income group have also received substantial assistance. Until 1978, the most popular programme consisted of the distribution of plots of land by Kuwait Municipality to families who would then go to the Credit and Savings Bank for thirty-year, interest-free loans for the nominal cost of the land (between 750 and 1000 square metres were allocated per plot) and for the construction of the actual 'villa', as Kuwaitis call their houses. The snag was that as costs rose, the borrowers found that the loan was not large enough to enable them to complete construction and, consequently, the last land area to be designated under the scheme was left with half-finished houses. The Government decided to make a further grant to the families which found themselves in this embarrassing predicament to enable completion of the homes, and it then halted any further allocations. Now the only way for people in the average income group to get government housing assistance is through a programme operated by the National Housing Authority. The authority actually builds the villa, and the head of the household applies to the Credit and Savings Bank for a loan with which to buy it. By 1979, the NHA had more than 2000 houses under construction and was also experimenting with a project to put Kuwaiti families into luxurious high-rise complexes. Other plans have been outlined to provide single Kuwaitis with apartments, while complexes for pensioners have also been constructed.

Another scheme has concentrated on housing bedouin who, having left the desert for city jobs, had set up home in makeshift houses which soon became shanty towns. These unsanitary eyesores have disappeared as a result of determined government policy to put these people into new homes under the Rural Housing Programme. By the end of 1980 about 10,000 houses will have been built under this scheme, many of them along the lines of traditional, one-storey Arab houses which are rented out for nominal amounts. In 1979 more than 4000 of the Arab-style houses were scheduled for distribution. The residents become eligible for other housing when and if they are accepted for

Kuwaiti nationality, priority being given to bedu in the armed forces, the police or in government service.

Despite the enormous efforts being made, there remains a lengthy housing list in a country where the native population is increasing at an estimated 3.5 per cent a year. By the beginning of 1979 some 30,000 houses had been built by the Government, many of them in the previous three years, but the housing waiting-list was holding steady at around 20,000 people. At the time, the Ministry of Housing believed that up to 90 per cent of these would be housed within two years, but it now seems certain that continuing large-scale building programmes will be needed at least until the year 2000. The problem is that private housing is beyond the means of many Kuwaitis: land prices have rocketed in the last ten years, while there has been a similar if not greater increase in the cost of materials. The private sector may be able to meet the needs of half the people coming on to the housing market in the next twenty years, but that still leaves the state with substantial responsibilities in the construction field.

For the most part, expatriates are not allowed to own property unless they are nationals from Arab countries with reciprocal arrangements. Of the few who are entitled, even fewer can afford it and the vast majority of the foreign workers live in apartments owned by Kuwaitis. Many workers, particularly foreign labourers of bachelor status, find it better to go in for shared accommodation, and at the other end of the scale skilled foreigners brought in under contract are usually given company housing.

The finest housing of all is owned by upper-middle-class Kuwaitis and wealthy merchant families who have built large, individually designed homes along the wide boulevards of the suburbs of Kuwait City. These delightful residential areas have been built up on grid patterns which include schools, community shopping centres, health centres and other facilities. They represent the pinnacle of housing developments in Kuwait – developments which even fifteen years ago would have been unimaginable.

On the Air

Kuwait's first public radio service started in 1951 with two men sitting in a hastily converted room transmitting for two hours a day. Now, in the eighties, the country has two TV channels and six radio services, all housed in a sprawling Ministry of Information complex which represents perhaps the best example of modern architecture among the state's 'new wave' of public buildings. The ministry has a wide range of functions but, inevitably, the broadcasting services attract most attention in an age when virtually every home has at least one television set and a couple of radios.

The ministry's new centre became a going concern in 1978 when the radio staff, then totalling more than 700, moved in and promptly added an Iranian service to their two Arabic, one English, one Urdu and one FM, all-music, stereo service. They were followed by administrative and technical personnel housed in the 14-storey administration block, the focal point of the centre located among lawns and fountains just across from the historic Shamiya Gate, a reminder of days when Kuwait City sat small and snug behind an encircling wall. And then came the thousand TV employees, bringing with them the nation's second PAL-colour channel. Its arrival found a warm welcome among the populace, a dedicated and often critical band of watchers.

Until the completion of the centre, neither radio nor television services had been able to enjoy facilities purpose-built for the job. Radio's home in an old barracks on Sour Street – the spot chosen for the new complex – had been in service since those lowly beginnings in 1951. Although broadcasting hours were increased to three in 1953, it was not until 1958–9 that radio received special government attention and that both staff numbers and broadcasting hours started to rise significantly. In 1961 the state took over a private TV station which had been started a couple of years before by a group of merchants who bought a second-hand transmitter from the United States and began putting out 'canned' programmes, mostly imported from the West.

The Government's first task was to install a more powerful transmitter (at the time, nobody outside Kuwait City could receive the weak signals), and then they began building studios – or rather, converting them at an old army premises near the seashore at Dasmah. The idea of an integrated, custom-made complex for radio, TV and the Ministry of Information as a whole was first mooted in 1964 and a detailed report was submitted two years later. The Ministry of Public Works in conjunction with the Ministry of Information and the Planning Board (now Ministry of Planning) signed a contract with a firm of international consultants to make a project study. Years of negotiation followed, with Ministry of Information experts travelling the world to study operations in other countries. At last a construction contract was signed and in 1974 work began, along with a series of intensive training courses to ensure that all personnel would be sufficiently qualified to take over the running of the complex when it became a reality. That day came in 1978 with the completion of the main administration building, flanked on one side by the two main television units and on the other by the radio centre. There are also workshops, a garage and a large, circular concert hall counterpoised to the sweep of the main buildings. The site will also in due course include a so-called cinema building which will act as the centre for production of feature and other films for television and cinema. Other facilities have had to be built away from the complex, such as a massive antenna system on Failaka Island which, like so much else connected with the centre, is remote-controlled. In the bowels of the complex amid tight security is the heart of the entire operation: the power supply. Two separate stations provide electricity to give an alternative source should one of them break down; should they both do so, there is a huge emergency generator giving the ministry complete power independence – and should that in turn fail for any reason, there is a bank of batteries to keep essential broadcasting services on the air. The Kuwaitis are taking no chances.

Overleaf: One of the ultra-modern TV production studios in the new Ministry of Information complex. Completion of the new broadcasting facilities has led to the opening of the state's second colour TV channel.

The types of programme broadcast vary greatly. The main radio service comes in the form of a twenty-hour-a-day Arabic station which features everything from home-produced dramas to current affairs programmes. A second Arabic service is on the air for six hours in the afternoon, while English-language programmes (news, music, magazine shows and so on) are relayed first thing in the morning and from about 8 to 11 p.m. The various minorities receive Iranian and Urdu programmes during other two-hour time slots, and the stereo FM service plays music non-stop for eighteen hours a day, starting at 8 a.m. The music is mainly light and popular but may also include Arabic, Indian, French, Spanish, classical and other types. The new facilities offer the producers, technicians and artists great scope: they include such features as two large drama studios, an FM studio, a 180-square-metre music studio, various rehearsal and listening rooms, eight smaller units for recording and montage, and a dozen transmission studios (any eight of them capable of being used simultaneously) for news, medium-wave, FM and short-wave services. There are three fully automatic control and observation networks, and three others for production studios, engineering supervision and effects. But the most impressive feature on the radio side is the concert hall with its plush seating for 300 guests where, in the pleasantest of surroundings, concerts can be recorded in quadraphonic sound or transmitted live.

As to the facilities available for television, the 800-square-metre production studio offers, by itself, a far larger area than the total production facilities previously available – and it is just one of the three main units. Each, of course, boasts the latest fully automatic equipment, backed up by manual controls for every phase of the operation. There are also two transmission areas, each divided into two studios, plus a host of control systems, huge workshops, wardrobe departments and much else besides. The technical side of Kuwait television can safely be said to have few, if any, equals in the developing world.

The television programmes relayed to viewers in Kuwait cover a host of subjects. On the original channel most programmes are produced locally; a third of them are of a specialist or cultural nature, a quarter are general entertainment, and the remainder cover religion, news and current affairs, drama and sport. Supplementing the local productions are those imported from other Arab states, as well as some from further afield, mainly the United States, Britain and, in the case of films, India. The new channel, which is normally on the air for four hours each evening, consists of mainly foreign fare imported from a variety of sources: Russian films, American series, British documentaries and so on (all non-Arabic imports are sub-titled). In the absence of published audience ratings, it is impossible to say what type of programme the audience enjoys most. Certainly, the never-ending flow of letters to the Ministry of Information lets officials know what the public finds objectionable, and in keeping with Islamic beliefs, TV screens are free of the sex and violence seen on television in the West.

Educational broadcasts are of special importance, the Ministry of Education being active in devising its own programmes in conjunction with television staff. Special transmissions are also made for students approaching important exams, while during the long summer breaks the general programmes are expanded to include four hours of shows in the morning with wide family appeal. The first fruits of the efforts of a unique venture called the Arabian Gulf States' Joint Programme Production Institute are now being seen, too. The institute was established in Kuwait because of the level of expertise available there and because of the facilities at the new complex. With a Kuwaiti as director-general, the institute – comprised of TV services from Saudi Arabia, Iraq, Qatar, the UAE, Bahrain and Kuwait – aims to produce programmes for the Arab market. The initial $7 million project was a series of 130 programmes called 'Iftah Yasimsim', literally 'Open Sesame' – no less than an Arabic version of 'Sesame Street', Muppets and all (except that old favourites like Bert and Ernie became Badr and Anees and completely new characters like Melsun the parrot emerged). Most of the programmes in this educational series for tots were shot on a lavish set in Kuwait, while others were filmed throughout the Gulf.

News plays an important part in the ministry's operations: not just on television and radio, either, although there is a central, 24-hour news service which monitors all leading international news bureaux, local events and news broadcasts from all over the Middle East and elsewhere in the world. The ministry also has a responsibility for the international dissemination of news and information and, to this end, produces *Al-Araby* magazine whose 200,000 copies a month circulate from the Gulf to the Atlantic. This magazine covers such topics as science, politics, economics, literature, history, religion and psychology. Each edition is compiled by writers and photographers based in Kuwait, and the magazine is printed on the ministry's own press. The press itself is a mammoth undertaking, printing about 65 million items a year from school textbooks to government forms, magazines to driving licences. Among the ministry's publications are *Al-Kuwait*, which appears in Arabic twice a month and deals with life and times in the country; *Alam-Al-Fikr* (World of Knowledge) which appears quarterly and whose 300 pages are read mainly by academics; the *World of Drama* which features Arabic translations of foreign playscripts; and the weekly *Official Gazette*. Annual publications include the *Kuwait Yearbook*, which details achievements in the state during the previous twelve months, and many other books, magazines, brochures and even maps.

The ministry's duties also entail keeping a watch on the nation's press. There is no pre-publication censorship in Kuwait but the seven daily newspapers – five Arabic and two English – can be suspended if they break a government-established code covering defamation, libel, and some ill-defined areas such as attacking individuals or conjecturing government business. Leading newspapers and magazines from the world are flown in daily, and the ministry normally restricts its censorship of these to cutting out indecent pictures.

Government funds have also gone towards the establishment of Kuwait News Agency (KUNA), which became a going concern in 1978 and which offers newspapers, publishing houses, large companies and institutions a round-the-clock flow of news and information. The agency, run on the lines of the major bureaux, provides a local news service in Arabic, an international service put together by monitoring radio and international news agency output, and specialist reports such as business and finance. KUNA has been progressively putting out a wide network of foreign correspondents with the aim of offering both Arabic and English teleprinter services, and it is envisaged that the agency will grow to include photographic, features and research departments.

Film censorship also falls to a committee under the supervision of the Ministry of Information, although it includes representatives from other government departments, religious bodies and the Arab Office for the Boycott of Israel. The prime targets, once again, are explicitly sexual scenes.

The Ministry of Information therefore has wide powers which it uses sensibly, and wide responsibilities which it pursues diligently. The results are radio and television services of tremendous variety and appeal; an information service ranking among the most comprehensive anywhere; and a broadly based press which is freer than it is in the vast majority of developing nations.

Keeping in Touch

On 15 July 1775 the first postal despatch from Kuwait was recorded. The letter from a business agency in Persia to its directors in London went by camel to Aleppo on the first 'Desert Express' run which, for the next twenty years, was to form a vital link in communications between Europe and

India. Today in the heart of Kuwait City stands the massive Telecommunications Centre with an antenna tower which dwarfs all around: this, two hundred years after that first letter, is the hub of Kuwait's worldwide communications network. The service run by the Ministry of Communications today ranks as one of the most efficient in the world and has become the envy of many Middle East nations where simply making a local phone call can be a lengthy and arduous business.

The story of the modern service really begins in 1904 when Kuwait gave permission for an assistant surgeon in the Indian Medical Service to open a post office in the country which he would run in addition to performing his medical duties. Even so, it was not until 1915 that a post office was actually opened, the mail coming into and leaving Kuwait up to that time being handled by clerks of the British Political Agent. The mail came and went by steamship until the late twenties when it was routed through, first, Basra and later Sharjah. Direct airmail services came to the country in 1933, with an Imperial Airways flying-boat calling in *en route* to Karachi.

A telex room in the Telecommunications Centre. The telex system is used extensively by Kuwaiti companies in international dealings.

Indian stamps used during the war were replaced in 1948 by British ones overprinted with the word 'Kuwait' and, two years later, a second post office opened in Ahmadi. After that expansion was rapid, and in 1961 Kuwait became a sovereign state and took over full responsibility for its own postal service, joining the Universal Postal Union and issuing its own stamps in Kuwaiti currency. Today there are about 50 post offices in the state and 22,000 letterboxes. In 1977 about 85 million pieces of mail were handled by the Post Office, which now has modern headquarters in Kuwait City and at Kuwait International Airport.

Telephone services have expanded in similar fashion, and almost a million international calls were handled in 1977. There is no way of knowing how many local calls were made as the internal service in Kuwait is free. Direct dialling has been introduced to countries as far away as Great Britain, although to obtain the service a subscriber has to put down a

Although subscribers can now dial direct to much of the world from Kuwait, the international telephone operators still have plenty of work.

deposit of KD 300, a figure arrived at late in 1978 after complaints that the original deposit of KD 1000 was too high. Most companies also keep in touch with international business contacts through a widely used telex service, now as much part of Kuwaiti office furniture as desks and chairs.

At Umm Al-Aish, about 70 kilometres north of Kuwait City near the main road to Iraq, stands the Satellite Communications Earth Station with its 355-tonne steel dish trained on Intelsat IV, a communications satellite stationed over the Indian Ocean. This complex enables Kuwait to keep in touch with such nations as Japan, India, Pakistan, Bahrain, Lebanon, Great Britain, Spain, France and other European nations, all of which have reflectors pointing at the same satellite to receive or send phone calls, telegrams or television pictures and sound. The station receives its power from mains supply but has a bank of batteries which float on charge to ensure a steady delivery of current. Two standby diesel generators are maintained within the complex for emergency use in the event of a mains failure. The station is linked to the Telecommunications Centre, from where messages emanate, by an underground coaxial cable and two micro-wave links. When Umm Al-Aish went into service with a 132-channel capacity its value was soon realized, and the decision was made to erect a second station further south which would be trained on the satellite over the Atlantic, thus giving Kuwait direct, single-hop contact with about two-thirds of the world. The extent of the nation's communications system and its links with the Ministry of Information centre has made Kuwait the logical headquarters of pan-Arab operations in the exchange of television news and programmes.

Instantaneous contact via space satellite with someone 5000 kilometres away is just one of the benefits of a system which began when a solitary letter took two weeks to travel from Kuwait to Aleppo.

The antenna tower of the Telecommunications Centre has become a distinctive landmark in Kuwait City, where it dominates the busy downtown area.

Light, Life and Water

Kuwait's rapidly increasing population poses many challenges, not least how to provide sufficient electricity and water to meet the daily needs of hundreds of thousands of domestic, business and industrial users. The demand for water alone has increased from less than 4 million litres in 1958, to 18 million in 1965, 90 million in 1970, and more than 230 million today – and this in a country which has so few freshwater wells that even a century ago it was having to import potable water by dhow from the Shatt Al-Arab.

It is no coincidence that electricity and water come together under one ministry, as both are derived from a common fuel which Kuwait is fortunate to have plenty of: natural gas. It is this gas that superheats the steam to temperatures which drive the turbo-generators to produce electricity and which may be distilled to meet domestic water needs. The Ministry of Electricity and Water is the world's largest distiller of water; it has two major sources of power and desalinated water at the port complex of Shuweikh and at the Shuaiba Industrial Area, plus a new power station at Doha just across the bay from Kuwait City.

Only in 1934 did the first privately owned, oil-powered generator begin supplying a limited number of private customers with electricity. This also marked the arrival of the nation's first air-conditioners – now common in practically every household and office. A 930-kilowatt system had been developed by 1951 when responsibility for power supply was taken over by the newly formed Department of Electricity. Growth became rapid after that: three alternating current generators were installed at Shuweikh, each with a capacity of 750 kilowatts. By the late seventies this had been increased to 160,000 kw each, while generating units at Shuaiba had been installed to produce 1400 megawatts. With the addition of the four 150-mw units at Doha (from a power station which has been designed to run on a variety of fuels) and the completion of five 40-mw units at Shuweikh, Kuwait will have met its target for 1980 of having a total generating

The modern power station and water distillation plant at Doha, 30 kilometres from Kuwait City, has been designed to run on a variety of fuels – including, of course, oil.

capacity of 2500 mw. This involves in addition, of course, having the necessary support facilities – cables, transformer stations, etc. – to cater for 10,000 or more new customers per year.

The story is much the same with water. Apart from a few sweet wells, the only natural source was the brackish water heavily contaminated with magnesium sulphate. By 1950 a privately established sea-water distillation plant was in operation, supplying about 2.7 million litres a day. At this time the Government ordered its own plant to be built in Shuweikh, and in 1953 ten evaporators went into action, each capable of producing 455,000 litres of distilled water a day. Another plant went into operation in 1955 but, within a decade, both had become obsolete with the arrival of multi-stage flash evaporation systems. This new type of plant was incorporated at both Shuweikh and Shuaiba in order to increase production steadily towards the target figure set at 214 million litres a day by 1980.

The clean, elegant lines of water storage towers silhouetted against the setting sun. Their value is more than aesthetic, though, in a country where large-scale evaporation makes conventional reservoirs useless.

The Oil

A view of part of the ammonia plant at Shuaiba run by the Petrochemical Industries Company which is helping to open up the lucrative downstream market in Kuwait.

It is, of course, oil that makes it all possible – oil that has financed Kuwait's phenomenal development in the past thirty years, that provides the nation with its international clout. Kuwait has astonishingly large amounts of petroleum, with proven reserves which can be bettered only by Saudi Arabia and the USSR. And, for a variety of reasons, it is the cheapest oil to produce anywhere in the world. So the occasional visitor to Kuwait might find it odd to encounter a virtual obsession which, far from concentrating on the abundance of petroleum resources, centres on the fact that one day the oil will run out.

The problem is that while these resources may last a lifetime, it will be the lifetime of a human being, not a nation. So it is not perhaps surprising after all that the country with more oil per head of population than any other should be concerned with deriving the absolute maximum from what is tantamount to its sole natural resource.

Official estimates of how long Kuwait's oil will last are not available, but the period most usually quoted is 70-plus years. This, though, is based on 'guesstimates' of proven reserves (there may be new finds), on present recovery methods (improved technology seems bound to be developed in coming years), on current production rates, and on a host of other factors which will either shorten or extend the life of the country's oil.

The Kuwaitis naturally want to make it last as long as possible, and they have embarked on a conservation policy which, during 1978, limited production to an average of two million barrels a day from the Kuwait Oil Company producing areas. The limit was briefly exceeded in 1979, but in early 1980 production was cut to 1.5 million barrels per day. The nation has been steadily moving away from a situation in which it is entirely dependent on the sale of crude oil: an active policy of developing downstream industries has been pursued, not only to ensure maximum utilization of petroleum resources but also to widen the industrial base of the oil sector and increase the level of technical know-how.

Kuwait Oil Company (KOC) is the main producing arm, responsible for more than 90 per cent of all crude oil extraction. Much of it comes from the huge Burgan Field, the world's second largest oilfield, but well concentrations can be found practically everywhere in the country except the extreme west, an area which has still to yield a commercial find. The only offshore production at the moment is off the Partitioned Zone, an area between Kuwait and Saudi Arabia which is now divided for administrative purposes but where all oil production remains shared equally.

It is not simply oil that is important, however. Gas is playing an increasingly significant part in the petroleum industry, and Kuwait maintained its position at the forefront of 'associated' gas utilizers in 1979 with the inauguration of the billion-dollar Gas Project, one of the largest of its type anywhere. The aim is to ensure that the gas, which is produced mixed in with the oil and which has hitherto been flared off in the atmosphere, receives treatment so that valuable butane, propane and natural gasoline can be extracted as liquids from the mainly methane stream.

Apart from technical developments, the most significant moves in recent years have been concerned with the national take-over of all the major entities in the petroleum industry. This came as the result of many direct and indirect pressures: the growing national awareness since the achievement of full sovereignty in 1961; the increasing availability of indigenous skills; the realization of the importance of Kuwait controlling its solitary natural resource; and, not least, the 1973 oil crisis which proved such an eye-opener to both importing and exporting nations. The era of cheap oil came to an end and the world was never to be quite the same again.

The results can be seen in the country's oil industry of today – an industry which in all its diversified facets is owned and controlled by Kuwaitis.

A common sight in Kuwait: a well head with 'Christmas tree' valves which control the flow of oil coming up the shaft from deep under the desert.

The Early Days

Surprisingly, perhaps, the Kuwait oil industry took a long while to get off – or under – the ground. The first, somewhat half-hearted attempt to obtain a concession was made by the Anglo-Persian Oil Company (APOC), now British Petroleum, in 1911. At the time Britain had responsibility for Kuwait's external affairs under the agreement of 1889, and the British Political Agent decided the time was not right to forward the oil company's request to the ruler, Sheikh Mubarak. Two years later, in 1913, a team from the British Admiralty visited the Gulf and noted that the chances of discovering oil in Kuwait were 'not unfavourable' – this understatement apparently being based on bitumen seepages found in Burgan. In the same year the ruler agreed that any concession would go only to a company nominated by the British Government, an agreement which was later to give rise to some heated exchanges between British and American oil interests.

The Kuwait oil concession remained on a back burner until 1923 when APOC finally began negotiations with the new ruler, Sheikh Ahmad. That same year, the Eastern and General Syndicate (EGS) received approval to begin negotiations, and the battle for the concession began. Sheikh Ahmad, the founding father of Kuwait's oil era, proved as shrewd as he was tough, and for five years he rejected as inadequate all the terms offered. By 1928 EGS had become linked with Gulf Oil of America and, as elsewhere in the Gulf, the British started to insist that the nationality clause be observed, thus effectively blocking any participation by non-UK oil concerns. It was a transatlantic argument which was to go on, sometimes acrimoniously, for several years, and negotiations did not fully resume until 1932, by which time the British had conceded an open-door policy to American companies. Even so, no conclusion of a concession contract looked likely as the two oil giants progressively improved their terms, but still not to the satisfaction of Sheikh Ahmad. Then, in December 1933, the British and Americans decided to pool their resources and formed Kuwait Oil Company Limited, each side holding equal shares. With just one contender in the field, it seemed only a matter of time before the Kuwaitis would be obliged to sign a concession.

The first KOC proposals were put and rejected early in 1934. In March, Sheikh Ahmad not only turned down a revised set but also stunned the negotiators by telling them that another, '100 per cent British' company had recently asked for permission to enter a bid for the contract and that the initial terms were better than anything KOC had offered. The ruler suspended all talks until the end of that summer after further unsatisfactory discussions.

The new entrant in the concession stakes turned out to be Traders Limited, and the terms offered proved to be good enough for Sheikh Ahmad to agree, in September 1934, to sign a contract with them on condition the firm received approval from the British in accordance with the 1913 agreement.

In an incredible sequence of events which followed, the American side of the KOC negotiating team apparently dreamed up the story that the Traders bid was nothing more than a double-cross by APOC. They convinced the Kuwaitis that APOC actually controlled Traders and that the whole affair was simply a ploy to ensure that the Kuwait concession fell wholly to the British. At the same time Traders Limited was running into opposition from the UK Government which was annoyed with the company for not getting permission to approach the Kuwaitis prior to making a concession bid. The upshot was that in December KOC told its negotiators to meet all Sheikh Ahmad's terms and, finally, a contract was signed. Undoubtedly, it had been a long and involved struggle – a fascinating tale which this brief outline can scarcely do justice to, but one which is told in admirable detail in *The First Kuwait Oil Concession*, a book written by A.H.T. Chisholm, chief APOC negotiator.

KOC began to move men into Kuwait in 1935, when preliminary studies got under way. A year later the first well

Changing Times

At the start of 1970 there were eleven Kuwaiti university graduates working full-time for KOC. A year earlier, there had been one. In addition a growing number of skilled Kuwaitis were being employed in operational divisions, the growth of educational facilities in the late fifties and sixties having made available young men who had completed high school. They were taken on in increasing numbers by the company and placed on special training programmes which in turn produced a nucleus of technically competent home-grown operators within KOC. And there was an expanding corps of Kuwaitis in administrative posts. The ramifications of these developments could hardly have been appreciated at the time: for one thing, they ended the 'splendid isolation' of the company as Ahmadi suddenly became an acceptable place for middle-class Kuwaiti sons from the city to work. The arrival of local graduates accelerated the trend, and the links formed between oilfield and city led to the establishment of a fast-growing and often vocal body of Kuwaiti opinion anxious to gain greater national control of the oil. There were also murmurings that Kuwait had been denied a fair price for the commodity for too long. Things reached a head in 1973 when an oil embargo and the tripling of prices made the world realize that oil really was finite, and that power over such a precious article was held not by the multi-national companies but by the sovereign states sitting on top of the reservoirs.

Inevitably, negotiations were begun between the Kuwait Government and BP/Gulf which resulted in 1974 in the signing of an agreement giving the state a 60 per cent share in KOC. A year later, terms were reached by which the Government took over the remaining 40 per cent and Kuwait Oil Company Ltd became Kuwait Oil Company (Kuwait Shareholding Company) – a national undertaking which gave the country control over its major oil producer and, hence, over its future. It is important to remember that KOC was not nationalized but bought out by the Govern-

Exploratory drilling still goes on in Kuwait, the most recent efforts concentrating on the search for gas many thousands of metres underground.

The KOC refinery at Mina Al-Ahmadi is currently undergoing a $600 million modernization entailing the construction of a desulphurization plant, scheduled for completion in 1984.

30,000 barrels a day at Mina Abdullah, while KOC had increased its own refining capacity to 250,000 barrels a day (later upped to almost 300,000). The deep-berth North Pier was commissioned in 1959 to accommodate larger tankers, although within ten years the arrival of very large crude carriers (VLCCs) had made even this facility inadequate; KOC responded with the construction of the two-berth Sea Island, a pier some thirteen kilometres offshore supplied by a gigantic submarine pipeline and capable of handling the biggest ships.

As world demand soared, the sixties saw the expansion of virtually every sector of the industry. By the end of the decade, KOC was producing 2.5 million barrels a day, 80 per cent of it from the Greater Burgan area. Plans were being laid which would soon see production pass the three million barrel mark, and Gulf and British Petroleum were eagerly anticipating another bumper decade in the seventies. But already the wind of change was blowing.

(1951), Ahmadi (1953), North Kuwait (1955) and Minagish (1959) coming into production. These were joined by the Umm Gudair Field in 1962 although, from the start, Burgan established itself as king of them all. The very first production well drilled there continues to turn out oil to this day: its total so far is well over 17 billion barrels.

Another development of the fifties centred on the arrival of a Japanese concern, Arabian Oil Company, as holders of the concession for the offshore area of the Partitioned Zone (again, with Kuwait and Saudi Arabia sharing the benefits equally). Despite a blow-out and fire on its first rig, a second wildcat well found commercial quantities in January 1960, and a year later the first export of crude was made from gathering and terminal facilities at Khafji on the Saudi side of the zone.

It was a time of considerable activity on the Kuwait oil scene. Aminoil had built a refinery with an initial capacity of

Pipelines carrying crude oil to a waiting tanker at North Pier, one of four loading terminals operated by Kuwait Oil Company.

was sunk on the north shore of Kuwait Bay, but it came up dry after boring almost 2500 metres. In 1938 a second well was sunk at Burgan, and out gushed the oil. Kuwait Oil Company was a going concern. Finds came thick and fast after that and, by the time eight more wells had been drilled around Burgan in 1942, the existence of large oil accumulations had been confirmed at comparatively shallow depths of between 1027 and 1480 metres. A three-year hiccup in operations was caused by the Second World War, but soon after the resumption of drilling in 1945 a production capacity of 30,000 barrels a day was reached. Appropriately, it was Sheikh Ahmad who turned the silver valve in June 1946 to start the oil flowing aboard the tanker *British Grenadier* at a ceremony to mark the first export of Kuwait crude oil.

Little time was lost in building the necessary infrastructure for the fledgeling industry, KOC establishing its operational headquarters at Ahmadi, an area on the edge of the Burgan Field named in honour of the ruler. A tree-lined township soon started to take shape and, at nearby Mina Al-Ahmadi ('mina' simply means port in Arabic), KOC's first terminal, South Pier, was built along with a 25,000-barrel-a-day refinery. Between 1946 and 1949 roads, shops and a host of associated services appeared, as well as homes, offices, workshops and recreational facilities.

By this time other oil companies were bidding to become involved in the Arabian oil bonanza and, in 1948, the American Independent Oil Company (Aminoil) won the concession for the Kuwait portion of the Partitioned Zone. Getty Oil was awarded the Saudi Arabian concession under an agreement whereby any oil would be divided between the two undertakings. Aminoil established its headquarters at Mina Abdullah, just south of the KOC terminal, and Getty chose a spot a few kilometres to the north of the dividing line in the zone. Although Aminoil started drilling in 1949, it proved to be several years before the company made a commercial find. KOC had no such problems. During the fifties more oil was steadily uncovered, with wells at Magwa

A workover rig at Ahmadi on the edge of the famed and prolific Burgan Oilfield, the second largest in the world.

ment; British Petroleum and Gulf retain favoured status as far as agreed liftings are concerned and also supply KOC with technical back-up. The company itself, however, has become fully 'Kuwaitized', an awkward word for a policy of positive discrimination aimed at putting as many nationals as possible into positions of responsibility. At KOC today, about half the 4700 workforce consists of Kuwaitis, many of them filling top administrative and technical posts, with the tally of local graduates now pushing towards the 200 mark. Outside specialists are still needed in some areas but their numbers have been dwindling, and the company continues to improve its record as one of the most efficient oil undertakings in the world.

A network of pipes at one of the KOC oil gathering centres which operate 24 hours a day, 365 days a year in the heart of an inhospitable desert.

The take-over of KOC led to the Government successfully concluding negotiations with Arabian Oil Company which gave the state 60 per cent of its half-share of the offshore operations in the Partitioned Zone (the other half of the concession still belongs to Saudi Arabia). Negotiations then began with Aminoil for its concession of the Kuwaiti portion of the onshore zone, but talks became hopelessly bogged down over the question of cost and so, in 1977, Kuwait nationalized the American firm, the Government paying compensation on the basis of an official estimate. Aminoil became Kuwait Wafra Oil Company until 1978 when its refinery and terminal at Mina Abdullah were handed over to Kuwait National Petroleum Company (KNPC) and its operations in the Wafra Field became part of KOC.

With an eye to conservation, a limit on KOC production was imposed in 1976 which restricted daily oil production to a maximum of two million barrels, averaged out over a year. (The Government cannot restrict activity in the Partitioned Zone because of the shared nature of the operations.) The ceiling was not tested for almost three years, mainly because of the levelling out of world demand, Kuwait being particularly susceptible to market changes as its heavy, high-sulphur crude oil is inclined to be less desirable in times of relative glut. Kuwait responded to the loss of Iranian production in the early months of 1979 by raising output to a rate of something over 2.7 million barrels a day which, if nothing else, proves the flexibility of Kuwaiti production, which has a nominal maximum capacity of around 3.5 million barrels per day. However, production was subsequently eased back to the old level and in April 1980 it was cut further, to 1.5 million b.p.d. The last year for which complete statistics are available is 1978, when KOC exported more than 586 million barrels of crude and 33 million barrels of refined products. More than 45 per cent of the crude went to Europe, the United Kingdom being by far the largest customer on that side of the world, while Japan accounted for another 23 per cent.

Tapping the Gas

Since the coming of oil, an ever-present feature of the desert landscape has been the circles of fire rising tower-like into the sky – the gas which is produced along with every barrel of oil that comes out of the ground. For years this highly valuable product was flared off in the atmosphere simply because there was no other way to use it – a situation which, obviously, no government could tolerate indefinitely. So Kuwait embarked on a programme which, by the mid-seventies, had established the nation as one of the main gas utilizers, about 60 per cent of it being used. Some of it went to power generation for domestic users, some went to industry, a little

The Kuwait National Petroleum Company refinery at Shuaiba is one of the largest in the Middle East and pioneered the way as the first commercially successful all-hydrogen plant in the world.

was processed at KOC's two small gas liquefaction units, and most was re-injected into the oilfields to maintain pressure on the oil below and thus improve recovery rates. But this was still not regarded as good enough, and a start was made on a gas utilization scheme, known simply as the Gas Project, which entailed the construction of a massive three-train gas processing plant at KOC's Mina Al-Ahmadi terminal and the building of a gas gathering and transmission network across the country.

The fact is that in addition to oil, Kuwait has massive associated gas reserves. The idea behind the Gas Project was to take all this gas and process it so that the stream could be stripped of its butane, propane and natural gasoline before the lean gas went on for other uses. Those towers of fire, it was decided, had to disappear, although contrary to a belief still prevalent in Kuwait they will never be snuffed out completely simply because there is always a certain amount of waste which has to be flared. A start on the Gas Project was made in 1976, and in February 1979 the Amir inaugurated the system at a ceremony at Mina Al-Ahmadi, the focal point of the whole operation.

But it is deep in the desert that the story really begins. At twenty-five gathering centres in the south-east, north and west producing areas the gas is collected and eventually separated from the oil. It is transmitted in gas and liquid streams to the terminal, the western product being relatively high in impurities and first requiring treatment at the 'acid' gas removal unit at the KNPC refinery at Shuaiba. The gas comes together in one of the three identical trains of the liquefaction plant where it is processed into a liquid stream before undergoing fractionation in a de-ethanizer, de-butanizer and depropanizer. As the propane and butane contain impurities, they are passed through a product-treating plant in which sulphur compounds are adsorbed. Finally, a 37,000-horsepower refrigeration plant cools the products before they are stored: in liquid state, propane requires a temperature of $-45°C$ and butane $-6.7°C$. Only natural gasoline can be stored at ambient temperatures. In addition to the main processing unit, nine LPG (liquefied petroleum gas) storage tanks have had to be built, ranging in size from 457,000 to 267,000 barrels, in addition to special pipelines and loading facilities on KOC's South Pier. At the peak of construction in 1977 more than 7000 men were engaged on the project, most of them building the actual LPG plant. Now that it is complete the operational workforce totals 250, the majority of them Kuwaitis who underwent two years' training before the system actually became a going concern.

At present the plant is working at nothing like full capacity because it was designed to process all Kuwait's gas at a time when it was envisaged that daily oil production would be around 3.5 million barrels a day. The conservation policy has drastically reduced this but, making the most of the situation, Kuwaiti officials point to its scope for future growth. The whole gas market is in fact fiercely competitive, and it remains to be seen how commercially successful the plant will be. Such success, however, is not the only yardstick. The project is important to Kuwait not only because it offers the opportunity of long-term financial gain but because it has resulted in a major step towards diversification in the industry and has continued the vital process of the acquisition of technical know-how. It has also offered employment opportunities to Kuwaitis and, most important, means that a freely available yet increasingly valuable product is not being wasted.

One of the tanks in which the liquid product from the recently completed LPG plant is stored prior to shipment.

The coming of the Gas Project has caused something of a headache for the men concerned with producing the oil. It has always been desirable to match oil extraction rates with tanker loading: if, say, tankers were available to take aboard two million barrels on any given day, then the wells on that day should ideally produce two million barrels and not much more. Practically speaking, daily liftings can vary between about one million and three million barrels. The problem caused by the Gas Project centres on the fact that it needs a fairly constant stream of gas which, because all the gas is mixed in with the crude, means in turn a steady rate of oil production. KOC's monster tank farms with a total storage capacity of 10.5 million barrels of oil give some leeway but, despite the apparent size, not much. So a reservoir of gas over and above the 'associated' supplies needs to be found. One short-term answer lies in the gas which has been re-injected into the oilfields over the years, and the Government has given approval for these reserves to be tapped should it be necessary to balance high gas demand with low oil production. This though is something of a standby, with limited long-term applications. What is needed is a source of entirely unassociated gas – and that is just what Kuwait is striving to find.

Iran has discovered two of the world's biggest concentrations of free gas existing in a geological phenomenon known as the Khuff Formation. Geologists believe that this huge source of unassociated gas extends across the Gulf and runs under Kuwait some 6.5 kilometres down, considerably deeper than any drill has penetrated before in the state. So, in 1977, a start was made on the exploratory Deep Test Well with an expected rendezvous at 6250 metres beneath the surface of the Burgan Field in the spring of 1978. This initial effort was bedevilled by problems and, running months behind schedule, suffered a blow-out in the summer of 1978, demonstrating yet again the ever-present risks of any drilling operation. The consequent fire eventually burnt itself out several weeks and more than KD 10 million later. Undeterred, a new Deep Test Well was spudded-in early in 1979 and a second one followed it a few months later. The chances of finding a major source of unassociated gas have been officially described as 'hopeful'. Only time will tell.

Life Downstream

The 'downstream' industries – refining, petrochemicals, even maritime transport – have traditionally been the preserve of the importing nations. But Kuwait has spelled out its position loud and clear: it intends to break into the downstream markets and, with other producers, would consider restricting crude oil supplies if it found the way blocked. These industries are important for the same reasons as those given for LPG; they represent diversification of the industry, more jobs and technical advances, and the opportunity to get away from the position of being a residual supplier of crude oil.

Refining in Kuwait is well established. The largest unit is KOC's refinery at Mina Al-Ahmadi which can produce up to 292,000 barrels per day of such products as motor spirit, kerosene, gas oil, diesel, and light and heavy fuel oils. In 1979 construction started on a catalytic reformer which will produce 864,000 tonnes of motor gasoline per year. There is also KOC's new LPG plant, plus a bitumen plant which opened in 1978 and is capable of producing, storing and despatching 254,000 tonnes a year of various grades for both domestic use and export. The KOC refinery remains basically a topping-up operation – the sophisticated end of the market falls to Kuwait National Petroleum Company operating one of the most advanced refineries in the world at Shuaiba, the southerly neighbour of the Mina Al-Ahmadi complex.

KNPC went into business in 1961, with the Government holding 60 per cent of the stock and private shareholders the remainder. Initially its task was to manage the local marketing of products from the KOC refinery but by 1968 plans had been finalized for the construction of its own refinery. Instead of opting for tried and tested designs, the company plumped for the world's first all-hydrogen complex to go into commercial operation. The disadvantages of such a system were that it was costly and complicated; the advantages were that it gave KNPC scope and flexibility, for the process would enable, at the top end of the hydrocarbon spectrum, the production of high-grade, low-sulphur products and, at the bottom end, the conversion of tar-like residues from the refining process into saleable products. The first stage of the refinery was built in 1968 and boasted such features as the world's heaviest single vessel erected in one place (a 600-tonner for the isomax unit), a hydrogen plant with a capacity of 40 million cubic metres a day, and two units each with a capacity to process 35,000 barrels of residue per day. At the time, sceptics doubted KNPC's ability to handle such a revolutionary refinery but, relying mainly on local skills, the company has confounded the critics. Today, through expansion and improved operational techniques, the capacity of the complex has risen to some 200,000 barrels a day, the actual record for one month being achieved in September 1978 when a daily average of 194,751 barrels of oil was processed. In all, the refinery produces about 30 grades of product tailored to specific companies' requirements and has its own lube oil plant. The company also has the monopoly of petrol stations in the country and, with its 3000 employees, currently produces all the premium grade (98 octane) petrol consumed in the country and two-thirds of the regular (90 octane) fuel, the remainder coming from the KOC refinery.

KNPC has taken over the operation of the ex-Aminoil refinery at Mina Abdullah, which itself is the southerly neighbour of the Shuaiba Refinery Industrial Area. Unlike the Shuaiba refinery, which gets all its crude oil from the original KOC fields, Mina Abdullah gets its crude from the Wafra area in the Partitioned Zone. This oil is notoriously high in sulphur content and the refinery's primary task is to remove this undesirable element. Basically, it consists of a 144,000 barrels-per-day crude unit, a 35,000 b.p.d. desulphurization process, a hydrogen unit, and a 320-tonnes-a-

day sulphur recovery unit. An offspin of the operation is that Mina Abdullah does a healthy business selling liquid or flaked 99.9 per cent pure sulphur. The refinery and terminal, which has a workforce of about 700, currently exists independently of other KNPC endeavours apart from the higher echelons of management, although there are plans to link the two neighbours by pipeline.

Another important element in the downstream scene is the Petrochemical Industries Company (PIC), which came into being in 1963 when it was established as a joint venture with government, private and foreign shareholdings. By 1975 all foreign and private interests had been bought out, and the company became 100 per cent state-owned although still run along highly commercial lines. PIC has concentrated on producing fertilizer, which many people consider will be of prime importance in the coming decades; it has plants at the main Shuaiba complex concerned with the production of liquid ammonia, ammonium sulphate, concentrated sulphuric acid and, most important of all, urea. Ammonia, produced on a larger scale than any other chemical derived

PIC's urea plant at Shuaiba where much-needed fertilizer is produced for developing countries on several continents.

from petroleum, is the source of the nitrogen in urea production, and it is this easily used and versatile fertilizer which accounts for the bulk of PIC sales. In 1978 some 582,000 tonnes of ammonia were produced, from which 679,000 tonnes of urea were derived (liquid ammonia is only exported when it is surplus to the requirements of fertilizer production). PIC urea comes in clear white pills with a nitrogen content of around 46 per cent.

But fertilizers have not been PIC's only concern in recent years. In 1974 the company was put in charge of the salt and chlorine works at Shuweikh, formerly the responsibility of the Ministry of Electricity and Water. Most of the products from this division are consumed locally and include the domestic bleach 'Chlorsal'. Also produced are table salt, caustic soda, hydrochloric acid, compressed hydrogen, chlorine gas and liquid, and distilled water. But it is the petrochemical side which holds out most promise for the future, and plans are already on the drawing-board for an aromatics plant which in a few years could be producing 284,000 tonnes of benzene, 61,000 tonnes of ortho-xylene and 87,000 tonnes of para-xylene per year. An olefins plant is also planned which, using ethane-rich gas from KOC's gas plant, could produce an annual total of 132,000 tonnes of polyethylene, 137,000 tonnes of ethylene glycol, or 344,000 tonnes of styrene monomer. The Ministry of Oil, however, intends to ensure the viability of these projects before giving the final go-ahead to PIC to increase its plants and its 1700 workforce.

The actual shipping of the hydrocarbons has not been ignored, either. The Kuwait Oil Tanker Company has made remarkable strides since it purchased its first tanker in 1959 – a 49,000 tonner which at the time was regarded as one of the world's biggest! Times have certainly changed: today KOTC's *Al-Andalus* tips the scales at 361,000 tons and is still a long way from the heavyweight records. KOTC is also operating LPG tankers built to carry the output of the Gas Project: the first of four 328,000-ton tankers, *Gas Al-Kuwait*, was delivered in 1978. KNPC has its own 13-strong fleet to carry its products, in addition to a bunker berthed strategically in the Gulf to sell fuel to passing tankers. Additionally, there is one very large crude carrier (VLCC) carrying the Kuwaiti flag in the fleet of the Arab Maritime Petroleum Transport Company, a joint venture formed by members of the Organization of Arab Petroleum Exporting Countries.

Despite the size of the Kuwaiti fleet, the largest in the Arab world, it cannot cope with more than 10 per cent of crude exports and must still rely primarily on foreign crews and officers. Similarly, the amount of refined products and petrochemicals Kuwait can produce barely scratches the surface in terms of total world demand and the country's own sales of crude oil. Nevertheless, any temptation to write off Kuwait's downstream industries as an expensive exercise in self-indulgence would be wrong. Not only is there a determination to proceed with the development of refineries and other processes, there is also a growing pool of skill and expertise working towards making them viable and competitive in the long term. And the industries enjoy something of an advantage over their counterparts in the developed nations, the traditional downstream bastions – the raw material in Kuwait is free.

Moving the Goods

The sheer volume of oil and related products exported from Kuwait in the course of a year is monumental. In a typical month, KOC might despatch 50 million barrels of crude and a million barrels of refined products; KNPC will send abroad a million tons or more of products from the port of Shuaiba; and PIC might easily chip in with 50,000 tonnes or more of urea. And during that month the cargoes will be bound for countries all around the world.

It falls to Kuwait Oil Company to handle the monster crude carriers, most of the burden being shouldered by Sea Island, a two-berth steel pier some 13 kilometres offshore and fed with oil at a rate of 15,250 tonnes an hour by a 122-

Hundreds of kilometres of pipeline run across the desert bringing crude oil and gas condensates for processing or direct shipment. The crude is then pumped aboard the world's supertankers via massive loading arms (above). Part of the deck of a 350,000-ton oil carrier is shown below. The completion of the single point mooring means that Kuwait can handle ships of half a million tons ... or more.

centimetre submarine pipeline. Sea Island, completed in 1968, deals with about two-thirds of crude oil exports and has been visited by the *Bellamya*, a floating monster of an oil tanker tipping the scales at 553,662 dwt. The pier was not really designed, however, to accommodate ships in the half-million ton bracket, and to ease the burden a single point mooring some 3000 metres from the pier was commissioned in 1979. This mooring, linked by a crude pipeline to Sea Island, can cope with the largest ships in the world, the vessels floating with the tide as they take on oil. In all, KOC has fifteen berths for tankers: two at Sea Island, one at the mooring, four at North Pier and eight (including the new ones for LPG exports) at the original South Pier at the Mina Al-Ahmadi complex. South Pier has become mainly a pier for oil products, only 10 per cent of crude oil now being exported through a facility first built more than thirty years ago. It not only handles liquid gas and products from the oil company refinery but is also linked by pipeline to the Shuaiba refinery to enable loading of KNPC products. Also in the Mina Al-Ahmadi complex is a bitumen pier, completed in 1979, which handles the various grades and blends produced by KOC's new bitumen plant. The particular importance of this pier is that it will boost the nation's capacity to export the product to other Gulf nations. Further up the coast is the four-berth, twenty-year-old North Pier built to meet the requirements of increasingly large tankers, but now, with its 18-metre maximum draught, capable of exporting only about 25 per cent of crude exports. By comparison, the sea depth at Sea Island is 28 metres.

Oil in Kuwait is kind to the producers as it comes out of the ground under its own pressure and, because the tank farms north and south of Ahmadi are some 122 metres above sea level, it can be gravity loaded on to tankers at a rate of 800 tonnes an hour at Sea Island. In fact, pumps are used to boost this to 15,000 t.p.h., the figure for North and South Pier (with their smaller pipelines) being 10,000 and 6,000 t.p.h. respectively. The record for exports stands at more than five million barrels in one day, yet such a high rate is not what the terminal operators are striving for. What they attempt to achieve is an even flow of loadings to enable a steady production flow in the field. Although the 10.5 million barrel capacity at the tank farms sounds huge, it could prove woefully inadequate if crude liftings occurred in surges. Computers play a large part in the operation, deciding what ship should berth when and where, what the oil production rate should be, what tanks should be loaded, and so forth. Any tank on any of the farms can be switched to serve any of the crude oil berths, and the whole process is presided over by just two men at the central control-room in Ahmadi.

Far from all the crude oil is earmarked for export: much goes to the KOC refinery while, in 1978, an average of 167,484 barrels a day went to the KNPC refinery. The principal oil facility at Shuaiba is the 320-metre products pier which has four berths capable of handling tankers up to 100,000 tons. Loading rates at the pier – which, like all KOC piers, has bunkering facilities at every berth – vary from between 1400 tonnes per hour for the lighter, 'white' products and 3000 t.p.h. for 'black' ones. In addition to products from the KNPC refinery, the pier handles a limited amount of liquid ammonia from the PIC plant. The commercial harbour at Shuaiba deals with most of the other PIC exports. Travelling a little further south, one encounters the two sea-berths which serve the Mina Abdullah refinery. The maximum size of tankers which can be handled stands at 200,000 tons at the outside berth and about 35,000 tons at the inside one. Storage tanks at Mina Abdullah have an operational capacity of about five million barrels, and there is also one of the world's largest open-air reservoirs with a capacity of more than one million barrels.

Where does it all go? Most of Mina Abdullah's products are sent to Japan, while China and India are among the best PIC customers. Both KOC and KNPC send their products all over the globe, KNPC being responsible for Kuwait's product marketing and maintaining offices in New York,

London, Tokyo, Hamburg, Karachi and Singapore. Product exports include highly specialized fuels for the sophisticated markets of Japan and the West and more conventional products for the Indian sub-continent and East Asia. Record exports from the Shuaiba refinery were notched up in December 1978 when the total passed the 1.2 million tonne mark, and 1978 also proved a bumper year for PIC with almost 700,000 tonnes of fertilizer being sent abroad.

There is also a flourishing home market, a recent survey showing that on a *per capita* basis Kuwait uses more fuel than any other nation, including the United States. As already noted, KNPC has the monopoly of filling stations in the country and, during 1978, sold more than 850 million litres of regular fuel and about 114 million litres of top grade, representing increases in demand in excess of 15 per cent. A new tank storage complex fed directly from Shuaiba was completed in 1979, and KNPC's local customers include its own subsidiary, Kuwait Aviation Fuelling Company, which sells aviation turbine kerosene to the Kuwait Airways fleet and visiting airliners at the international airport. The company recorded a 17.2 per cent jump in demand in 1978.

Sales of crude oil are conducted by the Ministry of Oil and, as the Government insists on contractual liftings, there are no spot sales as such in Kuwait. The main customers are British Petroleum and Gulf – one-time owners of KOC – and Shell. Under the contracts, Gulf lifts 500,000 barrels per day, plus or minus 10 per cent averaged over a year; BP's base is 450,000 b.p.d. plus or minus 10 per cent; and Shell's is 360,000 b.p.d., plus or minus 45,000 b.p.d. The OPEC decision to reduce the price of heavy oils has benefited the country as, of course, has the drop-off in Iranian production. As far as LPG goes, discussions continued throughout 1979 to attract more customers, Kuwait remaining adamant that the expected surplus of liquid gas in the eighties is a myth. One difficulty concerning the LPG sales has been the nation's insistence on contracts tied to LPG being exported in the four specially built Kuwaiti tankers. This has not proved such a problem with oil, and the ministry remains intent on tying sales to the use of the seven crude carriers currently sailing under the banner of the Kuwait Oil Tanker Company. KNPC has also started building up its own fleet of product tankers, in addition to the bunker ship which it has 'parked' further down the Gulf.

The Ministry of Oil is not simply concerned with the sale of crude oil and gas. Its technical section has responsibilities which include developing policy recommendations and making planning studies of all technical activities within the industry; providing guidance, counsel and supervision in the fields of exploration, drilling, production, reservoir engineering, transport and computer systems; and overseeing effective implementation of Kuwait's conservation policy. The department of economic affairs is in charge of gas and oil marketing; optimizing the use of available resources and Kuwait's investments in oil-related projects; and directing and co-ordinating relations with international organizations such as OPEC and OAPEC. Other responsibilities include the development of human resources within the oil sector, with particular emphasis on the training of Kuwaitis. A legal department safeguards the interests of the ministry and industry, while tenders and contracts of all state oil companies are vetted and supervised by officials in conjunction with the Central Tenders Committee. In 1978 the ministry also took over responsibility for all the nation's mineral (including non-petroleum) resources; at the moment there is precious little outside the hydrocarbon field except sand, but it is possible that the search for minerals under the sea will now get a new lease of life.

Obviously, though, the emphasis will remain very much on oil. During 1978 average daily production from KOC fields amounted to almost 1.9 million barrels, with another 160,000 coming from Kuwait's half of operations in the Wafra field. Production at Arabian Oil Company, operating offshore in the Partitioned Zone, amounted to about 400,000 barrels a day split fifty-fifty between Kuwait and Saudi Arabia.

Yet, as they often tell you in the country with the third largest proven oil reserves in the world, the stuff is worth more in the ground than out of it. Not surprisingly, Kuwait does not intend to underwrite the extravagances of others at the expense of its own future.

Trade, Commerce & Industry

Equipped with every modern comfort and facility, the new commercial centres in Kuwait City are answering the business demands of the eighties.

The Kuwaitis' reputation as shrewd businessmen pre-dates the oil era by at least a century, and this experience has been of great value to them during recent rapidly changing times. In every sphere of business life in Kuwait – commerce, banking, industry, retailing – there has been the most phenomenal growth over the last twenty years. As the economy has expanded so opportunities have opened up in a host of fields, with service industries leading the way. Long-time merchant families have been in the vanguard of the trading boom, while in Kuwait City and elsewhere the proliferation of modern stores has made available goods from all over the world. The financial sector has had its ups and downs, one of the latter coming in 1977 when the Government felt obliged to bail out Kuwaiti losers on the stock exchange to the tune of KD 160 million. The Government's fiscal policy, in fact, remains the most important element in the economy, and the stock exchange slump came as a direct result of a government decision to cut back land purchases.

The state has also been the prime mover in industry, although its pre-1973 influence was mainly one of restraint because of worries about market prospects and the fact that more industries only increased the need for expatriate labour. The Industrial Bank of Kuwait was established in 1974 and has since then backed well over a hundred projects, concentrating on manufacturing industries, especially the production of building materials. These projects have taken advantage of the growing home and Gulf markets and have given Kuwaitis more investment opportunities. But despite the cheap capital for industry and subsidized rates for such things as water and power, the end of the seventies brought a downturn in industrial lending.

The Amir has spoken forcefully about the role of the private sector. In 1978 he said: 'We shall continue to consolidate and develop the national economy and seek to expand the scope of activities both internally and externally. The private sector has had a memorable role in the service of our society, but we do visualize a more constructive role for it in the Kuwait of the future. It is expected of the private sector to make a greater contribution to the service of our new society which has ensured its freedom of activity and was never sparing towards it with help and encouragement.'

At the time of writing, the watchword is caution, spiced with a liberal dollop of consolidation. Even in the oil industry the only major project embarked upon in 1979 was the improvement of KOC's refinery – plans for a new petrochemical plant were expected to get the go-ahead for the 1980s, but as a whole the industry seemed to be taking a breather after its big diversification effort between 1968 and 1979, which culminated in the opening of the Gas Project.

For all this, Kuwait's industry today is alive and well. Despite the limitations of a nation whose sole natural assets are hydrocarbons, a variety of small manufacturing industries are thriving. In the service field there seems no sign of the bubble bursting, while the financial scene is far healthier than it was just a couple of years ago.

Encouraging the development of local industry, such as this asbestos plant, has been the primary concern of the government-owned Kuwait National Industries Company.

Industry

The foundations of Kuwait's non-oil industrial base were laid primarily in the sixties when, around the port of Shuweikh, an area of mainly service industries grew up. The emphasis of manufacturing concerns has always been on meeting local needs, only goods surplus to requirements finding export markets in the Gulf or elsewhere in the Arab world.

Much activity has centred on supplying the building industry, and it has been the Government which has given the lead. Kuwait National Industries produces asbestos pipes and sheets, as well as sand–lime and cement bricks for local construction companies such as the Kuwait Pre-Fabricated Building Company which was established in 1964 and is now

The limestone brick factory, also owned by Kuwait National Industries, has helped the state meet the local needs of the construction industry during the past two decades of frenetic activity.

Kuwait Metal Pipe Industries produce pipes in large quantities for both the home and export market. The company played an important part in supplying 350 kilometres of pipeline for the recent nationwide gas-gathering project.

owned by three equal partners: the Kuwait Industries Company, Kuwait Investment Company and the Savings and Credit Bank. Apart from constructing conventional buildings, the company has played an important part in the erection of prefabricated homes under the Government's limited-income housing policy. There is also the small but flourishing Kuwait Foundry Company which was formed in 1961 and makes such items as rainstorm gullies, sanitary ware, manhole covers and pressurepipe fittings. And two years after the Kuwait Metal Pipe Industries was founded by Amiri Decree, welded pipes had started to roll off the production line. The firm played an important part as sub-contractors on pipeline construction for KOC's Gas Project.

There are several hundred small and not-so-small industries around the Shuweikh area which are helping Kuwait to cut down reliance on finished goods. They range from the Kuwait Flour Mills Company, which produces much of the nation's bread, biscuits and flour, to the Kuwait Oxygen and Acetylene Company, supplying industrial and medical gases.

There is also a car-battery factory, a brickworks and, elsewhere, manufactories of aluminium window frames and other building materials, all providing thousands of job opportunities and giving Kuwaitis the chance to learn new skills from electronics engineering to competitive business administration.

For a long while though it remained the oil industry which supplied the most dramatic examples of diversification, the arrival of the Kuwait National Petroleum Company serving to show the world that the state was determined to break into the growing downstream market. It was no coincidence that KNPC's revolutionary all-hydrogen refinery was built at Shuaiba, for this strip of land between the KOC and what was then the Aminoil terminal had become the focal point of the nation's big industrial push.

An Amiri Decree established the Shuaiba Industrial Development Board (now the Shuaiba Area Authority) in May 1964, and construction started that would transform a desolate stretch of sand and sea into a multi-industry complex. The priorities were the building of a commercial harbour, industrial plots and the all-important services, which today include two huge water and power plants operated by the Ministry of Electricity and Water. These were designed to provide pumped water for both industrial and domestic use. Other facilities include the liquid products pier which serves the KNPC refinery built at Shuaiba in 1968 and liquid ammonia exports from the Petrochemical Industries Company.

The efforts of the authority to attract major industrial developments have paid off. Apart from KNPC and PIC the following concerns are among those now successfully operating at Shuaiba:

Kuwait Cement Company, established by Amiri Decree in 1968, became operational in 1972 with the capacity to produce 305,000 tonnes of ordinary Portland cement and two types of sulphate-resisting cement. Two additional grinding units and handling systems for bagged and bulk cement came on line in 1977, and the annual capacity of the plant is now estimated at about a million tonnes, all of it marketed locally. Despite a search for suitable minerals within Kuwait's borders, the necessary clinker and gypsum for cement production still has to be imported, most of it from Iraq.

Kremenco (Kuwait Industrial Refinery Maintenance and Engineering Company) was formed in 1969 in conjunction with Foster Wheeler International. The first company of its type in the Middle East, Kremenco undertakes such work as the manufacture, erection and repair of steam generating units and heat exchangers; the maintenance of refineries; pipework fabrication and pressure vessel manufacturing; the erection and maintenance of distillation plants; and offshore repair work.

Kuwait Sulphur Company became a going concern in 1973 with an annual capacity of 40,000 tonnes of pulverized sulphur. The aim of the company is to use the sulphur extracted in KNPC's refining of crude oil and to market the product internationally.

United Fisheries of Kuwait, as we saw earlier, has become one of the biggest names in commercial fishing. Its Shuaiba facilities include production warehouses for processing shrimps, an ice plant with a daily capacity of 12 tonnes, a refrigeration room for the storage of 500 tonnes of frozen shrimps, and a fish-grinding plant.

Other concerns currently operating from Shuaiba include the *Refrigeration and Oxygen Company*, which produces oxygen, nitrogen and argon; *Dresser (Kuwait) Company*, producing barite, spersene, drilling detergent, bentonite and other drilling fluid products; *Packaging and Plastic Industries*, producing millions of polythene and woven propylene packing bags; and the *Industrial Gases Establishment*, producing liquid nitrogen, liquid oxygen and argon for industrial use.

Other industries are being attracted to Shuaiba, but it would be unrealistic to expect Kuwait ever to become a large-scale exporter of manufactured goods. For one thing there are not the essential raw materials, although the search for minerals is about to be stepped up. For another thing, Kuwait is expensive both in terms of the capital required and in terms of labour costs. Only on the home market and, to a limited extent, in the Gulf can industries hope to be cost-effective, and even that success depends very much on development generated by government policies. The state bestows on these industries other benefits such as cheap development loans, cheap land, cheap services, cheap power and water. And the absence of taxes is a considerable bonus. At the moment the loosely defined aim is to encourage industrial growth which will assist Kuwait in terms of self-sufficiency, broaden the nation's technical base and offer wider scope for the opportunities of Kuwaitis themselves.

Industries relying on hydrocarbons, on the other hand, have a great deal going for them. They have the raw material at cost price – the lowest cost in the world. The common yardsticks of jobs for Kuwaitis, diversification and the acquisition of technical know-how, still apply, but the market for these industries stretches round the world.

Sea Links

Port congestion has been one of the facts of life which most oil-producing nations have had to live with since they embarked on massive development projects. The importation of goods into countries without the resources to furnish either raw or finished materials has been reflected in the lines of ships which have been waiting for months upon end outside over-worked port facilities. In some countries during the seventies vessels had to hang about for more than a year and, while the situation never got as bad as that in Kuwait, the state did at one time find itself with about 200 freighters waiting up to two months to berth. Clearly, something had to be done.

The answer was supplied in three stages: first, the main port of Shuweikh was expanded; then outside consultants were introduced to reorganize the port; and, for the longer term, facilities at the port of Shuaiba were extended. At Shuweikh, the back of the problem was broken in 1977. At the start of the year 170 ships were waiting. Eight months later the line had been halved, and by the end of the year there were just four vessels queueing up. And 1977 was a record year, when something like 4.5 million tonnes of goods were unloaded at Shuweikh (in 1978 the figure dropped by about 500,000 tonnes, illustrating the levelling off of development activity).

Shuweikh has a 'notional maximum' capacity of 3.5 million tonnes now that the initial phase of expansion is complete, and the port can offer eighteen deep-water berths for ships up to 210 metres in length. Plans have been drawn up which could increase the number of large berths to forty-four – and this from a port which twenty years ago had only one berth and one wooden jetty and even as recently as 1973 was handling not much more than a million tonnes a year. The load on Shuweikh lessened with the opening of a container depot in 1977 at Doha just across the bay, but the main credit for the dramatic improvement must go to the port authorities under the Ministry of Communications. Their tactics to ease congestion included the construction of warehousing near Shuweikh and at Doha, the ordering of more cranes and other handling equipment, and the establishment of stiff regulations to prevent merchants stockpiling goods on the dockside. Another move was to reduce the amount of transit goods accepted. Under new rules, any ship which arrived with proportionately more transit cargo than Kuwaiti cargo was not allowed to discharge at Shuweikh and could only offload the Kuwaiti part of the shipment on to barges. Similarly, no vessel with less than 600 tonnes of Kuwait cargo was allowed alongside a berth, and the import of motor vehicles was shifted entirely to Shuaiba. Open-air storage of non-perishables was introduced and, even before

new berths were finished, ships were putting in alongside them, unloading by their own derricks or by mobile cranes. Within a matter of months the convoy of vessels in the bay had started to disappear.

Actual facilities at Shuweikh since the completion of the western extension include fourteen berths which can take ships up to 10.6 metres draught at low water and four berths where the depth is 8.5 metres or less. The largest of the main berths is 211 metres long though the majority, including two set aside for cement imports, are between 183 and 200 metres. There are also two dolphins, three fishing berths and a variety of smaller berths.

At Shuaiba, work started in the summer of 1977 to increase capacity from 1.2 to more than 3 million tonnes. At present the port has five berths within the commercial harbour with draughts ranging between 7 and 8 metres. There are five cranes on the main mole, with limited warehousing and a fairly large barge harbour which serves as the home for fishing boats, tugs and other small vessels. Under a KD 32.5 million contract, the port has been transformed by the completion of the first phase of a project early in 1980. Construction has concentrated on one multi-purpose marginal and three main berths on a new mole which will serve to protect the harbour from high seas. The second phase entails the building of six berths, each with a 14-metre draught, although the three external ones will only be used when weather conditions are suitable. The port will then be capable of receiving ro-ro ships, as well as having Kuwait's first specialized container dock and the capacity to handle vessels of up to 80,000 dwt that require a high standard of handling techniques.

Shuaiba has never encountered the warehousing problems of Shuweikh, as the port was constructed in 1967 purely to serve the industries within the Shuaiba Industrial Area and, until 1974, the unloading of general cargo was prohibited. Since then the pressure on Shuweikh has press-ganged Shuaiba into service, but even now importers have to remove

A vessel undergoing repairs in a dry dock at Shuweikh. The port has been extensively modernized and enlarged during the past few years to cope with the growing volume of imports.

all goods the minute they are imported or run the risk of having them confiscated.

As for actually shipping the goods, Kuwait has established itself as one of the Arab world's leading maritime nations – indeed one would scarcely expect anything else given the Kuwaitis' history as merchants and mariners. On the oil front, Kuwait Oil Tanker Company has seven crude carriers of its own and has responsibility for operating the new LPG tankers. The company, 51 per cent government-owned, also currently operates the expanding Kuwait National Petroleum Company fleet which, it is hoped, will eventually carry up to 60 per cent of KNPC exports. The nation is also an active participant in the Arab Maritime Petroleum Transport Company, a joint venture formed by the Organization of Arab Petroleum Exporting Countries.

The Kuwait Shipping Company was established in 1965 to deal with dry cargo; the Government had an initial 60 per cent stake, although the undertaking was expected to run on commercial lines from the very start. It began with a handful of chartered and second-hand freighters and today has a fleet of over fifty vessels, the company having weathered the worldwide downturn in shipping activity better than any other. The name of the company changed to the United Arab Shipping Company in 1975 following an agreement with Saudi Arabia, Iraq, Bahrain, Oman, the UAE and Qatar to establish a joint venture with a capital of KD 500 million. So far participation by concerns from the other states has remained negligible. The company's ships – many built in Japan, the United Kingdom and Spain – now cover the world, with regular runs to the USA, the UK, European ports and Japan. Senior officers have traditionally been hired from Britain, but the company maintains an active training programme aimed at providing Kuwaitis to operate the fleet in due course. The concern has various subsidiaries, including the Kuwait Shipping Agency; it has a half-share in a chartering company and participates in a forwarding company, Aratrans, with Kuwait Airways Corporation.

The Kuwait Shipbuilding and Repairyard Company won a contract in 1975 for the construction of repair facilities at Shuweikh as part of the expansion plans at the port. The company now maintains a dry dock in Shuweikh and also has a one-third stake in Gulf Dredging Company, a specialist firm formed in conjunction with Contracting and Marine Services – another local firm in which the Government has a major shareholding – and a Dutch group of marine engineers. GDC won an important part of the contract for the improvement of Shuaiba and also got the dredging job for the basin and channel at Kuwait's new naval base in the south of the country. As its flagship, the company has one of the most powerful dredgers in the world, and hopes to expand its operations throughout the west side of the Arabian Gulf and, perhaps, further than that.

Skyways

Kuwait enters the eighties with a brand-new airport terminal which has the capacity to meet the needs of up to two million passengers a year and some of the most advanced cargo-handling facilities anywhere in the world. The opening of the complex comes some thirty years after the first control tower went into operation – a ground-to-air radio housed in a tent. In those days, Kuwait Oil Company operated a DC-3 Dakota used for bringing fresh fruit and vegetables from Cyprus and the Lebanon and for taking workers on to India. The only way for members of the public to fly out of Kuwait in 1948 was by boat: a flying-boat of the old BOAC would call in twice a week.

Construction of the first phase of the international airport was finished in the early sixties and, ever since, the makeshift terminal buildings have been struggling to keep pace with the continually increasing number of passengers. In 1978 the total of arrivals and departures stood at one million, twice what it had been only five years before. Similar increases had been recorded in the number of aircraft: about 7300 non-military planes landed in 1973 and about 15,000 in 1978. By

The passenger terminal of the new Kuwait International Airport, completed in 1979 to handle the huge increase in air traffic experienced throughout the seventies.

that time the new terminal buildings were taking shape; construction had begun some four years earlier but the completion date was finally put back to 1979–80 following a series of delays.

The futuristic design for the new terminal was first put forward in the late sixties, but the idea was shelved for several years until it became obvious that the already hard-pressed passenger buildings would not be able to cope indefinitely. So the Japanese designs were dusted down and the Ministry of Public Works awarded the main contract to a Dutch company. From the air, the main passenger terminal resembles the outline of a plane, and even from the ground it has a profile not dissimilar to a 'jumbo'. It is situated closer to the main runways than the old terminal and, apart from being architecturally exciting, offers passengers the latest word in facilities and services. The 25,000-square-metre floor area includes a ground-floor arrivals lounge and a first-floor departures lounge complete with a large visitors' restaurant and a most attractive mosque in its centre. An 800-metre loop road, Kuwait's first elevated highway, takes traffic to the departures area which itself is spanned by a massive, 15,000-square-metre roof made of 1800 tonnes of steel supported on just 24 columns. This roof forms the 'wings' of the design while the 'fuselage' houses departures and arrivals gates, waiting areas and so on. Planes taxi to the terminal apron where passengers board via one of thirteen telescopic, air-conditioned bridges from the terminal, the construction of which was originally put at KD 28 million. Within the main building are numerous facilities ranging from offices and airline desks to refreshment areas and a special VIP lounge. Baggage handling facilities are fully automatic, the electronic information system is among the best available, and a network of escalators ensures speedy movement around the building. There are also shops, ample toilet facilities, health services, information centres, rest areas, lounges and a control tower to supervise movement on the apron.

In all, more than 150,000 cubic metres of concrete have been poured into the new airport (delivery delays of cement were one reason for the late completion); some 50,000 cubic metres were used on the terminal building itself and a similar quantity on the apron. Underground pipes have been laid to enable airliners to refuel without resorting to the customary fleet of tankers. The first part of the complex to be finished was the freight depot, handed over to the Civil Aviation Authority late in 1978. Handling processes at the depot are fully computerized, smaller items being brought in by rail-borne cars and deposited on a KD 2 million conveyor-belt system which automatically stores and registers them without any human handling. Forklift trucks are used for large items brought in from aircraft on the depot's own apron, which can accommodate up to five aircraft the size of Boeing 707s. The amount of freight imported by air has soared in recent years: even before the completion of the new depot, the totals had jumped from 6 million kilograms in 1972 to about 27 million in 1977.

Commercial aircraft visiting Kuwait International Airport now include representatives of most of the world's great airlines, the runways being long enough to handle the very largest planes. The national carrier is Kuwait Airways Corporation (KAC), an organization which traces its roots to a day in 1954 when a group of businessmen got together and formed the Kuwait National Airways Company. The first services used trusty DC-3s operating from a rough landing strip which had Nissen huts as a terminal and an engineering depot situated in Beirut. In 1962 Kuwait Airways Corporation came into being and has since been establishing itself throughout the Arab world, Europe and Asia. Boeings have been the mainstay of the now nationalized fleet, 707s fulfilling intercontinental duties until the arrival of the first of three 747s in 1978. These specially designed jumbos have extended KAC's range as far as Copenhagen and are proving one of the most popular features on an airline which makes up for the absence of in-flight booze with high standards of service, particularly cuisine. Among the dozens of cities on regular routes are London, Paris, Frankfurt, Rome, Athens, Jeddah, Baghdad, Amman, Beirut, Dubai, Bahrain, Karachi, Bombay and Delhi. In the summer of 1980 the airline increased its scope by ordering its first European Airbus.

KAC has a record as one of the safest airlines in the world and, according to one international aviation magazine, the airport is 'superbly equipped technically'. There is a large complex of hangars and workshops manned by a staff which includes an increasing number of Kuwaitis trained by such companies as Boeing, Rolls-Royce, and Pratt and Whitney. KAC is capable of completely stripping and reassembling an entire 707 within the strict international regulations, and one hangar can accommodate up to three 707s at a time. Maintenance represents one of the company's largest expenditures, and the standards required are normally far higher than those imposed by international regulations. As KAC says: 'The kind of maintenance we carry out is preventive rather than corrective. Every one of the thousands of components in our Boeings is regularly monitored for wear in accordance with a programme recommended by the manufacturers. We keep a detailed life history of every single component on each of our aircraft so that we know exactly when it was inspected and when it must be replaced.'

A New Zurich?

The Kuwaitis have always been good at handling money – their history as merchants provided the base on which today's comprehensive financial sector has been built. The expertise has been joined by the brute force of the money from oil, a flow of cash which grows ever larger with each rise in the price of crude oil. The by now familiar question, though, is what happens after oil: can Kuwait really establish itself as an advanced capital market and thus become what one journalist described as 'the Zurich of the Arab world'?

Undoubtedly, impressive progress has already been made towards this goal, although the process of establishing adequate market regulators is still far from complete. There have been increasing signs in recent years, however, that the business and financial sectors were moving far nearer towards being able to stand on their own feet, rather than (as has happened more than once) being forced into a position where they have to seek urgent government help to bail out investors or institutions. As one senior Ministry of Planning official put it: 'We think our economic institutions are now moving into manhood and must make their own resources. They should look to government now as a parent, perhaps, but no longer as a sugar daddy.'

There remain several hurdles to be overcome before the nation can lay claim to any mini-Zurich title. For a start, an international financial centre needs an international currency, and there have been few indications so far that Kuwait is keen to see the dinar exposed to the roller-coaster of the currency market.

It has not been easy to break the habit shared by many investors of simply looking for profits from straightforward speculation in shares or property – and as land prices have been known to increase more than 200 per cent in a two-year period, the reticence in many cases is understandable. 'This deep-rooted tradition of trading and financial realism', according to *The Times*, 'is the Kuwaiti strength. But if the business and financial structure is to mature, the country's institutional traditions will have to become increasingly complex and more regulated as well as more able to tap the power of Kuwait's private wealth.'

Nevertheless, the capital market has been developing strongly, particularly since the Central Bank of Kuwait was given the power to fix interest rates where before they were prevented from rising above 7 per cent because of traditional Islamic interpretations of usury laws (in effect, commercial banks were able to offer about $8\frac{1}{2}$ per cent by adding handling charges). The abolition of the ceiling is regarded as a major step towards fiscal reform. Several other moves have helped the overall situation, especially the beginning of reform of the stock exchange which for a long while was strictly informal. Incidentally, although only about forty companies are quoted, the exchange's turnover has sometimes matched the daily total in London. A secondary market is beginning to develop as well, and – most important – there are strong grounds for believing that the necessary skills are becoming available to support Kuwait's bid as a centre of Middle East business affairs. Others, of course, are after the same prize: Beirut's credentials were already well established until civil strife tore the Lebanon apart, while Cairo's financial ambitions suffered after the estrangement between Egypt and the rest of the Arab world in 1979. The offshore banking business has been developing nicely in Bahrain, but Kuwaiti financiers do not necessarily see any competition between the two: they believe that Kuwait can fulfil its role as a capital providing centre and Bahrain that of a capital transfer centre. This opinion is not universally held, however, although it could be well into the eighties before any real financial rivalry develops between the Gulf nations.

In the field of banking, there are eight commercial banks (the National Bank of Kuwait, Al-Ahli Bank, Gulf Bank, Commercial Bank of Kuwait, Burgan Bank, Kuwait Finance House, Bank of Kuwait and the Middle East, and Bank of Kuwait and Bahrain); several property loan specialists (most notably the Real Estate Bank which is quoted on the stock

Since restrictions were lifted on the height of buildings in Kuwait City, the skyline has become dotted with towering office blocks.

exchange); and a number of investment companies led by the Kuwait Investment Company, the Kuwait Foreign Trading, Contracting and Investment Company, and the Kuwait International Investment Company. There are plenty of other financial services, too, ranging from money brokerage and insurance to stockbroking and exchange dealing.

The Central Bank attempts to control credit expansion by taking in time deposits from the commercial banks and also requiring them to retain a high liquidity ratio. Many of the banks' foreign assets are kept with foreign banks, mainly in short-term deposits and negotiable certificates of deposit. Although the banks welcomed the lifting of the interest-rate ceiling they were not keen to lose the extra they could add on in handling charges, and they are still not in a position to compete with the banking units established in Bahrain.

Yet although they have problems, Kuwait's banks have proved themselves capable of meeting requirements in the country, often employing high-level foreign skills to cope with increasingly complex transactions while at the same time developing local talent and sharpening their inherent business acumen.

As far as the man in the street is concerned, the banks have become an important part of everyday life, with branches being established throughout the country. In Kuwait City particularly these branches tend to be in spacious, attractive premises, while the actual head offices resemble the prestigious buildings of top financial institutions elsewhere in the world.

Inside new commercial centres, shoppers can search for goods in air-conditioned comfort – or simply relax by the side of a fountain.

The Future

Kuwait looks to the future: an engineer operating a sun ray collector as part of the Solar Energy Project run by the Kuwait Institute for Scientific Research.

What will the eighties bring for Kuwait? It is a question of particular moment not only to the rulers and inhabitants of the state but also, perhaps, to the world as a whole. Any nation with massive reserves of oil (and there are precious few of them) in a decade which will probably see large-scale shortages of such a vital commodity, is bound to play a crucial part in decisions which will affect countless millions in every corner of the globe. The price of a barrel of crude oil rocketed in 1973 and soared again in 1979, yet the industrialized nations still continued to gobble up oil while attempting to cajole the producers to supply more to satisfy their need – or is it greed? Maybe the decisions reached at the Tokyo summit of the industrialized nations in the summer of 1979 will have proved the turning point. Kuwait, for one, has reason to hope it will for, along with several other OPEC members, it knows it cannot observe the problems of the developed countries with total indifference: it has a very real interest, financial and otherwise, in the fate of these nations.

The conservation ceiling which now limits production to an average of 1.5 million barrels a day is well below the potential of the KOC-controlled fields. Yet even if Kuwait felt at some time during the eighties that production should be raised to meet a particular need, can anyone be sure that such a capacity might not be needed even more in the 1990s or beyond the year 2000? It is a very real dilemma. For the moment, the Kuwaitis adopt the financially sound standpoint that the oil is worth more in the ground than out of it. Financial thinking can change, however, not least because of longer-term political considerations. And the plight of developed nations is far from the only concern – Kuwait has always fulfilled ambitious and selflessly motivated undertakings to Third World and developing nations, and their increasing needs for ever higher-priced oil will continue to raise questions of supply and ability to pay.

As to the actual level of resources in Kuwait, there is plenty of room for speculation. Will exploration resume off the nation's coasts, for instance? Can the deep test wells yield the sort of unassociated gas reserves which will make Kuwait an LPG world leader? How far will the downstream industries expand, particularly refining and petrochemicals? These are just some of the vital questions which will need to be answered in the next few years.

Undoubtedly, the blessing of oil has placed an enormous responsibility on nations such as Kuwait. The determination of the decision-makers to put their own nation first is understandable, but the difficulty will be in ensuring that decisions taken for domestic reasons do not produce a backlash from further afield. So far the Kuwait rulers have steered a careful, pragmatic path.

Politically, the nation's links with Gulf, Arab and other Islamic states look bound to strengthen even further. The treaty signed with Saudi Arabia towards the end of 1978, for example, was not merely an affirmation of friendship but a commitment to follow compatible and mutually beneficial paths. The break in ties with Egypt in 1979 also demonstrated

Kuwait's active involvement in the Islamic bloc opposed to any Middle East 'solution' which does not include a restoration of Palestinian rights and the return of Arab Jerusalem, the third holiest city in Islam.

The question of Gulf security looks like being a recurring theme of the eighties. Real or imaginary threats to the security of Kuwait from outside are tucked away somewhere in the folds of international intrigue. Kuwait has made it clear that it wants no big-power interference in the Gulf, and sister nations on the peninsula have echoed this sentiment. While staunchly rejecting Communist philosophy, Kuwait is determined to stay apart from any super-power bloc, preferring to pool its political resources with the Arab and Islamic nations and with the rest of the world's developing countries. Bilateral relations with nations great and small look like continuing to develop on the lines of mutual respect, equality and friendship.

Kuwait appears certain to remain active in international organizations, not least OPEC, and developing nations can undoubtedly look forward to receiving the sort of assistance which has won Kuwait so many admirers around the world. Of course, Kuwait gets richer as the price of oil increases, and the problems of how to use this wealth for the benefit of the post-oil generation will remain uppermost in the planners' minds. There is, it is true, the Fund for Future Generations, although – admirable as the idea behind the scheme is recognized to be – recent voices have been raised arguing that the money might be better poured into development projects now to build up the industrial and commercial base for the future, rather than having it lie dormant for a quarter of a century. By the same token, Kuwait could argue that it is already proceeding with development plans at the fastest rate desirable.

Development is certainly continuing at a steady pace. Not at the helter-skelter, almost chaotic pace that seemed such a feature of Gulf life in the sixties and seventies, but at the sort of rate tailored to the steady, progressive growth which

Pearling, fishing, trade and now transportation of oil and hydrocarbon products – the sea has represented and continues to represent Kuwait's essential link with the rest of the world.

Kuwait's human and material resources can handle. The emphasis has swung away from prestige projects and pie-in-the-sky proposals – the Kuwaitis have been learning and maturing, and the results can be seen in the people, in society and in the evolving landscape.

There is no doubt that the Kuwaitis are working hard for that future. Yes, money keeps rolling in thanks to the oil, but it takes no small amount of judgement to make sure that the benefits of the wealth are felt in the tangible form of hospitals, roads, industry, schools, social justice and so much else. And it bears repeating again and again that, vast as Kuwait's oilfields are, they are but a drop in the sea of time. In a couple more generations, the oil era is likely to be just another passing phase to be read about in history books.

Yet it is upon this passing phase that Kuwait must build her entire future. That is how much a barrel of oil is worth to Kuwait. Its value is not in hard cash but in the sort of life it holds out to tomorrow's children. Apart from her people, hydrocarbons really are Kuwait's sole natural asset.

Index

Page numbers in italic refer to illustration captions

Abdullah Gulum Ashkanani Mosque, 7
Agriculture, 63
Ahmad, Sheikh, 53, 100, 130, 131, 133
Ahmadi, 2, 11, 28, 34, 50, 53–4, 60, 119, 133, 136; *133*
Ahmadi Natural History Group, 35, 70, 71, 74
Ahmadi (formerly Southwell) Hospital, 105
Airport *see* Kuwait International Airport
Alam-Al-Fikr, 116
Alexander the Great, 37, 38
Al-Andalus, 148
Al-Araby, 116
Al-Jahra Gate, *33*
Al-Khalifa family, 12
Al-Kuwait, 116
Al-Sabah dynasty, 2, 12
Al-Sabah Hospital, 101–2; *87, 102, 103*
American Independent Oil Company (Aminoil), 133, 134, 139
American Mission Hospital, 99
Amiri Hospital, 100, 102
Anglo-Persian Oil Company (APOC), 130, 131
Arab Bank for Economic Development in Africa, 85

Arab Fund for Economic and Social Development, 85
Arab League, 82
Arab Maritime Petroleum Transport Company, 83, 149, 168
Arab Shipbuilding and Repair Yard, 83
Arabian Gulf States' Joint Programme Production Institute, 115
Arabian Oil Company, 66, 134, 139, 154
Aratrans, 168
Arts, the, 18–20

Bahrain, 12, 174, 176
Banks, 174, 176
Basra, 13, 14
Beach clubs, 26, 27–8, 29, 56; *31*
Beach development, 55–7
Bedouin, 24, 35, 75; *58*
Bellamya, 151
Birds, 70–2; *72*
Boatbuilding, 16, 42, 55; *5, 17*
British East India Company, 13
British Grenadier, 133
British Petroleum (BP), 130, 135, 136, 137, 153
Broadcasting, 110–16
Bubiyan, 36
Buchanan Report, 40, 52
Building industry, 160 (*see also* Housing)
Burgan oilfield, 53, 128, 133, 134, 135, 144; *133*

Camels, 31, 35–6, 75
Central Bank of Kuwait, 79, 174, 176
Chisholm, A.H.T., 131
Cinema, 20, 29, 117; *31*
Commerce, 173–6
Contracting and Marine Services, 169
Credit and Savings Bank, 108

Dasman Palace, 42
Desert, 2–3, 33, 34, 35
'Desert Express', 13, 117
Dhows, 13, 42, 44, 67; *12, 17*
Dickson, Colonel H.R.P., 47
Dilmun civilization, 36–8
Doha, 16, 55, 123, 165; *17, 123*
Downstream industries, 128, 145–54
Dress, 21; *21, 22*
Dresser (Kuwait) Company, 163

Eastern and General Syndicate (EGS), 130
Education, 88–98
 beginnings, 88
 facilities, 92, 98; *91*
 girls', 92
 growth of, 90–2
 special, 98
 university, 93–8
 vocational, 98; *94, 97*
Electricity, 123–4; *123*
Experimental Farm, 64, 66; *63, 64*

Fahad Al Salem Mosque, *11*
Fahaheel, 34, 54, 102

184

Failaka Island, 29, 36, 37, 38, 55, 111
Falconry, 26, 31, 51
Fertilizer, 85, 147, 148, 153; *147*
Financial Times (London), 83
Fintas, 53
First Kuwait Oil Concession, The, 131
Fishing, 13, 27, 63, 67–8; *13, 68*
Flora, 35, 75
Food and Agriculture Organization, 85
Foreign aid, 83–5
Foreign policy, 81–3, 181
Freeth, Zahra, 8

Gas, 128, 140–5
  liquid, 128, 142–3, 145, 151, 153; *143*
  refineries, 141, 142
Gas Project, 128, 141, 142, 144, 148, 158
Gas Al-Kuwait, 148
General Authority for the Arabian Gulf and South Arabian States, 85
Getty Oil Company, 133
Government, 77–85 (*see also* Ministries)
Gulf Dredging Company, 57, 169
Gulf Oil Corporation, 130, 135, 136, 137, 153

Hawalli, 42, 102
Health, 98–105
  child centres, 101
  clinics, 105
  health services, 99
  hospitals, 99–103
  medical staff, 103
Highways, 2, 40, 42, 53, 57–60
Horses, 26, 31; *26*
Hospitals, 99–103 (*and see under individual names*)
Hotels, 48–50
Housing, 41, 42, 47, 54–5, 106–9; *41, 44*
  assistance, 107–9
  for expatriates, 109
  low-income, 106–7; *107*

  skating, 24–5; *24*

Industrial Bank of Kuwait, 158
Industrial Gases Establishment, 163
Industry, 78, 157, 160–4; *158, 160, 161*
Insects, 72
International Fund for Agricultural Development, 85
International Monetary Fund, 85
Iran, 82, 139, 144
Iraq, 2, 14, 35, 82
Irrigation, 64–6
Islam, 6–11
  influence of, 10, 11, 19
  principles of, 5, 7, 8

Jaber Al-Ahmad, Sheikh, 3, 42, 45, 77, 78, 158
Jahra, 2, 34, 53, 55, 58, 64

Kobbar, 36
Kremenco, 163
Kuwait Airways Corporation, 50, 168, 171–2
Kuwait Aviation Fuelling Company, 153
Kuwait Cement Company, 162
Kuwait City, 38–52 (*and passim*); *39, 40, 120, 157, 174*
Kuwait Flour Mills Company, 161
Kuwait Foundry Company, 161
Kuwait Fund for Arab Economic Development, 79
Kuwait Foreign Trading, Contracting and Investment Company, 80
Kuwait Fund for Arab Economic Development (KFAED), 83–4
Kuwait Hotels Company, 49, 50
Kuwait Industries Company, 161
Kuwait Institute for Scientific Research (KISR), 66, 67, 70; *179*
Kuwait International Airport, 60, 119, 169–72; *170*
Kuwait International Investment Company, 80
Kuwait Investment Company, 80, 161
Kuwait Investment Office, 80

Kuwait Metal Pipe Industries, 161; *161*
Kuwait National Industries Company, 160; *158, 160*
Kuwait National Petroleum Company (KNPC), 50, 139, 142, 145–6, 149, 153, 162, 168
  refinery (Shuaiba), 142, 145–6, 152, 161, 162; *141*
Kuwait News Agency (KUNA), 117
Kuwait Oil Company, 27, 53, 70, 105, 128, 131, 133, 135, 136, 149, 154, 169
  refinery (Mina Al-Ahmadi), 141, 145, 152; *135*
Kuwait Oil Tanker Company, 148, 154, 168
Kuwait Oxygen and Acetylene Company, 161
Kuwait Pre-Fabricated Building Company, 160
Kuwait – Prospect and Reality, 8
Kuwait Shipbuilding and Repairyard Company, 169
Kuwait Shipping Agency, 168
Kuwait Sulphur Company, 163
Kuwait University, 6, 23, 33, 70, 75, 93–8, 105; *92*
Kuwait Wafra Oil Company, 139

Leisure activities, 24–31

Mammals, 74–5
Maritime transport, 149–53; *151*
Marriage, 23
Mecca, 7, 8, 9, 10
Mina Abdullah, 135, 139, 146, 152
Mina Al-Ahmadi, 133, 141, 142, 145, 151; *135*
Ministries:
  Awqaf and Religious Affairs, 10
  Commerce and Industry, 49
  Communications, 118, 165
  Education, 19, 92, 115
  Electricity and Water, 35, 123, 148, 162
  Finance, 78, 80
  Foreign Affairs, 41, 45, 83
  Housing, 109

Information, 19, 40, 50, 110, 111, 115, 117; 77, *111*
Oil, 148, 153, 154
Planning, 63, 111
Public Works, 60, 64, 111
Social Affairs and Labour, 18
Mohammed, 6, 7, 8
Money, 78–81
  expenditure, 79
  inflation, 78
  investment, 80
  reserves, 80
  taxation, 79–80
Mosques, 52; *7, 11, 88*
Mubarak the Great, 44, 47, 130
Mubarak the Great Hospital, 102; *103*
Mubarakiyah School, 88
Mylrea, Dr Stanley, 99

National Assembly, 41, 77
National Council for Culture, the Arts and Letters, 19
National Housing Authority, 107, 108
Niebuhr, Karsten, 13
North Pier, 135, 151; *134*

Official Gazette, 116
Oil, 127–55; *129, 133, 134, 138, 151*
  companies *see under individual names*
  concession, 130–1
  crisis of 1973, 129, 136
  development of industry, 133–5, 181
  discovery of, 130
  downstream industries, 145–54
  future policy, 154–5, 183
  national ownership, 129, 136–7
  organizations, 82–3
  reserves, 80–1, 127–8, 179, 180
  responsibilities resulting from, 2, 85, 179
  wealth as result of, 12, 79, 90, 127
Organization of Arab Petroleum Exporting Countries (OAPEC), 83, 149, 154, 168
Organization of Petroleum Exporting Countries (OPEC), 82, 153, 154, 179, 181

Packaging and Plastic Industries, 163
Palestine, 81, 90, 181
Palestine Liberation Organization, 85
Pearling, 13, 14–16, 19, 90; *15*
Petrochemical Industries Company (PIC), 147–8, 149, 152, 162; *127, 147*
Petrochemicals, 145, 147–8, 149, 158
Pollution, 68
Population, 2, 52, 78, 87, 90
Port facilities, 164–9
Postal service, 117–19
Press, 116–17
Public transport, 87

Radio, 110, 114
Rainfall, 35
Ramadhan, 8, 9, 10
Refining:
  gas, 141, 142
  oil, 145–6
Refrigeration and Oxygen Company, 163
Relief and Works Agency for Palestinian Refugees, 85
Reserve Fund for Future Generations, 78–9, 80, 181

Salmiyah, 34, 41, 42, 48, 55, 102, 105; *7, 11, 40, 56*
Satellite Communications Earth Station, 120
Saudi Arabia, 2, 58, 61, 82, 83, 85, 127, 128, 133, 134, 139, 180
Savings and Credit Bank, 161
Sea, importance of to Kuwait, 3, 12, 16
Sea Island, 135, 149
Seif Palace, 41, 44–45, 47, 78; *47*
Shamiya Gate, 41, 110
Shatt Al-Arab, 14, 35, 68, 123
Shell Petroleum Company, 153
Shrimping, 67; *66*
Shuaiba Industrial Area, 34, 54, 123, 124, 164, 167
  KNPC refinery, 142, 145; *141*

PIC petrochemicals plant, 147; *127, 147*
  port, 165, 167
Shuaiba Area Authority (formerly Shuaiba Industrial Development Board), 162
Shuweikh, 41, 48, 58, 94, 100, 123, 124, 148, 160, 161
  port, 165, 167, 169; *167*
Snakes, 72–3
Souk, 50–1; *51*
South Pier, 133, 142, 151
Southwell Hospital *see* Ahmadi Hospital
State General Reserve, 79, 80
Subiya, 53
Sulaibikhat, 102

Telecommunications Centre, 50, 118, 120; *118, 120*
Telephone service, 119–20; *119*
Television, 10, 29, 31, 110, 114–16; *111*
Temperature, 8, 34–5
The Times, 173
Touristic Enterprises Company, 27, 50, 55
Traders Limited, 131
Traffic, 39–40, 57–60; *61*
Travel, 29

Umm Al-Aish, 120
United Arab Shipping Company (formerly Kuwait Shipping Company), 168
United Fisheries of Kuwait, 163
United Nations, 82
UN Emergency Assistance Fund, 85

Water:
  supplies, 35, 63, 64, 123, 124, 162; *124*
  distillation, 35, 123, 124; *123*
Wildlife, 70–5
Winstone, Victor, 8
Women, position of in society, 11, 23–4, 47
World Bank, 85
World of Drama, 116

Zor Hills, 33, 70